W9-ACV-873

WITHDRAWN

No longer the property of the
Boston Public Library.
Sale of this material benefits the Library.

SOCIAL GROUPS IN POLISH SOCIETY

Social Groups in Polish Society

Edited by

DAVID LANE
Reader in Sociology in the University of Essex
and
GEORGE KOLANKIEWICZ
Lecturer in Sociology in the University of Essex

Columbia University Press
New York
1973

© David Lane and George Kolankiewicz 1973

All rights reserved. No part of this publication
may be reproduced or transmitted, in any form
or by any means, without permission.

First published 1973 by
THE MACMILLAN PRESS LTD
London and Basingstoke
Associated companies in New York Toronto
Dublin Melbourne Johannesburg and Madras

ISBN 0–231–03729–5

Printed in Great Britain

* HN 539
.5
.S6 L35
1973 b

BOSTON PUBLIC LIBRARY

Publishers' Note

The series of eleven volumes entitled 'Political and Social Processes in Eastern Europe' is the result of a British inter-university, inter-disciplinary comparative study, sponsored by the Social Science Research Council. Professor Ghiţa Ionescu was the organiser and co-ordinator of the research work (1968–71).
The volumes are as follows:

Ghiţa Ionescu (University of Manchester): The Evolution of the Socialist State
Jane Cave (University of Birmingham), R. Amann (University of Birmingham), L. Blit (University of London), R. W. Davies (University of Birmingham), T. Podolski (Portsmouth Polytechnic), and G. Sakwa (University of Bristol): Politics and the Polish Economy
David Lane (University of Essex) and George Kolankiewicz (University of Essex) (*editors*): Social Groups in Polish Society
Jaroslav Krejčí (University of Lancaster): Social Change and Stratification in Postwar Czechoslovakia
Vladimir V. Kusin (University of Glasgow): Political Grouping in the Czechoslovak Reform Movement
A. H. Brown (University of Oxford) and G. Wightman (University of Liverpool): The Communist Party in Czechoslovakia
J. F. N. Bradley (University of Manchester): Czechoslovak Politics 1948–68
Phyllis Auty (University of London): The Changing Role of the Yugoslav Communist Party
R. K. Kindersley (University of Oxford): The Yugoslav Federal Assembly: Relations between Executive and Legislature
F. Singleton (University of Bradford): The Yugoslav Social Groups and Institutions
D. Matko (University of Glasgow) and D. J. R. Scott (University of Glasgow): Career Patterns of Yugoslav Decision-Makers

The individual volumes have different titles and each of them is a self-contained, independent study on a separate subject.
Together they form a tripartite analysis of three given Socialist states of Eastern Europe: Czechoslovakia, Poland and Yugoslavia, as follows:

Subject of study	Poland	Czechoslovakia	Yugoslavia
The changing role of representative institutions	Jane Cave G. Sakwa	J. F. N. Bradley	R. K. Kindersley
The changing role of the Party	Jane Cave	A. H. Brown and G. Wightman	Phyllis Auty
The changing role of the groups in the interplay between the government and the economy	L. Blit, R. W. Davies, R. Amann, and T. Podolski David Lane and George Kolankiewicz	Jaroslav Krejčí Vladimir V. Kusin	F. Singleton D. Matko and D. J. R. Scott

See for a complete description of the project in the Appendix of _The Evolution of the Socialist State_, by Ghiţa Ionescu in this series.

Each book in the series will carry its own index of names and subjects. When all eleven volumes have been published a complete synoptical index to the series will be published.

Contents

List of Tables

List of Diagrams and Map

List of Tables in Appendixes

APPENDIX 4

Preface

The subject of this book is the study of social groups in Poland. By a 'group' in its widest sense we mean an aggregate or category of persons having relationships with each other, possessing common qualities or features which sometimes give rise to shared norms and values. We do not claim that social groups are the only or necessarily the most important aspect of social and political change. But we do believe that a fuller appreciation of politics may be afforded by an understanding of the group structure. In the past, studies of East European societies after the Second World War have overwhelmingly concentrated on *political* groups and processes to the exclusion of the social. We hope that this book will help redress the balance as far as Poland is concerned. We take the view that the study of the formation of social groups is important in its own right as well as providing insight into the political process. The industrialisation process carried out by the Communist élites in the State socialist societies of Eastern Europe has had a momentous impact on the social structure of these countries which we seek to describe and thereby to show the interaction of political and social forces.

The book is arranged in the following way. The first chapter is a general introduction to the changing social, political and economic structure of Poland both before and after the foundation of the People's Republic of Poland. Whereas this chapter is a macro study, the ones which follow are micro studies, each dealing with a particular social group: the working class, the peasantry and the intelligentsia. We have organised the study around social groups, rather than on themes, to facilitate comparative study of these phenomena in the other two countries which comprise this series (Yugoslavia and Czechoslovakia). These general social groups have been found to include many sub-groups which have made a complete description impossible. We have, therefore, in addition to a general introduction on each group, focused in some chapters on a more detailed study of one sub-group: in the case of the cultural intelligentsia, we have considered the writers and their expression through the Polish Writers' Association; the technical intelligentsia has been limited to engineers and directors of enterprises. Each study attempts to describe the changing structure of the group. We have indicated the ways demands are made on the political system, and in the chapter on local political authorities we have studied the interaction of social groups in the locality. We hope that a following volume in this series will emphasise the more political significance of these studies as it concentrates more on political institutions and processes. In this following book too is a study of the Roman Catholic Church in Polish society. The time period covered for each subject in this volume is from 1945 to the assumption of the leadership of the Polish United Workers' Party by Gierek and the emphasis is on the later Gomułka epoch. In the conclusion some tentative points are made about changes which have taken place in 1971 as well as a general summing-up of the significance of the various studies.

We are indebted to many people and institutions who have made this book possible. The monograph was inspired by Professor Ghiţa Ionescu, who has acted as the co-ordinator of the comparative study on Poland, Czechoslovakia and Yugoslavia of which the study is a part. The British Social Science Research Council played a major part in providing finance which enabled George Kolankiewicz to work full-time as a research fellow on the project and facilitated visits to Poland to collect information by him and Ray Taras. We would like to express our thanks to the following for help given to the authors in the course of their work: the Institute of Sociology of Warsaw University, the Institute of Administration and Management of Warsaw University, the Polish Library, London.

We are also grateful to David Bouchier, Christel Lane, Ray Taras, Ros Patton, who have read parts of the manuscript and have made many useful suggestions, and to Ilse Browne and Luise Dobson, who typed the manuscripts.

Department of Sociology   DAVID LANE
University of Essex   GEORGE KOLANKIEWICZ

CHAPTER ONE

Structural and Social Change in Poland

By David Lane

The government which came to power with Soviet backing in Poland in 1945 sought to create a new socialist order based on that of the Soviet Union. In the years immediately following 1945 the Soviet model of State socialism was extensively copied, but the ruling élites found that the Poland of the late 1940s and early 1950s was in many ways different from where the model had been evolved – Soviet Russia of the twenties and thirties. Like all governments seeking to build anew they were faced by constraints rooted in the past – by values which men have learned in childhood and by structures which have sustained the population for generations. Men do not lightly and easily change such attitudes and ways of life and their values and expectations play a most important part in determining what a new government may do, even though it may have considerable force at its disposal to ensure compliance to its will. The objective economic conditions which may be technically determined (such as the level of industrial development, the educated stock of population) also determine the economic policies considered desirable by the new élites. In this chapter then we shall firstly consider the kind of society Poland was before the socialists came to power and this may give us a greater understanding of the problems they faced and the policies they implemented from 1945 onwards. Secondly, we shall turn to the impact the Communists made after the war on the structure inherited from prewar Poland.

Before the Second World War Poland had been influenced by the industrialisation process of Western Europe. But economic growth, following rapid industrialisation in the late nineteenth century, had been very slow in the inter-war period. Private

entrepreneurs had set up many factories in Silesia, Warsaw and
Łódź in the late nineteenth century, but, like Tsarist Russia at
the same time, large-scale industry was foreign-owned and
managed and by 1937 just over 40 per cent of the capital of
joint stock companies was in foreign ownership.[1] In addition to
foreign business activity, the State also played an important
economic role: it owned the railways and airlines and it had a
monopoly in the production of alcohol, tobacco and arma-
ments. Approximately half of all bank credit originated from
government banks, and the State had a large financial stake in
chemicals, coal and iron and steel.[2] It has been estimated that
in 1932–3 State enterprise accounted for about 17 per cent of
the general turnover of industry and commerce.[3] Social change
had also proceeded as a corollary of the economic: the urban
population increased and an extensive network of schools was
set up so that by the 1931 census it was reported that some
three-quarters of the population was literate.[4] But despite this
intrusion of foreign capital and State activity, Poland before the
Second World War was still predominantly a rural society:
the urban population in 1931 was only 27·4 per cent of the total.[5]
Agriculture was the most important economic sector, contributing some 45 per cent of the net material product in 1937, and
in 1939 about 55 per cent of the employed population worked in
agriculture.[6]

We shall see later that in theory the legitimacy of the new
Communist régime was based on the working class. But the
relatively low level of industrial productivity meant that the
working class constituted a small part of the total population:
out of a population of 34·5 millions in 1937 only 828,900 were

[1] *Pétit annuaire statistique de la Pologne 1939* (Warsaw, 1939) p. 108.

[2] See A. Jezierski, 'Warunki rozwoju przemysłu w Polsce międzywojennej
(1918–39), in *Uprzemysłowienie ziem polskich w XIX i XX wieku* (Warsaw,
1970).

[3] J. Taylor, *The Economic Development of Poland 1919–1950* (Ithaca, New
York, 1952) p. 92.

[4] *Pétit annuaire statistique* . . ., p. 29.

[5] *Pétit annuaire statistique* . . ., p. 10.

[6] O. Lange cited by Nicholas A. Spulber, 'National Income and Product',
in *Poland*, ed. Oscar Halecki (New York 1957) p. 276. The share of agriculture in commodity production was 54 per cent in 1938: Alfred Zauberman, *Industrial Progress in Poland, Czechoslovakia and East Germany* (London,
1964) p. 60.

employed in industry and mining.[1] In addition, there were 374,000 licensed artisans usually self-employed in small establishments.[2] It has been estimated that overall about 20 per cent of the population derived its livelihood from industry.[3]

Prewar Poland was nationally and ethnically a mixed society and the various national groups had figured prominently in certain occupations and statuses. Of the 32 million population of Poland in 1931, by nationality only 22 million were Poles; there were 3·2 million Ukrainians, 2·7 million Jews, 1·2 million Ruthenians, nearly a million Byelorussians, some three-quarters of a million Germans and 138,000 Russians.[4] This mixed population reflected the fact that Poland's borders had been subject to considerable changes in previous centuries. These cannot be discussed in any detail here. In brief, after 1815 Poland had been partitioned between Prussia, Austria and Russia (who had under her jurisdiction the largest part, Congress Poland) and it was not until February 1923 with the recognition of the Polish–Lithuanian border that Poland regained her territorial integrity when some of her previous territory and juridicial authority were returned to her. But much of the territory she then regained was now populated by non-Poles.

The minority groups in prewar Poland played an important part in the development of commerce and industry. The 1931 census, for example, showed that whereas the Jews constituted only 9·8 per cent of the total population, they made up 58·7 per cent of those engaged in commerce, 21·3 per cent of persons in industry and they also figured prominently in the professions.[5] While Germans constituted prosperous groups in agriculture and industry, the Slavonic nationalities (Poles, Byelorussians and Ukrainians) made up a large part of the peasantry[6] though the Poles had a powerful squirearchy and

---

[1] *Concise Statistical Yearbook of Poland 1939–41* (London 1941) p. 50.

[2] Ibid., p. 44.

[3] J. Taylor, *Economic Development . . .*, p. 83. Comparative figures for Germany and Yugoslavia were 38 per cent and 11 per cent respectively.

[4] *Pétit annuaire . . .*, pp. 22–3.

[5] *Pétit annuaire . . .*, pp. 32–3. About half the number of lawyers and 46 per cent of doctors were Jewish. J. Żarnowski, *Struktura społeczna inteligencji w Polsce w latach 1918–1939* (Warsaw, 1964) pp. 223, 262.

[6] Of the peasants 69 per cent were Polish speaking, 13 per cent spoke

the remnants of an aristocracy. The majority of Slavonic Catholic rural Poles constituted the bulk of the small-holding peasantry. But industrial development was largely performed by foreigners and nearly three-fifths of Poland's own commercial class was Jewish. These facts about the social composition of the population help to pin-point some of the cleavages in prewar Poland and the weak support of the Communists.

For the Communists, who were effectively in power after 1945, there was no wide basis of support for them in prewar Poland. This was for many reasons. In the first place, as we have seen above, the industrial working class, which generally provides a base for the Communists, was small. Secondly, the communist party of Poland and its predecessors had never had a wide basis of support among the Polish working class, which was largely attracted to the Polish Socialist Party (PSP).[1] Of the party's peak inter-war membership of 12,000, 59 per cent were classified as intellectuals, only 1,200 or 10 per cent were industrial workers and of the remainder, 28 per cent were peasants and 3 per cent farm labourers.[2] One of the main reasons for the rejection of the Communists was their emphasis on internationalist and pro-Russian values in a country where Polish nationalist feeling was strong. Thirdly, the Communists had been declared illegal since 1919 and the party was weakened even further by being dissolved under pressure from Stalin in 1938. These social and structural difficulties meant that the communist party traditionally had a weak social basis of support. The party itself was revived during the war (1942) and renamed Polish Workers' Party (*Polska Partia Robotnicza*). It joined forces with the newly founded pro-Soviet Polish Patriots Union, giving a joint membership of 20,000 in 1944.[3]

The political culture of prewar Poland was not of the western democratic, participatory type. An unsuccessful parliamentary system, set up after the First World War, came to an

Ukrainian, 5 per cent Ruthenian and 4 per cent Byelorussian. J. Szczepański, 'Zmiany w strukturze klasowej społeczeństwa polskiego', in *Przemiany Społeczne w Polsce Ludowej*, ed. A. Sarapata (Warsaw, 1965) p. 50.

[1] See M. K. Dziewanowski, *The Communist Party of Poland* (Cambridge, 1959).

[2] J. A. Regula, *Historia Kommunistycznej Partii Polski* (Warsaw, 1934) p. 259. Cited by Richard F. Staar, *Poland 1944–1962* (Louisiana, 1962) p. 72.   [3] Staar, p. 80.

end in 1926 when Piłsudski took effective control of the executive. He made the political parties impotent and later instituted controlled elections. The régime of Piłsudski and his successors was conservative and lacking in drive and policy; probably the best description of it is 'ineffectual authoritarianism'.[1] Its ineffectiveness as a government is indicated by the stagnation of Poland's economy between the wars[2] and by the inability of the government to prevent the simultaneous invasion of Poland by both of her powerful neighbours in 1939. Hence Poland lacked a firmly based liberal-democratic tradition and had had a disastrous experience of right-wing authoritarianism. Furthermore, the events of the Second World War significantly weakened the liberal and right-wing forces but strengthened the hand of the Communists.

THE EFFECTS OF THE WAR

The Second World War and its immediate settlement had both a social and political impact. The most striking feature of the war was the destruction of human life itself: it has been estimated that 6 million Polish citizens died in the area of prewar Poland.[3] Most of those killed were civilians among whom the Jews were widely exterminated. The Nazis also pursued a policy of destroying the Polish intelligentsia, bourgeoisie and landowners. By 1941 some two-thirds of the Polish population of 1939 came under German jurisdiction and the remainder under that of the USSR.[4] Approximately 1 million Poles were forcibly moved to the USSR, and 1½ million to Germany. German officials and businessmen took over confiscated workshops in Poland's western territories and, after 1941, with the German invasion of the USSR, the territories were absorbed into the Reich.

The immediate effect of the ending of the war was a significant realignment of Poland's prewar boundaries. She lost to

---

[1] Halecki, p. 101.

[2] Rather exceptionally the central industrial region was developed in the post 1936 period.

[3] E. Szyr *et al.*, *Twenty Years of the Polish People's Republic* (Warsaw, 1964) p. 42.

[4] Taylor, *Economic Development . . .*, pp. 158, 165.

the USSR territories to the east of Brest-Litovsk including the town of Lwów. On the other hand, she gained Silesia, Pomorze and parts of East Prussia from Germany. (See map.) Economically, the period the Second World War witnessed a decline in the productivity of Poland's agriculture and industry.

MAP I. POLAND AFTER THE SECOND WORLD WAR

The postwar settlement, however, resulted in important industrial acquisitions located in former German territory. The gains are shown in Table I. Also, in exchange for the mainly poor agricultural land lost to the Russians, the Poles gained the fertile land area of prewar eastern Germany which had provided a quarter of Germany's food production.[1]

[1] Ibid., p. 173.

TABLE 1. POLAND'S INDUSTRIAL RESOURCES
(PREWAR AND POSTWAR)

Category	Prewar	Postwar	Percentage gain
Coal			
Production area (sq. km.)	3,880	4,450	15
Number of mines	67	80	19
Production (thousand tons)	32,600	64,650	98
Coke plants	9	20	122
Production (thousand tons)	2,124	5,353	152
Brown coal mines	7	20	186
Production (thousand tons)	18	7,611	3,220
Briquette plants	4	8	100
Production (thousand tons)	17	386	1,270
Zinc and lead			
Number of mines	2	9	350
Production (thousand tons)	492	1,214	147
Iron ore			
Number of mines	20	21	5
Production (thousand tons)	792	865	7
Crude oil			
Number of wells	812	190	−77
Production	501	118	−76
Potassium salts			
Number of mines	3	0	—
Production (thousand tons)	522	0	—

Source: Taylor, *Economic Development* . . ., pp. 179–80.

The transfer of territory was also accompanied by population movement: between 1946 and 1949 about two and a half million Germans, Ukrainians, Russians and Byelorussians had left Poland for the West.[1] Hence the total population inhabiting Poland had fallen from 34,849,000 in 1939 to 25,507,000 in 1951[2] and the ethnic–religious composition by the latter date was over 98 per cent Polish and over 95 per cent Catholic. The political effects of the war on balance were to the Communists' advantage. While the Soviet invasion in 1939

[1] E. Strzelecki, 'Rozwój ludności Polski w dwudziestoleciu 1944–64', in *Przemiany społeczne w Polsce Ludowej*, ed. A. Sarapata (Warsaw, 1965) p. 89.
[2] G.U.S., *Rocznik Statystyczny 1970* (Warsaw, 1970) p. 21.

and the controversial massacre of Polish officers at Katyń offended Polish nationalism, the war had other more positive attributes for a future Communist government. Many of the non-Communist Polish political leaders emigrated to the West and others were killed in the Warsaw uprising which preceded the liberation of the city by the Red Army. Also, many of the prewar aristocracy and bourgeoisie either did not return from emigration or fled before the advancing Communist forces. Politically the London-based Polish *émigré* government was outmanoeuvred by the Russians, who were able to secure international recognition for their own protégés now organised under the Polish Committee of National Liberation – the Lublin Committee. In 1945 a government was formed with sixteen out of twenty posts filled by the Soviet-backed Lublin Committee. Poland's history cannot be seen independently from that of Germany and Russia: in 1945 the USSR was intent on bringing postwar Poland under the Soviet sphere of influence and this entailed the imposition of a socio-political order of the Soviet type. The absence of any significant support by Western foreign powers for a non-Soviet solution of the Polish problem made a *de facto* Communist seizure of power and a government of the Soviet type inevitable.

POLITICAL AND SOCIAL CHANGE AFTER 1945

Against a background of internal opposition the political changes which took place in the late forties were designed to consolidate the power of the Communists. Perhaps the most important internal political event was the unification of the Polish Workers' Party, PWP (*Polska Partia Robotnicza*), with the Polish Socialist Party, PSP (*Polska Partia Socjalistyczna*), in December 1948. After that date, a new party, the Polish United Workers Party, PUWP (*Polska Zjednoczona Partia Robotnicza*) (in which former members of the PSP were given a significant but minority share of top positions) effectively ruled the country. The incorporation of the PSP in the PUWP not only weakened possible counter-revolutionary groups but also provided the ruling party with many more administrative and executive activists who were urgently needed by a party intent on rapid industrialisation and social change. Membership of the PWP, which was some 210,000 in 1945, rose to 1,240,000 (or 5 per cent of the total population) for the PUWP in 1950.[1] In addition, other minor parties, the United Peasant Party (*Zjednoczone Stronnictwo Ludowe*)[2] and the Democratic Party (*Stronnictwo Demokratyczne*), maintained a separate existence though they played a minor political role.

Changes in the international environment, which cannot be pursued in detail here, contributed to the more intense political control after 1948. The Cold War intensified: Czechoslovakia was incorporated in the East bloc following the seizure of power by the Communists in 1948 and Yugoslavia was expelled from it. Political relations with the West hardened: NATO was formed in 1949 and, following Soviet pressure on the Poles, Marshall aid was restricted for use in Western Europe.[3] In Eastern Europe there followed greater military and economic integration which made Poland and other East European States more dependent on the Soviet Union. These changes set the scene for industrialisation and rapid social change which were to take place in the early fifties.

As in Russia after the October 1917 Revolution, nationalisation and full central control were not introduced in one fell swoop. From the beginning, the economy had three sectors: state, co-operative and private enterprise. The immediate tasks to be carried out between 1945 and 1948 were to integrate the annexed territory from Germany, to settle the displaced population and to carry out a minimum programme of agricultural and industrial reform which would secure an economic and social basis for the new Communist-controlled government. Much of the land left by the fleeing German population was claimed by Polish peasant proprietors and consequently worked in small batches. This process was rationalised by the land reforms of 1946 and 1947. Large estates (over 50 hectares or over 100 hectares, depending on the region) were divided for private cultivation among some 1 million peasants.[4] At one

---

[1] B. Bierut, 'II Zjazd PZPR', in *Nowe Drogi* 1951, no. 4 (April) p. 69.

[2] See Ch. 2.

[3] UNRRA aid between 1945 and 1947 came to 476·3 million dollars. It ceased in 1947.

[4] See United Nations Food and Agricultural Organisation, *F.A.O. Mission for Poland* (Washington, D.C., 1948), pp. 39–40. Andrzej Korbonski,

stroke the Communist leaders neutralised the opposition of the peasants and destroyed what remained of the land-owning classes. But the economic results of the reforms encouraged the proliferation of small units (under 10 hectares) which could hardly support their owners and did not provide a surplus for the market.[1] The Polish Peasant Party (*Polskie Stronnictwo Ludowe*), which was founded in 1945, had considerable support among the peasants and was one of the main political forces opposing the Communists. In 1949 it joined forces with the pro-Communist Peasant Party (*Stronnictwo Ludowe*) to form the United Peasant Party (UPP) (*Zjednoczone Stronnictwo Ludowe*), which has continued to the present day. The UPP, unlike its predecessor, was pledged to support the worker–peasant alliance and the political leadership of the PUWP. During 1950 and 1951 many of the anti-Communists in the UPP were made to resign and some were arrested. Henceforth the UPP was to be a party with mainly peasant support working within the framework laid down by the Communists.[2]

Nationalisation of industry in 1945 was concentrated on firms owned by former German nationals and after the first Congress of the PWP (6–13 December 1945), a decree was passed on 2 January 1946 nationalising firms employing more than fifty production workers per shift[3] – in effect nearly all mining, the best part of medium- and all large-scale industry. Control of nationalised industry was centralised under fourteen central boards which had authority over materials and sales. Some private enterprise continued in these early postwar years, though it played a secondary and subservient role to the nationalised sector. It was also of diminishing importance: by 1950 the share of private firms in industry and handicrafts had dropped to 6 per cent (21 per cent in 1946) and that of private

The Politics of Socialist Agriculture in Poland 1945–1960 (New York, 1965) ch. 3. G.U.S., *Rocznik Statystyczny 1949* (1950) pp. 54–9, 61.

[1] By 1950, 88 per cent of farms, covering 69·9 per cent of the cultivated area, were under 10 hectares in size. See Appendix 2, Table 3.

[2] For further details see Andrzej Korbonski, *Politics of Socialist Agriculture in Poland: 1945–1960* (1965) ch. 4. We consider the significance of the UPP below in Ch. 2.

[3] J. W. Gołębiowski, 'Problemy nacjonalizacji przemysłu', in *Uprzemysłowienie ziem polskich w XIX i XX wieku* (Warsaw, 1970) p. 533.

trade had fallen to 15 per cent (78 per cent in 1946);[1] more important still is the fact that by 1947 the socialist sector accounted for 99·5 per cent of total gross industrial output.[2]

In addition to these changes in the ownership and control of industry was the growth of Poland's industrial capacity resulting from an increase in capital accumulation. Whereas in 1938 only 12·5 per cent of the gross national product was used for gross public and private investment, by 1952 the figure had risen to 23 per cent.[3] Before the Second World War Poland had a low ratio of capital accumulation: expressed as a percentage of national income it was 3·2 in 1930, 0·6 in 1931, negative for 1932 to 1935, nil in 1936 and 6·8 in 1938.[4] From the late 1940s, when Poland had reached the prewar level of output, large increases in capital formation occurred as a result of the industrialisation drive: between 1946 and 1950 gross investment increased by 60 per cent; between 1951 and 1955 it rose by 34 per cent; for the periods between 1956 and 1960 and 1961 and 1965 it increased by 32 per cent and 23 per cent respectively.[5] The largest proportion of this investment (on average 40·7 per cent annually between 1946 and 1969) was in the industrial sector,[6] and mainly in heavy industry. The economic effects of this investment programme were to more than double by 1953 the share of industry in the national income: in 1938 industry contributed 4·08 billion złoties, whereas by 1953 the figure had risen to 10·37 billion złoties (expressed at constant 1938 prices): agriculture contribution, on the other hand, fell from 6·90 billion złoties to 5·20 billion.[7]

One area in which private enterprise continued to play an

[1] Figures cited in W. J. Stankiewicz and J. M. Montias, *Institutional Changes in the Postwar Economy of Poland* (New York, 1955) p. 20.

[2] *Rocznik Statystyczny, 1949*, p. 21. The handicraft trades still remained in private hands. Though the number of workshops declined from 140,000 in 1948 to 93,884 in 1950, the number rose in the 1950s and 1960s to reach a total of 170,000 in 1969 when total employed was 355,000. *Mały Rocznik Statystyczny 1970* (1970).

[3] U.S. Congress, Joint Committee on the Economic Report, *Trends in Economic Growth: A Comparison of the Western Powers and the Soviet Bloc* (Washington, D.C., 1955) p. 290.

[4] Figures cited by A. Zauberman, *Industrial Progress . . .*, p. 42 n.

[5] *Mały Rocznik Statystyczny 1971*, p. 67.

[6] *Rocznik Statystyczny 1970*, p. 97.

[7] U.S. Congress, *Trends in Economic Growth . . .*, p. 287.

important role was agriculture. Collectivisation of peasant plots was not part of Communist policy in the immediate post-revolutionary era and had been denied as an aim of the government by Gomułka in 1946. From 1949 to 1956, however, for reasons which will be discussed in a later chapter, a collectivisation drive took place: in 1949, 243 collective farms were founded, a figure which rose to 10,600 in the autumn of 1956. Even so, at the height of collectivisation only 8·6 per cent of the total cultivated area was collectivised. In 1956 policy again changed, membership of the collectives was made voluntary and over 80 per cent of the farms were dissolved, leaving by 1962 a total of only some 2,000 farms covering 1·2 per cent of the cultivated area.[1] Hence agriculture remains an important area, not only of private ownership but also of what it implies for the Communist government – a source of non-Communist values and potential opposition to the government.

The overwhelmingly Roman Catholic composition of the Polish population singles Poland out from the other States of Eastern Europe which have, at most, Catholic minorities. The significance of the Church in Poland is two-fold. First, it may provide the population (or part of it) with a belief system which is an alternative and to some extent a competitor with Communism; to this extent it may undermine the legitimacy of the ideology and symbols used by the ruling party – for instance, it denies the theoretical primacy of Marxism–Leninism. Second, it provides a structure which may aggregate and articulate interests and in this respect it may function as an important political group. The Church too had been given a prominent place in Poland before the Second World War: the 1921 Constitution referred to it as occupying 'a pre-eminent position in the state among legally equal religions'.[2] While it is not our prime concern to conduct research into the Roman Catholic Church in this book,[3] a brief outline of the relations between Church and State is in order.

The policy of the Communists in the early postwar years was not to destroy the Catholic Church: it sought to placate rather

---

[1] Staar, pp. 88–90. See also Ch. 2, below.
[2] Cited by Halecki, p. 199.
[3] The role of the Church will be studied in a following volume of this series by J. Cave *et al.*, *Politics and the Polish Economy*.

than to antagonise religious feeling. But the role of the Church in the society was increasingly restricted.[1] The formal agreement between Church and State signed in 1950 gave the Catholics many formal rights; the teaching of religion in schools, the continuation of the Catholic University of Lublin, the conduct of charity work, participation in religious pilgrimages and processions, the publication of religious matter, religious care in the armed forces and other institutions. Such rights, of course, were within the framework of Polish State laws which in practice restricted the freedom of activity of the Church. It was required not to participate in anti-government campaigns, to support reconstruction, to teach respect for State laws and not to obstruct collectivisation.

The actual relations of Church and State have fluctuated. In the early 1950s the State tried to undermine the authority of the Church: it attempted to control ecclesiastical appointments, and priests were required to swear an oath of allegiance to the State. Religious propaganda was brought under the control of groups sympathetic to the Communists. Communist pressure culminated in 1953 in the arrest of Cardinal Wyszyński, who was deprived of his ecclesiastical position. After October 1956 State control weakened. Arrested ecclesiastics, including Wyszyński, were freed and the government relaxed its control of Church appointments. A wider range of Catholic views was allowed publication and in the elections of 1957 twelve members of the Catholic Znak group were elected to parliament. But the early 1960s witnessed minor clashes between Church and State. In 1961 a law was adopted to abolish all religious instruction in schools though the Church was able to continue with religious instruction through its own network of catechism centres.

---

[1] In 1946 civil marriage became universal and the conditions for divorce were defined by State law; all statistical records concerning deaths, births and marriages were transferred from Church to State; religious instruction in schools was to be performed by clergy and not by religion, and the hours of religious instruction were limited. In 1950 followed another blow which weakened the Church's economic power: with the exception of land used by parish priests for their own subsistence, all land and property were nationalised – though the Council of Ministers had power to allow the Church to use and administer such property. In 1971 the State returned ownership of ecclesiastical property to the Church in the Western Territories.

Another controversy was over birth control where both sides took up opposing ideological stances. After 1956, despite differences and open disagreements, both sides sought to avoid direct confrontation. The State believed that secularisation would follow industrialisation and would be reinforced by the materialist values inculated in the educational system. The Church for its part had concessions by which it could maintain its links with Rome and spread its beliefs: it could work within the confines of a Communist society as it could within those of the capitalist.

Thus the relative failure of collectivisation, the existence of more than one political party and the relative autonomy of the Roman Catholic Church are the main structural differences between People's Poland and the USSR.

Let us now turn to consider factors, such as the demographic background, which are relatively (but not completely) independent of political control, and others such as the occupational structure which have been influenced more directly by the Communist polity. In the first place we shall describe the size, composition and growth of the population and then define the income, status and education of the major occupational groups. The industrialisation process brought in its train significant changes in the structure of the population. There was a stimulus to the movement of population from village to town, and there took place important changes in the educational levels of the population. The existence of a Communist government also had important effects on the prewar pattern of emigration and on the role of women in the economy. Finally, we shall mention some of the main cleavages in the social structure.

POPULATION GROWTH AND MOVEMENT

As we saw earlier, the Second World War and its immediate aftermath resulted for Poland in a net population loss of 10·2 million people – a fall from 34·8 millions in 1938 to 24·6 millions in 1949. By 1966, however, this vital loss had nearly been made up, for the population totalled 31·8 million. As we may see from Appendix 1, the postwar years witnessed a very high though declining birth rate and a much lower but also falling death rate. The former fell from 30·7 in 1950 to 16·7 in 1970 and the latter from 11·6 to 8·1 in the same period, giving a population growth rate of 19·1 in 1950 and 8·6 in 1970. Particularly remarkable is the drop in the infant mortality rate – from 111·2 in 1950 to 33·4 in 1970. The figures, in common with those of other societies, also show a higher birth rate in the countryside than in the town.

The deaths incurred during the Second World War together with the high postwar live birth rate led to a highly skewed population structure. Even before the war there had been a considerable surplus of women over men: in 1931 there were 106·9 women for 100 males: in 1946 the figure had risen to 118·4 and in the towns it was 130·9.[1] Turning to the age structure, we see that 29·5 per cent of the population in 1950 was under 15; 62·3 per cent was between the age of 20 and 60 and 8·2 per cent was over 60; by 1969 the proportions were 27·2 per cent, 60·1 per cent and 12·7 per cent respectively.[2] In the early postwar years the working population had to support a large, unproductive population, while during this time opportunities for occupational promotion to fill the depleted managerial, technical and administrative ranks were very great for the newly qualified.

We have already noted the shift westwards of Poland's borders after the war. The realignment was accompanied by massive population movement. Between 1946 and 1949 two and a quarter million inhabitants, mainly Germans, left the western territories, another 1·5 million arrived in Poland from the east and about the same number returned from Western Europe. The total influx to the 'reclaimed' western Polish territories between 1946 and 1949 was 2·5 million persons, most of whom were young. In fact between 1950 and 1961 the population of the western territories increased from 5·7 million to 7·7 million mainly as a result of natural growth.[3]

These mass geographical population movements had stabilised by 1950, when internal migration became characterised by a movement from village to town. Despite the fact that the largest war losses were in the towns and the greatest natural population increase was in the countryside, the urban population by 1950 was 36·9 per cent of the total – 1·8 per cent more

[1] E. Strzelecki, 'Rozwój ludności . . ., p. 87.

[2] *Rocznik Statystyczny 1970*, p. 37. [3] E. Strzelecki, pp. 89–122.

than it had been in 1939. The figures slightly underestimate the
extent of urbanisation, for many inhabitants of the villages
supported themselves by non-agricultural work – 26 per cent
in 1950, compared to only 19 per cent in 1931. During the
1950s the urban population increased by 5·3 million. Only
some 1·1 millions was accounted for by incoming migration,
while natural growth made up 2·3 millions and administrative
changes 1·9 million.[1] By 1960 48·3 per cent of the population
was officially defined as 'urban'. During the 1960s the urban
population increased by 19·6 per cent and the rural population
increased by only 2·6 per cent.[2] By 1970 the urban population
(52·2 per cent) outnumbered the rural (47·8 per cent).

THE CHANGING STRUCTURE OF OCCUPATIONS

Let us now turn to consider the stratification of the population
into various class and occupational layers. A broad summary of
the main postwar changes may be seen in Table 2, which shows
the major occupational social groups in 1931 and 1960.

There are four main points which are illustrated by the table.
First, the proportion of handicraftsmen and petty traders fell
six-fold (from 10·7 per cent to 1·5 per cent); second, the share
of non-manual workers rose three times (from 5·6 per cent to
17·8 per cent); third, independent farmers remained in 1960 the
largest occupational group (when family helpers are included)
though manual workers constituted the largest group in paid
employment (44·2 per cent); fourth, in contradistinction to the
USSR, a very small proportion (at most 3·3 per cent) was in
co-operative farms.

More detailed figures of employment by economic sector is
shown in Table 3. Here the decline over time in the role of
agriculture (the 1970 census results show that 29·5 per cent of
the population in that year depended on agriculture for their
main source of income – a drop of nearly 10 per cent on the
1960 figure)[3] and the rise of industry, building and transport

---

[1] Strzelecki, pp. 99, 111.
[2] W. Kawalec, 'Narodwy spis powszechny 1970: pierwsze rezultaty i
pierwsze wnioski', in *Nowe Drogi*, April 1971, no. 4, p. 36.
[3] Kawalec, p. 37.

is clearly brought out. (Unearned income is attributed to pensioners and scholarship holders.)

The rapid postwar growth of industry combined with the effects of political change resulted in the emergence of a working class different in composition to that of inter-war Poland. The lack of expansion of Polish industry between the wars led to a stable working class community during that time. After the Second World War leading administrative, executive and technical positions were filled by former workers and the massive influx of peasants to the factories meant that the working class was now composed to a large extent of inexperienced and

TABLE 2. OCCUPATIONAL STRUCTURE OF THE POLISH POPULATION 1931 AND 1960

Social group	*1931* Gainfully employed and family members maintained by them (*per cent*)	*1960* Gainfully employed and helping family members (*per cent*)	*1960* Gainfully employed (*only*) (*per cent*)
Handicraftsmen and petty merchants	10·7	1·5	1·8
Independent farmers	51·8	44·0	27·8
Non-manual workers and free professionals	5·6	17·8	22·9
Manual workers	28·6	34·2	44·2
Non-income disposing	3·3	—	—
Members of rural and urban labour co-operatives	—	2·5	3·3
	100·0	100·0	100·0
Absolute numbers	31,915,800	13,875,000	10,755,300

The data in Table 2 are not fully comparable. The studies group the population somewhat differently, and while the data for 1931 pertain to gainfully employed and family members maintained by them, the data for 1960 refer to the structure of gainful employment. Cited by W. Wesołowski, 'Changes in the Class Structure in Poland', in J. Szczepański, *Empirical Sociology in Poland* (Warsaw, 1966).

country-born men. By 1962, for instance, only 17 per cent of the total industrial labour force and 19 per cent of building workers had been in those categories before the war.[1] This meant that traditional working class trades, which had a tendency to recruit within certain families, were broken up. In the State fishing industry after the war, for example, 70 per cent of recruits came direct from the villages.[2] Painting lost its skilled craft character and became more a job of work – performed by relatively unskilled men from the countryside.[3]

TABLE 3. POPULATION BY MAIN SOURCE OF INCOME (PER CENT), 1931, 1950, 1960*

Economic sector	*1931*	*1950*	*1960*
Agriculture	60·0	47·1	38·2
Industry	12·7	20·9	25·0
Building	1·3	4·8	6·3
Transport and communication	3·2	5·2	6·1
Trade	4·8	5·4	4·9
Education, science, culture	1·0	2·2	2·8
Social welfare, health	0·6	1·2	1·8
Other sectors	7·4	9·2	8·4
Living on unearned income	2·9	4·0	6·5
	100·0	100·0	100·0

* Source: *Rocznik Statystyczny 1970*, p. 40.

The process of social mobility was influenced by the Communist political élites who sought in the early postwar years to recruit men from the working class to positions of authority. Thus a typical feature of the period until about 1955 was that heads of industrial enterprises and local government officials were often promoted manual workers. From the mid-fifties, however, these men began to fade into the background and

[1] W. Wesołowski, 'Changes in the Class Structure in Poland', in *Empirical Sociology in Poland*, ed. J. Szczepański (Warsaw, 1966).

[2] Aurelia Jankowska-Polańska, 'Rybacy morscy jako grupa zawodowa', in *Przegląd Socjologiczny*, vol. xv, no. 1 (1961) p. 119.

[3] Edward Lenkowski, 'Badanie nad strukturą i postawami pracowników fizycznych zawodu malarskiego', in *Przegląd Socjologiczny*, vol. xv, no. 1 (1961).

to give way to younger men educated in People's Poland.[1]

The place of women in the economy also underwent important changes. A much higher proportion of women entered industrial employment than before the Second World War and many fewer were engaged in domestic service. Many women began to receive higher technical education and by 1961, as shown in Table 4, they constituted 20 per cent of the graduates

TABLE 4. FULL-TIME GRADUATES OF HIGHER
TECHNICAL SCHOOLS BY SEX, 1946–61

Year	Total	Women	Per cent women
1946	908	33	3·6
1951	4,759	507	10·7
1956	10,594	1,264	11·9
1961	7,738	1,547	20·0
1967	9,858	1,197	12·1

Source: Data supplied by: Międzyuczelniany Zakład Badań nad Szkolnictwem Wyższym (1969).

of technical high schools, though the figure had dropped significantly by 1967. Having graduated, however, few women were appointed to posts of director, chief engineer or assistant director: of 4,656 factory directors in 1964, only eighty-nine were women. In the pure sciences and medicine, women were much better represented than in applied technology. In 1964 they accounted respectively for 49·5 per cent and 56·7 per cent of the graduates; and by 1968 53·3 per cent and 59·4 per cent.[2] In other non-manual occupations women could expect considerable advancement. In 1964, for example, one third of the chief accountants were female.[3]

Another characteristic of the occupational structure was the mixing of peasant–worker population: after the war, a greater

---

[1] This process is discussed in detail in Chs. 3, 5 and 6.

[2] *Spis Kadrowy: Pracownicy z wykształceniem wyższym*, no. 2 Zatrudnienie 1968 (Warsaw, 1969) p. xv. G.U.S. (Warsaw, 1968) p. xv.

[3] *Rocznik Statystyczny Pracy*, p. 322.

number of non-agricultural personnel (teachers, health and communication workers) lived in the countryside and an estimated third of rural residents were travelling to work in the town. Ziółkowski has estimated that of half the families giving agriculture as their source of support at least one person is employed outside agriculture.[1] Compared to prewar time there has occurred a decline in the number of agricultural labourers (in 1950, 1·9 per cent of the rural population was employed on private farms and 3·4 per cent on State farms, compared to 11·9 per cent in 1931 on private farms).[2]

The shortage of housing in the towns led to the development of hostels for the newly arrived rural male immigrants, and these were often of a 'familial–neighbour' type, recruiting men from a certain rural area.[3] In this way pockets of 'rural folkways' were perpetuated in the towns making adaptation to city life more difficult. The significance of the peasant nature of the 'new' working class will be commented on later.

Here, before turning to consider the more sociological aspects of the system of stratification, we may conclude: first, that the effects of war and politics led to the advancement of many previous workers to executive and technical positions; second, that the rapid industrialisation created a new mainly peasant-recruited working class in the towns and a less exclusive peasantry in the countryside; and third, that the peasant background of the working class gave rise to problems of labour discipline and turnover.

The industrialisation process was accompanied by profound changes in the educational system. By 1960 a minimum schooling of seven years was universal. This was regarded as one of the most effective ways to provide a widespread pool of labour with the minimum skills and the 'right' attitudes to industrial employment. Vocational and secondary education was expanded. In 1937–8 only 13·5 per cent of the 14–17 age group was at school,

[1] J. Ziółkowski, 'Miejsce i rola procesu urbanizacji w przeobrażeniach społecznych w Polsce Ludowej', in *Studia Socjologiczne*, 1965, no. 18, pp. 65–6.
[2] *Wieś w liczbach* (1962) p. 25.
[3] Before the war nearly half of rural emigrants went to take up household work in the town; after the war some 60 per cent went into industry. S. Nowakowski, 'Hotel robotniczy na tle procesów urbanizacji', *Przegląd Socjologiczny*, vol. xii (1958) p. 33.

by 1956–7 this figure had risen to 46 per cent and again to 72·8 per cent in 1962–3.[1] As shown by Table 5, between 1949 and 1964 the number of pupils in elementary vocational schools increased threefold and the number in secondary vocational schools rose sixteen times.

TABLE 5. NUMBER OF VOCATIONAL SCHOOL PUPILS

School year	Elementary vocational schools	Secondary vocational schools
1937–8	184,000	10,000
1948–9	218,000	40,000
1950–1	317,000	270,600
1963–4	591,800	631,700
1969–70	656,199	824,188

Source: Rocznik Statystyczny 1970, p. 414.

TABLE 6. NUMBER OF STUDENTS IN HIGHER EDUCATIONAL INSTITUTIONS (000's)

Academic year	No. of students	Academic year	No. of students
1937–8	49·5	1958–9	156·5
1946–7	86·5	1959–60	161·0
1947–8	94·8	1960–1	165·7
1948–9	103·5	1961–2	172·4
1949–50	115·5	1962–3	190·3
1950–1	125·1	1963–4	212·6
1951–2	141·7	1964–5	231·2
1952–3	131·3	1965–6	251·9
1953–4	140·0	1966–7	274·5
1954–5	155·4	1967–8	288·8
1955–6	157·5	1968–9	305·6
1956–7	170·3	1969–70	322·5
1957–8	162·7	1970–1	329·4

Source: Polska w liczbach 1944–1966 (Warsaw, 1966) p. 86. Rocznik Statystyczny 1970, pp. 400–1. Mały Rocznik Statystyczny 1971, p. 267.

[1] Figures cited by W. Wesołowski, 'Changes in the Class Structure . . .'.

In higher education a relatively smaller expansion occurred. As shown in Table 6, between 1949–50 and 1969–70 the number of students in higher educational institutions nearly tripled. The largest rise – a tenfold increase – occurred in the number of engineering students while students of humanities increased only four-fold. From 1945 to 1962 a third of a million students graduated from Polish institutes of higher education[1] and they were considered by the Communist authorities as forming the basis of a new socialist intelligentsia – by 1962 80 per cent of all persons having higher education had graduated after the war. Furthermore, quite a large proportion of the graduates originated from the working class. The changing social composition of the student body is shown in Table 7. Here we see that in 1960–1 29 per cent of students originated from manual worker strata compared to only 9·5 per cent in 1935–6. Non-manual children, however, still constituted the largest group.

TABLE 7. SOCIAL COMPOSITION OF STUDENTS IN HIGHER EDUCATION (PER CENT)

	1935–6	*1960–1*
Manual workers	9·5	29·2
Peasants	5·0	18·5
Petty proprietors and handicraftsmen	12·0	4·6
Non-manual workers	38·0	46·5
Other occupations (including free professions)	35·5	1·2
	100·0	100·0

Source: A. Sarapata, 'Stratification and Social Mobility in Poland', in J. Szczepański, *Empirical Sociology in Poland* (Warsaw, 1966) p. 46.

So far we have considered the statistical categories into which the social structure may be classified and have ignored the group structure: that is, we have not considered the extent to which the categories described are aware of any group identity, the degree to which they are differentiated and the pattern of relations between them.

[1] J. Szczepański, 'Zmiany w strukturze klasowej społeczeństwa polskiego', in *Przemiany społeczne w Polsce Ludowej*, ed. A. Sarapata (Warsaw, 1965) p. 32.

The discussion of the actual nature of the social structure in any society is bedevilled by the way the ideology of that society defines the way that social strata, and particularly social classes, *should* behave. Such notions play a pivotal point in Marxist sociology and politics: class defines the legitimacy or otherwise of a social order and the boundaries of political conflict. Here we may focus on the income and status of the four groups defined in the 'official' ideology: the manual working-class, the intelligentsia, the peasantry and private businessmen.

In the political theory which legitimises the Polish People's Republic, the 'working class', employed in State-owned enterprises, is distinguished as the political ruling class. It is differentiated, however, by its relations to the means of production of its component parts and the 'intelligentsia' forms a separate stratum by virtue of the essentially *non-manual* nature of its work activity. The definition adopted by sociologists in State socialist countries implies only the inclusion of all technical, executive and administrative non-manual workers rather than having the connotation of 'independent thinkers' or a cultural élite which the term has in the West. It is recognised by Polish sociologists though that non-manual workers may be divided into different categories.[1] In this study we shall restrict the term 'intelligentsia' to those concerned with creative cultural and scientific work and with the organisation of work requiring higher education.[2] The intelligentsia, then, is a separate stratum which is considered by the ideologists of modern Polish society to be superior in its economic performance to the remainder of the working class. The peasantry[3] and businessmen form a distinct 'class' because they still own their property, tools and produce and their income is determined by what they sell on the market. They are recognised as having a different outlook and interest to the working class, and such class differences form one of the major cleavages in the society.

To some extent these class differences are reinforced by the differentiation of incomes. It is true that one of the most important social effects of Communist control was an immediate

---

[1] See Ch. 3.

[2] J. J. Wiatr, 'Inteligencja w Polsce Ludowej', in *Przemiany społeczne w Polsce Ludowej*, ed. Sarapata (Warsaw, 1965) p. 459.

[3] See Ch. 2, pp. 29–35.

reduction in the income differential between non-manual and manual labour. In 1937 non-manual workers earned on average three times as much as manual workers, whereas by 1960 the differential was only 9 per cent.[1] Wesołowski[2] has shown that 41 per cent of non-manual workers in 1963 earned over 2,000 złoties, compared to 33·1 per cent of manuals; though it should be noted that manual workers outweighed non-manual personnel eight times in the lowest wage group (701–800 złoties), and that there were one and a half times as many non-manuals in the highest groups as manuals. (For a more detailed and extensive study see Chapter 3.) In addition the real income

TABLE 8. EXPENDITURE OF MANUAL AND NON-MANUAL WORKERS IN 1966 AND 1968

	Manual		Non-manual	
	1966	*1968*	*1966*	*1968*
Total spent (złoty per year per person)	11,398	12,763	15,182	16,819
Items of expenditure	*Per cent*	*Per cent*	*Per cent*	*Per cent*
Foodstuffs	50	49·5	43·1	42·5
Alcohol and tobacco	4·2	4·1	3·2	3·1
Footwear and clothing	16·1	16·1	17·0	17·2
Accommodation	9·6	9·4	11·5	11·5
Hygiene and health	4·1	4·2	5·8	6·0
Heating and lighting	4·5	4·4	4·5	4·3
Education and culture	6·8	7·1	9·2	9·2
Communication and travel	2·1	2·4	3·2	3·6
Other	2·6	2·8	2·5	2·6
	100	100	100	100

Source: Budżety rodzin pracowników zatrudnionych w gospodarce uspołecznioniej, no. 53, 1969, p. xvii.

of the lower groups was considerably raised compared to prewar by subsidised housing, health and other social services. However, significant differences in consumption persist: in 1960 only 8·6 per cent of the households of manual workers had vacuum

[1] L. Beskid, 'Dochody robotników i pracowników umysłowych', *Przegląd Statystyczny*, 1963, no. 3.
[2] Wesołowski, 'Changes in the Class Situation', p. 27.

cleaners, whereas the figure for non-manual employees was
31·1; similarly, the figures for refrigerators were 2·8 and 9·9 per
cent.[1] Also, from data collected in Table 8, we see that in 1968
non-manual workers spent more of their income on accommodation, hygiene, health, communication, travel and culture
than did manual workers. An even more important distinction
between manual and non-manual is their educational background, the details of which are shown in Table 9. Obviously,

TABLE 9. EDUCATIONAL LEVEL OF EMPLOYEES IN THE NATIONAL
ECONOMY IN 1958 AND 1968 (PER CENT)*

Educational level		Total (per cent)	Manual (per cent)	Non-manual (per cent)
Higher	1958	3·8	—	12·1
	1968	13·8	—	13·8
Secondary vocational	1958	6·9	0·5	21·0
	1968	11·3	0·8	31·8
Secondary general	1958	4·3	0·5	12·9
	1968	4·5	0·3	12·5
Incomplete secondary general	1958	4·9	1·5	12·4
	1968	3·8	1·2	8·7
Elementary vocational	1958	8·2	8·2	8·2
	1968	15·3	16·9	12·2
Complete elementary	1958	40·8	45·9	29·6
	1968	44·0	56·3	20·2
Incomplete elementary	1958	31·1	43·4	3·8
	1968	16·4	24·5	0·8
		100	100	100

* *Rocznik Statystyczny Pracy 1945–68*, p. 260, Table 3.

the more highly educated are almost exclusively concentrated
among the non-manual strata – though a sizeable number of the
'lower' non-manual group in 1958 only had an elementary
education.

Of course, 'non-manual' and 'manual' are very general
categories and it is necessary to define a little more carefully
how certain strata have a prestige relative to others. Wesołowski
and Sarapata utilised the results of 753 interviews conducted in

[1] Ibid., p. 30.

Warsaw to generalise about the hierarchy of occupations in Poland. They divided occupations into five groups: intelligentsia (leading administrative and cultural personnel), skilled workers, those in private business, white collar (lower clerical and executive) and unskilled manual. The groups were ranked according to 'material benefits', 'job stability' and 'social prestige'. The results are shown in Table 10.

TABLE 10. STATUS OF VARIOUS OCCUPATIONAL GROUPS

Socio-occupational group	Material Benefits		Job stability		Social prestige	
	Ranking	Middle pt.	Ranking	Middle pt.	Ranking	Middle pt.
Private business	1	1·81	3	2·76	3	2·81
Intelligentsia	2	2·35	1	1·60	1	1·74
Skilled worker	3	2·40	2	1·70	2	2·33
White-collar	4	3·30	5	2·86	4	3·17
Unskilled worker	5	4·12	4	2·85	5	4·06

Criteria: Scale 1 – material benefits. Scale 2 – job stability. Scale 3 – social prestige.

Source: W. Wesołowski and A. Sarapata, 'Hierarchie zawodów i stanowisk', in *Studia Socjologiczne*, no. 2 (2), 1961, p. 104.

The main inferences to be drawn from Table 10 are that the scale of material benefits do not correlate exactly with job stability and prestige. Private business provides high income (Rank 1) but is rated below the intelligentsia and skilled worker in prestige and security. Turning to the scale of social prestige we see, rather surprisingly perhaps, that skilled workers are ranked second after the intelligentsia and above entrepreneurs and (unskilled) white collar non-manual workers. Hence one of the important aspects of a *communist* pattern of industrialisation and political change is that private entrepreneurs, as a class, have less status than men in State employment and that the skilled manual worker has greater prestige than the *lower* clerical (white collar group). Educational and occupational qualifications would seem to be the most important criteria determining the status of an occupational group.

The five occupational groups defined above comprise rather a large range of occupations and further research conducted by Sarapata (see Table 11) links up actual material benefit and actual social prestige with 'postulated remuneration' (i.e. what respondents believe occupations should receive as opposed to what respondents believe they do receive).

TABLE 11. RANKING OF OCCUPATIONS

	Evaluation according to views on				
Evaluated occupation	Actual material benefit (1)	Actual social prestige (2)	Difference col. 1– col. 2 (3)	'Postu-lated' remuner-ation (4)	Difference col. 1– col. 4 (5)
Minister	1	5	−4	2	−1
Doctor	2	2	0	3	−1
Locksmith – private business	3	12	−9	12	−9
University professor	4	1	+3	1	+3
Qualified steel-worker	5	6	−1	5	0
Priest	6	7	−1	14	−8
Engineer	7	4	+3	4	+3
Metal worker in factory	8	9	−1	9	−1
Professional officer (regular)	9	13	−4	7	+2
Private farmer	10	10	0	13	−3
Book-keeper	11	11	0	8	+3
Salesgirl	12	15	−3	16	−4
Militia	13	14	−1	11	+2
Teachers	14	3	+11	6	+8
Unskilled building worker	15	16	−1	17	−2
Nurse	16	8	+8	10	+6
State farm worker	17	18	−1	15	+2
Cleaner	18	17	+1	18	0

Based on: A. Sarapata, 'Justum Pretium', in *Studia Socjologiczne*, no. 3 (6), 1962, p. 106.

The second column of ranks (actual social prestige) spells out in more detail what we learned above. At the top come the 'intellectual' positions (professor, doctor, teacher, engineer), at the bottom are the unskilled (worker on State farm, cleaner, unskilled building worker). Gross differences between the remuneration and prestige of these occupations is brought out by comparing the ranks in columns 1 and 2, shown in column 3. Here a positive number shows actual prestige higher than material benefit and a negative number indicates lower prestige than material benefit: note that large discrepancies between the ratings of private locksmiths, teachers and nurses. In column 5 we have again computed the difference between actual and 'postulated' material means. One observes large divergencies between the actual and 'postulated' remuneration of private locksmiths, priests, teachers and nurses. These differences may be the basis of social tension between the various urban occupational groupings.

Later in this book we shall bring out in more detail the characteristics of these groups and discuss their operation in the political process. Here we may sum up the more important points. First, the social structure after the Second World War was more ethnically and religiously homogeneous than it had been before. Second, private enterprise continued after the war: in the towns it played a diminishing role, though in the countryside in agriculture it flourished. One of the main social tensions which exists is between the property interests of private farmers and the nationalised sector. Third, the working class itself was differentiated. While the Communist pattern of social change has led to a narrowing of differentials between manual and non-manual strata, the rise of a 'socialist intelligentsia' has brought new and powerful groups to the social scene. The technical and cultural intelligentsia then may in some respects have an interest distinct from the working class. Also, the access to specialised knowledge which these groups have puts them in a crucial position, for the political élites are dependent on their technical expertise and their administrative and executive efficiency. Fourth, the rapid social changes accompanying industrialisation and the hegemony of the Communist political élite could not but lead to manifestations of unrest. There have been notable mass political upheavals in Poland in October 1956 and December–January 1970–1; and there was a lesser outburst, mainly confined to groups of intellectuals, in February 1968. These upheavals will be discussed in later chapters.

CHAPTER TWO

The Peasantry

By Paul Lewis

THE SOCIAL SITUATION OF THE PEASANTRY

As a social type the peasant is a country-dweller of low status who supports himself primarily from small-scale agriculture conducted more as a way of life than as a commercial enterprise. In both production and consumption, the family is the basic unit and is the fundamental social institution of the little community in which he lives. The formally peripheral aspects of this summary 'typical' picture, however, are more likely to determine the actions of the peasantry as a group within the particular society: the pressure that the demands of the occasional market transactions put on the family economy; the nature of the peasant's access to the land on which he conducts his small-scale agriculture; the lowness of his status in relation to other groups and the direction of its change. It is his response to these variations in the basic conditions of existence and his ability or willingness to adjust to them that are most indicative of the position the peasant holds within the society. In this light the peasantry is a group frequently subject to far-reaching social change. From the beginning peasants as a social group have been in contact with urban societies, they have had to provide them with food in return for tools and commodities though they have lived beyond the pale of its most obvious social forms. Being both more and less than a part of the whole society, peasants themselves form a 'part-society'. Less than a part of society because it was within the urban sector that the culture of literacy, the greatest development of social heterogeneity and forms of association enabling rapid social and technical change, arose. In this sense, at least, the peasantry has remained outside the conventional history-making centres of human society. A peasantry is also something more than just a part of the whole. It almost constitutes a world of its own, apart and quite different from that of the towns and rural non-agricultural groups. The separateness of peasant society has been most emphasised in its cultural dimension: 'In a civilisation there is a great tradition of the reflective few, and there is a little tradition of the largely unreflective many. The great tradition is cultivated in schools or temples; the little tradition works itself out and keeps itself going in the lives of the unlettered in their village communities.'[1] The distinguishing characteristic of a peasant's life is that it is largely bound by the confines of the village and by the experiences and ideas he meets within it. Those who embody the great tradition and take on functions of government, for example, wield power within a society, not authority within a community. The broader social range of non-peasant groups makes for them a different kind of society, and it is only when this kind of differentiation occurs, represented in the power aspect by the rise of the State, that cultivators can be said to constitute a peasantry.[2]

Interdependence exists between peasants and their urban or manorial counterpart not just in a material sense, through the transfer of agricultural surpluses, but also in the social and political spheres. One of the distinguishing marks of a peasantry in contrast to a tribal society is its awareness of belonging to a society ruled by other groups and of its own low status in relation to them. The peasants' mean existence is usually regarded by them as part of the natural order of things. No political remedy for it is at hand because peasant society is politically 'truncated', with the power centres lying outside its compass and the techniques and capacity for political action of societal scope unlikely to be developed within the local community.[3] In Europe the sole contact of the villager with the national society and the literate culture that was the prerogative of supra-local groups – those whose social horizons were not bound by small communities – was mainly the Christian Church. Insofar as

---

[1] R. Redfield, *Peasant Society and Culture* (Chicago, 1960) pp. 41, 42.
[2] E. Wolf, *Peasants* (Englewood Cliffs, N.J., 1966) p. 11.
[3] G. M. Foster, 'Peasant Society and the Image of Limited Good', in *Peasant Society*, J. M. Potter *et al.* (Boston, 1967) pp. 39–40.

peasant revolts were directed against local oppression and individual tyranny, often in support of the central authority and the traditional social order, they did not necessarily weaken the structures that bred them. In this sense rebellious, as opposed to revolutionary, activities can be seen as functional to the system.[1] Thus, from the initial interdependence that lay at the historical roots of peasant-based societies, on the basis of the agricultural surplus, arose urban centres of social, political and cultural subjugation. The food-producing revolution that gave rise to the peasantry was also a social division of labour that fostered not only (as a broad generalisation) the social inequality of rural producer and urban consumer, but also social structures which institutionalised the social dependence this inequality pressed upon the peasant. Marx may be said to describe a primitive 'mass society' when he wrote that the French peasantry were as 'formed by simple addition of homologous magnitudes, much as potatoes in a sack form a sack of potatoes'.[2]

Within the part-society framework peasants would appear to have little capacity for political action of societal significance. The subsistence nature of peasant agriculture and the isolation of village life make the peasant an unlikely participant in the class relations of a national society. But the process of social modernisation leads to the growth of social heterogeneity and the proliferation of roles within specialised structures of social, economic and political activity. Market transactions play a greater part in the peasant economy, enfranchisement leads to involvement in organised political activities, and contacts with the urban world bring the need for adaption to a different kind of social relationship from that found in the personal, unformalised life of the little community. Social status becomes more a matter of individual achievement and is determined by performance in a variety of roles which are not necessarily closely related. The intensification of forms of economic domain over the peasant and the increased importance of market relations in an economy magnify the peasant's role as agricultural

---

[1] A distinction made by M. Gluckman in the Introduction to his *Order and Rebellion in Tribal Africa* (London, 1963).

[2] K. Marx, 'The Eighteenth Brumaire of Louis Bonaparte', in Marx and Engels, *Selected Works*, vol. 1 (Moscow, 1962) p. 334.

producer and the function of the farm as an agricultural enterprise. But within the peasant community the farm is as much a
social as an economic unit. Its agriculture is geared not to the
maximisation of profit but to the satisfaction of the needs of
the family, as are the economic activities of its members.[1] If the
pressures of the market run counter to their consumption needs
the increased demands on the peasant economy as a production
unit, therefore, may be perceived not as a stimulus to more
efficient production but as a form of social oppression disrupting
the peasants' way of life. In more socially heterogeneous communities with specialised structures of social activity roles are less
interdependent and the possibility of adaption to change greater.

What came to be known at the end of the nineteenth century
as the 'peasant problem' does not stem just from the obstacle
met within the peasant economy to the need for greater agricultural productivity and to sensitising a basically subsistence
agriculture to the pressures of the market. As already noted,
within the peasant community the social and economic aspects
of behaviour cannot be differentiated in terms of their meaning
within peasant society. The integration of the peasantry is thus
both a social, economic and political problem compounded by
the different interrelations of these activities at different levels
of the social whole. The intensification of demands on the
peasant sector lays bare the incompatibility of the traditional
peasant community with the spread of urbanism and the
emerging industrial economy as representatives of opposed forms
of social organisation. As characteristics of the little community
Redfield mentions: (*a*) its distinctiveness ('where the community
begins and where it ends is apparent'); (*b*) its smallness – it can
be directly known and experienced as a totality; (*c*) its homogeneity, in that 'activities and states of mind are much alike for
all persons in corresponding age and sex positions'; and (*d*) its
self-sufficiency, the fact that it is a 'cradle-to-the-grave arrangement'.[2] The social implications of 'smallness', moreover, make
for a different kind of society. Primary (face-to-face) relations
are, of course, not exclusive to the rural community and it is
impossible to conceive of a human society in which they would

[1] See, on peasant agriculture as a form of consumption economy, A. V.
Chayanov, *The Theory of Peasant Economy* (Homewood, Ill., 1966).
[2] R. Redfield, *The Little Community* (Chicago, 1960) p. 4.

not play a major part. What makes a little community different
is the fact that the predominance of primary relations is such
that the structure of relationships itself is of a different type. In
a closed community a small number of people interact in a
variety of roles and are less identified with particular ones.
They are seen more as individuals. Relations are in this sense
more personal and there is less necessity to place people as
members of a social category or class.

The erosion of the inclusiveness of community life during the
process of modernisation and its disruptive effects on the traditional way of life of peasant society bring to the fore the
archaicism of the peasant group. It is drawn into closer relations with systems of production and distribution which originate
in urban centres from which the nature of its part-society had
kept it relatively insulated. The peasants are confronted by, and
increasingly participate in, forms of social organisation which
their own society had little capacity or necessity for evolving.
Strain mounts as the peasant finds himself unable to live by the
contradictory demands and expectations that the merging of
the two worlds entails. The roots of peasant society are threatened when more than at any other time the peasant is in a
situation of greater awareness of his position in society and has a
greater capacity for political action. The nature of later developing societies also brings him into alliance with class forces of
opposition while the peasant is still committed to the traditional
way of life that is constantly being eroded by the social and
economic course of urban-industrial growth.[1] Alavi, for example, has shown how it is pre-eminently the middle peasant
who is prone to take revolutionary action.[2] He has not gained
from transactions with the greater society as much as the rich
peasant, nor has he lost his freedom of material action in the
same way as the poor one: 'This greater autonomy allows him
to voice more easily his sense of imbalance, while the increasing
uncertainty of his social relations forces him to do so.'[3] The

[1] The importance of this coincidence is emphasised by V. G. Kiernan,
'The Peasant Revolution', in *The Socialist Register 1970*, ed. R. Miliband
and J. Saville (London, 1970).
[2] H. Alavi, 'Peasants and Revolution', in *The Socialist Register 1965*, ed.
R. Miliband and J. Saville (London, 1965).
[3] E. Wolf, *Peasant Problems and Revolutionary Warfare*, Paper prepared for
the Third Annual S.S.C. (New York, 1967) p. 3.

isolation of the peasant and his relative self-sufficiency here become advantages. The fact that, nature willing, he can at least survive on his own resources means that he can withdraw temporarily from contact with alien organisations. If the price of needed industrial goods is too high, or are expected to be lower in the near future, the peasant farmer need not take his goods to the market to get the cash to buy them. The broadened material interdependence of modern society, creating links between people unknown to each other and necessitating constant participation in a variety of impersonal relations, can therefore put the peasant in a position of strength in the economy. It also, as in pre-collectivisation Soviet Russia, makes him a prime target for reorganisation and a source of capital reserves for a hungry developing economy.

The power that a peasantry has is one of resistance, more of a delaying tactic than an alternative to the way of life of urban industrial society. It is not until modernity itself has become established in a society and begins to impinge on the peasantry that it fights back and presses for a different kind of political order. Where a peasant movement has shaken the foundations of a State it has done so in alliance either with the urban working class or with members of the intellectual strata who articulate an ideology of opposition and perform organisational and leadership functions. Thrown back on its own resources, the opposition of the peasantry expresses itself in civil disobedience (the refusal to pay taxes, the Russian peasant soldiers voting with their feet against the First World War) and by withdrawal into the little community. The archaicism of peasant society, its resistance to change and the individual nature of peasant agriculture are seen as a threat by rulers consolidating their political control through the creation of new State organisations, and mobilising economic resources not only to maximise existing production but also to restructure the organisation of production to raise productivity. The more traditional character of the East European peasantries thus left them more isolated and, with the end of serfdom and the persistence of a subsistence farm economy, more individualistic in their agriculture than Western farmers. But while there still remained peasant communities to withdraw into and traditions still to be defended, they presented the Communist rulers with an agriculture badly in need of reorganisation and potentially disruptive for a planned economy. Let us now turn to consider the place of the peasant in Polish society.

THE PEASANT IN MODERN POLISH SOCIETY

With the birth of the Polish republic after the First World War peasants at last became citizens of a Polish State. Their attitudes to it, however, were equivocal and some feared the re-emergence of a gentry-State and their return to their former status as serfs.[1] The idea of the State ('państwo') remained etymologically and politically associated with the dominance of the 'gentleman' ('Pan'). The conditions of the peasantry in the twentieth century were, of course, far removed from those of eighteenth-century serfdom, but still demanded radical improvement. Hopes of general technical improvement in agriculture and of land-reform (at one end of the scale, in 1921, some 20,000 estates took 45 per cent of the land, while at the other, 15 per cent was held in over 2 million peasant holdings of under 5 hectares) were largely unrealised. The effects of the inter-war depression and of rural and urban unemployment hit the peasants hard. Witos, the peasant leader, comments in his memoirs: 'All agricultural products fell to one third of their former price, while those of industry remained the same. There were no jobs. The richer farmers do not take on labourers because they cannot pay the wages.'[2] By the thirties the dictatorship of the Colonels was well entrenched and in response to it the Peasant Party and other leftish groups combined in opposition. Although figures for political party membership amongst the peasants are non-existent for most of the thirties, there is no doubt that the Peasant Party, formed in 1931 out of smaller political groupings, held prime place in terms of numbers and influence throughout the countryside. It was emphatically a peasant-based party, for no more than 10 per cent of its politically active members were drawn from other social strata. In 1931 its leaders claimed a membership of 300,000, but even a third of this total is likely to be an exaggeration. Due to the

[1] J. Słomka, *From Serfdom to Self-Government* (London, 1941) p. 268.
[2] W. Witos, *Moje wspomnienia*, vol. 1 (Paris, 1964) p. 65.

loose nature of political organisation at this time and the difficulties put in the way of non-government political activities, the most accurate membership figures are likely to be those collected towards the end of the decade by the Ministry of the Interior for security purposes. Its estimate in 1938 was 150,000. As many as another 100,000 were members of the associated peasant youth organisation, *Wici*. On the radical right, the National Party made consistent efforts to gain peasant support but on the whole made little headway. There was, perhaps, more success in gaining the support of the rural clergy who in turn would influence the electoral choice of the peasants from the pulpit. Support for workers' political organisations was even less common amongst the small-holding peasantry although it was more widespread amongst agricultural labourers and estate workers. It is unlikely that more than a few thousand farm-owning peasants were members of socialist and Communist political organisations.[1] In the previous decade the leaders of the peasant parties, sensitive to the needs of national solidarity within the new republic, had tended to make right-wing alliances to mute opposition. Thus it was at a time when reformist solutions were unlikely to be considered (and when many peasant leaders were in jail or had emigrated) that organised political opposition developed among the peasants. The repression, affecting even the moderate parties, had a great effect on the political involvement of the peasants. Witos describes their response in the early thirties: 'The campaign I conducted in West and Central Małopolska became an enormous surge of support, such as I had never seen before. The number of registered members rose to a hundred thousand; the meeting at Limanowa exceeded 30 thousand people.'[2] A mass agricultural strike was organised in 1937, but it was the outbreak of war and not internal opposition that eventually brought down the government. The strike, however, was the culmination of a long period of hardship and of the frustration of its expectations of the modern Polish State. 'In its unity were combined the

---

[1] J. Borkowski, *Postawa polityczna chłopów polskich w latach 1930–1935* (Warsaw, 1970) pp. 411–38.

[2] W. Witos, op. cit., vol. 3, p. 329. Witos was not only the leader of the Peasant Party but also himself from a peasant small-holding family.

basic sources of strength and the mass nature of the rural democratic movement, the conditions for the great patriotic breadth of the peasant struggle of 1937.'[1]

The rise of a particular form of national consciousness among the peasantry during the nineteenth century had significantly affected its conception of political democracy within the republic and later its attitudes to the Communist government of People's Poland. Peasants became conscious of belonging to a national community during a century in which Poland did not exist as a State structure but only as a cultural tradition. Not surprisingly, its literature dwelt obsessively on the theme of nationhood and it was through the growth of literacy amongst some of the peasants that they developed a feeling of identity with the greater social entity. The role of the press is emphasised by Thomas and Znaniecki as being one of the few means available for building a secondary-group system within the Poland of the partitions and, moreover, a system that took the form of a wide community.[2] To a large extent the peasants' demands for political rights were based on the recognition of their cultural status as the body of the nation. Early political activities did little to satisfy these demands. They were often of a demagogic nature in which bribery and deceit were common. The political repression and machinations of the inter-war dictatorship did not diminish their political cynicism: 'In consequence it all evoked in the countryside a feeling of powerlessness, deep disillusion and, together with this, political prostration.'[3] In short, the political experience of the Polish peasantry had not encouraged them to place much faith either in the efficacy or the value of national political institutions. The peasant parties that had gained their trust and popularity were repressed in the thirties and their followers harassed by the State. This sphere was rarely one in which the peasant could feel his membership of the nation to be operative. The social division between town and country remained unusually strong and the 1937 strike took on an exceptional character in that it expressed the rural

---

[1] W. Matuszewska, *U źródel strajku chłopskiego w roku 1937* (Warsaw, 1962) p. 187.

[2] W. Thomas and F. Znaniecki, *The Polish Peasant in Europe and America*, vol. 2 (New York, 1958) p. 1368.

[3] S. Pigoń, *Z Komborni w świat* (Kraków, 1957) p. 61.

antagonism to the towns as a whole.[1] The continuation of the features of a part-society within the peasant sector made the adherence to peasant traditions and the way of life of the small community a condition of the peasants' survival. Having suffered less destruction during the war than other groups, these traditions after the occupation embodied a strong element of the nation's resistance to the imposition of a Soviet-style régime. In an article written years after the Stalinist period of Polish socialism the positive side of the peasant's 'conservatism' is emphasised: 'The peasant masses have more than once acted as a "moderator" of social progress, blocking excessively radical impulses, tempering the effects of radical and revolutionary activities. It can be said that they preserve those values whose worth is not always appreciated, but without which a nation loses its foundation.'[2]

With the ending of hostilities in Eastern Europe, the Polish Peasant Party (PPP) (*Polskie Stronnictwo Ludowe*) rapidly became the focus for anti-Communist forces in Poland. Traditional conservative and liberal forces, barely detectable in the postwar society, were politically exhausted by the failure of the interwar republic and could offer no political alternative to the Communists.[3] Thus support for and membership of PPP grew rapidly, most notably among non-peasant groups who opposed the Communists, giving rise to an anomalous group of pseudo-peasantists dubbed 'the peasants of Marzałkowska Street' (as strange-sounding a title as the 'Communists of Park Lane' would have been).[4] The PPP, under perpetual harassment from Soviet and Polish Communist organisations, could hardly cope with the task it found itself bearing almost alone. Its postwar leader, S. Mikołajoczyk, premier of the Polish government-in-exile after 1943, did not carry the authority and personal support of Witos and, it seemed, was over-confident of his ability to beat

[1] See F. Zweig, *Poland Between the Wars* (London, 1944) p. 129.

[2] J. Szczepański, 'Rola chłopów w rozwoju społeczeństwa polskiego', in *Wieś Współczesna*, Nov. 1966.

[3] On agricultural policy in prewar Poland see W. Stankiewicz, 'The Agrarian Problem in Poland between the two World Wars', *Slavonic and East European Review*, 43 (1964).

[4] One peasant leader at least seemed to regard this unusual source of support rather ambivalently. See S. Korboński, *Warsaw in Chains* (New York, 1959) p. 55.

the Communists at their own game. He and others had spent the war-time years in emigration and were probably not fully aware of peasant expectations of the postwar order.[1] Quite a significant part of the support for Mikołajczyk himself seems to have stemmed from the belief that he had firm American support and financial backing which would ultimately guarantee Polish independence in the same way that Wilson's emphasis on national self-determination had done twenty-five years previously.[2] Under constant pressure internally too from crypto-peasantists and those holding a variety of opinions on the extent of necessary co-operation with Soviet Russia and the Communists, the PPP found it increasingly difficult to maintain its organisation and rapidly disintegrated after the 1946 referendum and the succceeding election.

The Communists, however, had the task of unifying the country under their rule and extending control throughout a society which, by virtue of historical circumstance, had never in the modern period achieved any firm measure of political integration. It was not enough to take over the 'command posts', as just possessing them did not ensure command. There were still guerilla bands in many areas and a form of civil war continued into 1948. In this year, with the formal consolidation of Communist power and the emergence of signs that the régime was indeed contemplating the collectivisation of agriculture despite previous statements to the contrary, underground activities even intensified. This was particularly so in the rural east, which had already experienced a period of Russification between 1939 and 1941 and where its return was now most feared. The losses caused by wartime destruction and the shifting of Poland's borders, resulting in the movement of millions of its population to the devastated 'western territories', made the immediate expansion of agricultural production within its present structure a pressing necessity. These facts were patently obvious to Gomułka, Secretary-General of the PUWP, whose communism was modified by recognition of the limitations that existed within Polish society on such a path of development.[3] As agriculture had developed in the immediate postwar

---

[1] R. Halaba, *Stronnictwo Ludowe* (Warsaw, 1966) p. 224.

[2] S. Korboński, op. cit., p. 43.

[3] Even in his recantation he never fully disavowed the conviction that

years, collectivisation did not in any way seem to be inevitable. By 1948, however, its path was being mapped out by the Communist Party and the following year the collectivisation campaign began. Previous to this its necessity and advisability had been strenuously denied, and up to the 1947 elections the need to work out a policy based on the careful Marxist consideration of national conditions had been emphasised. This had been associated particularly with Gomułka and his idea of a 'Polish road to socialism'. But at the August–September 1948 plenary session of the Central Committee both the resignation of Gomułka from the party leadership and a detailed programme for collectivisation were announced. The growing Sovietisation of the country decided the fate both of the national road to socialism and of the peasants. Numerically, however, the effects of the campaign were never striking. Even by the end, in 1955, only 189,000 families were reorganised into the collective structure.[1] After Stalin's death in 1953 the tempo of the transformation and the ideological emphasis placed on it slackened. On the other hand, the peasant sector made a substantial contribution to the investment fund needed for the plan of socialist industrialisation (1950–5). During the six-year period agriculture had received only 10 per cent of total investment resources (and most of that went to the collectives) compared with over the peasants were reluctant to improve their farms or even maintain them, and some decapitalisation occurred during this period. In 1956 gross agricultural production topped the pre-war figure by barely 9 per cent.[3]

PEASANT ACTIVITY IN 1956

The social and political effects of the collectivisation campaign were no less serious than the economic. Although a brief honeymoon period was to follow Gomułka's return to power, peasant forced collectivisation would be a great mistake for the party. See N. Bethell, *Gomułka: His Poland and His Communism* (London, 1969) pp. 151–9.

[1] *Rocznik Statystyczny 1956* (Warsaw, 1956) p. 156.

[2] B. Strużek, 'Przemiany w społeczno-ekonomicznym podłożu ruchu ludowego w PRL', in *70 lat ruchu ludowego*, ed. J. Szaflik (Warsaw, 1967) p. 374.

[3] *Rocznik Statystyczny 1956* (Warsaw, 1956) p. 128.

caution reasserted itself when it became evident that he too was anxious to extend party control over the countryside. Similarly, the use of administrative pressure and overt coercion to carry out the policy led to the peasants' withdrawal from State organisations, which they regarded as organs of manipulation. It was all too obvious that the transmission belts ran in only one direction and with frequent changes in policy they almost ceased to run at all. Local party officials became confused and, eventually, hamstrung in the absence of unambiguous directives from above.[1]

A United Peasant Party (UPP) had been set up in 1949 from the remains of the PPP and the Peasant Party (the postwar Communist-sponsored Peasant Party); this new party, the United Peasant Party (UPP) (known in Poland as the ZSL, *Zjednoczone Stronnictwo Ludowe*), acted as a tool of the government during the collectivisation campaign. One of its most negative results was the disenchantment and cavalier treatment of even sympathetic peasant activists. In one rural district many peasant activists even had been pushed aside as 'kulaks' and in 1953 only 972 members of UPP remained there out of 7,000 at the time of the unification of the peasant movement.[2]

Thus, in 1956, as radical changes in both leadership and policy became more likely, the credibility of the State *apparat* evaporated. In addition, habits of institutionalised obedience were insufficiently strong to maintain the operations of the organisations in contact with the peasantry. Within a matter of a few weeks, while officially the fate of collectivised agriculture still hung in the balance, 85 per cent of the collectives were dissolved on the initiative of the peasants themselves. One of the reasons why the collectivisation drive did not continue was that such a policy was becoming more and more difficult to implement and the government was in no position to back up

---

[1] A. Korbonski, *The Politics of Socialist Agriculture in Poland 1945–60* (New York, 1965) p. 256.

[2] W. Fołta, 'Z wyborczych analiz', in *Zielony Sztandar*, 23 May 1956 (41). This article had been sent to the peasant party paper in 1953, but waited three years for publication. Even the original total of 7,000 UPP members is surprising (of a likely rural population of about 40,000) and indicative of the 'non-reactionary' political activeness of the peasantry, for PPP had been practically non-existent at the time of the 1947 election, its members, the article states, had been declared public enemies.

its decisions with coercion. The intensity of the dictatorship had already declined in 1953 after Stalin's death. In 1955 tentative moves to restrict the power of the security organs were made and, after the twentieth Congress of the CPSU in 1956, a process of considerable liberalisation was under way. Thus, in the fluid situation of late 1956, officials were wary of undertaking any action that would antagonise the population and could classify them as 'Stalinists'.[1] At this time, over a month after Gomułka's return to power as First Secretary, the power of the State at local levels had still not been strengthened. Local officials of the United Peasant Party were apportioning blame for the 'errors and distortions' that had occurred in their sphere and were deciding who should leave the organisation. While they dared not show their face in the villages their peasant supporters became totally isolated, in effect leaving many rural areas 'political deserts'.[2] Levels for quota deliveries (the equivalent of a tax in kind) for grain, meat and milk set by the State had simply been disregarded.[3] The output from the agricultural sector had fallen below 1930 levels.[4] Apart from the purely economic difficulties involved in the party's agrarian programme, then, the social and political obstacles to its implementation were such that the policy had become meaningless in Poland at the end of 1956.

Gomułka's statement in October that 'A chain is only as strong as its weakest link. We want to give [aid] – and we must give – quickly to the countryside'[5] led to a recognition of the fact that somehow the State and the peasants had to evolve some working relationship. For only by operating more within the peasant's perception of his economic needs would it be possible to inject the resources necessary to bring about agricultural modernisation and to extract produce with the degree of efficiency and stability necessary in a modern economy. The

---

[1] S. Ignar, speech to the Sejm, reported in *Zielony Sztandar*, 14 Nov. 1956 (91).

[2] P. Ziarnik, *Zielony Sztandar*, 16 Dec. 1956 (100).

[3] See the Resolution of the VIII Plenum KC PZPR (Oct. 1956), reprinted in *National Communism and Popular Revolt*, ed. P. Zinner (New York, 1956) p. 252.

[4] T. M. Piotrowicz, 'The Polish Economic Pendulum', in *Communist Economy under Change*; M. Miller *et al.* (London, 1963) p. 110.

[5] Address to the VIII Plenum KC PZPR, P. Zinner, op. cit., p. 206.

attempt to win the trust of the peasants to the extent of their having some confidence in their future as peasant farmers and their recognising their responsibilities to the State was the cornerstone of the declarations issued at the end of 1956 and the beginning of 1957.

In the 'Declaration of the Principles of PUWP/UPP Co-operation' the positive role of the United Peasant Party in the State was affirmed and its future independence, even though already subject to qualification, guaranteed.[1] The peasantry was recognised as one of the two basic classes in the building of socialism. In the collectivisation period the worker–peasant alliance had been subject to various 'distortions' in the 'exceeding of the voluntary motive in the setting up of production co-operatives',[2] the 'liquidation of the numerous forms of activity in the cultural and economic self-government of the peasant masses' and the conception of UPP as a 'Party transmission-belt'. The superiority of collective forms of agriculture was recognised but the immediate problem was 'assuring the growth of agricultural production by stimulating the material interest of the producer and by developing peasant initiative' without specifying that structural reorganisation would be necessary for this. 'Anarchism' was strongly condemned and 'an especially pressing task' was said to be the 'execution by the countryside of its obligations to the State'. Arrears of land-tax and quota deliveries had to be made good. The extent of these arrears was made clear in a second declaration published a month later stating in detail the path that agricultural development was to take.[3]

A large proportion of the deliveries of meat, milk, grain and potatoes had been retained by the peasants. In the case of the last two the arrears amounted to 20–25 per cent of the deliveries that had been made in 1955.[4] In 1957 quotas of grain were to be cut by a third, and deliveries of milk were to be abolished completely. Transactions with the State would take place

[1] 'Deklaracja o zasadach współpracy między PZPR a ZSL', in *Trybuna Ludu*, 10 Dec. 1956.

[2] In Polish usage the same as collective farm. While the co-operative movement has a long and worthy history in Poland, 'kolektyw' sounds all too much like a Russian transplant.

[3] 'Wytyczne w sprawie polityki rolnej', in *Trybuna Ludu*, 9 Jan. 1957.

[4] Figures for 1955 from *Rocznik Statystyczny 1967*, p. 293.

through the 'free' market. However, these relaxations were conditional on arrears being made up in full, at the latest by the end of 1958. This meant that, with grain, the State was demanding 630,000 tons less for its tax in kind but requiring 400,000 of this back as a 'debt'. Restrictions on production in large farms[1] were to be lifted, their scale of taxation reduced and a free market in land permitted. Thus future forms of production would 'result from . . . the conditions and concrete needs of the farmers, whose own experience and freedom of choice will determine the progress of the transformation and the development of the socialist economy'. But again, while the price paid for the grain quota had doubled, unspecified rises in the price of industrial goods for agriculture were made. Building materials, artificial fertilisers, machinery, tools and coal were all to be more expensive. Some machines were to be made available to private farmers but tractors were not mentioned among them. Even the revised figures for the supply of building materials, the 'Directives' stated, would not be enough to stop the further dilapidation of rural buildings. The peasants had to use their own initiative here and industry was 'called on' to step up production. The lifting of restrictions, therefore, that marked the outset of Gomułka's new agricultural policy was accompanied by heightened State demands. The concessions the peasants received were not unconditional, but the ground was prepared for the creation of more stable peasant–State relations and, despite problems, a considerable improvement in peasant agricultural production could now take place.

THE SOCIO-ECONOMIC STRUCTURE OF THE PEASANTRY

Observers in rural areas in late 1956 and 1957 noted quite spectacular changes in the reclamation of fallow land and the increased care taken in farm work as peasants responded to the change of leadership and became more confident that they would reap the benefit of their work at the end of the year.[2]

---

[1] Apart from high levels of taxation and quota produce to be supplied, peasants on farms of above average size had been subject to all manner of political and economic discrimination regardless of whether they actually 'exploited' anyone as kulaks.

[2] F. Lewis, *The Polish Volcano* (London, 1959) pp. 234–8.

But more basic changes in production were necessary to ensure the long-term efficiency of peasant agriculture. Since 1956 no remedy has been sought in collectivisation. Although Gomułka had never been led to disclaim it as the ultimate form of socialist agriculture, it was indefinitely shelved in practice in favour of a policy of agricultural modernisation within the existing structure of private farm-holdings. Through the internal pressures of the development of mechanisation and specialisation and through the influence of the market, it is held that the peasant will be led to abandon his self-sufficiency and join with others in forming large-scale production organisations. Ideological justification for this policy could be readily found in Lenin's emphasis on the voluntary principle in inducing change amongst the peasants.[1] Ideological justifications apart, however, the policy is very much a Polish response to Polish problems, conditioned by the fact that it follows an economically unsuccessful and politically dangerous attempt at an agricultural 'revolution from above'. The priority, indeed, was less to improve farming than to prevent its worsening, and to avoid the peasants' relations with the State from breaking down completely.

The number of farms was still growing, partly due to the continuing fragmentation of what were already very small farms.[2] Alongside some 2,000 collective farms and 8,000 State farms in 1960 were over three and a half million peasant holdings, the vast majority of them under twenty-five acres (approximately 10 ha.) in size. Collectivised forms of agriculture were and are more commonly found in the central-western and northern territories of Poland, thus leaving large areas almost exclusively under private peasant cultivation. Agricultural Poland is highly differentiated both in terms of the area of land under collective cultivation and also within the private farm group itself. Based on the results of survey work carried out in 1956–7, the Institute of Agricultural Economics divided the country into six socio-economic regions of private farms. The poorest and most peasant-dominated rural areas were those of the south-east and the centre-east, roughly covering the wojewodstwos of Białystok, Warsaw, Łódź, Kraków,

[1] H. Chołaj, *Leninizm a polityka rolna PZPR* (Warsaw, 1969) pp. 8–13, is the most recent example.

[2] See Appendix 2, Tables 2 and 3.

Rzeszów, Kielce and Lublin. The south-east has the largest proportion of small farms (those below 5 ha.). The average annual value of commodity production in this area was only 9,000 złoty, compared with 26,000 in the centre-west (Poznań and Bydgoszcz wojewodstwos). In the centre-east there are larger farms but they are not very productive. Farming brought in an average cash income of 18,000 złoty. The value of the means of production on the average farm there was 25,000 złoty in contrast to 37,000 in the centre-west. The centre-west, then, is the area of the most prosperous private agriculture and it is here that nearly all the 'capitalist' farms, using a substantial amount of hired labour, are concentrated, although they are still by no means numerous. Western and northern areas, those taken over from Germany after 1945, have more State farms, those along the northern coast occupying nearly half the farming area. Despite initial difficulties, with ruined farms, scarce equipment and lack of investment funds, the Poles who took over the land from the German population conduct their agriculture at a higher level than the indigenous Polish peasant areas of the south, centre and east, considerable improvement having occurred after 1956.[1] The rise in the number of very small farms of under 2 ha., which accounted for three quarters of the new farms appearing between 1950 and 1960, was more intensive following the abandonment of collectivisation. Nearly 400,000 new dwarf-holdings were created between 1952 and 1962, 60 per cent of them being set up in the second half of the period.[2] By 1963 the party took measures to combat further diminution in the size of the average farm which, it stated, lowered the production capacity of agriculture by diminishing the possibility of mechanisation and of improving the balance of crops. Tentative restrictions had been placed on land-transactions in 1957 and 1960, but now it was considered necessary to take 'more radical measures to put an effective end to this . . . unhealthy process'.[3] Small and medium farms were no

[1] IER, *Zmiany społeczno-ekonomiczne wsi* (Warsaw, 1961) pp. 63, 99–100.
[2] A. Szemberg, *Przemiany w strukturze agrarnej gospodarstw chłopskich* (Warsaw, 1966) p. 23.
[3] Report of the Politburo at *XII Plenum KC PZPR: W sprawie zwiększenia inwestycji w rolnictwie i zapewnienia dalszego wzrostu produkcji rolnej* (Warsaw, 1963) pp. 65, 68.

longer to be subdivided, the minimum size permissible being fixed at 8 ha. Further steps were taken in 1967 to speed the process of commassation (the integration of a 'farm' made up of small plots spread over the village, as in the strip system), another disturbing phenomenon in Poland's farm structure.[1] The 1968 figures, however, show that the process of farm division was continuing unabated, the total number of farms by then nearing 4 million[2] (see Table 3, Appendix 2).

During the fifties, as young people were drawn into non-agricultural occupations, the agricultural work-force aged considerably. In 1950 58 per cent were aged thirty-five years or over; ten years later this had risen to 67 per cent, the greatest rise being recorded for the over-sixties.[3] Fewer women than men were being drawn off the farms and in the ten-year period the number of women in charge of peasant farms nearly doubled.[4] The total rural emigration between 1945 and 1957 has been estimated to have reached a total of 10 per cent of the 1957 village population. The exodus was greatest during the forties and the period of postwar reconstruction when a number higher than the natural increase of the rural population was drawn off.[5] All in all, Pohoski concludes, the economic effects of migration have not been wholly beneficial. The migration itself provided the agricultural sector with great opportunities for improvement, but the selection of migrants acted against these advantages.[6] Most of the migrants left before their twenty-fourth year, the proportion of men leaving was higher amongst the agricultural population than the rural population as a whole, and (bearing in mind the deleterious effects of the

[1] L. Cegielski, 'Nowe ustawy agrarne uchwalone przez Sejm', in *Wieś Współczesna*, 133 (March 1968) pp. 88–9.

[2] B. Strużek, 'Problematyka podstawowych procesów rozwojowych wsi i rolnictwa w okresie 25-lecia PRL', in *Roczniki Dziejów Ruchu Ludowego*, 11 (1969) p. 35.

[3] *Rocznik Statystyczny* (1967) p. 47.

[4] Ibid. The processes were not unconnected, for women who are the heads of families tend to be older. See A. Wyderko, 'Zmiany w strukturze wieku ludności wiejskiej', in *Roczniki Socjologii Wsi*, 2 (1965) p. 114.

[5] M. Pohoski, *Migracja ze wsi do miast* (Warsaw, 1963) pp. 46–7. Due to the nature of the survey data used this does not include the migration of whole families who moved to the town. They probably made up over 15 per cent of the total rural movement.

[6] Ibid., p. 75.

growth in dwarf-holdings) migration was correlated positively with the size of farm the migrant left. One alarming aspect of the population shift was the fact that the rate of decrease in the numbers of those engaged in farm production was higher than that of the total classified as agricultural but inactive on the farm. Thus in the peasant sector alone relatively fewer producers were supporting more consumers. The process seems to have continued through into the sixties, resulting in a total decline of the agricultural population by some million and a half for the twenty-year postwar period.[1]

Many farms in the fifties were only in the process of being established as on-going concerns. One in four of the total of peasant farms had arisen on the basis of the postwar land reform.[2] Not all agricultural workers were capable of running their own farm independently, nor were the plots they had received always able to sustain a productive form of agriculture. Thus, as Gomułka launched his new policy in agriculture, a set of factors combined to put considerable strain on the production resources of the peasant farmer and to complicate the process of modernisation and economic intensification he hoped to introduce.

SOCIALISM WITHOUT THE SOCIALIST TRANSFORMATION OF AGRICULTURE?

While there may have been some truth in *Pravda*'s comment that the Poles seemed to think they could build socialism without the socialist transformation of agriculture, it could not be said that they were sponsoring the development of rural capitalism.[3] The January 1957 'Directives' abolished the grain and potato quotas for farms of less than 2 ha. and made social insurance compulsory for the small number of workers who did sell their labour to the richer farmers. The continuing shortage of industrial goods and building materials combined with the impossibility of private purchase of much of what was available hardly promised a rosy future for the richer peasant hoping to take the road of capitalist development. Rural capitalism, that

[1] I. Frenkel, *Zatrudnienie w rolnictwie polskim* (Warsaw, 1968) pp. 168–9.
[2] *Rocznik Statystyczny* (1967) p. 251.
[3] 'V derevnie polskoi', in *Pravda*, 4 Feb. 1957.

is, the development of commercially oriented agriculture using hired labour to a significant extent, had only developed within certain areas of Poland. Over most of the country social divisions within the peasantry were minimal compared with the social gulf between country and town. The stagnation of its economy throughout the nineteenth and into the twentieth century had had a levelling effect on the peasantry, which had acted against the emergence and persistence of a commercial agricultural stratum. The social characteristics of late-developing capitalism and its uncertain course strengthened in certain ways its undifferentiated character in prewar Poland.[1] Thus the most common evidence of rural poverty was the poor peasant rather than a landless proletariat, for the condition of agriculture did not permit the development of a group regularly hiring labour and therefore sufficiently strong to transform the rural community in this way. The peasant family had remained the basic social unit in Poland and the basis of agriculture. Few social characteristics of class polarisation could be found in the results of the survey conducted in 1957.[2] However, the new policy was running into difficulties in that year precisely because its workings initially favoured the large peasant. It was not due to 'rural capitalism' but to the new system of supply and prices set by the State that some peasants found themselves worse off. It had not been the intention to 'worsen the position of the weaker farmer, but that unfortunately is what it has come to', said the new secretary of UPP as opposition to this state of affairs grew within his party.[3]

At the same time the new policy has not been favourable for the growth of large-scale capitalist farms as a long-run tendency. The land tax is progressive and taxation on the use of hired labour prohibitive. Therefore, the enterprising farmer is theoretically being guided to intensive and mechanised methods which bring him into dependence on State and co-operative organisations. It is reckoned that by these means it does not pay to hire more than 25 per cent of the labour required for farm

[1] B. Gałęski and J. Ryng, 'O społeczno-ekonomicznej strukturze wsi polskiej', in *Lenin a kwestia agrarna*, chief ed. H. Chołaj (Warsaw, 1967) p. 367.

[2] B. Gałęski, *Społeczna struktura wsi* (Warsaw, 1962) p. 49.

[3] B. Drzewiecki, Report to VII Plenum NK ZSL (Warsaw, 1957) p. 32.

work and the number of capitalist farms (that is, those using full-time hired labourers) does not exceed 50,000.[1] Also there are now fewer people in the village who are only part-employed and looking for jobs than there were before the war. The growth of industry has drawn many peasants into non-agricultural occupations, even if all have not fully severed their links with the farm. Subsidiary employment is most widespread among poor peasants, defined in this case as the inhabitants of farms less than 4 ha. in size (or 3 in better farming areas). Of the poor peasants over a million farm-owners work outside their own farm and nearly 2 million families in this situation have at least one member working in this way (1957 estimates).[2] This accounts for, respectively, 29 per cent of all farm-owners and 33 per cent of peasant families living on private farms. The role of farming is not the same for all members of this group. Occupants of farms of up to 0·5 ha. (5,000 sq. metres, or just over an acre) are more precisely defined as plot-holding workers. Ninety per cent of them work full time outside agriculture and farming supplies only a marginal part of their income. Worker-peasants are those on farms of between a half and 2 ha. (3 in poor areas). Sixty-seven per cent of the occupationally active population here work outside agriculture. Only on farms above 2 ha. does farming play a significant part in the family economy. Here the mixed income group can more properly be called peasant-workers with the emphasis on the 'peasant'.[3]

Caution needs to be used, therefore, when taking the structure of farm holdings as a guide to the state of agricultural production. The farms of plot-holding workers and worker-peasants are strictly non-agricultural. These are, moreover, farm units whose numbers grew enormously between 1950 and 1960 (by nearly half a million). Even in the second group – worker-peasants owning farms of between 0·5 and 2 ha. – most of the 'agricultural' farms, that is where the farm was the major

---

[1] B. Gałęski, *Socjologia wsi* (Warsaw, 1966) p. 27.

[2] M. Dziewicka, *Chłopi-robotnicy* (Warsaw, 1963) p. 70.

[3] Differentiation made by R. Turski, *Między miastem a wsią* (Warsaw, 1965) pp. 207–13. The numbers comprising the first two groups are 0·35 and 0·83 million units (farm-holdings) respectively. Figures from the 1960 census returns.

means of material support, were one-person enterprises, which led Turski to conclude that they were only a temporary phenomenon and were likely to die out.[1] On the other hand, even farms of peasant-workers (between 2 and 4 ha.) were less efficient from the point of view of the utilisation of farm land. Although covering 3·6 per cent of the farming area they accounted for 2·4 per cent of commodity production (i.e. that part available for sale outside of the agricultural sector).[2] Off-farm employment for peasant-workers seemed to be a substitute for agricultural work rather than a complementary source of income. For all farms below 3 ha. where non-agricultural work provided the main source of income the consumption fund per family member was only 20 złoty a year higher.[3]

Of the population living on private farms in 1960 a large proportion did not work in agriculture. Only 58 per cent of farms were wholly agricultural in the sense that the family relied on it as the sole source of income. Amongst the other farm-owning families the small-holding supplied only a minor part of their livelihood in 85 per cent of the cases, the family being more dependent on off-farm earnings to support itself.[4] Thus, as well as the population as a whole,[5] the farm population itself has undergone considerable differentiation. The main groups can be defined as follows. First are those for whom the farm provides only an auxiliary source of income. Among holdings over 0.1 ha. there are approximately a million (27 per cent) of this type, 80 per cent of them under 2 ha. Second is a group for whom the farm provides the main source of income – 700,000 farms (20 per cent), mostly from 2 to 5 ha. Third are those for whom the farm provides an exclusive source of income and which are worked only by the family that owns it. This typical form of peasant farm accounts for just over half of the Polish total. Fourth are farms whose running depends on regularly hired labour. The 50,000 of these make up only 1–2 per cent of the farm total. Fifth, there are multi-family farms – the production co-operatives (collective farms) which take in 26,000 families. Finally, there are the large farms of a non peasant

---

[1] Ibid., pp. 207–10. [2] M. Dziewicka, p. 76.
[3] M. Czerniewska, *Gospodarstwa rolne i ludność o mieszanym źródle dochodu* (Warsaw, 1964) p. 55.
[4] Ibid., p. 26. [5] See Appendix 2, Table 1.

character, mostly State farms (called PGRs – *Państwowe Gospodarstwa Rolne*), with 320,000 workers.[1]

On the basis of economic dependence the relative isolation and self-sufficiency of the village population would seem to be a thing of the past. The rapid growth of peasant employment outside the village after the war has taken up a lot of rural unemployment and underemployment. In some areas the flow of labour out of agriculture, especially due to the selective nature of migration patterns, threatens an acute labour shortage, although it is not as widespread as Polish press reports foreseeing wholesale rural depopulation seem to suggest. But in 1968 a law was passed enabling farm-owners to assign their land to the State in exchange for a monthly pension. It was pointed out that a third of all farms are owned by people over sixty and that a third of these are without successors. The problem was becoming particularly acute at this time because 40 per cent of farm-owners without successors were over seventy years old.[2] The change in the labour situation has altered the structure of socio-economic relations in the village. One writer has described how relations of dependence have become less one-sided and are entered into more as a formal exchange of services, even to the extent of being calculated in cash terms. A farmer who has a horse lends it to a poorer peasant simply to enlist his neighbour's aid on the occasions when working his land requires the labour of two people.[3] But, while the class-like character of relations between richer and poorer may have declined and the peasant with more land is not automatically in a position of dominance, the area of land a peasant owns is still a good guide to his material situation. The value of what the member of a small-farm family consumes is on average a third less than that of a 'large peasant', while investment resources are far more sharply differentiated.[4] Size of land holding is by no means the sole determinant of wealth, but the process of economic intensification has not gone far enough for it to cease being the major part of the peasant farmer's capital. One of the main aims of the new policy of 1957 was to encourage the farmer to produce

[1] B. Gałęski, *Socjologia wsi – pojęcia podstawowe*, pp. 23–30.
[2] L. Cegielski, p. 89.
[3] M. Biernacka, *Potakówka* (Warsaw, 1962) p. 222.
[4] *Rocznik Statystyczny* (1967) p. 541.

more by intensifying production and raising productivity rather than by increasing land and labour inputs. This meant he would have to become more dependent on supplies from the State (e.g. for the purchase of fertiliser, seeds) or to join co-operative organisations to gain access to machinery. The change in the price-structure which this implied was based on more realistic costing and was designed to introduce stronger incentives to produce efficiently, led to its being criticised in political and social terms as both a pro-peasant and anti-peasant policy.

A future minister of agriculture took pains to defend the policy against the 'baseless and demagogic' accusation – 'recently heard very frequently' – that agriculture was to be improved at the cost of the peasantry. It was true that the attempt to introduce criteria of profitability into the peasant economy had meant rises in the cost of building materials, fertilisers, machinery, etc. to the value of 3,070 million zł. in 1957. These were to be more than outweighed by the reduction in land tax and of quota deliveries, for the policy was not designed specifically to raise or to lower the peasant standard of living. It was concerned with ensuring that peasant income would henceforth be tied to the level of gross and commodity production within the peasant sector. On the other hand, he argued that the rise in peasant income that was likely to occur was not to be taken as submission to peasant pressure. The complex relationship between peasant consumption and investment, the need for economic reserves to run a peasant farm, and the fact that a peasant does not receive any wage for his labour were mentioned here.[1] The success of the policy in developing a commercial peasant agriculture by building stable market and production relations between the peasant sector and the socialist economy was not outstanding during the rest of the fifties. The proportion of goods produced by industry for use on the farm did not in fact rise at all in the period 1957–61, and it is unlikely that the underinvestment of the early fifties was made up during these years, for the rise in peasant income encouraged the government to raise the price of fertiliser again in 1959 and then the level of farm taxation.[2]

[1] M. Jagielski, *O nowej polityce partii na wsi* (Warsaw, 1957) pp. 16–18.

[2] A. Korbonski, op. cit., p. 258, explains the small increase in production by political fears of punitive taxation and by the greater concern of the

By 1959 it was evident that there was a severe imbalance between livestock production and the development of arable farming. The rise in animal rearing since the war had been double that of arable output, resulting in a fodder shortage and the using up of grain that would otherwise have supplied the urban population. The low level of mechanisation meant that Poland's stock of horses (the highest number per hectare in Europe and still growing) further depleted fodder supplies. While the investment situation had improved, mechanisation was proceeding at a very slow pace, as were other pressing problems of land amelioration and building construction. The new policy was proving incapable of tackling the basic problems of the agricultural structure: the economic backwardness of the eastern rural areas and the unequal distribution of production resources within the village. Thus mechanised equipment was 'accessible only to a small stratum of richer farmers, which inevitably would accentuate the social inequality of the countryside and create the conditions for the exploitation and loss of material independence of the poorer part of the village'.[1]

The answer was to concert the development of agriculture in these spheres within the framework of the Agricultural Circles which the peasants had set up of their own accord in 18,000 villages since 1956. In a decree on 'Key Tasks in Agriculture' these circles became the main agent of agricultural transformation. A Fund for the Development of Agriculture was set up, financed by the surplus revenue gained from quota deliveries (the amount by which the price paid for the deliveries differed from the market price).[2] The peasants responded with suspicion to the State patronage of their movement. Hints about the State take-over had already reputedly led to the slaughter of livestock from fear of collectivisation.[3] Their development was hampered again by the lack of buildings to house the machinery, and the shortage of spare parts and other industrial products.[4]

peasant for more basic investment than that which would have had a direct result on production levels.

[1] 'Uchwała KC PZPR i NK ZSL w sprawie węzłowych zadań rolnictwa w latach 1959–65'. Reprinted in *Programy stronnictw ludowych*, ed. S. Lato and W. Stankiewicz (Warsaw, 1969) p. 564.   [2] Ibid., pp. 564–6.

[3] M. Celt, 'Another Round: Peasant and Party in Poland', in *East Europe*, 2, 1968.

[4] *Uchwała II Plenum NK ZSL* (Warsaw, 1960) pp. 9–10.

Three years after the inauguration of the measure the member-ship of the movement had only doubled; after one year of full-scale mechanisation Gomułka's comment was only that results were 'not bad'. The cost of the machines' exploitation was turning out to be prohibitive.[1] After several years of the policy fears of eventual collectivisation still discouraged one peasant in three from joining.[2] In 1965 the number of tractors owned by the circles was exactly half the total the party had initially envisaged in 1959.[3]

The premise of the new policy, and the consequence of poli-tical and economic pressure exerted by the peasantry that neces-sitated its adoption, is that the peasant must co-operate volun-tarily with government agencies to encourage the growth of an economically intensive agriculture. Until the peasant farmer is sufficiently dependent on production resources controlled by the State and until his farm loses its self-sufficient character, the most the State official can do is to persuade or cajole the peasant into changing his system of production. This is a slow process because of the peasant's suspicion of State initiatives, the time needed for production changes to take effect, the common lack of basic resources on which to build this kind of agriculture and, lastly, the habit of State institutions to fail to deliver the goods expected of them. At the same time the political situation makes the standard of living of the peasantry a weapon of the political struggle, while the recurring problems of the national economy lead it alternately to ease and intensify the demands made on the peasant sector, both processes disruptive of the creation of stable peasant-State relations. Conflicts such as these were largely responsible for the difficulties experienced in the im-plementation of the second five-year plan (1961-5).

Farm output in 1960 was at a fairly satisfactory level. The grain/fodder imbalance had been eased by further imports and the peasants' unease over the Agricultural Circles seemed no longer to threaten production activity. The harvest of 1961 was even better than that of 1960. But the resulting rise in peasant income, although reflecting rises in both gross and commodity

---

[1] W. Gomułka, *Przemówienie dożynkowe* (Warsaw, 1962) p. 19.
[2] Z. Adamowski, 'Stosunek chłopów do członkostwa w KR', in *Wieś Współczesna*, Oct. 1969, p. 64.
[3] *Rocznik Statystyczny*, 1967, p. 277.

production, brought criticisms of the 'rural privilege' that was said to pertain under the new policy. Consequently, the price of grain and potatoes was cut back and meat prices were frozen, bringing a 15 per cent drop in peasant income in 1962, which was not recouped until 1965.[1] The fall in prices had driven the peasants to market fully 13 per cent more of their produce than in 1961, a better harvest year. Production levels remained low for several years. As Gomułka said in his harvest speech in 1962, it was 'not the easiest of years'. He noted that every fourth slice of bread eaten in Poland was made with imported wheat. There was not much cause for rejoicing in the fact that livestock production had risen, for supplies of fodder were lower than they had been in 1961.[2] This hiatus contributed to the failure of the five-year plan and also to the end of the idea that any rapid expansion could be hoped for from peasant agriculture under the new policy. In 1965 only 12 per cent more produce was marketed than in 1960, compared with a rise of 23 per cent during the first five-year plan over 1955 levels. It was estimated that peasant real income had risen by 27 per cent in the first period and 16 per cent in the second (1961–5). After a slight reduction in the volume of quota deliveries in the fifties their level proceeded to rise faster than both gross and commodity production (although theoretically the proceeds were now returning to the peasantry through the Agricultural Circles).

Summing up the achievements of the first ten years of the new policy, an editorial in the journal of the Peasant Party pointed to 'its positive results [lying] mainly in the assumption by the peasants of their proper place in society', rather than to any degree of success in tackling the basic structural problems of Polish agriculture.[3] In 1967 the disparity between rural and urban standards was still estimated to be about 30 per cent, most noticeably in the indivisible communal benefits which are at a very low level in the countryside. The nature of peasant life itself and the pressures of the family economy still often act against what are regarded as the basic amenities of social welfare. For instance, in 1961 95 per cent of rural children were in

[1] *Rocznik Polityczny-Gospodarczy* (Warsaw, 1966) pp. 289 and 524.
[2] W. Gomułka, *Przemówienie dożynkowe* (1962) pp. 4–5.
[3] *Wieś Współczesna*, Jan. 1967, p. 3.

a position to complete the basic seven-year school (up to the child's fourteenth year). Only 65 per cent did so, despite the fact that they could not legally work until they were sixteen. A national survey made by a department of UPP at the same time discovered that on average the child of a peasant family worked every day from four to five hours on the farm in the summer.[1] Members of peasant families are generally not automatically entitled to free medical treatment. In 1968 8·2 million rural inhabitants had not insured themselves for treatment and of these only 35 per cent were eligible to use the free State service. Rural inhabitants attend a local medical centre on average five times less frequently than the town-dweller.[2] Despite their rural residence[3] comparison of family budgets shows that the peasant eats less well than the urban worker. Meat consumption (this is not confused with purchase) is lower and is replaced in the diet by cheaper foods like potatoes.[4] The sanitary conditions of one village and the state of health of its inhabitants were exhaustively studied in 1956[5] and the results totally contradict any conceptions that might remain of the healthy rural life. The continuing low status of the peasantry is thus attributable both to socio-cultural factors within peasant society and to its economic role within the nation.

POLITICAL LIFE UNDER THE NEW POLICY

While economic improvements were slow to emerge from the change of policy of autumn 1956, its results in the political sphere were immediate and similarly contradictory to the hopes of the party. The new-found liberalism was never intended to present the peasants with an opportunity to oppose socialism or collective agriculture. What was offered was the freedom to canvass opinions on the means by which the ultimate aim was to be achieved, particularly on the paths of social and economic

[1] S. Leczykiewicz, 'Zadania ZSL w związku z reformą systemu oświaty i wychowania'. Report at *IV Plenum NK ZSL* (Warsaw, 1961) pp. 60, 69.

[2] H. Rafalski, 'Chłopskie zdrowie', in *Polityka*, xiv, 14 (18 April 1970).

[3] And the assumptions of Western writers of the privileged status of the Polish peasant. See R. and B. Laird, *Soviet Communism and Agrarian Revolution* (Harmondsworth, 1970) p. 77.

[4] *Rocznik Statystyczny* (1968) pp. 530, 541.

[5] Z. T. Wierzbicki, *Żmiąca w pół wieku później*, pp. 408–33.

development that were to lead the country towards full industrialisation within a socialist framework. Most relevant to the peasantry, and what determined its 'interests' under socialism, would be the tempo of this development and the maintenance of equilibrium in the relative development of the agricultural and industrial sectors.[1] Under a policy of encouraging peasants to make voluntary contracts with the State for the production and delivery of farm goods the producer had to be defended from the arbitrary coercion of local officials and the Stalinist methods of administration. In future the peasants were to be encompassed by the norms of socialist legality. What was most threatening to the success of this policy was the peasants' withdrawal from all forms of contact with government institutions and their suspicion of all State agencies, for if force was no longer a viable means new relations had to be built up to enable the State to influence and inform the peasant farmer. With regard to the Communist Party, its authority could hardly be built up overnight so soon after collectivisation. The UPP, however, having been so obviously excluded from power during collectivisation could with more conviction mediate peasant–State relations.

After the regularisation of PUWP and UPP relations and the affirmation of the political independence of the peasant party its membership grew rapidly.[2] Former PPP leaders and activists were encouraged to join in rejuvenating the party as a political force and in promoting the interests of the peasantry as a 'co-founder of the socialist State'. Even those who previously had fought 'on the other side of the barricades' were welcomed, providing of course they accepted what seemed to be the current terms of the worker–peasant alliance.[3] In Lublin [województwo], a previous source of strong PPP support, 290 activists were reinstated, 450 new village UPP circles set up and 10,000 new members accepted, nearly doubling the 1955 membership.[4] But the first few months of the new policy failed

[1] See 'Wytyczne w sprawie polityki rolnej', in *Trybuna Ludu*, 9 Jan. 1957.
[2] See 'Wytyczne w sprawie polityki rolnej'. For membership figures see Appendix 2, Table 4.
[3] Ożga-Michalski, 'O aktualnej sytuacji i zadaniach ZSL', Speech at *V Plenum NK ZSL* (Zielony Sztandar, 23 Dec. 1956; 102).
[4] T. Wilk, Discussion at *III Kongress ZSL*, Stenogram (Warsaw, 1959) p. 185.

to bring about an improvement in the situation of many already hard-pressed peasants. The mobilisation of the old peasant democrats to the cause of a peasant-oriented socialism thus brought more experienced and critical political activists on to the scene at a time when the PUWP leadership was least anxious to have the shortcomings of its new policy aired. The policy of mobilisation came to be blamed for the expression of a dangerous combination of economic and political grievances, leading UPP to become the mouth-piece for outspoken criticism of the Communist Party and its right to rule the nation.

Stefan Ignar, who took over the chair of the Supreme Committee of UPP in October 1956, was himself emphasising the political character of the peasant party and criticising the previously held conception of it as a temporary organisation fulfilling administrative functions for PUWP at this time. At the same plenary meeting numerous political demands were made, for example, for UPP participation in agricultural decisions, and the abolition of the unconstitutional government Presidium, as well as others directed against the exploitation of the peasantry (a call for abolition of compulsory labour duties such as a statutory obligation to mend or build roads without payment).[1] In November, the UPP claimed the credit for obtaining the reversal of a decree restricting peasants moving to towns in search of work which, it stated, infringed the constitutionally guaranteed right of the citizen to work.[2] Opposition within UPP, however, was soon overstepping the permissible borders of the party's 'sovereignty'. According to Gomułka it had become infiltrated by 'alien elements' and was ceasing to be a matter of internal UPP discipline.[3] The new opposition did not stop at attacking the role of PUWP but went on to criticise the current UPP leaders for their acceptance of a predetermined socialist future for the country. It held that all those who had held power during the Stalinist period were more or less compromised and should step down. This group was calling for the

---

[1] S. Ignar, 'Stanowisko ZSL w sprawach politycznych, gospodarczych i kulturalnych oraz wynikających stąd zadań', Speech at *IV Plenum NK ZSL* (Warsaw, 1956).

[2] *Zielony Sztandar*, 25 Nov. 1956 (94).

[3] Speech at *IX Plenum NK ZSL*, Reprinted in *O naszej partii* (Warsaw, 1969) pp. 297–8.

'second stage' of the liberalisation process – the abandonment of socialism in Poland.[1] This was later attributed to a resurgence of PPP-ite 'agraryzm', opposing countryside to town, the peasantry to the workers and UPP to the party.[2] This opposition was all the more serious as it came not only from within the peasant party but from the *apparat* workers themselves.[3] This kind of political controversy made nonsense of UPP's role in bridging the gulf between the State and party leadership and the peasants, and it put the leaders of the peasant party in an extremely precarious position. It undermined the whole justification for an 'independent' peasant party, while in the eyes of the proponents of the second stage the peasant party leaders were as much compromised as the Communist leaders.

In the process of quietening the dissident voices in the UPP its membership was reduced – by 43,000 in 1958 alone. By the time of the third Congress of the UPP in 1959 organisational consolidation had caused membership to decline almost to the level of 1956. The congress marked the transformation of UPP into a 'peasant party of the socialist type' based on the principle of democratic centralism. It was not, however, the end of changes in the party, for in 1962 Ignar was replaced by Czesław Wycech. On taking over he did not deny the existence of a right-wing opposition, which had persisted even after the third Congress, nor did he deny the need for ideological vigilance. On the other hand, he was concerned about the effects on the UPP of continuing political conflict and hoped 'to prevent the falling away of many colleagues, often deserving and worthy people, from the leadership and from active party work'. He also hoped to save the party 'from unnecessary upheavals'.[4] The lack of ideological unity within the party and continuing disagreement over its role in the socialist State had been weakening the united front the national leaders had been hoping to present in the countryside. The coexistence of the parties in the countryside was not intended to offer the means of expression

[1] Materials from *VII Plenum NK ZSL* (Warsaw, 1957).

[2] Gomułka's address to the Third Congress PZPR (1959), *O naszej partii*, p. 438.

[3] Report of the Presidium of NK ZSL to *III Kongres ZSL*, p. 55.

[4] C. Wycech, 'Aktualne zadania polityczne i organizacyjne ZSL', in *VI Plenum NK ZSL* (Warsaw, 1962) pp. 12–13.

for differing political opinions but simply to provide a greater scope for State influence. Wycech seemed to imply that party work and the maintenance of channels of communications and influence between the peasants and the State leadership was more important than the party's ideological character. Less than an ideological shift from left or right, Wycech's leadership meant the depoliticisation of UPP and its concentration on the most important of tasks: getting the farm produce from the peasant sector and encouraging it to produce more.

In 1958 and 1959 there were indications that the peasants had not accepted the terms of State–peasant co-operation in agriculture. There were complaints that they were not 'fulfilling their obligations as citizens', that is, paying taxes and delivering their quotas.[1] It was hoped that the policy of decentralisation of local government and administration would make the peasants feel sufficiently a part of the State structure to respond more to its demands. As local structures were built up to co-ordinate production and promote economic intensification at the local level, the political parties (PUWP and UPP) began to pay more attention to local rural work and to concern themselves more with the economic problems of the village.

The peasants' relations with the PUWP had slowly been improving since the debacle of 1956. In 1958 Gomułka noted that a third of new members admitted at the beginning of the year had been peasants, a fact which called for special attention, as his new policy in agriculture had not ceased to be criticised as a withdrawal in the face of peasant pressure. He therefore called for special vigilance on the part of the rural branches and organisations of PUWP 'as objective economic and socio-political conditions are favourable to an influx of peasants into the Party'.[2] But at the time of the third Congress (1959) peasant membership was still far below that of 1956. During the sixties they continued to join, PUWP in fact having a higher growth rate and absolute increase in peasant membership than the Peasant Party itself. With this increase (about 70 per cent) some progress appears to have been made in combating what was seen as the major threat of the peasantry to the working of the socialist State, its passivity and persistent capacity to withdraw

[1] *III Kongres ZSL*, Stenogram, p. 702.
[2] W. Gomułka at XII Plenum KC PZPR, *O naszej partii*, pp. 543–4.

from economic transactions with the national economy.[1] With the reassertion of party discipline in both UPP and PUWP after the 1959 congresses and the growing involvement of both in the stubborn problems of agricultural improvement rather than political conversion, class-type criteria for the mobilisation of peasants passed into the background. At the fourth Congress of PUWP (1964) Gomułka stressed the need for enrolling, among others, agricultural innovators and the economic intensifiers among the peasantry, those who could be held to wield authority in the village by virtue of their economic success.[2] Social differences between UPP peasant members and those of PUWP with respect to land-ownership could still be seen in the mid-sixties but since the State 'controlled' the market by purchasing 80 per cent of the total produce and determined the supply of most production aids there was no longer any need for that kind of social discrimination.[3]

Differences in the social composition and organisation of PUWP and UPP are, however, quite marked in rural areas. Ideologically UPP differs little in its programme from the PUWP and is noteworthy in this respect only in the emphatic tribute paid to the progressive nature of the peasant movement.[4] Its political mandate is its special concern for the development of rural areas. It has more recently been termed an 'environmental' party, in distinction from the general role and leadership functions of the PUWP.[5] Although it is not regarded officially as a temporary institution, some fear that the UPP is losing its political character and will slip into oblivion as the peasantry became more urbanised. It has already been noted that peasants with large holdings are more frequently to be found in UPP than in the PUWP. It is only among peasants with farms of less than 2 ha. that the PUWP has a majority over the peasant party and this is the group in which peasant *farmers* are in a decided minority. The UPP member is also likely to be

[1] D. Gałaj, *Aktywność społeczno-gospodarcza chłopów* (Warsaw, 1961) p. 228.

[2] W. Gomułka, Report of KC to the Fourth Congress, *O naszej partii*, p. 601.

[3] See Appendix 2, Table 5.

[4] See Wycech on the new ZSL Declaration of its Programme and Ideology, *III Kongres ZSL*, Stenogram, p. 242.

[5] M. Sadowski, 'Przemiany społeczne a partie polityczne PRL', in *Studia Socjologiczne* (1968) 3–4, p. 105.

older. Table 6 in Appendix 2 compares the age structure of
PUWP and UPP rural members, in which the proportion of
peasants varies considerably (38 per cent and 68 per cent).
In 1967 33 per cent of the 39,822 headmen[1] belonged to PUWP
and 27 per cent to UPP. Of those who were not even part-time
farmers 50 per cent were in PUWP and only 15 per cent in
UPP. Amongst those over sixty years of age 26 per cent were
PUWP members and 33 per cent UPP. In all other age-groups
PUWP membership was the commoner.[2]

While UPP membership reflected the ageing of the agricultural population that had been taking place under industrialisation this was less true of the feminisation process. Perhaps due to
the idea that politics is a man's occupation and to the traditional
representation of the family farm as a social unit by its (male)
head, only 15 per cent of Peasant Party members were women.
The second plenary meeting of the Supreme Committee (1960)
had been partially devoted to their lack of involvement, but
little progress had been made by the fourth Congress.[3] Apart
from women and 'leading farmers', the recruitment campaign
of the sixties has been directed at young farmers and the rural
intelligentsia. The latter group – teachers, administrative
employees, agronomists, zoologists and other specialists –
were particularly needed within UPP to stimulate political
work among the peasants and to counteract the emphasis on
agricultural problems which was threatening a virtual depoliticisation of the party. In 1963 there were 89,000 teachers in
rural areas, 17,000 workers with higher education and at least
that number with a full general (secondary) or occupational
education.[4] But these numbers are for those working in the
villages, and it is not known how many live there. A large
proportion probably travel from a more attractive urban
residence to their rural work-place (especially since rural
professional groups have priority in the purchase of motor

[1] Headmen are rural members elected every three years by the village
meeting to represent its interests in the gromada People's Council and to
act as the go-between of the authorities to the community.

[2] *Sołectwa i sołtysi* (Warsaw, 1968) p. xviii.

[3] *IV Kongres ZSL*, Przemówienia-Referat-Uchwała (Warsaw, LSW,
1965) p. 165.

[4] M. Kozakiewicz, 'O kryzysie społecznej pozycji nauczyciela wiejskiego',
in *Wieś Współczesna* (May 1963) p. 99.

cars), an arrangement unlikely to increase their social influence within the community. In 1966 it was found that only 51 per cent of UPP members among the intelligentsia were resident in rural areas.[1] Specialist workers among the technical intelligentsia tend to be drawn more to the PUWP. A survey in one wojewodstwo found 60 per cent of agronomists in the PUWP and 26 per cent in UPP.[2] Apart from office and administrative workers (not necessarily with a high level of education) the largest group among the non-peasant membership of UPP were rural teachers: 16,350 (22 per cent). Agronomist and other specialist members totalled less than 8,000.[3] The strength of the Peasant Party lies, therefore, predominantly in the groups of full-time farmers and is particularly strong among those farming more than 10 ha. The strength of PUWP, which has over 0·5 million non-peasant members in rural areas, lies primarily with the non-agricultural population.[4]

But the case for the UPP, representing the most significant social and production forces of Polish agriculture, becomes stronger when one examines the more marginal farming groups. The Peasant Party does not operate at all within the State farms; these remain the territory of PUWP and exert little influence on the individual farming communities. Their level of agriculture has done little to impress the small-scale farmer of their superiority (although they showed signs of improvement in the latter half of the sixties) and their employees are still to a large extent made up of old estate workers who were not able or willing to take up the responsibilities of individual farming. In several ways they have inherited the status of the prewar agricultural labourers.[5] Of the collective farmers only 2,550 belong to UPP, which represents about 10 per cent of all

[1] W. Dąbski, 'O niektórych sprawach organizacyjno-politycznych Stronnictwa w województwie łódzkim', in *Wieś Współczesna*, Jan. 1966, p. 17.

[2] A. Potok and G. Madej, 'Pozycja służby rolnej w gromadzie', *Wieś Współczesna*, Dec. 1969, p. 104.

[3] W. Dąbski, 'ZSL w latach 1949–65', in *Wieś Współczesna*, April 1966, p. 158.

[4] See Appendix 2, Tables 4 and 6.

[5] J. Poniatowski sees them as almost the drop-outs of the agricultural sector. See 'O społeczno-ekonomicznych procesach integracji w PGR', in *Roczniki Socjologii Wsi*, v (1967).

collective farmers. Their direct influence on rural society is minimal. Similarly peasant-workers play only a small part in the Peasant Party and account for some 10 per cent of UPP membership.[1] Involvement in the social life of the rural community is made difficult by the sheer fatigue involved in travel – if the non-agricultural employment is outside the village – and the additional hours put in on the family farm. As the author of a village study has put it: 'As we move from the category of farmers to peasant-workers and that of worker-peasants, participation in both the formal and informal life of the rural community gradually declines.'[2]

Figures for peasant enrolment in UPP (comparative data for PUWP peasant membership are not available) show membership to be strongly differentiated on regional lines. In six of the seven wojewodstwos that make up the central-eastern and south-eastern socio-economic regions, membership in 1965 was at a level of 2·1 or less per hundred of the population dependent on private agriculture.[3] These were the six lowest indices for the seventeen wojewodstwos in Poland. At the same time 68 per cent or more of the population in these six wojewodstwos lived in rural areas, and of the rural population 67 per cent or more were dependent on individual peasant agriculture.[4] In the areas, then, which were most rural in character and where peasant farming was most widespread, support for the Peasant Party was at its lowest numerically. Moreover, these areas were the strongest areas of support for the peasant movement before the war. As farming here was of a more traditionally subsistence character the local peasants were the worst placed to take advantage of

---

[1] Z. Mikołajczk, F. Patryn, *Struktura i funkcje partii chłopskiej* (Warsaw, 1969) pp. 124–5.

[2] D. Markowski, 'Zagadnienia zróżnicowania społecznego', in *Studia Socjologiczne*, 27 (1967), 4, p. 85.

[3] See IER *Zmiany, Społeczno-ekonomiczna struktura wsi w Polsce Ludowej* (Warsaw, 1961), for criteria of socio-economic classification. The regional differences emerge more strongly than the social differentiation of the local peasant society. For the membership indices see W. Dąbski, *ZSL w latach 1949–65* and *Rocznik Statystyczny 1966*, p. 407 from which they were calculated. The six wojewodztwos in question (only roughly approximating to IER regions whose classification is not based on administrative units) are: Kraków, Białystok, Łódź, Warsaw, Rzeszów, Kielce.

[4] *Rocznik Statystyczny*, 1961, pp. 15, 23; *Rocznik Statystyczny*, 1966, p. 40.

the material incentives the freer market offered the commercially oriented farmer. Therefore they had the least to gain from the reforms. The fact that other regions, as well as only certain farmers in these traditional areas, were better placed to benefit from State aid and the more lucrative State contracts for produce left a reservoir of bitterness among those less privileged. This emerged at the 1967 powiat conferences of UPP where attacks were made on State policy and on the inactivity of the party in defending peasant interests.[1] Similarly at the 1969 conferences of the Centre and East 'PPP-type' criticisms were reported of the peasant–worker alliance.[2] Although these were the areas with the lowest index for peasant party membership, by virtue of the small-scale nature of their agriculture and the low level of industrial development some of the wojewodstwos held the highest absolute figures for UPP membership.

On the basis of the membership indices for UPP it appears that farmers are more likely to join from regions more advanced both in industrialisation and in the development of more intensive agriculture. Similarly both PUWP and UPP have membership indices rising with the area of land owned, at least up to 10 ha. Both show a greater degree of support among peasants with farms of over 5 ha. than among the small peasants. In the Peasant Party those with over 5 ha. have an absolute majority among the farm-owning members. From this point of view institutional mobilisation shows some association with the more productive groups. The value of farm-produce marketed is approximately over four times greater for farms of over 5 ha., although 70 per cent of the 5 ha. and over group do not exceed 10 ha.[3] By the mid-sixties then, some degree of political mobilisation had been achieved among the full-time farming peasants. The policy of the parties was to concentrate attention on the everyday problems of agriculture in an attempt to integrate through the market the peasant producers with the socialist economy. No inevitable contradictions are seen in this process, which is officially regarded as one of gradual transformation.

---

[1] I. Adamski, L. Makiela, 'Zjazdy powiatowe Stronnictwa w 1967 roku', *Wieś Współczesna*, in June 1967, p. 15.

[2] R. Maćkowski and R. Wysocki, 'Z myślą o skuteczniejszym działaniu, in *Wieś Współczesna*, April 1969.

[3] A. Szemberg, *Przemiany w strukturze agrarnej*, pp. 133–5.

The influence of the socialist economy which 'gradually penetrates the countryside [and] does not force the peasants to a choice between socialism and capitalism. . . . Because of this it forms the basis for a gradual transition from traditional agriculture and the traditional society founded on the individual farm, permitting the assimilation of elements of the socialist structure.'[1] Gałaj finds the crucial variable differentiating the peasant society of modern Poland to be 'socio-occupational activeness'. Peasants who take advantage of State credits, make more contracts with State-purchasing agencies and react to State incentives by changing their form of production were found to be the leading farmers of the village. Status was found to be contingent on such activity. Participation in social organisations and the formal institutions of the community was a further index of this activeness. Another study of social and occupational activities found them to be inter-related but the inevitability of a gradual socialist transformation was questioned.[2] The realisation that the development of capitalist farming is not possible 'may, but does not necessarily, lead to the acceptance of a socialist future'.[3] But if it is the most profit-oriented and enterprising peasant farmer, the potential capitalist, who is most likely to feel the pinch of the economic restrictions that do still exist under the new policy – for example the scarcity of machinery and building materials, the retention of the progressive land tax, the difficulty of hiring labour, etc. – the greater level of political mobilisation that has been achieved may be of dubious benefit to the State. If the thesis of socio-occupational activeness means that the political parties have made most headway in enrolling peasant members amongst the most rationally minded, the more commercially oriented, those with larger farms and the more prosperous (all empirically inter-linked variables) the State is in the anomalous position of depending for the implementation of its policy in the countryside on those who in fact may well be most critical of its economic restrictions.[4]

[1] D. Gałaj, *Aktywność społeczno-gospodarcza chłopów*, p. 227.
[2] F. W. Mleczko, *Z badań nad aktywnością zawodową i społeczną chłopów* (Wrocław, 1964) p. 230.
[3] Ibid., p. 217.
[4] R. Maćkowski and R. Wysocki, 'Z myślą o skuteczniejszym działaniu....'

The switch in policy in 1956 from relations of administrative coercion over the peasants to those based more on persuasion and incentive meant that local organisations of both parties had to be more responsive to the needs and attitudes of the peasants. The emphasis that came to be put in 1960 on the village organisations again meant that central control was weakened and more responsibility put on the local members for the implementation of the programme, for there were not enough party functionaries (as full-time workers) to co-ordinate activities. The increased mobilisation of the peasantry during the sixties, therefore, may reflect not its changing attitude to socialist agriculture but simply the fact that the parties are to a lesser extent the representatives of opposed interests and that the peasants find them easier to control. The authors of an article in the UPP journal were complaining in 1969 that direc-tives from the district party centre seemed to get lost en route to the village branches. Twenty-five per cent of the branches did not seem to conduct any political work at all and in those that did the frequency of 'educational' meetings was in some cases as low as three a year.[1] The lack of political work in rural PUWP cells was also criticised,[1] and there were complaints that political criteria were not being considered in the Agri-cultural Circles, which were dominated by the wealthier farmers.[2] Also, while membership of the Peasant Party was growing it was becoming increasingly difficult to recruit activists for party work.[3]

The dangers of overextending the network of State agencies in rural areas and losing control over the local party organisa-tions had been recognised by the leadership in the late fifties. During the discussion of the extension of the powers of the gromada councils, the possibility of informal groups within the bureaucracy monopolising its activities was considered a major threat. Thus it had to be accompanied by strict planning and control procedures 'to prevent arbitrary measures within the

[1] F. Siemiankowski and J. Grajewski, 'W POP na wsi województwa poznańskiego', in *Nowe Drogi*, Jan. 1962.

[2] J. Majchrzak, 'O pracy politycznej na wsi województwa bydgoskiego', in *Nowe Drogi*, Oct. 1965.

[3] M. Wilczak, 'Dlaczego coraz mniej społeczników?', in *Zielony Sziandar*, 29 June 1969.

individual organs of the state administration and to combat all manifestations of the misuse, waste and theft of social property and the spread of bribery and corruption'.[1] Two years later UPP devoted a plenary session to the problems of gromada administration and declared its deficiencies to be one of the chief obstacles to the planning of agricultural production.[2] Despite the mass of legislation on the formal tasks and procedures of the councils their actual co-ordinating effect had been comparatively small.[3] Official business was transacted by informal groups and plenary sessions were quietly bypassed.[4] The theoretical sovereignty of the gromada unit could hardly be more than a fiction, for it did not even carry out formal functions of legally ratifying the contracts made by peasant farmers with State agents which were generally the most important transactions made by the farmer with the State. It is also doubtful whether it had in fact gained independence from the powiat authorities. These authorities were in practice loath to delegate powers to the gromada councils within their jurisdiction, for the funds the powiats receive were dependent on their previous record of plan fulfilment which might be put in jeopardy if responsibility for the councils was passed.[5] The measures introduced in agriculture after 1956 have not resulted in any far-reaching political liberalisation and economic decentralisation in the countryside.

THE PEASANT PROBLEM UNDER SOCIALISM

Since Poland has been under Communist rule two methods of controlling the peasantry and commanding the agricultural surplus have been attempted – one basically political (collectivisation) and the other economic (greater reliance on market factors). Both have met with difficulties of a social nature. In

[1] *III Kongres ZSL*, Stenogram, p. 703.

[2] *IV Plenum NK ZSL* (Warsaw, 1961) p. 43.

[3] C. Bielecki and B. Winiarski, *Gospodarka rad narodowych* (Warsaw, 1960) p. 57.

[4] S. Asanowicz, 'Z problematyki sesji gromadzkich rad narodowych', in *Wieś Współczesna*, Sept. 1968, p. 122.

[5] The rural decision-making process is elaborated in J. Tarkowski, 'A Study of the Decisional Process in Rolnovo Poviat', in *Polish Sociological Bulletin*, 16 (1967).

the first case collectivisation in Poland suffered from the same defects as elsewhere: high investment outlays, low productivity and the apathy of its work-force. However, particular difficulties in implementing the policy were encountered owing to the assumption of a degree of polarisation between a capitalistic *kulakry* (or rich peasantry) and the agricultural labourers or poor peasants that did not exist in the Polish countryside. As noted (see p. 49), circumstances had not been favourable to the development of rural capitalism in Poland. Where such forms of class differentiation were more advanced (in the German-influenced west of prewar Poland) collective farms have remained more numerous and are economically stronger.[1] But generally the anti-kulak campaign served to reinforce the peasants' suspicion of State policy and their fears of Russification. As there were frequently no real kulaks to be found in a village the peasants simply took the campaign to be a further stage in the oppression of the countryside and an attack on the peasant way of life itself. Nowakowski writes that it had similar effects amongst the urban population in worsening rural/urban relations, as the denigration of kulaks was extended to include the whole peasant population.[2]

In the case of Gomułka's new policy in agriculture, material incentives were insufficiently effective within a peasant sector where immediate profit maximisation and pure economic calculation were not the only features deciding the organisation of the family-run farm economy. The slow pace of agricultural development caused the policy to follow a ziz-zag path as the party tried to accommodate the diverse interests of industry and agriculture, of the workers and peasants, as well as conforming to ideological requirements. The dispersion of peasant agriculture into nearly 4 million production units made co-ordination and supervision of production a well-nigh impossible task. That is not to say that the increased attention the State paid to peasant agriculture after 1956 left the peasant economy unaffected nor that it did not influence the social structure of the peasantry. The supply of production resources was stepped up

[1] In 1966 nearly half the total acreage of collective farms was located in the provinces of Poznań and Bydgoszcz. *Rocznik Statystyczny* (1967) p. 262.

[2] S. Nowakowski, 'Przemiany postaw w stosunkach wieś-miasto w Polsce', in *Ruch Prawniczy, Ekonomiczny i Socjologiczny*, 1 (1963) p. 271.

while distribution – of credits, machines, fertilisers, high quality seeds, etc. – remained largely in the hands of functionaries in powiat and gromada institutions. As the 'free' market for produce remained a State monopoly (buying 80 per cent of the commodity production of private farms and effectively determining prices) it was through access to this range of production inputs and to the lucrative contracts with the State for specialised lines of production that the peasant farmer was most able to improve his material status. Because of the dual nature of the peasant household, being a unit of consumption as well as one of production, the allocation of production resources has had a considerable influence on the social structure of the community. Due to the State's retention of control over these crucial elements of production in what is otherwise a free peasant economy, it has been assumed (with varying degrees of confidence) that the stage was thus set for the gradual socialist transformation of the countryside, a change that would be brought about by the growth of the peasants' 'socio-occupational activeness'. As peasants entered freely into a greater number of economic relations with the State, joined the political organisations in greater numbers and in other ways participated in the formal institutions of modern society they would cease to be peasants and would become socialist farmers.

The trouble with this idea of rural change, at any rate in its more determinist forms, is that it is over-reliant on the stereotypical conception of the peasantry as a conservative, apathetic and unchanging group. It is, however, the very fact of peasants' capacity to adapt to change in the greater society that has enabled them to survive as a group for such a long time and to emerge in modern society as 'conservatives'. There is a difference between a group's capacity to change in order to perpetuate tradition and to conserve certain values, and its undergoing transformation involving the adoption of new sets of norms and values. Only in the latter case could a thoroughgoing change in the social nature of group be said to occur and the group itself to be 'transformed'. Only if Marx's comments on the French peasantry of the last century[1] are taken to

[1] That 'they form a vast mass, the members of which live in similar conditions but without entering into manifold relations with one another. Their

constitute an adequate definition of the peasantry could the simple growth of production associations, of economic ties between peasants and State agencies and peasant participation in formal institutions be said to signal such a transformation. The evidence from Poland, on the other hand, indicates that the peasants are indeed adapting to the conditions set by the socialist State, but their 'activisation' is not a sign of the adoption of new norms and values – paramount among which would be a decline in the importance attached to the social and economic independence of the peasant household.

A monographic study by Adamski illustrates the complexity of the process of rural modernisation and its multi-faceted character. The differentiation between traditionalists and rationalists, he wrote, was 'currently the main area for the crystallisation of two types of social attitude amongst the rural population'. Rationalists were those more sensitive to the 'demands of modernity and the influences of contemporary life patterns'. The distinction manifested itself in patterns of expenditure on consumption and production goods, in receptivity to technical and organisational innovation and in the level of socio-political activeness.[1] A second form of socio-economic differentiation established groups of common situation. In this the families of the village were identified with aggregations differentiated by source and level of income. These groupings included, in order of descending income, those whose situation was determined by the size of the farm they owned in conjunction with the extent of labour hire,[2] size of farm in conjunction with the amount of credit drawn from State funds and size of farm with income from industrial employment. The rationalist–traditionalist differentiation emerged within all groups, including the peasant-workers, and it is significant that in conflict situations the contending groups were both rationalists (in fact the rationalist sub-group of each group of common situation). What Adamski saw as the prime sphere of attitudinal dif-

---

mode of production isolates them from one another. . . .' K. Marx, 'The Eighteenth Brumaire of Louis Bonaparte', p. 334.

[1] W. Adamski, *Grupy interesów w społeczności wiejskiej* (Wrocław, 1967) pp. 129–30.

[2] The study was made in a village of the Bydgoszcz region, where labour-hire is still more prevalent.

ferentiation referred to a basically normative distinction (although this may be less true with respect to the place of consumption within the household). Certain families were more inclined to act within patterns of behaviour that enabled a more effective pursuit of goals determined by given value-orientations. The rise of groups benefiting from State credits and industrial employment is as obviously attributable to the process of socio-economic modernisation initiated by the Communist government as the adoption of rationalist views is a part of social modernisation. It implies that the modernisation process has a varying impact over the range of social attitudes and activities. Tensions, moreover, develop between groups differently affected by such aspects of modernisation, and 'rationalism' affects the articulation of interests rather than creates a common interest in some aspect of the process or in modernisation as such. There does not, for example, seem to be a single social force within the peasantry that can be said to spearhead the process of modernisation within the socialist context. Survey material has shown that peasant farmers with stronger traits of 'entrepreneurship' (response to material incentives, acceptance of innovation) in fact hold firmer views on the private ownership of land.[1] Mleczko's monograph also demonstrates the differences that emerge in attitudes and reactions to social and economic change. Four peasants in his study were identified as kulaks and held themselves apart from village politics. Two others, however, were generally opposed to the direction of change initiated by the Communist government but showed a high level of socio-political activeness in which their aim was to 'oppose the on-going changes by passive resistance or by conducting agitation against them in favour of the social relations of the past'.[2] Yet this did not preclude participation in State organisations or endorsement of such general improvements as the electrification of the village.

Sources of opposition among the peasantry are generally located, as Gałaj points out, in 'the group owning larger, prospering farms. . . . Some of them listen to voices encouraging them to take the path of development normal under capitalism,

---

[1] B. Gałęski, *Chłopi i zawód rolnika* (Warsaw, 1963) p. 123.
[2] F. W. Mleczko, *Z badań nad aktywnością zawodową i społeczną*, p. 203.

which has real meaning in the political activities of the country-side'.[1] As development along these lines is curtailed in Poland, how do such farmers react? It is evident that peasants who meet with obstacles to the operation and development of their farms within the framework of private ownership respond in different ways. Some appear to opt out and avoid contact with State institutions and the socialist sector as far as possible. A few accept the logic of the Communist policy with its ultimate negation of traditional peasant values. Others join the political and economic organisations operating in the countryside but more with a view to pursuing traditional (anti- or, at best, non-socialist) objectives through the institutional means available. With continuing State control over key elements of farm production the entrepreneurial peasant is by no means likely to eschew contact with State agencies, as increasingly it is a prerequisite for running an economically successful farm. Most notably this is the case with the more profitable contracts and the use of machinery (private purchase of which was virtually impossible until recently) – so long as access to it can be guaranteed by the Agricultural Circle at the necessary time and providing its management can make sure that the Circle does not become the thin end of the socialist wedge. In this respect the decentralisation of the administrative structure and the emphasis in political organisations on practical, peasant-oriented work has helped the rural community to preserve its peasant identity. The extension of State bureaucracies into the locality has led to a dilution of the procedures of formal control, a peasantisation of formal organisations with numerous local institutions overlapping both in function and membership and with the spread of diverse formal and informal ties throughout the institutional network. The drive to involve the village's 'leading' farmers in State institutions further contributes to the representation of peasant interests within them. Thus an institutional group, or local élite, emerges whose members are frequently personally involved in the matters decided. They are, therefore, open to the personal influences and informal pressures of the local community.

The maintenance of relations of influence and mutual benefit between community figures and local office-holders (in the

[1] D. Gałaj, *Chłopski ruch polityczny w Polsce* (Warsaw, 1969) p. 45.

Circles, People's Councils, the political parties and occupational organisations), insofar as they can be functionally differentiated, is one way the entrepreneur secures access to scarce economic goods. Formal channels for the pursuit of economic interests frequently founder on bureaucratic inefficiency and threaten the future status of the peasant farmer as an individual proprietor. The usefulness of an ally in the administration turning a blind eye to certain irregularities is not to be ignored. A considerable divergence was found by Gałaj between the structure of land-holdings according to the gromada's tax returns and that obtained from the empirical data he collected. Many 'owners', predominantly of very small farms, worked outside the village and had no intention of returning. They therefore had rights to a 'family payment' as their share of the inheritance and on this basis were willing to be recorded as *de jure* proprietors of their share in the farm, a measure that avoided the payment of the higher scales of the land tax.[1] Similarly, recent research has shown that 39 per cent of land transactions made between 1957 and 1967 in a sample taken were not legalised. This was partly done to avoid legal costs (up to 4 per cent of the land's value) and bureaucratic entanglement. In many cases, though, rights of ownership were not definite, either because of the lack of records caused by Poland's troubled history and frequent border changes, or because rights were more traditional and not endowed with legal validity. In either case, even in such fundamental matters as land transfer, the informal mechanism of the peasant economy persists, remaining beyond the scope of formal institutional regulation.[2]

It is hardly surprising that formal bureaucratic procedures do not reflect the actual form of rural administration in the rural locality. But where the balancing of industrial and agricultural interests, as representatives of different systems of production, is a constant struggle the discrepancy becomes more significant. In a situation where, as J. C. Scott has pointed out, the divisive nature of peasant society obstructs large-scale organisation, where legislation is formalistic and its implementation erratic, and where the under-group is not able to act with full legitimacy as a group force, demands are more likely

---

[1] D. Gałaj, *Aktywność społeczno-gospodarcza chłopów*, pp. 35–6.
[2] S. Podemski, 'Jak po grudzie', in *Polityka*, xiv, 24, 13 June 1970.

to reach the political system at the enforcement stage. In this sense the evasion of bureaucratic procedures, the predominance of personal relationships and manifestations of petty corruption become a form of political influence.[1]

There are further signs that these forms of influence lead to the monopolisation of resources and attempts by the broader élite group to maintain its position by restricting access to others. For those excluded this becomes a further source of dissatisfaction, and it was against such cliques that opposition from the poorer groups in the backward eastern provinces was heard in 1967 within UPP. It was stated that 'in the countryside there has emerged a farming élite, a small stratum of producers, some of whom have allied themselves with representatives of the rural trade agencies, with those of the food-processing industry and, here and there, with representatives of the local State administration. Due to this they always have access to the most lucrative lines of production and to "regulated" contracts.'[2] The assimilation of this group into the local power structure, for reasons both of social status and of short-term economic efficiency, is not necessarily an effective way of transforming the peasant economy. For the benefits of this association may simply be assimilated to the existing advantages of higher status and may become a means of perpetuating it in a different form. For this reason participation in State organisations does not in itself indicate agreement with their formal objectives or further the socialist modernisation of agriculture. A series of correlations carried out by K. Ostrowski and A. Przewórski has established that mobilisation as a process of institutionalisation is distinct from the growth of activeness within the organisations.[3] What party membership actually means for the process of rural modernisation and what kinds of activity it is associated with depends on what particular functions the organisations perform in the local society. The study made by Adamski illustrates functions resulting from

[1] J. C. Scott, 'The Analysis of Corruption in Developing Nations', in *Contemporary Studies in Society and History*, xi, 3 (1969) p. 326.

[2] J. Adamski and L. Makiela, 'Zjazdy powiatowe Stronnictwa w 1967', p. 14.

[3] 'A Preliminary Inquiry into the Nature of Social Change: the Case of the Polish Countryside', *Studies in Polish Political System*, ed. J. Wiatr (Wrocław, 1967) pp. 100–1.

the activities of rural interest groups and the integration of the agricultural élite.

Adamski traces the development of the interest groups to the scarcity of material benefits in the countryside and to inequalities of access to the local power-holders who were instrumental in deciding their allocation. The scarce goods which helped bring about their formation were: the awarding of some State contracts for farm-produce; the location and order of use of Agricultural Circle machinery; the use of State-owned land; access to middle- and long-term credits; the distribution of building materials, and the distribution of local non-agricultural jobs. Interests in these matters differed according to the groups of common situation already mentioned.[1] The existence of the groups emerged most clearly at a crisis point in the village which laid bare the contradictory long-term interests of the groups. This concerned the management of the Agricultural Circle, which, until 1964, was chaired by a member of the labour-hiring group. Having a large farm and holding numerous State contracts, the chairman represented the 'private future' interests concerned with keeping ties with the State at a minimum; for him existing links were lucrative yet they did not pose any threat to private property. This state of affairs, however, was less satisfactory for other farmers who personally owned less equipment and who resented the fact that under the pre-1964 management only one tractor had been purchased, despite the availability of funds for more. It was particularly irksome for the State-credit group which had largely developed its farms on the basis of the postwar land reform. This group was, therefore, in the eyes of the traditionally wealthy a 'new' group, and it was more irritated by the fact that the circle should be run by the old élite rather than by the actual lack of machines and the restrictions put on State aid. Both motives played a part, though. Several of the 'new' group were leading activists in the UPP branch and, in association with PUWP members and supra-local authorities which had for some time been dissatisfied with the progress made by the circle, conducted a campaign to show up the shortcomings of its management. This resulted in sufficient support to vote the old chairman and

[1] W. Adamski, 'Koncepcja "grupy interesu" w środowisku wiejskim', in *Studia Socjologiczno-Polityczne*, 19 (1965).

chief of machinery disposal out of office at the next meeting of
the circle members. These offices were then occupied by the
State credit group (i.e. 'new' farmers), now commanding a
majority on the board, who were then able to initiate a new
policy of extending the amount of machinery in the ownership
of the circle. This was a victory not only in economic terms, for
the change saw the departure of the former tractor mechanic
(who had lodged with the former chairman) as well as the old
chief of machinery. As the new chairman quickly purchased
three new tractors he then had to engage four new mechanics,
who were all eager for the jobs and whose gratitude further
raised the status of the chairman as a quasi-employer and patron
for several of the village's poorer families. The consequences of
the complex relationships between personal ties and formal
relations, between social prestige, political power and economic
strength, did not end with this. Suffice it to say that the change
in management of the circle put the chairman very much in
the good books of the authorities. Thus he was soon able to get
the job of agent for plant contracts in the village (with the help
of his son-in-law who worked in the beet plant) and then a
30,000 złoty long-term loan (in this case thanks to a comrade
in the powiat body of the peasant party).[1]

In this case the Peasant Party acted in alliance with PUWP,
in line also with State policy and with the support of the powiat
authorities. While the affair with the Agricultural Circle was a
defeat for the old, wealthy élite of the village it can be seen that
a new élite was in the making, and likely to become in the future
a guardian of the vested interests which were rapidly accumulat-
ing around a mixture of prestige, power, friendship and kin-
ship relations. A second case study from the same region and
in the same period illustrates again the dominance of a traditional élite, which found institutional legitimation for its
interests against State policy within the Peasant Party but so
monopolised the institutional life of the village that it retained
its supremacy. This was possible both because of its ability
to assume control of a variety of institutions and, in the last
analysis, because of the reactive nature of the powiat authorities
so long as it was seen to be in control of the community. A

[1] W. Adamski, *Grupy interesów w społeczności wiejskiej*, pp. 108, 135,
185–9.

further contributory factor was the weakness of the Communist Party. It had been outmanoeuvred rather ingeniously in 1954 when it had attempted to set up a collective farm. This was forestalled by non-party peasants setting up one themselves of a lower type, i.e. involving a lower level of common ownership and basically involving only collective cultivation. By this action the local party branch lost face in the village and the confidence of the superior authorities, for the powiat officials henceforth considered the leaders of the collective as the representatives of the village. Its administration in fact was mostly composed of rich peasants, although most collective members were middle peasants. Thus slighted, the PUWP cell was the first to come out for its dissolution in 1956. When this had occurred the collective farm's chairman – the largest farmer in the village – became chairman both of the gromada People's Council and of the newly set up UPP branch, which was externally recognised again as *the* village institution. Most dissatisfied at this stage were the middle peasants – again owning most of their land by virtue of the land reform and possessing few production resources – who had seen considerable advantages in the collectives. But they were even more disillusioned with PUWP and UPP, both of whom had shown scant concern for their interests since 1954. More as a political move than an economic one, a middle-peasant collective was set up in 1958 in order to gain some form of political recognition from the powiat authority. This was again successful and the wealthy chairman of the GRN was eased from office. Two more collectives were soon set up in other parts of the village, eventually involving all PUWP members and most of the UPP (the largest peasants remained independent). This, however, again presented the authorities with the problem of whom they were to regard as village leaders. As a result the collectives were asked to amalgamate. As the point of their existence was largely a political one the request was refused, leading to their disbandment. While the author of this study makes the point that this sequence of events had proved that such enterprises required middle-peasant support to succeed, this could hardly have been a great satisfaction to them. UPP was by this time fully compromised as an 'egoistic' organisation – but still controlling the Agricultural Circle – while PUWP was only slowly overcoming its lack of concern for the agricultural interests of the village.[1] Gałęski's[2] doubts about the socially modernising effects of socialist industrialisation on rural populations seems, therefore, well justified. In view of the last case study, made in the region which before the war had the most capitalistic and commercial form of agriculture, his hypothesis that its effects could well be disruptive of market-oriented agriculture and its associated social structure is at least partly substantiated, for the disunity of the village society was quite evident. Electrification plus People's Councils has not meant communism for the Polish peasantry. It has led rather to the adaption of the peasant economy and society to a set of conditions established, and frequently changed, by the State without injecting any dynamic likely to bring about the transformation of its basic structures. Polish agriculture still remains a peasant economy, neither capitalist – i.e. involving the extension of labour-hire and the free accumulation and disposal of capital – nor socialist. Indeed, the restrictions on capitalist development may well be aiding the preservation of peasant agriculture, for left to its own momentum of development it would be likely to evolve spontaneously new relations in production at a rate faster than the growth of socialist agriculture. The effects of the growth of State dependence, however, have not brought any basic division within the rural community. With Adamski's schema of cross-cutting social differentiation the forms of division necessitate the spread of social ties throughout the various groups and result in a multiplicity of factions that appear in different forms according to the situation. Ties between the rationalist and traditionalist sections of each group of common situation are strengthened over an issue such as the operation of the Agricultural Circle which hinges on the conflict of their long-term interests. In the short run the members of each common situation grouping are in conflict with one another, and each therefore seeks to consolidate support in various ways with the members of the other groups. Thus a whole network of integrating relations is created between all groups of the community.

The social structures of other traditional communities have

---

[1] Z. Żebrowski, 'Społeczno-zawodowa aktywność chłopów', in *Studia Socjologiczno-polityczne*, 19 (1965) pp. 188–93.

[2] 'Typy uprzemysłowienia', *Studia Socjologiczne*, 4 (1967).

been found to be well integrated despite the effects of industrialisation. In her study of 'An Industrialised Village' Olszewska concludes that 'the course of industrialisation and urbanisation may not run so deep as is usually thought'.[1] In saying this she refers not to the obvious material and superficial changes in the appearance of the village, but to the quality of community relations and the values they express. Dominant among valued institutions were work and the family. Work was valued above the level of instrumentality and it remained one of the prime functions of the family unit. Week-long absences in urban 'workers' hotels' on the part of worker-peasants were accepted with equanimity. Occupational qualities were still the prime criterion in the choice of a spouse as was good health. Weddings were large-scale community ceremonies and every villager was assumed to have the right of entry to the reception. Despite the rising cost of such celebrations, 'family weddings' were very much the exception. Inactivity was generally looked on with moral disapprobation, as was lack of thrift and the expenditure of income on items and activities whose benefit was only short-lived. Expenditure on religion, on the upkeep and care of graves and the restoration of the church, was high and evidently regarded as well worthwhile.[2] Economic modernisation, however, has not left community life unchanged. Rising cash incomes provide the means to sustain social activities – both traditional and modern – at a higher level. The growth of secular activities has complemented rather than displaced religious activities in the community. Secular activeness in one study was found to intensify with that of parish institutions.[3] The functions of religion seem to be changing, though, with respect to the situation of different groups within the peasantry. In one village typical of the backward eastern part of the country the parish remained the central institution of integration, encompassing even the local power-holders who sat on the parish council. In this area, which has not progressed markedly under the new policy, it is interesting that church 'activists' are increasingly drawn from the youth of groups less touched by

[1] A. Olszewska, *Wieś uprzemysłowiona* (Wrocław, 1969) p. 146.
[2] Ibid., pp. 126–40.
[3] K. Adamus-Darczewska, 'Z zagadnień aktywności społeczno-gospodarczej wiejskiej parafii w Polsce', in *Roczniki Socjologii Wsi*, viii (1970) p. 63.

the emigration process.[1] It is only 'reactionary clericism' and 'parish activism' that are officially frowned on by the political parties. The role of party member is easily assimilable to the others played by the peasant, despite an apparent formal incongruity (at least in the case of PUWP). In one sample 40 per cent of party members amongst the peasants were regular churchgoers and another 3 per cent irregular attenders.[2]

Not all groups, however, have responded in the same way to the new conditions of social life in the Polish countryside. For those less committed to the agricultural occupation and the peasant way of life the need is less strongly felt to accommodate the values of peasant society with the institutional means for their implementation within the socialist State. This applies particularly to the younger generation brought up in postwar Poland, more vulnerable to the pressures of modernisation with its avenues of social and geographical mobility and exposed at a younger age to the radically different outlook expressed by Communist ideology. The hopes and aspirations in this are in sharp contrast to the realities of rural life, still backward and underprivileged in contrast to the urban milieu. Not only are social conditions actually worse in the countryside, but the conviction remains that the nation as a whole holds the peasant in low esteem. Given the fact of (or belief in) the existence of greater opportunities for mobility this is a further disincentive for commitment to the agricultural life. A survey carried out in the early sixties established that both rural and urban dwellers gave the private farmer a fairly high ranking in the hierarchy of occupations. The peasants still mostly held, though, that the rest of the nation placed the peasant where he had traditionally been – at the bottom of the scale. This conviction, moreover, was linked with fears for the future of private farming. Over half the respondents expressed worry about its prospects.[3] Given this combination of factors rural youth have good reason to be dissatisfied with farm life, and the future holds little hope for its

[1] E. Ciupak, *Kult religijny i jego społeczne podłoże* (Warsaw, 1965) pp. 316–320.

[2] A. Pawełczyńska, 'Postawy ludności wiejskiej wobec religii', in *Roczniki Socjologii Wsi*, viii (1970) p. 82.

[3] W. Makarczyk, 'Czynniki stabilności i aktywności zawodowej rolników w gospodarstwach indywidualnych', in *Studia Socjologiczne* (1961) 2 (2) pp. 132 and 139.

rapid improvement. The consequence has been the spread of the process of emigration – both 'external' and 'internal'. It was noted in 1966 that RYU (the Rural Youth Union) was enrolling a disproportionate number of teenagers.[1] Membership was highly unstable and of short duration: before its fourth Congress in 1970, a quarter of its 1 million membership was being renewed each year, sapping its organisational unity and leading to the depoliticisation of its activities. Anxiety was aroused by this process in that 'from lack of experience the youngest are particularly vulnerable to alien . . . opinions and ideas'.[2] The reaction of the rural youth to the combination of social and cultural cross-pressures has been the growth of dissatisfaction with their surroundings, exemplified by the events within RYU. Their response to the spread of urban values and certain patterns of behaviour in the countryside has not been to challenge traditional rural society but to avoid it, either through migration or by attempting to emulate urban cultural patterns in the village. But this has rarely involved attempts to transform the village as an occupational, social or political community and has been more of an anomalous attempt to graft rather superficial elements of urban life on to the peasant society. The creation of semi-urban enclaves within the village is associated more with a process of 'internal emigration' prompted by such feelings as 'it was boring at home . . . PYU had become a lot more popular since it opened a club'.[3] One study has shown that membership in the movement holds attraction because of an orientation towards urban life and aspirations to migration and not because of activities leading to the social transformation of the village.[4] Membership was correlated with both occupational and geographical mobility. Due to their susceptibility to the changes that have taken place in postwar Poland the younger generation's awareness of the higher standards of consumption and of the better amenities of town life held up as incentives to the rural population has

[1] *III Krajowy Zjazd Związku Młodzieży Polskiej* Iskry (Warsaw, 1966) p. 441.

[2] J. Kraśniewski, 'Gdy organizacja odmładza się', in *Trybuna Ludu*, 21 May 1969.

[3] A. Strońska, 'Życie i okrycie', *Polityka* 16, 18 April 1970.

[4] W. Makarczyk, *Czynniki stabilizacji w zawodzie rolnika i motywy migracji* (Wrocław, 1964) p. 159.

exacerbated the consciousness of rural/urban differences and the drift from the land.[1]

The consequences of the continuing obstacles to the re-modelling of peasant society and its farming in socialist Poland were dramatically illustrated in 1970, twenty-two years after an attempt to remove them by collectivisation had been launched and fourteen years after the tactics that make up the new policy were devised. Due to bad weather, the harvests of 1969 and 1970 were both very poor. As a result their effect was disastrous, leading to a sharp rise in the cost of food-stuffs which sparked off the riots on the northern coast in December 1970. The run of bad weather was not of course responsible for the riots and the fall of the government leaders and neither were the prob-lems of agriculture the sole cause. But in conjunction with other factors they played a large part in discrediting the leader-ship. Having instituted a policy less anti-peasant and less orthodox than those of the other European Communist States the Polish leaders were constantly subjected to charges of revisionism (both internal and external), and critics were ready to seize on any shortcoming in private agriculture that could be used against the leadership. At the end of 1970 the peasant party journal, *Wieś Współczesna* (*The Contemporary Countryside*), published an editorial defending the policy against critics who remained unmentioned but whose line of attack was identified quite clearly. The non-capitalist nature of Polish agriculture and the capacity of the State to control the market were em-phatically underlined. 'Even in the Soviet Union', it said 'where there is a forty-year old kolkhoz tradition and State farms predominate, there appears a marginal private market in agricultural produce not much smaller than that in Poland (15 per cent of marketed produce compared to 20 per cent in Poland)'.[2] There was little positive argument for the Polish system of agriculture and its socialisation policy, and its defence rested largely on the difficulties of Polish development and the fact that her acute lack of capital resources precluded forms of socialisation which were not based on the exploitation

[1] For the reaction to consumer incentives see M. Pohoski, 'Interrelation Between Social Mobility of Individuals and Groups in the Process of Economic Growth in Poland', in *Polish Sociological Bulletin* 10 (1964) pp. 25–6.   [2] *Wieś Współczesna*, 166, Dec. 1970, pp. 4–5.

of the labour reserves that peasant agriculture maintained. 'If in Poland there was no individual peasant agriculture but only the State and co-operative system, the growth in agricultural production achieved over the past dozen years would have cost the nation . . . several times as much.'[1]

The nature of the industrialisation process in Poland and its effects on the peasant sector had, however, made peasant agriculture (despite considerable expansion of output) a very weak link in Poland's economy. The avoidance of a capital-intensive path of economic development had meant that productivity per agricultural worker was still very low and had increased by a minimal amount compared to the situation in industry. Between 1950 and 1967 the proportion of the national income produced by agriculture had declined from 40 per cent to 17 per cent. In this period the proportion of the labour force active in agriculture had fallen only from 57 per cent to 42 per cent.[2] The low overall standard of living of the Polish population (a further association with labour-intensive development) made it especially susceptible to changes in food-prices: in 1969 food still accounted for 40 per cent of the average family budget, while amongst the lower paid it accounted for well over half their total expenditure.[3] But it is hardly possible to see how peasant agriculture could have fulfilled the expectations that were imposed on it, combining the satisfaction of the needs of the population at a higher level with the goal of national self-sufficiency in grain production.

It had been planned to eliminate grain imports by 1970 and the campaign to achieve this had been the major theme in agricultural pronouncements throughout the sixties.[4] This was a target unlikely to be achieved within the existing land-structure and extremely ambitious by any criterion.[5] Due to the

[1] Ibid., p. 6.

[2] B. Strużek, 'Polityka rolna a nowy plan 5-letni', in *Wieś Współczesna*, 166, Dec. 1970, p. 21.

[3] 'Gospodarstwa indywidualne a sytuacja w rolnictwie', in *Wieś Współczesna*, 166, Dec. 1970, p. 8.

[4] The short-fall in the 1970 grain harvest is calculated variously at between 2 and 4 million tons from 1969 levels. As 1·5 million tons were imported in that year as much as 5·5 million tons may have to be purchased to maintain supplies at the 1969 level.

[5] S. H. Franklin, *The European Peasantry* (London, 1969) pp. 215–16.

competition within agriculture between grain cultivation and the production of fodder supplies for livestock this meant a restriction on meat production. With the failure to introduce sufficiently intensive methods of farming among the peasants the grain campaign led to a continuous fall in the proportion of animal products in farm-output after 1962.[1] The effect of the second bad harvest (1970) was to convert this fall into an absolute drop in the supply on the market (as happened also with grain), leading to the attempts at the end of the year to restore market balance by adjusting food prices.

The end of Gomułka's rule, then, was marked by a situation in agriculture as desperate as that which had helped his return to power in 1956. Unlike 1956, however, the countryside remained politically quiescent. Gomułka's policy had provided a structure in which the more pressing frustrations of the peasants could be eased; poor peasants who were unable to support themselves from agriculture could generally find off-farm work in the non-agricultural sectors of the economy. Enterprising peasant farmers had certain lucrative outlets for their produce and could find ways to circumvent formal restrictions within the decentralised bureaucracy that the scattered nature of peasant agriculture had forced on the State. As the political and economic systems that had been introduced in 1956 in the countryside coalesced into an amorphous administrative bureaucracy, their institutions proved increasingly amenable to various forms of peasant influence and pressure. It was the working class rather than the peasantry as a whole that reaped the consequences of the inefficiency of such a system. That is not to say that the peasants found it satisfactory. It was, however, irksome for them rather than oppressive. But the hopes of UPP that it will become a party independent of PUWP and free to express specifically peasant interests do remain. These views were rejected at the first meeting of the new UPP leadership in February 1971.[2] In their view the future lies with co-ordinated inter-party work and with the structure of their activities improved to ensure a higher degree of effectiveness. Changes in the agricultural policy are to be economic rather than overtly political. Initial measures, nevertheless, include the removal of

[1] B. Strużek, 'Polityka rolna a nowy plan 5-letni', pp. 17–19.
[2] *Trybuna Ludu*, 11 Feb. 1971.

the essentially political controls that Gomułka had retained over agriculture from fear of rural developments getting out of hand. This particularly concerns the abolition of quota deliveries for meat, grain and potatoes (to take effect from 1972) and the reductions at the higher end of the land-tax scale, a concession to the larger farmer.[1] In this respect the measures represent a logical continuation of the new policy and the broadening of its scope. It remains to be seen whether it will be sufficient to foster the development of a fully market-oriented agriculture and produce the demise of the continuing elements of self-sufficiency in peasant agriculture that perpetuate the peasant problem in Poland.

[1] *Trybuna Ludu*, 18 April 1971.

CHAPTER THREE

The Polish Industrial Manual Working Class

By George Kolankiewicz

What we have to deal with here is a communist society,
not as it has developed on its own foundation but,
on the contrary, as it emerges from capitalist society;
which is thus in every respect, economically, morally and
intellectually, still stamped with the birth marks of
the old society from whose womb it emerges.[1]

INDUSTRIALISATION AND URBANISATION IN POSTWAR POLAND

Postwar Poland inherited a developed and active working class
from the inter-war society. The industrial manual labour force
had been primarily located in the.heavy industrial sector of
mining and iron and steel as well as in the traditional metal and
textile industries.[2] During the years of the depression it was
particularly the workers in the latter industries who exhibited
signs of militancy in reaction to unemployment and to a fall in
their standard of living.[3] For example, the first recorded use of
the occupation strike (as a counter-measure to lock-outs) in
Poland was in a textile factory in January 1931 and it rapidly
became the most popular form of industrial militant action.
Statistics show that, in 1936, 2,056 strikes occurred, involving

[1] K. Marx, 'Marginal notes to the programme of the German Workers'
Party', in Marx and Engels, *Selected Works* (London, 1968) p. 323.

[2] M. Ciechocińska, *Położenia klasy robotniczej w Polsce 1929–39* (Warsaw,
1965) p. 20, and *Mały Rocznik Statystyczny, 1939.*

[3] For a discussion of the deteriorating material situation of sections of
the industrial manual workers see W. Bielicki and K. Zagórski, *Robotnicy,
wczoraj i dziś* (Katowice, 1966).

675,000 strikers and 22,016 factories, with the loss of nearly 4 million man hours. This must be judged against the fact that, in 1938, there were 808,400 workers employed in medium- and large-scale industry.[1] Writing on this subject some twenty years later, Jan Szczepański echoed the words of Marx quoted above when he wrote:

> Old traditions and images intertwine with a new social reality. Older workers are prone to viewing management/worker relations in terms of the class-conflict schema of the past.[2]

We mention the size and the industrial militancy of the prewar manual working class in order to suggest that there existed in prewar Poland a section of the industrial proletariat which was both aware of its collective interests and was experienced in their articulation. The 'old traditions and images' of these workers were not entirely compatible with those of the new communist leadership. The priorities of the State in the area of industrialisation and urbanisation (as well as 'political stabilisation') frequently left the industrial worker in a disadvantageous position, and consequently evoked from him the 'traditional' attitudes and actions.

This incompatibility between the old traditions and the new social order was first demonstrated in the immediate postwar period with the fate of the union factory councils, and furthermore foreshadowed how 'workers' democracy' was to be interpreted in the context of the 'new' social reality. However, the industrial structure founded by the communists initially opened up new possibilities for participation by the working class.

With the withdrawal of the Nazi occupation forces from Polish territory the Polish Workers Party (PWP) and the State administration acknowledged the right of the workers and their representative organs, the factory council and factory committee, to participate in decision-making on all matters affecting the factory. Temporary management formally consisted of three members: the factory director and representatives of the people's

---

[1] M. Ciechocińska, *Położenia . . .*, p. 145. It is only the medium- or large-scale industries which could contain an 'organised' labour force.

[2] J. Szczepański, 'Robotnicy', in *Odmiany czasu teraźniejszego* (Warsaw, 1971).

council and the factory council. The intention was to draw together the professional, political and social interests respectively involved within the factory.[1]

It soon became obvious that management–worker relations had to be clarified. In October of 1944 a provisional decree was drafted in Lublin concerning the role of the factory councils of the trade unions, which was subsequently rejected by the Polish Committee for National Liberation (PCNL). The amended version, more 'revolutionary' in content, acknowledged the right of the councils to supervise the management of the factory and working conditions, to participate with management in the ratification of pay norms and work regulations, as well as the right to direct control over employment and dismissal.[2]

The PCNL had already been shown to be opportunist in its treatment of the 'nationalisation' question when it had dropped the latter slogan from its manifesto lest it should not obtain the support of the small proprietors and peasants.[3] The plans for the factory councils were similarly used by the PCNL, not only to gain support from the workers but also to strengthen the PWP in its confrontation with the London government. The decree was promulgated through the press and over the radio and had '. . . a great mobilising impetus for the thousands of workers who at the time of the liberation of the country rose to the battle for the seizure and protection of the factories'.[4] But as the initial fervour of liberation receded, the management–worker conflict was again seen to be crystallising along the traditional lines. Factory councils controlled by party and union activists constantly counterposed themselves to decisions made by management, particularly in matters relating to production. The unions adopted this traditionally aggressive stance against management because as the Central Committee of the Trade Unions in April 1945 maintained:

[1] J. Gołębiowski, 'Problemy nacjonalizacji przemysłu', in *Uprzemysłowienie ziem polskich w XIX i XX wieku* . . ., p. 509.

[2] Ibid., p. 510.

[3] See also A. Korboński, *Politics of Socialist Agriculture in Poland 1946–1960* (New York, 1965) p. 72.

[4] The as yet unratified decree relating to the role of the union factory councils was used quite clearly as a propaganda instrument in the industrial region of Silesia to hasten the departure of the Nazi forces as well as to align this vital region with the communists. J. Gołębiowski . . ., p. 511.

In many factories co-operation between management and the factory councils has had positive results. At the same time, management recruited primarily from specialists and functionaries of the old mould are often incapable of resolving conflict, working as they do with old methods, disregarding the new attitudes of the working-class, as well as ignoring the representatives of the working-class in deciding upon fundamental problems.[1]

The Industrial Department of the Central Committee of the PWP was in favour of widening the rights of the factory councils and increasing the sphere of public control though at the same time it supported the principle of 'one man management'.

On 20 May 1945 this decree concerning the role of the factory councils was finally ratified, having meanwhile lost most of its original content. The power of the director had been widened to include all matters relating to the production activity of the enterprise and the factory council, whereas the workers had been deprived of direct influence on the management of the enterprise. The decree not only went back upon the resolutions of the Central Committee of the PWP and the trade unions but also quite clearly disregarded the rights attributed to the councils in January and February of 1945. The rights relating to the regulation of wage levels and norms were omitted and the only conferences which were retained were the 'technical' ones from which the factory councils were excluded.[2] The reasons given for this *volte face* were the 'anarcho-syndicalist' demands of the factory councils and the pressures exerted by the prewar management and technical intelligentsia who were hostile both to political intrusion in their affairs and to the party itself. The deteriorating economic situation provided a further justification for restricting the role of the councils.

Let us now turn to consider the support enjoyed by the communists after the Second World War. In 1945 the Polish Workers Party had a membership predominantly of manual workers and peasants with only 11·0 per cent of its membership being non-manual workers. By October 1949, only 57·0 per cent

[1] 'Sprawozdanie KCZZ z działalności i stanu związków zawodowych w Polsce XI 1944–XI 1945'. Quoted in J. Gołębiowski . . ., p. 514.
[2] J. Gołebiowski . . ., pp. 515–16.

of the total membership of 1,368,759 were manual workers.[1] The unification of the PWP and the Polish Socialist Party (PSP) in December 1948 drew many non-manual workers into the ranks of the party[2] and the intra-generational mobility of the initial postwar period (when many manual workers moved into non-manual positions) tended to distort party membership figures.[3] The rapid growth in party membership in the first months of 1945 was due firstly to the fact that support for the government was expressed by support for the party, particularly on the part of the manual workers and the semi-proletariat in the rural areas, and secondly by the rather indiscriminate induction of new party members in the first months of 1945.[4]

The postwar period was one of rapid social mobility as well as political change. The extent of mobility of manual to non-manual status in the later forties and fifties may be illustrated by a study carried out in 1968 of 3,482 male heads of households employed in the industrial public sector. Of those who had commenced employment as industrial manual workers before 1939, 39·3 per cent were non-manual workers by 1968. In the

[1] A. Kurz, *Społeczna rola Polskiej Zjednoczonej Partii Robotniczej* (Warsaw, 1967) p. 58, and S. Widerszpil, *Skład polskiej klasy robotniczej* (Warsaw, 1965) p. 306.

[2] A study by Malanowski showed that by Jan. 1945 there were 145 members of the PWP in a town whose population was 13,000. By 1948 there were 621 members, of whom 43·4 per cent were manual workers, 21 per cent non-manual workers and 25 per cent petty-bourgeois in origin. The author notes that the majority of the non-manual members were originally manual workers who had moved into the ranks of the administration at the lower levels. J. Malanowski, *Stosunki klasowe i różnice społeczne w mieście* (Warsaw, 1967) p. 85.

[3] A study by J. Janicki of industrial clerical/administrative employees showed that the immediate post-1944 period had the highest level of manual to non-manual mobility. Fifty-five per cent of such non-manual employees had been 'manual workers'. Of those who had been *unskilled* manual workers, 25 per cent had been promoted as late as 1950–4. In J. Janicki, *Urzędnicy przemysłowi w strukturze społecznej Polski Ludowej* (Warsaw, 1968) p. 144.

[4] A study of a powiat north of Warsaw has shown that after only one month of activity the local party ranks had swollen from 16 to 1,000 members (28 Feb. 1945) and by March the figure was constant. Cf. A. Kociszewski, 'Powstanie władzy ludowej i walka o jej utrwalenie', in *Ciechanów w okresie władzy ludowej*, 1970, pp. 21–3.

case of those who had commenced active employment as industrial manual workers in the periods 1945–55 and after 1956, the figures were 22·5 per cent and 18·3 per cent respectively.[1] More than one Polish author has remarked upon the paradoxical situation in which the party was rewarding its most active and committed members by 'promotion' into the ranks of the 'white-collar' while it was at the same time strongly emphasising the leading role of the working class.[2]

The second form of mobility was geographical mobility, and included the rural to urban migration of the late forties and early fifties. On the basis of one estimate, during the years 1946–50, the migration to the towns accounted for nearly 95 per cent of the natural rural population growth.[3] By 1950 one third of the population of industrial Łódź was composed of postwar migrants from the countryside as was the case for one-quarter of the population of Warsaw.[4] During the period 1946–50 over 7 million people left their rural environment to take up residence and work in the towns. They settled mostly in the Western Territories and along the northern seaboard, occupying towns and villages which had been vacated by the German population. The migration after 1950, though larger in absolute terms, was not as significant in its intensity.

On the industrial front the years 1948–9 marked a point of change in direction of the industrial development of Poland. On 10 February 1949 the Central Planning Office, which had 'co-ordinated' the work of the various departments, was replaced by the State Economic Planning Commission. There followed a period of more centralised planning, a higher level of investment and State control over the three sectors of the economy (public, co-operative and private) and, most significantly, an increase in the tempo of industrialisation.[5] Taking 1949 as the base year (100), the index of industrial investment had leapt to 326 by 1953. The comparable figures for the

[1] L. Beskid and K. Zagórski, *Robotnicy na tle przemian struktury społecznej w Polsce* (Warsaw, March 1971) p. 45.

[2] W. Wesołowski, 'Prestiż zawodów-system wartości-uwarstwienie społeczne', in *Studia Socjologiczno-polityczne*, 1963, no. 15.

[3] M. Pohoski, *Migracje ze wsi do miast* (Warsaw, 1963) p. 51.

[4] 'Portret Klasy', in *Polityka*, no. 24, 13 June 1964.

[5] H. Jędruszczak, 'Odbudowa potencjału przemysłowego w latach 1945–49', in *Uprzemysłowienie ziem polskich*, p. 547.

period up until 1958, taking 1953 as the base, was only 114.[1]

The most striking single example of the effort which went into the industrialisation programme during the years 1950–3 was the construction of the Lenin steel works and the town of Nowa Huta. Not only did this emphasise the government's investment policy for heavy industry but it also reflected one aspect of the political character of the investment and urbanisation programme. Writing of the factors which influenced the placement of the town of Nowa Huta, Renata Siemieńska noted that it was intended

> ... to create a large new and strong socialist urban working class society, which would in time influence the development of the social structure and social relations in an old and extraordinarily staid population such as existed in Kraków.[2]

Large-scale industrialisation in Poland required a correspondingly high level of urbanisation to supply the requisite manpower. Employment in industry during the years 1950–3 increased by over 700,000 but this growth was not entirely a consequence of the requirement for industrial manpower but involved other social and political considerations. The eradication of unemployment was a priority, demonstrated by the fact that the growth in employment was 1·7 times the growth in the number of persons coming up to the age of employment.

The new industrial workers were recruited primarily into the traditional industries such as mining and textiles as well as into modern industries located in these areas. By 1960 two-thirds of the total increase in employment had been centred around the old industrial regions of Łódź, Warsaw, Silesia and the seaports of Gdańsk and Gdynia.[3] Recruitment into the traditional industries had primarily occurred before 1950, whereas it was the machine-tool and electrical engineering industries which

---

[1] R. Wilczewski, 'Rozwój przemysłu w latach 1950–1965', in *Uprzemysłowienie ziem polskich* . . ., p. 570.

[2] R. Siemieńska, *Nowe życie w nowym mieście* (Warsaw, 1969) p. 18.

[3] Mining, textiles and the foodstuffs industries accounted for 63 per cent of total production and employed 52 per cent of the total industrial labour force in 1950. S. Misztal, 'Zmiany w rozmieszczeniu przemysłu na obecnym obszarze Polski w latach 1860–1960', in *Uprzemysłowienie ziem polskich* . . ., pp. 647–54.

grew most rapidly during 1950–3, increasing the number of their employees by 90 per cent in some cases.[1]

It is generally held that it was only after 1953 that the real income of manual workers enjoyed significant growth. At the same time during the early fifties income differentials between industrial manual workers and technical intelligentsia were also diminishing. Whereas in 1950 the latter earned 79·5 per cent more on average than did the manual worker this difference had dropped to 56·4 per cent and was subsequently a cause of much discontent, particularly amongst the young technical intelligentsia.[2]

The low level of growth in real wages prior to 1953 was felt most strongly by the prewar manual workers and less intensely by the newly migrated peasant-worker or young graduate of a vocational school. We might hypothesise that the older worker, with his developed material and consumption aspirations, felt the stagnation of real wages most acutely. For many of the new workers the fact that they had moved from rural/agricultural employment into industry was for the time being, at least, a significant achievement.[3] The movement from country to town, as well as the change from agricultural to industrial employment without a change of habitation, was so popular that by the time of the IX Plenum of the CC PUWP in late 1953 the government had to put a brake upon the migration and at the same time cut investment in heavy industry.[4]

[1] R. Wilczewski, 'Rozwój przemysłu w latach 1950–1965', in *Uprzemysłowienie ziem polskich . . .*, pp. 596–601.

[2] K. Zagórski, 'Warunki materialno-bytowe robotników i inteligencji', in *Struktura i dynamika społeczeństwa polskiego* (Warsaw, 1970) p. 155.

[3] S. Widerszpil, *Skład polskiej klasy robotniczej* (Warsaw, 1965) p. 100, and M. Pohoski, *Migracje . . .*, p. 182.

[4] The policy of taxation and compulsory quota deliveries made productive agricultural work unattractive. Those who left agriculture were usually between the ages of 15 and 25 and were not given adequate training or introduction into industrial/urban life. This created tension of a more social kind reflected in drunkenness and hooliganism, as well as seriously affecting the productivity levels in industry.

STABILISATION AND CRISIS. THE PRELUDE TO AND EVENTS OF JUNE 1956

The second Congress of the PUWP in March 1954 decided to halt the movement of population into industry and raise the standard of living of those already working in industry. Consequently, rural to urban migration had fallen from 161,000 per annum in 1951 to 55,000 per annum in 1955. More specifically the increase in industrial employment had been about 164,000 in 1953, whereas in the following year it was only 110,000.[1] Industrial investment was almost completely halted and an effort was made to produce more consumer goods and to stimulate the agricultural sector.[2] During the years 1954 and 1955 the wages of industrial manual workers increased by 6·5 per cent and 5·2 per cent respectively though at the same time the number of hours worked per worker was greater than for the year 1953.[3] After 1953 many of the investments initiated under the six-year plan in 1950 came at least into partial production. The labour force became more stable and productivity increased with the gradual adaptation of the new workers to industry. In contrast, production in most of the light industries, such as textiles, clothing and leather, was the same in 1955 as it had been in 1950 in terms of its percentage share of total industrial production, though in absolute terms there had been some increase in quantity. With the increase in the proportion of the national income allocated to consumer goods and light industries there was also a decrease in the prices of some consumer goods and services in the years 1954, 1955 and 1956.[4]

We must, however, be cautious in drawing conclusions about the standard of living of 'the workers', for the internal differentiation of income in 1955 amongst workers in various sectors of industry was quite significant. Manual workers in the heavy industrial sector such as mining, iron and steel and machine industries received anything up to 44 per cent above

[1] R. Wilczewski, 'Rozwój przemysłu . . .', pp. 574–95.

[2] Investment as a part of the national income dropped from 28 per cent in 1953 to 24 per cent in 1954 and 21 per cent in 1956. *Rocznik Statystyczny 1970*, p. 77.

[3] *Rocznik Statystyczny Pracy 1945–1968* (Warsaw, 1970) p. 418. R. Wilczewski . . ., p. 576 and *Rocznik Statystyczny 1970*, p. 145.

[4] *Rocznik Statystyczny 1970*, p. 344.

the national average wage for industrial manual workers whereas those manual workers in light industry such as textiles, clothing and printing received up to 28 per cent below the national average.[1] A form of wage aristocracy existed within the ranks of the manual workers, which was related to the fact that in 1955 30 per cent of those employed in industry were women. The majority of these women were employed in the lowest-paid sectors of textiles, clothing and foodstuffs, thereby lowering the average wage earned in light industry.

The second Congress also considered the deteriorating political situation. By 1955 only 45 per cent of the party membership were manual workers, and 40 per cent non-manual workers. The Congress noted the lack of real links between the party and the masses.[2] In industry, the membership of workers in industrial party organisations had dropped from 80 per cent in 1952 to 72 per cent by the end of 1955.[3] There were certain factors which led to the decreasing share of manual workers in the party. First, as we have noted, there was a high level of upward mobility of manual workers who were party members into non-manual occupations. One author estimates that between 1945–59 over 69,000 manual worker party members joined the ranks of the white-collar workers. This was due to the fact that a large proportion of party members amongst manual workers were skilled and therefore were first in line for promotion to managerial, supervisory or other non-manual positions.[4] Second, with the development of industry, more industrial occupational groups such as engineers and economists, technicians and clerks were developed. Not only did the industrial manual working class increase in the years 1950–5 from just under one and a half million to just over two millions, but the engineering–technical cadres and the administrative–clerical employees doubled, from just over 200,000 in 1950 to over 400,000 in 1955.[5] These rapidly growing groups of

[1] K. Zagórski and L. Beskid, *Robotnicy na tle . . .*, p. 94.

[2] J. Olszewski, 'O niektórych biurokratycznych wypaczeniach w stylu pracy partyjnej', in *Nowe Drogi*, no. 1, 1955.

[3] S. Widerszpil, *Skład polskiej klasy . . .*, p. 305, fn. 31.

[4] By May 1946 5,000 workers had taken management positions at lower and middle management levels. See J. Janicki, *Urzędnicy przemysłowi w strukturze społecznej Polski Ludowej* (Warsaw, 1968) pp. 151–4.

[5] *Rocznik Statystyczny Pracy 1945–68*, p. 34.

non-manual workers frequently viewed the party as a legitimate channel for the expression of their demands and for the furtherance of their interests. During this period, while there was a marked increase in the percentage of party members with secondary and higher education, there was a corresponding decrease in membership amongst the less well-educated workers.[1] The fact that in 1950 there were six industrial manual workers for every non-manual worker, while by 1955 there were only four, would by itself have changed the composition and character of the party.[2]

The party was naturally concerned by these changes in the composition of its membership, as it was with the economic implications of such a vast growth in the 'unproductive' clerical and administrative sectors; already by 1955 there were signs that many of the promoted workers were being moved out of administration and back into their old manual occupations.[3] This process of trimming the bureaucracy was accelerated by the events of June 1956 in Poznań. Although these events resulted directly from specific local grievances, they would probably not have occurred at all if the system had more efficiently reflected the needs and demands of the industrial manual workers.

The dissatisfactions expressed in Poznań in 1956 highlighted many facets of the economic and political trends of that period. For some time the working conditions at the ZISPO works (formerly and currently called the H. Cegielski group of factories) had been deteriorating and the lack of raw materials had led to short-time working. To this was added a dispute about the size of tax deductions and the belief that changes in work norms which had led to higher productivity had not been reflected in appropriate wage increases.[4] Furthermore, as a result of the elimination of progressive piece work rates in the second half of 1955, earnings began to fall, creating an intolerable economic situation for the workers. According to Hiscocks,

[1] S. Widerszpil, *Skład polskiej klasy* . . ., p. 306.

[2] J. Kordaszewski, *Pracownicy umysłowi* (Warsaw, 1969) p. 123.

[3] J. Janicki, *Urzędnicy przemysłowi* . . ., p. 166. See also Ch. 5 on the technical intelligentsia.

[4] Productivity is a quality very difficult to measure in the socialist economic system, despite all the indicators available, and Polish sociologists are well aware of how it can vary in the opinion of workers. R. Dyoniziak, *Społeczne uwarunkowanie wydajności pracy* (Warsaw, 1967) p. 105.

The party leaders in the works having failed to obtain satisfaction from the local authorities sent a delegation to Warsaw where their claims were abruptly rejected by the Minister for Motor Industry, Julian Tokarski.[1]

To understand the 1956 Poznań events we need to consider certain distinctive features of metal workers in general, and the employees of Cegielski in particular. The manual workers in the metal and machine tools industry in 1955 were certainly on average in the top wage categories. The labour force in the metal industry had increased rapidly in size between 1950 and 1953 but had not expanded after 1953. At the same time production in this industry had grown quite considerably between 1954 and 1956 for both the domestic and the growing export market. Between 1954 and 1956, at the Cegielski factory, the growth in productivity per worker/hour had far outstripped the growth in wages per worker/hour.[2] As Hiscocks rightly pointed out, the Cegielski workers had a long-standing tradition for 'industry and integrity' but they also had a tradition stretching back to the prewar days for industrial militancy.[3] The industry also had the largest percentage of workers with prewar experience. (We have already noted that the prewar industrial manual workers were most affected by the tensions of the six-year plan.) From the beginnings of People's Poland the miners', the railway workers' and the metal workers' unions were a political force.[4] The accumulation of factors mentioned above was finally brought to a head by the insensitivity of first the local and then the central authorities. A strike was called at the Cegielski works on 28 June and spread rapidly to other factories, the strike being carried by the workers, who sometimes forcibly shut down other enterprises.[5] The situation rapidly

---

[1] R. Hiscocks, *Poland: Bridge For an Abyss* (London, 1963).

[2] K. Doktór, *Przedsiębiorstwo przemysłowe studium socjologiczne zakładu przemysłu metalowego 'H. Cegielski'* (Warsaw, 1964) p. 157, Diag. 16.

[3] See M. Cierchocińska, *Położenie klasy robotniczej* . . ., *Materiały*, no. 47, p. 218.

[4] The latter was particularly powerful, as it had been early reconstituted, and by Oct. 1945 it boasted 107,000 members. K. Ostrowski, *Rola związków zawodowych w polskim systemie politycznym* (Wrocław, 1970) p. 53.

[5] For one account of how the strike affected a factory other than H. Cegielski see A. Zimowski, 'Pracowałem w "Stomilu" ', in *Pamiętniki Inżynierów* (Warsaw, 1966) pp. 924–5.

escalated into a demonstration and eventual confrontation with the People's Militia and the violence which followed left a toll officially reckoned to be 53 dead and 300 wounded.

The initial reaction of the central party authorities and the government was to brand the demonstrations as the work of provocateurs and imperialist agents who, in view of Poznań's role as the setting for the international trade fair, were using it as the venue for their sordid machinations. On the following day representatives of the government and party hastened to Poznań. Included in this delegation were J. Cyrankiewicz and E. Gierek. Cyrankiewicz appealed to the people of Poznań and to their characteristic features of 'industriousness, fastidiousness and patriotism' in an effort to restore order. He admitted the justness of their grievances though at the same time he maintained that the situation had been exploited by 'murderous provocateurs'.[1]

In July the VII Plenum of the CC PUWP critically considered the events of June and it attacked the provincial party organs for their inability to adjust to the increased observance of Leninist norms of party and social life. The local party organisations, it was said, had lost contact with the industrial party organisations as well as with the central party organs. In the atmosphere of self-criticism and political relaxation initiated by the second Congress of the PUWP, the local party authorities were unclear as to what this entailed in terms of concrete action. As one very influential journalist and commentator notes, 'The criticism initiated by the party was not accompanied by sufficient efforts and consequential action in repairing the damage [of the previous period]'.[2] The party activists, despite the best will in the world and much hard work, had cut themselves off from the masses and had put their effort into policies which neglected the fundamental interests of the working people. They had in fact actively abetted a situation where production plan fulfilment overshadowed the immediate interests of the workers.

---

[1] *National Communism and Popular Revolt in Eastern Europe*, ed. Paul F. Zinner (New York, 1956) p. 127. Poznań had last carried out a successful revolt in Dec. 1918 in which it displayed its patriotism.

[2] A. Werblan, 'Od tragedii poznańskiej upłynął rok', in *Polityka*, 26 June 1957. He also attacked wastage, exhibitionism and sham finery of the élite which was a disgrace to a hard-working and relatively poor country.

To rectify this situation the VII Plenum declared that the basis of the forthcoming five-year plan would entail (i) the stepping up of real wages for workers and other employees by 30 per cent, with particular reference to the lower paid groups, and (ii) an improvement in the housing conditions of the urban population. The government was to release 7 billion złoties for these wage increases. Premises becoming vacant as a result of the cuts in the administrative apparatus were to be used to house working people. In addition the government promised that from January 1957 family allowances would be increased to help raise the standard of living of the lowest paid categories of employees, and that the revision of work norms would not be permitted if it involved a drop in wages. Conditions of work were to be improved and Sunday working in the mining industry was to be gradually abolished.[1]

The party had been aware, even before the summer of 1956, of the shortcomings of the trade unions and the under-representation of the workers by them. As one writer had put it

The activity of the trade unions should be strengthened. They should fight much more courageously and energetically for the full observance of collective agreements, for a better fulfilment of workers' needs.[2]

The Poznań events had brought out the need for some form of workers' participation and the subsequent wave of self-criticism which swept through the ranks of the unions generated resolutions concerning the expansion and improvement of the rights of the factory councils.

Despite these pressures the VII Plenum reiterated the principle of one-man authority of the enterprise director and justified it on the grounds that it was essential to the efficient management of the enterprise. At the same time, however, it agreed that the competence and rights of the union factory councils should be broadened.[3] The VII Plenum envisaged the

[1] 'Uchwała o sytuacji politycznej i gospodarczej kraju i zadaniach partii', in *Nowe Drogi*, nos. 7–8, 1956.
[2] J. Morawski, *Trybuna Ludu*, 27 March 1956, cited in P. Zinner . . ., p. 63.
[3] The rights of the enterprise director had already been extended by the resolution of the Council of Ministers and the CC PUWP on 9 April 1956. See Ch. 5 on technical intelligentsia.

restoration of some of the rights of the union factory councils
which had in fact been promised in 1945, namely the rights

> to participate in the solution of all matters connected with the
> material situation of factory personnel and working conditions
> and, in the solution of all matters pertaining to wages and
> norms, bonuses, working-time, . . . hiring and firing, work disci-
> pline and the allocation of housing . . . ; to participate in work-
> ing out the plan of the enterprise within the limits provided for
> the enterprise management.[1]

The management and the factory councils were regularly to
consult the workers on all essential matters concerning the
enterprise, as well as to report to the workers about the plan
and other such matters. This left a role for the unions similar to
that defined by the Leninist principle that the unions articulate
real information about the needs and demands of the masses
and in this way defend their interests.[2] The question of control
over the activities of factory management did not arise.

Following upon the VII Plenum of the CC PUWP, the
Central Council of Trade Unions held their VIII Plenum on
18 August. The most significant resolutions stressed the need for
greater democracy within the unions in the election of officers
and a greater independence for the unions as a whole.[3] In the
words of one commentator there had appeared within the
unions '. . . the strongest and most far advanced syndicalist
tendencies'.[4] The movement for democratisation within the
unions was, however, outstripped by the spontaneous formation
of workers' councils in some of the larger Warsaw factories.
Their formation demonstrated that the workers thought little
could be achieved through the discredited trade unions.

---

[1] *Trybuna Ludu*, 31 July 1956. In P. Zinner, Resolution of VII Plenum,
CC PUWP, 18–28 July.

[2] For a discussion see K. Ostrowski . . ., pp. 31–48.

[3] P. Zinner . . ., p. 190.

[4] A. Łopatka, *Państwo socjalistyczne a związki zawodowe*, 1962, quoted in
A. Owieczko, 'Ewolucja samorządu robotniczego', in *Socjologiczne problemy
przemysłu i klasy robotniczej* (Warsaw, 1967), no. 2, p. 119, fn. 52.

WORKERS' COUNCILS. DEMOCRATISATION VERSUS
RATIONALISATION (1956–8)

We wish now to examine the demands which led to the setting
up of the workers' councils and we shall then consider one consequence of these demands, namely the economic gains of the
industrial manual workers. What did the formation of the
workers' councils have in common with the demonstration in
Poznań? J. Chałasiński suggests that the Poznań riots finally
shattered the myth of the unity of the progressive intelligentsia
with the working people.

> The working masses demonstrated, and the significance of this
> demonstration was directed not just against the isolation of the
> leaders of the government and party from the masses, but also
> against the isolation from the masses of the 'progressive' intelli-
> gentsia who wrote about and propagated socialism . . . and
> against its social mythology which screened the reality from view.[1]

The setting up of the workers' councils was a way of exposing
the reality of the industrial situation, the bureaucracy of administration, the inexpert management and the subservient
trade unions. Because these councils were an attempt to cut, as
it were, the Gordian knot which had been tied over the past ten
years, they frequently appeared to exist in a vacuum, unrelated
to other organisations and bodies. One writer saw the significance of the workers' councils, as well as the source of their
problems to lie in the directness and 'synchronic' manner of
their formation.

> The problems of the workers' councils stem from the fact that
> the creation of these institutions was an act with primarily
> political character and not the crowning point in some longer
> organic process of formation of factory employee self-management.
> First the institution of the council was set up and only then did
> the enterprise organisation adapt itself and slowly, very slowly
> was the mentality of the interested parties transformed.[2]

[1] J. Chałasiński, *Przeszłość i przyszość inteligencji Polskiej* (Warsaw, 1958)
p. 15. For the author, the nobility-intelligentsia in the ghetto of their prewar
isolation from the masses did not differ significantly from the progressive
intelligentsia.

[2] A. Małachowski, 'Jutro rad robotniczych', in *Przegląd Kulturalny*, no.
31, 1957.

The party and its newly reinstated leader, Gomułka, overtly welcomed the initiative displayed by the workers in setting up the workers' councils. At the VIII Plenum of the CC PUWP in October 1956 the party leadership recognised that the demands of the workers exceeded the concessions granted at the VII Plenum, and that real changes were required which could not be avoided by promises of consultation. The Plenum resolved, therefore, that the tasks of the councils were to include deciding on matters concerning norms and wages, making decisions jointly with the director, drawing up the production plan, evaluating its fulfilment and prescribing plant expansion. The party leadership regarded the fundamental aim of these measures as a basis for a rise in productivity and quality which in turn would lead to an improvement in the standard of living of the workers. The Plenum also decided, quite significantly as it happens, that the councils were to participate directly in the appointment and dismissal of the enterprise directors.[1] Gomułka stressed that any raising of the standard of living of the workers depended upon improvement of the management system and upon greater productivity by the workers. It was in this context that he envisaged the role of self-management, if it was to have any role at all: 'The problem of workers' self-management currently being discussed by employees in the factories and by various party and state organs boils down to what I was saying about production and living standards.'[2]

In the months after Poznań, workers' councils and the meaning they had for the workers was linked to a specific political situation which had developed in Poland and only later was it to become intertwined with economic and organisational questions. Hannah Arendt considered the relationship of the 'council' to the organised revolutionary party. In her view,

> The fatal mistake of the councils has always been that they themselves did not distinguish clearly between participation in public affairs and administration or management of things in the public interest. In the form of workers' councils they have again and again tried to take over the management of factories and all these attempts have ended in dismal failure. 'The wish of the working class' we are told 'has been fulfilled. The factories will be managed

---

[1] 'O aktualnych zadaniach politycznych i gospodarczych Partii, in *Nowe Drogi*, no. 10, Oct. 1956, in P. Zinner.   [2] Cited by P. Zinner . . ., p. 212.

by the councils of workers.' This so-called wish of the working class sounds much rather like an attempt of the revolutionary party to counteract the councils' political aspirations, to drive their members away from the political realm and back into the factories. And this suspicion is borne out by the two facts: the councils have always been primarily political, with social and economic claims playing a very minor role, . . .[1]

On 19 November the Sejm formally recognised the rights of the workers' councils which had been put forward by the party leadership in October. A few days earlier, however, the Council of Ministers had declared the greater independence of the industrial enterprise as a unit in the planning and administrative system. The fact that these issues were treated separately showed just how wary the party and the government were of the council movement.[2]

In examining the significance of the workers' councils during the nearly eighteen months that they existed as relatively autonomous bodies it is necessary to highlight the impact of the councils on other power centres. For example, how did the workers' councils affect the position of the enterprise management at its various levels? What was the reaction of the party organisations to the apparent usurpation of their authority at shop-floor level? In what way did the workers' councils threaten the higher administrative organs at the ministry and intermediate levels? Could the unions survive as mass organisations when active worker interest seemed to have passed them by? Could one or all of these organs succeed in pushing back the workers' councils into the factories?

THE WORKERS' COUNCILS AND FACTORY MANAGEMENT

During the first enthusiastic months after October 1956 the workers' councils frequently encroached into matters related to the day-to-day running of the enterprise which in turn frequently led to conflict between the councils and the senior

---

[1] H. Arendt, *On Revolution* (London, 1963) pp. 277–8.

[2] S. Frenkiel, 'Czy te uchwały załatwiają sprawę', in *Z.G.*, no. 22, 1966. The author believes that the separation was caused by the government's fear of enterprise independence, associated too closely with workers' councils. The Yugoslav model was never far from their minds.

management.[1] The councils became the focus of workers' demands and although these latter were often trivial or impossible to fulfil, they nevertheless exemplified the October spirit.[2]

Possibly the most significant and certainly most highly symbolic gesture in the sphere of management–worker relations was the granting by the VIII Plenum of the right of workers' councils to participate directly in the appointment and dismissal of the director of the enterprise. Exerpts from the memoirs of enterprise directors show quite clearly that at least some of the workers' councils promptly seized this opportunity. They approached qualified persons from amongst their own factory personnel or from outside institutions or factories and offered them the posts vacated by the departing managers.[3] Subsequently advertisements for positions vacant appeared in the popular and professional press.[4] In this effort to have qualified and experienced directors at the head of management, the workers' councils had the full support of the young technical intelligentsia. The industrial values of the skilled manual workers stressed qualifications and experience. Furthermore authority and remuneration should be based upon a combination of these and not upon political power. These values in turn coincided with those of the technical intelligentsia.[5] That the workers' councils eventually came under the almost exclusive control of an alliance of these two groups can be partially explained by their common affirmation of these values.

The workers' councils could now propose persons for the post of director and assistant/deputy director, whereas until 1956 this had been the preserve of the ministry and the local party organisations. The combination of increased independence of

[1] M. Hirszowicz and W. Morawski, *Z badań nad społecznym uczestnictwem w organizacji przemysłowej* (Warsaw, 1967) p. 31.

[2] A. Owieczko, 'Ewolucja samorządu . . .', p. 106.

[3] L. Krzenek, 'Z życia inżyniera', in *Pamiętniki Inżynierów* . . ., p. 187.

[4] For example: 'The group of factories for the production of building materials at Żerań in Warsaw seeks a candidate for the post of chief director. Appointment will be made under competitive conditions. Very high professional qualifications are required as well as considerable experience in the sphere of organising prefabrication factories.' Sixteen candidates were reported to have applied for the post. 'O radach robotniczych', in *Polityka*, 27 Feb. 1957, no. 1, p. 7.

[5] See Ch. 5 on the technical intelligentsia, and H. Najduchowska, *Pozycja społeczna starych robotników przemysłu metalowego* (Wrocław, 1965) p. 53.

the industrial enterprise, the greater sphere of competence of the director, and the workers' council striving for control of both, provided a serious threat not just to the industrial management but the party and the administrative bureaucracy as well.[1]

The bureaucracy was well aware of this and had in fact made provision for such a situation in its legislation dealing with the workers' councils. First, the director had the right, even the duty, not to carry out resolutions of the councils where they were seen to be against the law or to be contravening the obligatory plan.[2] Second, where conflict occurred between the councils and the director both sides initially could appeal to the higher administrative organ or to the minister, who would decide the case. This policy was used to protect the interests of the State and was a means by which the administration could keep the workers' councils in check.[3]

The principle of workers' self-management was also traditionally associated with the division and allocation of profits. Some councils emphasised their 'political nature' by introducing a system entailing the equal division of profit in which the sole differentiating criterion was the length of time a person had served in a factory. This meant that a cleaning woman with three years' service in the factory might receive a greater share in the division of profit than a director who had only been there for two years.[4] Although the application of this principle was limited, the tendency towards a 'levelling out' of profits, if not income, was by all accounts widespread amongst the workers.[5]

The principle of 'levelling' was one example of the contradiction between the demand for the 'democratisation' of social and economic life and that for 'rationalisation' of the economy and management. This was illustrated by the fact that the majority

---

[1] See W. Krencik and C. Niewadzi, 'O właściwą rolę rad robotniczych w polskim modelu gospodarczym', in *Gospodarka Planowa*, no. 3, 1957, p. 4.

[2] H. Najduchowska, 'Dyrektorzy przedsiębiorstw przemysłowych', in *Przemysł i społeczeństwo w Polsce Ludowej* (Warsaw, 1969) p. 91.

[3] M. Tempczyk, 'O radach-praktycznie', in *Polityka*, 8 June 1957.

[4] A. Małachowski, 'Jutro rad . . .', p. 4.

[5] A. Owieczko, 'Ewolucja samorządu . . .', p. iii. The same demand was made in an equally highly charged political situation in Gdańsk in 1970. For an example of the same demand made in another context see D. Singer, 'Italy after the Miracle', *New Statesman*, 17 Sept. 1971.

of enterprises compromised on this point and introduced a system whereby the division of profits was related to the basic income. This compromise arose from the clash of interests between the intelligentsia and the skilled workers on the one hand, and the unskilled manual worker on the other. The former felt that the division of profits should be related directly to the value of input, which corresponded in their eyes to levels of skill. The easiest way to achieve this was to link profit-sharing to basic income. This was, however, disadvantageous for the unskilled manual worker, whose basic pay was low. It was not surprising, therefore, that, according to one author, over 80 per cent of the workers in some factories desired an equal division of profits.[1]

We would like to suggest one further hypothesis which would seem to fit the developments of the immediate post-October period. We would maintain that the 'urawniłówka' (levelling) demand was less an economically motivated and more a political expression insofar as it attacked the distribution of profits. It demonstrated to the workers their control over their economic situation, particularly in those cases where they had obtained the power to change the distribution of profits. Such a demand for the equalisation of profit-sharing was made in the Warsaw Automobile Factory. Though the difference in earnings between engineers-technicians and manual workers was quite large, that of the latter compared favourably to other factories in the same industry in Warsaw. However, the workers were not concerned with the earnings of other groups of manual workers but with differences within the factory. The success of their demand was shown by the fact that although during the years 1956–7 the increase in productivity was negligible the increase in the level of pay for workers was greater than that for the engineering-technical employees.[2]

---

[1] A. Małachowski, 'Jutro rad robotniczych . . .', p. 4. K. Doktór examines the conflict during the 1956–7 period centred about the division of profit in Cegielski. The case of the older skilled workers against the 'democratic' division of profit was very forcefully put to the workers' council and eventually triumphed. K. Doktór, *Przedsiębiorstwo . . .*, pp. 149–50.

[2] For a study of Warsaw Automobile Factory 1956–61 see S. Szostkiewicz, *Przemiany w strukturze załogi fabryki samochodów w latach 1956–61* (Warsaw, 1965). The majority of manual workers at WAF were skilled or semi-skilled (categories IV–IX).

THE WORKERS' COUNCILS AND THE HIGHER
ADMINISTRATION

Management and manual workers might find themselves at cross purposes but they were frequently allies in their dealings with the superior administration. Both workers' councils and senior management were anxious to free themselves from the excessive central control in matters of planning and administration exercised by ministries and other administrative bodies. Workers' councils desired decentralisation, since they felt it a necessary prerequisite for democratisation within the enterprise. Similarly, senior management argued for decentralisation, considering it a necessary precondition to expert and rational management.[1] By supporting senior factory management, the workers' councils threatened to make the enterprise more independent of the ministries. Moreover, by taking matters of planning and administration upon themselves as a result of the more decentralised economy, the councils could make large sections of the lower and higher administration redundant.[2]

The administration and ministries attempted to forestall this eventuality by being extremely slow in setting up workers' councils in those factories which had not formed them spontaneously. By May 1957, six months after the official sanctioning of the workers' councils by the central committee, very few concrete proposals had been worked out by administrative bodies for setting up such councils.[3] Despite the impression that the workers' councils were a widespread popular movement, Table 12 indicates that they were not as numerous as they might have been, suggesting that the administration was often successful in hindering their formation. We see that councils were formed primarily in the large enterprises, particularly those with over 1,000 employees. More surprising is the fact

---

[1] Lower management and supervisory staff as well as the technical intelligentsia were not so much concerned with questions of enterprise independence, as theirs was a 'science' orientation as opposed to the 'service' orientation of top managers. See ch. 5 dealing with the technical intelligentsia. Furthermore, not all enterprise directors saw the increased independence of the enterprise as desirable.

[2] S. Jakubowicz, 'Kierunek i zwiększona samodzielność przedsiębiorstwa', in *Polityka*, 14 Dec. 1957.

[3] M. Tempczyk, 'O radach-praktycznie . . .'.

TABLE 12. SIZE OF FACTORY AND NUMBERS OF WORKERS' COUNCILS*

Factories according to number of employees	Factories in which councils could be set up	Factories in which workers' councils were set up			
		Between 1956 and April 1957		By 31 December 1957	
		No.	Per cent	No.	Per cent
Total	11,355	2,924	26	5,619	50
Less than 20	1,019	16	1·5	93	7·0
21–250	5,517	800	14·9	3,000	54·5
251 500	2,516	884	36·0	1,141	45·0
501–1,000	1,448	607	41·5	687	47·0
1,001–2,000	533	350	63·0	396	72·0
2,001–3,000	156	135	86·5	156	100
3,001 plus	146	138	94·5	146	100

* L. Gilejko, 'Formowanie się i rola samorządu robotniczego', in *Struktura i dynamika społeczeństwa polskiego* (Warsaw, 1970) p. 180, Table 1.

that only 26 per cent of enterprises had formed workers' councils during the first half year in which they were officially sanctioned. Such a low percentage may have been due to the low value attached to councils by some groups of workers. It may also have been the result of unofficial opposition to their formation by those who were threatened by such organisations. It is only fair to add, however, that the larger enterprises suffered more from the kinds of problems of management techniques, organisational size and worker-participation, which made the formation of councils particularly necessary.[1] The enterprises were further hampered by the fact that the proposed reduction in the number of plan indicators was not being achieved. This led one journalist to note, 'It is difficult to believe that such tardiness is simply a matter of incompetence. It is not only bureaucratic opposition but opposition of a political nature also.'[2] In 1957 the popular paper *Polityka* carried a report of an

[1] For a discussion of 'alienation under conditions of socialism' see Z. Mikołajczyk, 'Rady robotnicze a alienacja', in *Z.G.*, 2 June 1957.

[2] M. Tempczyk, 'O radach . . .'.

explosive situation in the Lenin steel works. It explained how the workers' council and the enterprise management had appeared to decline from signing an experimental wages agreement with the ministry. This agreement had been formulated by the workers' council and particularly affected the skilled manual workers, as it would restructure the pay tariff in their favour. A letter to the above eventually clarified the situation: the management and council had not met the minister, it was claimed, because they had not been informed of the date and time of the meeting. The relevant communication had been 'mislaid' in a drawer at the ministry. It had also been alleged that strikes were taking place in those Warsaw factories which had been at the forefront of the workers' councils movement although everything in these factories was normal. In the same letter the writer maintained that workers had been planted in these factories for the specific purpose of stirring up trouble, which seemed to the writer as if

> . . . somebody was trying to compromise the workers' councils and everything they stood for. . . . It would be very convenient for certain parties if storms blew up in these factories and discredited the new system of management.[1]

The administration and those in the 'old-guard' management mould accused the workers' councils of seeking political power and of developing into an anarchistic force. By such arguments the former hoped to gain support amongst the higher political authorities, namely the party leadership. One director of a large Warsaw factory came to the defence of the workers' councils and pointed out that the workers were well aware of the opposition and of its intentions.

> According to the deepest convictions of the activists of the workers' councils these accusations against them were put forward by the bureaucratic elements who look upon workers' self-management in factories with a decided lack of enthusiasm and a good deal of distaste.[2]

The opposition to the workers' councils frequently found support for its case in the actions of the workers themselves during

[1] K. Wigura, 'Kto daje tę broń do ręki', in *Polityka*, 24 April 1957.
[2] J. Barski, 'Niemowlę chce rosnąć', in *Polityka*, 24 April 1957.

the confused and turbulent months of 1957. (We shall show
below that it was a particular sector of industry and the industrial manual workers who benefited most from the Polish
October economic concessions.) As a consequence of low pay,
strikes broke out in the summer of 1957 amongst the lower-paid
groups of workers.[1] Conflict between workers' councils and
workers, and between workers' councils and management, also
increased. It mainly concerned the role of the workers' councils
in the division of the factory fund, i.e. profits and basic wage
increases. This troubled the idealistic supporters of the councils
who felt that such action on the part of the workers was
playing into the hands of '. . . the dogmatist and sectarian
opponents of the new democracy who could point to these
events and say "I told you so"'.[2] Indeed this seemed to be the
case. For after mid-1957 discussion focused on the 'consciousness
of the working-class' and how it fitted in with workers' democracy. One author suggested that the young generation of
workers was possibly not mature enough to handle the great
responsibilities which democracy entailed.[3]

The same author recognised that one of the prime obstacles
to the development of the workers' councils as organs of control
by the direct producers over their work was precisely this differentiation within the ranks of the manual workers. Szczepański in 1959 observed that in new factories 20 per cent of
manual workers had prewar experience whilst in the old factories this figure was over 35 per cent. Between 25 per cent and
30 per cent of workers in factories, depending on whether they
were old or modern factories, were first-generation migrants
from the countryside. Again in some of the new factories as
many as 50 per cent of the manual workers were under twenty-
eight years of age and in some of the recently constructed metal
works as many as 25 per cent of manual workers were women.[4]

[1] G. Pisarski, 'Trzeba usunąć źródła zadrażnień', in *Z.G.*, 8 Sept. 1957.

[2] S.J., 'Nakaz chwili', in *Polityka*, 21 Aug. 1957.

[3] A. Werblan, 'Świadomość klasowa a demokracja', in *Polityka*, 28 Aug.
1957.

[4] J. Szczepański, 'Robotnicy', in *Odmiany czasu . . .*, p. 155. Two studies
bring this point out very well. The Warsaw automobile factory had 70 per
cent of its manual workers of working class origin and 75 per cent under
thirty-nine years of age. The steel works had 70 per cent of its manual
workers of peasant origin and nearly 90 per cent between the ages of

Skilled workers had expectations concerning the role of the workers' councils which were considerably opposed or inconsistent with those of the unskilled manual workers. Young workers, educated and brought up under the conditions of socialism, displayed attitudes to management, work relations and job content which were significantly different to those of their older colleagues. The questions of age difference, rural/urban origins and levels of skill influenced the representativeness of the workers' councils. Eventually the councils were robbed of the opportunity of being the organisation which could have unified the various interests within the factory and instead became the instrument of lower management and the technical intelligentsia.

The point which we wish to make is that the view espoused by the administration eventually triumphed over the view held by the 'left-wing'. One of the deciding factors was this internal differentiation of the manual workers as a social group. The demand for democracy for the workers, and for 'all power to the workers' councils' promoted by the 'Po Prustu' group was finally declared to involve too great a risk.[1] It implied the liquidation of central planning and administration – which was not feasible when the workers had shown themselves to be incapable of handling what freedom they already had – in a socially responsible fashion.

THE WORKERS' COUNCILS AND THE TRADE UNIONS

The situation within the trade unions had deteriorated quite rapidly after the VIII Plenum of the CC PUWP. Despite the barrage of criticism from within the party's own ranks, as well as from the workers' councils, the trade union organisation was

twenty-five and forty-four years. A. Stojak, *Studia nad załogą huty im. Lenina* (Warsaw, 1967) p. 19. The differences within certain factories were sometimes as great as those between certain enterprises.

[1] For an example of the type of discussion see 'Towarzyszowi w odpowiedzi', in *Polityka*, 1 March 1958. A. Werblan also attacks the 'left wing' or revisionists for their belief in the workers' councils as a political force which was to be counterposed to the type of socialism which led to the formation of a bureaucratic caste. See 'O socjalistyczny kierunek działalności kulturalnej', in A. Werblan, *Szkice i polemiki* (collected writings) (Warsaw, 1970) p. 36.

too complex a body simply to fade away and be replaced by the workers' councils. The organisation was able to maintain the factory councils (the decision-making union body at the level of the enterprise) intact until the tide turned against the workers' councils.

During the months which followed October, workers' councils were gradually transformed from a body having immediate links with the factory workers and concerned with everyday affairs into a body concerned more with production organisation, efficiency and productivity. With the passage of time the expectations of the workers concerning the role of the councils were in turn modified. In April 1957 the Sociological Research Centre of the Polish Academy of Sciences carried out research into expectations of workers in three factories concerning their councils. It found that 75·9 per cent expected the councils to achieve better work organisation, and 75·6 per cent also anticipated greater profitability from the factory. These were active expectations, linked to a productivity-type of mentality, which saw profitability linked to better management of work. A similar study was repeated in February of 1958, and the author summed up the results as follows:

> The wave of enthusiasm and optimism in relation to the councils is falling. The evaluation of their capabilities is a lot more sceptical and limited. This relates to . . . the possibilities of the councils in the area of work organisation in the factory, control over the administration, and relations between the workers and the management.

The primary concern of the workers was the question of the division of profit amongst the employees, not because re-organisation or other questions had become any the less important to the workers, but because

> . . . on the basis of their experience of the workings of the councils, only those hopes relating to the division of profit had been fully verified . . . whereas the solution of other problems was only in a limited sense within the capabilities of self-management, as the structure stood at the time.[1]

As the management role of the workers' council was trans-

---

[1] M. Hirszowicz and W. Morawski, *Z badań nad społecznym* . . ., pp. 34–6.

formed into its principal function, it became less an agent exercising control over the administration, and more a part of it. But whilst workers' councils were stressing their co-management functions, a body of opinion evolved which viewed the union factory councils as the real defenders of the interests of the workers.[1] At the IX Plenum of the CC PUWP held in May 1957 the party leadership left the workers' councils with their management function but gave responsibility for general policy to the trade unions. This was the first step in the merging of the councils into one body, which was to culminate in the setting up of the Conference of Workers' Self-Management in December 1958. One observer pointed out that from mid-1957 onwards: 'The further development of workers' democracy was closely interconnected with the style and method of trade union functioning.'[2] This meant that the workers' councils were not to mark out any new path in the field of workers' democracy; instead of attempting to alter the activity of the unions, they became supervised by them.

THE WORKERS' COUNCILS AND THE PUWP

During the October days and its aftermath the party had frequently taken an active part in the organisation and the setting up of the workers' councils. This was not surprising, since the principal forces behind the councils were the skilled workers, who also had a high level of party membership. We must, however, qualify our statement and draw attention to the fact that the gap between the lower party membership, particularly at the industrial level, and the leadership was greater than the gap between party and non-party workers. This disjunction between levels of the party organisation must be seen as crucial. In October 1956 the first secretary of the party committee at the Cegielski works emphasised the role played in the Poznań events by the breakdown in links between party leadership and the membership. Furthermore the party committee

[1] 'Nasze propozycje w sprawie odnowy ruchu związkowego', in *Głos Pracy* 1956, no. 265 quoted in A. Owieczko, 'Ewolucja samorządu . . .', p. 119.

[2] A. Owieczko, 'Ewolucja samorządu . . .', p. 122.

... instead of politically directing the party organisation had ... in practice sought to administer the factory, transforming the party organisations into ... aides of the directors and managers. ... The voice of the workers was not heard or heeded nor were the workers taken seriously. ... This state of affairs was nothing else than the expression of a lack of faith in the workers' ability to reason politically.[1]

Party organisations at the shop floor level were on the other hand often instrumental in the removal of incompetent managers and directors when they worked to break down the conservative forces within the factories.[2] As with the trade unions, however, the authority of the party fell sharply with the introduction of the workers' councils. Party activists had to depend upon personal, occupational or other attributes, such as experience, rather than their 'membership card', to influence the course of events during 1956–7. Again in the case of Cegielski, the first secretary of the factory committee declared:

On my return to the factories in 1956 ... I was unsure as to upon whom I could rely, we had to rebuild the [party] organisation. Our political work was mostly based upon non-party workers.[3]

To counteract this the Party Central Committee proposed in May 1957 to set up branches consisting of those party members who were also members of the workers' councils. The party wished to re-establish its authority within the factories through those members who had shown that they had the confidence of the workers, regardless of their party membership. At the same time the party had to reassume its leading role and distinguish itself from the non-party activists. As one writer put it:

At the moment the party is lost in the masses and does not constitute a distinct social force. This is shown by the fact that there is no significant difference in the views of the lower level of the party and those of the mass of the non-party population on matters concerning party policy and its execution.[4]

Between November 1957 and November 1958 the party carried

[1] K. Doktór, *Przedsiębiorstwo* . . ., pp. 109–10.
[2] J. Machno, 'O partii, samorządzie i dyrektorach', in *Polityka*, 20 Sept. 1958.
[3] K. Doktór, *Przedsiębiorstwo* . . ., p. 110.   [4] *Polityka*, 1957, no. 31/32.

out a review or 'verification' of its members and candidates which resulted in a significant decrease in membership, particularly amongst manual workers. Total membership of the party fell by some 300,000, and the percentage of manual worker members fell from 45 per cent in 1956 to 40 per cent by 1959. Verification resulted in the expulsion of some members, and encouraged others to leave. Such men 'had accidentally found themselves in the party over the past years', and others 'were opposed to and in conflict with its policies'.[1] Worker membership of industrial organisations had fallen from 72 per cent in 1955 to 65 per cent in 1961. This decrease did not augur well for the party, but by expelling some members it was able to increase its authority over others.

The IX Plenum in May 1957 rejected the idea that the workers' councils should develop into a vertical system corresponding to the industrial branches and having a structure similar to the trade unions. With such a structure the councils could have their representatives at all levels of the national economic, political and local hierarchies and eventually present an 'alternative' political grouping.[2]

A year later, at the fourth Trade Union Congress, the first secretary of the CC PUWP announced the formation of the Conference of Workers' Self-Management, which became law on 20 December 1958.[3] Not only did this return the 'formal' control of the workers' councils to the trade unions but it also silenced those who criticised the party for not limiting itself to strictly political activity.[4] The CWSM (Conference of Workers' Self-Management) resolution formally brought the party into self-management in a much more emphatic way than by simply grouping those who were firstly workers' councils members and then only party members. This more obviously freed party members from the difficulties which arose when they wished to be members of both the workers' councils and the PUWP. It was probably no coincidence that from 1960 onwards the membership of the party began to grow and the percentage of manual

---

[1] S. Widerszpil, *Skład polskiej* . . ., p. 306 and M. Sadowski, 'Przemiany społeczne a partie polityczne PRL', in *Studia Socjologiczne*, 1968, pp. 30–1.
[2] S. Krajewski, 'Samorząd zrzeszeniowy', in *Ż.G.*, 13 Jan. 1957, p. 6.
[3] See *Trybuna Ludu*, 1958, no. 105.
[4] These opinions were again expressed in 1971 after the Gdańsk riots.

workers during the year 1960 actually showed an increase over
the previous year. The influence of the workers' councils was
on the wane and the activists slowly returned to the party.

THE 'NEUTRALISATION' OF THE WORKERS' COUNCILS

The development and eventual demise of the workers' councils
as independent bodies was related to the debate about the role
of the party and central planning in the management of the
economy. The conservative elements within the administration
maintained that the distortions of the Stalinist period were a
result of poor administrative method, not of any inherent fault
within the system of centralised planning. At the other end of
the scale were those who were later dubbed as revisionists,
supporting a 'petty-bourgeois-anarchistic' tendency.[1] They believed that unless the workers were given real and far-ranging
power the only possible outcome would be another violent political confrontation.[2]

The proponents of the middle course eventually won the day.
Their outlook was a 'managerial' one, which did not emphasise either the 'central administration' or the 'free-market
viewpoint' and in this way excluded the more political aspects
of the argument. Instead they focused upon the problem of
rationalisation which entailed that decisions be taken by experts and that management of industry be a matter for specialists. They argued that though the socialist economy could be
centrally planned, it need not necessarily be centrally adminis-
tered. Furthermore, they viewed the industrial enterprise
primarily as an economic unit. A prominent economist of the
time commented:

> The political maturity of the workers does not predestine them
> to perform specialised professional functions. The enterprise is
> not a political creation but a rational, technological and economic
> one. The rational application of technology, organisation and
> economics requires professional qualifications. The workers as

[1] A. Werblan, 'O socjalistyczny kierunek . . .', p. 36.
[2] For a discussion of the various positions in this argument and its
development see M. Hirszowicz and W. Morawski, *Z badań nad społecznym . . .*, pp. 43–7.

direct producers understand these processes and should have the possibility of joint decision-making, but management belongs to the experts.[1]

Gradually, the workers' councils and their presidia came under the sway of the factories' technical personnel, particularly those in middle management. Although departmental workers' councils were introduced in 1959 and concerned themselves with problems of the workshop, the focus of power remained at the level of the presidium. The presidia, especially after the formation of the CWSM, were becoming increasingly isolated from the council and from the workers. In time, the decision-making body of the workers' councils came to be dominated by persons who maintained that since there was an inherent contradiction between 'professional management' and 'democracy' (and that since in the last analysis the expert was always right) then there was no need for decisions to be taken by a body such as the workers' councils.[2]

The events of October and the eighteen months after resulted in greater power for management but had very little consequence for the industrial manual worker in terms of direct control over his work situation. The observation of one author characterises the workers' disenchantment with post-October events:

> The workers felt like a horse tied to a cart which had had its blinkers though not its reins removed. . . . Whilst now being able to look to the right and to the left, it nevertheless still had to go forward, for where there are reins there is also a whip.[3]

[1] E. Lipiński, 'Rady robotnicze, przedsiębiorstwo i inne sprawy', in *Ż.G.*, no. 51, 1957, pp. 1–2.

[2] Hirszowicz and Morawski . . ., p. 52 and A. Owieczko, 'Ewolucja . . .', p. 118.

[3] J. Barski, 'Niemowlę chce . . .'. Some authors of course believed that self-management would of necessity enter into a more stable and less glamorous phase. Economic efficiency and technological innovation would predominate. This meant that a workers' council, successful in righting the blatant wastage and inefficiency of the Stalinist period, would have to be slightly more sophisticated when the industrial administration had been made more efficient. This in turn would require professional qualifications and experience which the manual worker did not possess. The blinkers were removed, but only to show that the reins were now held by enterprise management rather than the ministries. See W. Morawski, 'Funkcje samorządu robotniczego w systemie zarządzania przemysłem', in *Przemysł i społeczeństwo w Polsce Ludowej* . . ., p. 249.

Political developments between 1956 and 1958 had been limited when seen as a contribution to greater democracy for the manual workers (at least in terms of the workers' councils), but were the material gains any more gratifying? If 'bread and freedom' were the demands made by the Poznań demonstrators, had the party leadership and the government found the former easier to concede than the latter?

THE ECONOMIC GAINS OF THE INDUSTRIAL MANUAL WORKER IN 1956–70

The changes brought about after the Polish 'October' led to a significant growth in average wages as well as a growth in real income per person. Table 13 indicates the extent of the changes in the first five-year plan period, compared to the years that followed.[1] It shows a considerable rise in consumption for both periods.

TABLE 13. GROWTH OF CONSUMPTION PER INHABITANT, OF REAL INCOME PER PERSON AND OF AVERAGE REAL WAGES PER PERSON AND PER FAMILY

Particulars	Percentage average annual rate of growth during	
	1956–60	*1961–7*
Consumption from personal income in constant prices per inhabitant	4·6	3·7
Real income per person supporting himself from wages (including social benefits)	4·9	3·9
Average real wages per person employed	5·2	1·9
Percentage growth in real wages for each 1 per cent growth in real income for each person in a working family	1·06	0·49

During 1955–60 employment in industry grew by only 310,000 compared to 780,000 in the period 1961–7. Heavy industry, with 193,000 new manual workers, or 69 per cent of

[1] A. Karpiński, *Polityka uprzemysłowienia Polski 1958–1968* (Warsaw, 1969) p. 27, Table 2.

the total growth in this period, continued to be the greatest growth area. The high wage rates in heavy industry helped to account for the growth in real wages among manual workers, while in 1960 there was a drop in real wages for the economy as a whole and in the years 1962 and 1965 the real wages level was stationary.[1] These facts are hidden in the aggregates shown in Table 13. Investment was aimed at completing those projects commenced during the six-year plan which had been halted in 1953–4. However, in 1959–60 investment in heavy industry, which had been relatively unchanged for some years, increased rapidly. Conversely, the production of consumer goods reached its peak growth in 1957 and from 1958 increased at a falling rate.[2]

During the period 1956–60 the average gross monthly income of the industrial manual worker increased by 500 złoties, whereas that of the engineering-technical cadres rose by some 800 złoties. It would seem, therefore, that the trend towards equalisation apparent before 1956 had been reversed.[3] An important feature of the income growth of the manual workers was not how it compared to the technical intelligentsia but how it was distributed internally within the group of industrial manual workers. Already by mid-1957 there were complaints that the distribution had favoured those in heavy industry, in particular mining, at the expense of industries such as clothing and textiles.[4] Whereas the rate of growth of monthly income amongst manual workers in the light industries was, on the face of it, as great as that of their colleagues in heavy industry, it was much lower in absolute terms, as Table 14 shows.[5]

A study of the Warsaw Automobile Factory found that the

[1] S. Widerszpil, *Skład polskiej klasy . . .*, pp. 109–11.

[2] A. Karpiński . . ., p. 26. Between 1950 and 1958 the rate of consumption growth was 6·2 per cent p.a. compared to 3·3 per cent p.a. for 1958–67.

[3] *Rocznik Statystyczny Pracy 1945–68 . . .*, p. 149, Table 13 (155).

[4] B. Borkowski, 'Padają i takie pytania-no a robotnicy', in *Polityka*, 17 Aug. 1957. Manual workers in light industries received increases of 190 zł. per month, in heavy industry 290–330 zł. per month, in mining increases were as large as 780 zł. per month on average.

[5] It is perhaps interesting to note that those industries which received the highest income increases in the years after 1956, namely the miners, textile workers and printing-workers (10·4 per cent), were all represented by strong unions. L. Beskid and K. Zagórski, *Robotnicy na tle . . .*, p. 94, Table 7.

gross monthly income of the manual workers fell in 1960 and 1961, whereas that of the technical-engineering staff and the clerical-administrative employees had continued to rise steadily.[1] Was this a more widespread phenomenon? On the evidence available it does appear that the drop in growth of real wages which occurred from 1960 to 1965 affected primarily the industrial manual worker. Between 1955 and 1960 the gross monthly income of the average industrial manual workers, taken as a percentage of that of the industrial technical intelligentsia, fell from 64 per cent to 63 per cent. By 1965 it had fallen further to 61 per cent and in such industries as clothing and textiles it was as low as 51 per cent and 53 per cent respectively. More striking was the differentiation of income between industrial manual workers and clerical-administrative personnel. In 1965, the manual workers' earnings had compared very favourably with average gross monthly income of the clerical employees (it was 101 per cent on average). However, by 1960 the figure was 96 per cent, and by 1965 94 per cent.[2]

TABLE 14. GROSS MONTHLY INCOME OF MANUAL WORKERS, AND ITS GROWTH IN SELECTED INDUSTRIES

Industry	Złoties per month (*1955*)	Złoties per month (*1960*)	Average rate of growth in income, *1956–60* (*per cent*)
Fuel (includes miners)	1,669	2,666	9·9
Iron foundries	1,461	2,235	8·9
Electrical engineering	1,130	1,679	8·3
Textile	859	1,460	11·2
Clothing	830	1,217	8·0

The general improvement in the economic position of the non-manual worker was closely related to the policy expounded at the XI Plenum of the CC PUWP held in February 1958. This plenum emphasised the necessity of liquidating the serious over-employment of white-collar workers in industry. During

[1] S. Szostkiewicz, *Przemiany w strukturze załogi* . . ., p. 149.
[2] Beskid and Zagórski, p. 100, Table 11.

1955–62 there was a significant reverse mobility for those workers who had been promoted to white-collar positions in the preceding ten years. According to one estimate, 85·6 per cent of manual workers who had moved into industrial administration returned to their previous jobs.[1] Understandably this did not take place without a great deal of opposition from those who had 'served' the party and who had frequently not initially desired advancement.[2] This was part of the larger process of rationalisation of employment which will be discussed in chapter 5 – the technical intelligentsia. The process required an increase in income differentials so as to reflect more adequately the sharpened differentiation of education and status.

This increase in differentials came under attack from, amongst others, the workers in the Cegielski factories, who had been the vanguard of October 1956. They complained of the favouritism shown to the engineers and technicians in their factories in matters concerning wages and earnings. For their part, the engineers and other sections of the industrial intelligentsia maintained that inequality of income was necessary if it was to reflect the effectiveness and 'value' of input and that technological advance would only be hindered by what they termed as a 'faulty system of rewards', i.e. one not favouring those with technical and professional qualifications.[3]

The arguments of the industrial intelligentsia proved to be the more influential. For example, in the period 1958–62 the average per capita income within the family of the manual worker grew by 23 per cent whereas the growth in income for the non-manual family was 10 per cent greater.[4] The relative economic and material situation of manual and non-manual

---

[1] J. Janicki, *Urzędnicy przemysłowi . . .*, p. 166.

[2] For example, see letter M.T., 'Rozumiem gorycz robotnika', in *Polityka*, 17 Jan. 1959.

[3] See letter by J. Grzędzielski, 'Kompleksy inteligencji technicznej-Kogo się w Polsce favoryzuje', in *Polityka*, 31 Jan. 1959, and J. Winnicki, 'Spocić się można nie tylko przy dźwiganiu ciężarów', in *Polityka*, 31 Jan. 1959. As early as 1959, 77 per cent of manual workers in one study (1,164) were shown to be highly critical of the pay and norms system seeing it as unjust and inadequate. Eighty-three per cent of the party members amongst them were equally critical, particularly of the work norms, which they maintained indicated a lack of knowledge of shop-floor conditions. See A. Milecki, 'Robotnicy o normach', *Polityka*, 28 Sept. 1959.

[4] A. Tymowski, 'Zarobki w przemyśle', in *Polityka*, 20 May 1967.

workers in 1962 is of particular interest, since in that year real wages hardly rose at all, the cost of living grew quite considerably and even the nominal wage increases were lower than in previous years.[1]

This differentiation of manual and non-manual workers is supported by the data in Table 15, where we see that only

TABLE 15. INCOME PER PERSON PER MONTH IN MANUAL AND NON-MANUAL HOUSEHOLDS (1962)[2]

Income per person per month	Manual (per cent)	Non-manual (per cent)
Less than 600 zł.	8	0·7
600–1,000 zł.	39·5	22·6
1,001–1,500 zł.	33·2	41·9
1,501 zł. and over	19·3	34·8
	100·0	100·0

0·7 per cent of non-manual workers' families earned less than 600 złoties per person per month. In contrast, 8 per cent of manual workers' families were in this low income bracket. Moreover only 19·3 per cent of such families earned over 1,500 złoties per person per month, compared to nearly 35 per cent of non-manual workers' families.

We now bring together our findings concerning the two problems we have considered: first, the breakdown of the

[1] The Central Statistical Office carried out a study comparing the manual and non-manual heads of families employed in industry. Its sample included 2,000 manual workers and their families and 400 non-manual employees and their families. The average size of a manual worker's family was 3·35 persons per household, of whom 1·45 persons were actively contributing to the household. By comparison the non-manual worker's family was smaller, averaging 3·19 persons, but with 1·5 persons in employment. The size distribution of the manual family was generally a 1–2 person or 5-person plus family whereas the non-manual worker's household usually consisted of 3–4 persons. The smaller earning power of the manual worker's household was due to the fact that its children were more likely to leave home to study or work in another town. The non-manual worker's family had better and larger housing space and could permit its children to remain at home much longer. A. Tymowski, 'Zarobki . . .'.

[2] A. Tymowski, 'Zarobki w przemyśle'.

workers' councils as an organ of control by the manual workers over management and the administration; second, the gradual decline in the economic position of manual workers in comparison to other groups. We would like to integrate these related topics by examining a study of the means by which the division of profits has been regulated within a Polish enterprise. The apportioning of the enterprise fund, as we saw above, was a matter which had been of primary interest for the workers' councils. With the formation of the CWSM, however, it had come under the control of the management. Subsequently, it became an instrument for enforcing work discipline within the factory so that, for example, a worker might not share in this division of profit if he was absent from work for three days without due cause. A major Polish study[1] examined the division of profit within sixty-nine enterprises in 1962 and demonstrated how the enterprise fund could be used as a harsh sanction against the manual workers. In Table 16 we notice that the number of manual workers completely excluded from a share

TABLE 16. PARTICIPATION IN ENTERPRISE FUND ACCORDING TO SOCIO-OCCUPATIONAL CATEGORIES

Employees	Total	Manual workers	Engineering-technical employees	Administrative clerical employees
Entitled to participate in division of enterprise fund	68,425	53,906	6,841	6,441
Punished for breaking work discipline by reduced share of enterprise fund	6,621	5,931	287	179
Completely excluded from share of fund	4,494	—	152	182

[1] J. Balcerek and L. Gilejko, 'Ekonomiczne efekty działalności samorządu robotniczego', in *Przedsiębiorstwo w polskim systemie społeczno-ekonomicznym* (Warsaw, 1967) p. 452.

in the enterprise fund is missing. (This was not a misprint.) The author of the study does report, however, that 18·6 per cent of manual workers entitled to participate in the division of the fund were either totally or partially excluded. In the case of the engineers and clerical-administrative staff the figures were 6·3 per cent and 5·6 per cent respectively.[1]

It is also interesting to note that in only four out of the sixty-nine enterprises investigated were management personnel disciplined by means of exclusion from profit-sharing, for not fulfilling the resolutions of the CWSM. Management frequently received premiums solely by virtue of their formal position and not because of any concrete contribution to the profitability or success of an enterprise.[2]

This helps to demonstrate the effects of groups other than the workers themselves dominating the workers' councils and the enterprise. As early as 1962, only five years after the workers had initiated great political and economic changes, these newly dominant groups had directly affected the income and material position of the manual worker. There were other important differences between manual and non-manual workers, such as housing, which were not so closely related to income. We wish to examine these in the context of one industrial community.

Łódź is one of the traditional industrial cities of Poland. It has a high percentage of second and third generation industrial manual workers but it also has a large section of postwar migrants from the countryside. The city is a traditional centre of the textile industry with 50 per cent of its workers coming from textile families. Although the status of the textile worker is generally seen as quite low, primarily because of the low pay in the industry and because of the high proportion of female labour (64 per cent), in Łódź the opposite is the case. Here the high status was not unrelated to the fact that the local authorities had special educational and training facilities for those who

[1] According to our calculation the number of manual workers completely excluded from participation in the enterprise fund would be 4,095, though there could be other factors involved of which we are not aware.

[2] It could be argued that this was a foreseeable development from a situation where the production plan and its efficient fulfilment were predominant. Management made the enterprise fund either the 'stick or the carrot' for the workers rather than for the whole enterprise.

were thinking of entering the industry.[1] (It is also worth noting that in 1961 48·2 per cent of the party members in Łódź were manual workers, employed mostly in the textile industry.)[2]

A study conducted in Łódź in 1965 of 1,000 male heads of families and their families revealed a sharp differentiation in housing according to socio-occupational background. We can see from Table 17 the distinctly underprivileged character of all three manual worker categories and in particular the unskilled workers. Over 30 per cent of this latter group have to live three or more persons per room.[3] A second author studied housing in two modern towns. Neither town had an initial problem of over-crowding such as Łódź, which had inherited it from before the war. This author found that the number of persons per room for the non-manual urban dweller ranged from 1·2 to 1·4. In the case of the manual workers' family the figures were 1·8 to 1·9.[4]

Material differences between manual and non-manual workers extended into other spheres of life. Housing, educational opportunity, holidays and sickness benefits also differentiated manual and non-manual workers. We shall deal with educational opportunity in chapter 5 on the technical intelligentsia but some general points should be made here. In 1955 31·5 per

[1] J. Marczak, *Młodzież robotnicza w łódzkim przemyśle włókienniczym* (Łódź, 1969) p. 52 and p. 158.

[2] S. Widerszpil, *Skład polskiej klasy . . .*, p. 366.

[3] Another more nationally representative study had similar results and showed that whereas the 5-person manual family had 1·95 persons per room, in the case of a 5-person non-manual family there were 1·59 persons per room. This was despite the fact that the government limited the space per person to 5–7 sq. metres in 1960 compared to the previous 7–10 sq. metres. See L. Beskid and K. Zagórski, *Robotnicy na tle . . .*, p. 127.

[4] K. Słomczyński and W. Wesołowski, 'Zróżnicowanie społeczne: podstawowe wyniki', in *Zróżnicowanie społeczne . . .*, p. 109, Table 8. The authors found that unskilled workers in Łódź had a housing density of 2·4 persons per room whereas the more modern cities of Koszalin and Szczecin, settled primarily after the war, had a more egalitarian distribution. In the latter unskilled workers had 1·5 persons per room, which were in fact more favourable conditions than for the white-collar workers in Łódź. Another study of manual and non-manual workers in Łódź also showed differentiation of manual and non-manual workers by education, income, authority and prestige. See K. Słomczyński, 'Układy zgodności i niezgodności w natężeniu cech położenia społecznego', in *Zróżnicowanie społeczne*, ed. W. Wesołowski (Wrocław, 1970).

TABLE 17. STRUCTURE OF ACCOMMODATION DENSITY ACCORDING TO SOCIO-OCCUPATIONAL CATEGORY

Socio-occupational category	Accommodation of respondents according to number of persons per room (per cent)					
	Up to 2	2–3	3–4	4 or more	Lack of data	Total
Intelligentsia	93·4	4·4	2·2	—	—	100
Clerical workers	75·3	14·0	10·7	—	—	100
Technicians	75·8	19·0	5·2	—	—	100
Manual/non-manual workers	64·7	18·0	13·9	3·4	—	100
Foremen	81·0	11·4	6·3	1·3	—	100
Manual workers						
Skilled	57·0	21·5	12·6	8·5	0·4	100
Semi-skilled	49·1	25·4	15·2	10·3	—	100
Unskilled	44·4	24·4	20·1	11·1	—	100

Source: A. Kobus-Wojciechowska, 'Zróżnicowanie warunków mieszkaniowych i sytuacji materialnej', in Zróżnicowanie społeczne . . ., ed. W. Wesołowski, p. 195, Table 6.

cent of the first-year students receiving higher education were of working-class origin whereas by 1960–1 the percentage had dropped to 26·2 per cent. From 1965 the percentage continued to drop until 1968, when the State introduced a points system, placing great emphasis upon social origin. This system helped to raise the figure from a low of 25·8 per cent in 1967 to 31·9 per cent in 1968. As Table 18 shows, this caused a significant drop in the proportion of students from non-manual worker backgrounds.[1] The educational career path taken by young people was heavily dependent upon the type of secondary school attended. Vocational schools were generally chosen by working-class parents and children, whereas the general secondary schools, which usually led on to higher education, were the first choice of non-manual workers and their children.[2]

TABLE 18. STUDENTS IN THEIR FIRST YEAR OF FULL-TIME STUDY ACCORDING TO SOCIAL ORIGIN

				Social origin		
Year	Total	Manual worker	Peasant	Non-manual worker	Individual craftsman	Other
1960–1	100·0	26·2	18·3	49·1	5·0	1·4
1965–6	100·0	27·7	14·9	52·6	3·7	1·1
1966–7	100·0	26·6	15·3	53·1	4·0	1·0
1967–8	100·0	25·8	14·8	54·3	4·1	1·0
1968–9	100·0	31·9	16·7	47·4	3·2	0·8
1969–70	100·0	31·8	15·6	48·4	3·3	0·9

In 1969–70 only 14·7 per cent of the children accepted at general secondary schools were of manual working-class origin, whereas over 41·3 per cent came from non-manual backgrounds.

[1] L. Beskid and K. Zagórski, *Robotnicy na tle . . .*, p. 56.
[2] For a wider discussion and more data from the Warsaw study see Z. Kitliński, 'Popularność różnych kierunków kształcenia wśród młodzieży i rodziców w środowiskach społecznych Warszawy', in *Studia Socjologiczno-Polityczne*, No. 14, 1963, p. 181, and H. Kubiak, W. Kwaśniewicz, 'Niektóre aspekty procesu demokratyzacji szkolnictwa wyższego', in *Studia Socjologiczne*, 1967, no. 27. In this study 60 per cent of children at general secondary schools were of non-manual origins, 29 per cent of worker origin.

Amongst the school leavers from general secondary schools, of those with manual worker origins 25·5 per cent went into higher full-time education in 1969–70, and the proportions of those of peasant and non-manual background was 21·2 per cent and 27·9 per cent respectively.[1] The initial educational disadvantage is seen therefore to lie in the selection of secondary school. An important influence in these schools is whether they have an 'intelligentsia' or a 'worker' environment. A study by Kitliński showed that schools with a worker environment, i.e. with a majority of children from manual worker origins, lowered the aspirations of the intelligentsia children attending them.[2]

Other factors which differentiated manual and non-manual workers were holidays and sick pay. Manual workers commenced with on average twelve days' holiday per year and received twenty days' holiday after ten years. The non-manual employee, on the other hand, averaged one month (or thirty days) holiday per year, and also had the right to three months' illness benefit at full pay. The manual worker received only 70 per cent of his wage when sick. He could also be given two weeks' notice to leave compared to three months' for the non-manual workers.[3]

During the early and mid-sixties the manual worker became relatively worse off. Whereas during the years 1956–60 the gross monthly income of industrial manual workers had risen by an average of 9 per cent per annum, between 1961 and 1965 the rate had dropped to a mere 3·2 per cent.[4] Some manual workers in light industry, such as printers, had an average growth of only 1 per cent per annum over this period, reflecting the fact that in the years 1962 and 1965 the average real wages of those manual workers employed in the public sector did not rise at all.[5] We may suggest that the real income of the industrial manual worker dropped particularly sharply in light industry.[6]

---

[1] Beskid and Zagórski . . ., p. 55.   [2] Z. Kitliński, 'Popularność . . .', p. 189.

[3] 'Socjalistyczny kodeks pracy', in *Polityka*, 1968, no. 41. These regulations have been relatively unchanged since prewar years. In 1971 changes are planned; see Ch. 7.

[4] Beskid and Zagórski, *Robotnicy na tle* . . ., p. 94.

[5] A. Karpiński, *Polityka uprzemysłowienia* . . ., pp. 26–7. Instead of the planned 22 per cent real wages grew by only 8 per cent during 1961–5.

[6] Work norms were drastically revised upwards in 1960 which affected manual workers rather than non-manual. *R.S. Pracy*, p. 352.

Why did this not lead to discontent amongst the manual workers of the kind witnessed during the late fifties? One factor which may have served to ease the hardships of the years 1961–5 was the growth in employment.

During 1958–63 the increase in employment was smaller than during 1954–7; only 160,000 compared to 214,000. The relationship however between the growth in employment and the growth in those coming to the age of active employment was another matter altogether. During 1954–7 the growth in employment as a percentage of the increase in the number of those coming to employable age was 111·5 per cent. For the period 1958–63 the percentage was 163·3 per cent.[1] In this later period, therefore, there was (i) an absorption of the unemployment which may have occurred during the previous years,[2] or (ii) an increase in the number of youths going to work rather than into higher education,[3] or (iii) renewed migration from the countryside which was eradicating unemployment in the countryside.[4] In all three cases the years 1958–63 were an improvement for those newly employed regardless of the drop in real wages for some groups of manual workers. Income per head in the household grew quite significantly during 1958–63[5] and therefore cushioned the drop in wages.

Table 19 shows the growth in employment as a percentage of those coming to employment age up until 1969. The periods 1951–3 and 1958–63 are similar in that employment grew faster than the rate of growth of those of employable age. What appears significant, however, is the 'tight' situation which was developing during the years 1964–9, where growth in employment barely kept ahead of population pressure.[6] We wish to

---

[1] Beskid and Zagórski, *Robotnicy na tle . . .*, p. 68.

[2] The lower-paid industries such as textiles in particular felt the pinch of unemployment. In Łódź after 1956 there were ten applicants for every vacant post. See M. Wierzyński, 'Środek ale nie złoty', in *Polityka*, 16 Feb. 1963.

[3] The number of students in higher education dropped after 1957 and did not grow significantly until after 1963. *Rocznik Stat. 1970*, p. 420.

[4] 1958 and 1959 were years of outstanding urban migration, the level of which was not reached again until 1965. *Rocznik . . .*, 1970, p. 57.

[5] A. Karpiński, *Polityka uprzemysłowienia . . .*, p. 27.

[6] In 1964 net rural to urban migration was 114,000 whereas by 1970 it had risen to 161,500. *Mały rocznik statystyczny 1971*, Warsaw. Employment

conclude our discussion with an examination of this crucial period.

TABLE 19. RELATIONSHIP BETWEEN GROWTH IN EMPLOYMENT AND NUMBER OF THOSE COMING TO EMPLOYABLE AGE

Years	Growth in population coming to the age of employment (000's)	Growth in employment (000's)	Growth in employment as a percentage of increase in population coming to the age of employment
1951–3	238	407	171·0
1954–7	192	214	111·5
1958–63	98	160	163·3
1964–9	281	286	101·8

Between 1966 and 1969 the average rate of growth of gross monthly income for the industrial manual worker rose to 4·2 per cent per annum, and there was a particularly significant improvement for certain sections of the workers. The lowest and highest paid groups had remained the same since 1955. The former consisted of workers in the light industries, such as clothing and porcelain, and the latter were, predictably, workers in the fuel industries, i.e. miners.[1] The average gross monthly income of the industrial manual workers expressed as a percentage of that of the engineering-technical and administrative-clerical workers rose from 61 per cent and 94 per cent in 1965 to 65 per cent and 99 per cent respectively in 1969. The most remarkable growth was amongst the coal miners, who ranked below only automobile workers in having the most favourable ratio to the income of engineering-technical staff (69 per cent), and the most advantageous ratio compared to the administrative-clerical (134 per cent).[2] Whereas the electrical engineering

in industry in 1970 had risen by 66,000. Registered unemployment, though it is a dubious statistic, showed a remarkable increase during 1969 particularly amongst skilled workers. This latter fact is important, since registered unemployment amongst skilled workers had been steady over the previous six years and hence the winter of 1969 could be assumed to be a crisis point. The figures which are available for 1970 did not indicate any fall in unemployment.

[1] L. Beskid and K. Zagórski, *Robotnicy . . .*, p. 94.   [2] Ibid., p. 100.

industry had a large growth in employment of manual workers since 1955, the average monthly income of its manual workers, when compared to other industrial manual workers, had actually deteriorated since 1955. The same was true of the transport, metal and machine-tool industries, each of which employed an increased percentage of the total labour force.

Taking the income of the metal worker as 100 then the equivalent worker in mining earned 224·5, and for iron and steel the figure was 140·8. In the chemical and the machine industries the manual worker with the comparable skill levels had an income on the above scale of 84·4 and 93·5. The author of the study observed that those workers employed on piece rates had the highest earnings. Those employed on day rates and premiums, i.e. workers in indirect production, generally received 20–40 per cent less than those in direct production. Frequently, however, those workers employed in indirect production had higher qualifications than those in direct production. This may have been a source of tension at work.[1]

It is necessary to emphasise the fact that greater income was received by manual workers in the coal and fuel industry. These workers constitute over 10 per cent of the manual worker labour force. Even the electrical engineering and metal industries, which had increased their percentage of manual workers they employed since 1955 (i.e. from 2·8 per cent and 4·9 per cent to 4·9 per cent and 6·6 per cent respectively in 1969), compared poorly in income terms to the coal and fuel industry. From Table 20 we see that despite the all-round improvement in gross monthly pay for manual workers between 1965 and 1967 the greatest improvements by far were recorded in the fuel and iron industries. The large group of workers in the 4,000 + złoties per month bracket (28 per cent and 10 per cent) represents a manual workers' 'income aristocracy'. An indication of

[1] B. Fick, *Polityku zatrudnienia a płace i hodżce* (Warsaw, 1970) p. 306. The figures in the study relate to 1964, and if anything the disproportions are now still greater. The reason for the higher pay of those on piece work rates is believed to be due to the 'loosening of work norms'. In the fuel industry (mining) 66 per cent of the manual workers fulfilled their norms by between 150 per cent and 199 per cent and 7·5 per cent by over 200 per cent. The comparable data for the electrical engineering and the textile industry were 2·9 per cent and 0·2 per cent, and 9·9 per cent and 0·8 per cent. *Rocznik Statystyczny Pracy*, p. 354. See also K. Doktór, *Przedsiębiorstwo*, pp. 154–6.

TABLE 20. INDUSTRIAL MANUAL WORKERS AND THE DISTRIBUTION[1] OF GROSS MONTHLY INCOME FOR SEPTEMBER 1965 AND 1967

Industry	1965			1967		
	Up to 2,500 zł. (per cent)	3,001–4,000 zł. (per cent)	4,000+ (per cent)	Up to 2,500 zł. (per cent)	3,001–4,000 zł. (per cent)	4,000+ (per cent)
Fuel, including mining	30·4	28·8	22·7	24·6	31·2	28·8
Iron foundry	41·3	29·3	4·3	30·2	37·0	10·4
Metal	72·9	9·1	1·5	63·2	14·4	2·9
Electrical-engineering	75·6	9·1	1·7	67·9	12·9	4·0
Textile	92·8	1·4	0·1	84·3	3·6	0·2
Clothing	93·7	1·3	0·2	84·4	3·8	0·4

[1] Percentages are not exhaustive. *Rocznik Statystyczny Pracy* . . ., pp. 447–9, Table 39 (181).

the wage incentives offered in this industry is the fact that the percentage over-fulfilment of work norms has been increasing in the fuel industry since 1960. For all other industries it has been falling or remained steady.[1]

To conclude this section we would like to examine briefly the relative economic position of the manual and non-manual employees and their families in 1968. From 1962 onward the size of both manual and non-manual families had fallen. According to Central Statistical Office data,[2] one in three manual workers' wives went out to work compared to one in two non-manual workers' wives. In the manual households 7 per cent of the under-eighteen age group were at work whereas none of their non-manual counterparts were in full-time employment. For the nineteen to twenty age group 51·2 per cent of those in manual familes were by now at work compared to only 7·4 per cent of their non-manual opposite numbers. This was to be expected as it reflected the educational opportunities and aspirations of the two groups. There was an inverse correlation between family size and income per head which held more strongly for the manual workers' household (0·61) than for the non-manual employees' (0·52).[3] This supports our belief that manual-worker group membership leads a person to start work earlier in life than non-manual membership.

As we have indicated in Chapter 1 above, the expenditure patterns of the two groups differ quite considerably. Table 21

[1] *Rocznik Statystyczny Pracy* . . ., p. 352, Table 10 (125). Whereas between 1961 and 1965 the growth in norm over fulfilment was accompanied by an increase in productivity, 1966–7 saw a slowing down in productivity growth, yet norm over-fulfilment continued and indicates the power of this sector to maintain norms at a favourable level.

[2] *Budżety rodzin pracowników zatrudnionych w gospodarce uspołecznionej poza rolnictwem i leśnictwem* 1968, Warsaw, Nov. 1969. The study examined 3,468 households, representative of the country, 53·3 per cent manual, 31·2 per cent non-manual, the remainder a mixed category.

[3] The manual worker's household consisted of an average of 3·27 persons compared to non-manual 2·90. However, there were significant differences within the former, e.g. Warsaw metal workers' families had an average of 3·7 persons per family, Łódź textile workers 3·5 persons, Silesian miners 3·8 persons. Manual workers in the iron and steel industries had the largest families, 5 persons, which was primarily due to their recent or current rural connections. See H. Krall, 'Pobieżny szkic do portretu klasy', in *Polityka/Statystyka*, no. 5, Nov. 1970, p. 3.

indicates how expenditure patterns in foodstuffs and meat products differ according to family size and manual/non-manual occupational groups. We see that the non-manual worker spends a smaller share of income on foodstuffs and meat products than the manual worker, regardless of family size. Price increases in foodstuffs, therefore, would most readily be felt by the manual worker's household. This would apply not only because manual workers have larger families, but because even when income per head and family size are kept constant, the manual worker's household still spends more on food than does his non-manual counterpart.

TABLE 21. RELATIONSHIP BETWEEN FAMILY SIZE AND EXPENDITURE UPON FOODSTUFFS FOR MANUAL AND NON-MANUAL HOUSEHOLDS 1968[1]

| | Percentage of expenditure upon | | | |
| *Size of households* | *Foodstuffs* | | *Meat products* | |
	Manual	*Non-manual*	*Manual*	*Non-manual*
1 person	41·3	35·0	8·6	6·8
2 persons	46·8	38·4	13·6	10·3
3 persons	45·7	39·5	14·3	10·9
4 persons	47·6	40·9	14·5	11·7
5 persons	49·4	44·6	14·2	12·5
6 persons plus	51·0	44·3	14·0	12·1

The opinions of manual workers tend to substantiate our claims that certain periods were more favourable for them than others (Table 22). After the initial gains which benefited all in 1956–60 the manual workers, particularly the unskilled amongst them, regarded the following five years as particularly difficult. All groups felt the improvements during 1966–8 as partly due to the difficult preceding five years (1965 in particular), and partly due to the increase in real wages and standard of living[2] which extended to manual as well as non-manual workers.

[1] Calculations on the basis of information from *Budżety rodzin*. . . .
[2] K. Zagórski, 'Warunki materialno-bytowe robotników i inteligencji...', p. 173.

TABLE 22. YEARS IN WHICH RESPONDENTS FELT THEY
WERE BEST OFF (PER CENT)

Socio-occupational category	Total	1947–9	1950–5	1956–60	1961–5	1966–8
Unskilled workers	100	15·3	14·8	16·2	7·9	20·6
Skilled workers	100	15·9	15·9	16·1	9·8	22·3
Administrative-clerical workers	100	13·0	13·0	15·7	10·5	26·4
Specialists	100	10·8	11·0	16·4	14·7	27·7

An interesting corollary of the study as presented above is that about 30 per cent of both groups of manual workers felt that after 1956 there had been a deterioration in their standard of living. We suggest that these included particularly manual workers from the metal, electrical engineering, transport and machine-tool industries, whose gross average in relation to the average for the industrial manual workers' monthly wage had dropped since 1955. For example, the gross monthly income in 1955 of manual workers in the electrical engineering industry was 98 per cent of the average income for the industrial manual worker. By 1969 it had dropped to 90 per cent.[1]

In the light of what we have said above we can now ask whether the industrial manual worker during the sixties was able to control or influence his wider economic fate at the industrial shop floor level. We examine this question by focusing on workers' self-management after 1958.

TRADE UNIONS, WORKERS' COUNCILS AND THE
PUWP

The Conference of Workers' Self-Management created on 20 December 1958 marked the end of a period of fluidity in the pattern of relations between management, workers, unions and the party. In contrast to the initial formation of the workers' councils the CWSM was 'imposed' from above and included all the important formal organisations within the enterprise, i.e. the party, the unions, the workers' councils and the technical

[1] Beskid and Zagórski, *Robotnicy na tle* ..., p. 94. See also K. Doktór, *Przedsiębiorstwo.* ...

organisation, STO (Supreme Technical Organisation). The workers' councils, which had been a symbol of the spirit of 'October', had become only one organisation amongst many deciding the policy of the enterprise. The trade unions had competed against rather than co-operated with the workers' councils and they welcomed the councils' failure to live up to the expectations of the workers. At the fourth Congress of the Trade Unions in April 1958, where the principle of the Conference of Workers' Self-Management was first published, the leadership also accepted the *de facto* splitting-up of several unions, which increased their total from twenty-two (which had existed at the time of the third Congress in 1954) to twenty-nine. This 'decentralising tendency', as one author has called it, was considered to be dangerous to the trade union movement which was an organisation based on industrial branches. Critics of the decentralisation tendency saw in this an extension of the 'anti-Leninist' view that unions were to protect the interests of the individual groups of workers and that the workers' councils were to manage the factories on behalf of the workers.[1] Further evidence for this was provided by the decision that the unions might employ brief token strikes when faced by a recalcitrant management.[2]

A difficult problem for the party was how to legitimate its action in introducing the Factory Committee of the PUWP into the CWSM. The industrial manual workers had expressed their dissatisfaction with the party as a representative of their interests by setting up their workers' councils. The factory management also opposed the party because of its intervention in economic and production matters.[3]

The party argued that the working class was not sufficiently prepared to manage the 'workers' democracy' implied in the formation of the workers' councils. It emphasised its own role in preparing the 'new working class' for democracy and minimised the importance of immediately widening democracy. The party maintained that it had to be included in self-management because, it claimed, the demand that workers' councils should run the enterprise in sole partnership with the manage-

[1] K. Ostrowski, *Rola związków zawodowych . . .*, p. 54.
[2] J. Kofman, 'Związki zawodowe w świetle IV Kongresu', in *Nowe Drogi*, May 1958, pp. 3–14.   [3] See Ch. 5 on technical intelligentsia.

ment exaggerated the extent of the workers' socialist consciousness.[1] Subsequently the third Congress of the PUWP held in March 1959 ratified a change in the party statutes. The factory committee of the PUWP was made responsible to its superior for the economic condition and effective functioning of the industrial enterprise, a general responsibility which included practically everything that went on in the factory.[2]

Management, for its part, benefited greatly from the formation of the CWSM. It strengthened the position of the enterprise director *vis-à-vis* the workers' council. The presidium of the workers' council could now only give its opinion in the matter of appointment and dismissal of the director and his deputy. Previously it had been entitled to 'propose' (*wnioskować*) the appointment or dismissal of the director and his deputy.[3]

In 1959 the Conference of Workers' Self-Management included the following bodies: the workers' council, the factory committee of the PUWP, the factory council of the trade unions, representatives of the USY (Union of Socialist Youth) and of the branch association of the STO (Supreme Technical Organisation). The director and departmental managers were not formally included in the CWSM though they were obliged to attend its meetings. Apart from these bodies there were also problem commissions appointed by the workers' council and composed of experts. Two-thirds of the workers' councils was to be composed of manual workers. The Conference of Workers' Self-Management was equipped with rights in the following spheres:

(i) Laying down the basic direction of development of the enterprise; commenting upon and approving the plan; decision-making on more important matters related to decentralised investment, and giving its opinion and participating in the laying down of centralised investment decisions.

(ii) Supervision and control over the functioning of the enterprise and the activity of its administration.

[1] J. Wacławek, 'W sprawie koncepcji roli partii w zakładach pracy', in *Nowe Drogi*, Feb. 1959.
[2] R. Zambrowski, Report of third Congress of the PUWP, *Nowe Drogi*, no. 4, April 1959. [3] L. Gilejko, 'Formowanie się i rola . . .', p. 181.

(iii) The rationalisation of the activity of the enterprise. (To decide upon directions of technological innovation, work organisation, rationalisation and raising productivity.)

(iv) Deciding upon the division of the factory fund, upon work regulations and the monthly and quarterly operating plans.[1]

From the beginning the onus was placed upon the economic-production function of the self-management organs. As a result the wages of manual workers did not increase and in some cases fell after 1959. The workers' councils could no longer decide unilaterally, e.g. by popular vote upon the division of profits, and soon afterwards work norms were raised throughout industry.

By the early sixties it was apparent that the workers' councils had lost authority in the eyes of the industrial manual workers. One study in 1961 showed that 46·3 per cent of manual workers believed that the factory party committee had the greatest authority within the work-place. A further 25·2 per cent chose the union factory council, and only 8·3 per cent of the 3,363 workers questioned still believed that the workers' council had the most authority within the enterprise.[2]

Workers' perceptions of the growing authority of the party was closely related to the increasing party membership after 1958 of skilled workers. One study in 1959–60 found that of 8,555 new party members in large industrial enterprises 56·4 per cent were skilled manual workers and only 16·2 per cent were unskilled manual workers. By 1961 worker-members of the party were predominantly skilled workers in all industries (see Table 23).[3]

---

[1] L. Gilejko, 'Formowanie się i rola . . .', p. 183.

[2] It is interesting to note that 60·1 per cent of workers in the fuel industry (miners) believed the party to have the greatest authority whilst 34 per cent in the textile industry believed the union to have the most authority, yet the same study found that there was a greater degree of party membership amongst textile workers than amongst those employed in the fuel industry (12·0 per cent and 15·8 per cent). S. Widerszpil, *Skład polskiej klasy . . .*, pp. 322–3, and a study of four factories by A. Owieczko, 'Działalność i struktura samorządu robotniczego w opinii załóg fabrycznych', in *Studia Socjologiczne*, 1966, no. 22, pp. 83–5.

[3] S. Widerszpil, *Skład polskiej klasy . . .*, p. 308, Table 74.

TABLE 23. SKILLED WORKERS AS A PERCENTAGE OF TOTAL MANUAL
WORKER PARTY MEMBERSHIP BY INDUSTRIES

Industry	1960 (per cent)	1961 (per cent)
Fuel	78·1	79·9
Iron and steel	88·8	92·6
Machine and metal	86·9	88·6
Chemical	85·0	85·4
Textile and clothing	81·8	80·7
Foodstuffs	69·6	64·9
Building	48·9	50·0

On the basis of an intensive study of a factory in the machine-tools industry during the years 1960–3 one author found that all formal organisations within the factory were used by particular groups of employees for exerting pressure upon top management. The higher and middle production supervisors (managers) used the workers' council and the factory council of the trade unions. Predominantly skilled workers dominated the factory party committee. The young workers used the USY factory committee, and the female manual workers, the League of Women. Generally, the organisations utilised by manual workers were not used by non-manual workers and thus helped to sustain much intra-factory conflict.[1]

We may now turn to analyse the results of three studies dealing with a fairly representative cross-section of industry, namely heavy (aluminium works), medium (transport) and light industry (textiles) to see how and by whom the industrial manual worker was or was not represented in the various organisations comprising the CWSM.

Table 24 shows the distribution of manual workers among the various organisations within the textile factory. Despite the fact that the workers are well represented on the plenum of the workers' council (55 per cent of total membership), the actual decision-making organ, the presidium, has only one worker. The presidium of the workers' council is controlled by foremen, who in the textile industry are frequently promoted skilled manual workers. The party committee and the trade union

[1] R. Dyoniziak, *Społeczne uwarunkowanie wydajności pracy* (Warsaw, 1967) pp. 163–4, Diagram 7.

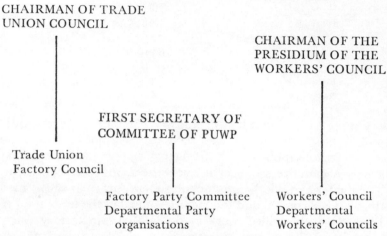

Diagram 1. The *Wielka Czwórka*: The Leading Group within the Enterprise

factory council appear to have a more balanced representation of the factory employees. Of course, such representation does not ensure that the manual workers will actually be influential. The factory party committee has one or more full-time party secretaries, and the union has one full-time chairman. This limits the influence which the part-time members can have on general policy decisions,[1] arrived at by the full-time policy making group. The latter, consisting of the enterprise director, the first secretary of the party committee and the chairmen of the union factory council and the workers' council presidium,[2] constituted the 'clique' frequently identified in Polish industry after 1958. The point we would like to make here is that the presidium of the workers' council appeared to be controlled by

[1] For a discussion of the development of the workers' councils in the textile industry in 1956–7 see J. Kolaja, *A Polish Factory – a case study of workers' participation in decision-making* (New York, 1960).

[2] See A. Jędrzejczak, 'Wielka czwórka', in *Polityka*, 30 June 1962. See Diagram 1.

TABLE 24. ORGANISATIONAL MEMBERSHIP BY INDUSTRIAL SOCIO-OCCUPATIONAL CATEGORY[1]

Organisational membership	Workers (per cent)	Foremen (per cent)	Engineering-technical (per cent)	Administration (per cent)	Per cent
Factory Committee of the PUWP (N = 28)	43	7	50	—	100
Conference of workers' self-management (N = 112)	53	14	19	14	100
Workers' council (N = 51)	55	22	13	10	100
Presidium of the workers' council (N = 14)	7	50	29	14	100
Trade union factory council (N = 27)	67	7	11	15	100

[1] J. Kulpińska, Społeczna aktywność pracowników przedsiębiorstwa przemysłowego (Wrocław, 1969) p. 109.

foremen, and engineering-technical personnel were the second most important group.

We next examine a study of the transport construction industry to see whether the composition of the workers' council presidium varies according to industry. In Table 25 we see that the presidium of the workers' council is dominated by managers, engineering-technical and administrative-clerical personnel as well as manual workers. As one author quite rightly pointed out,

> . . . numerical superiority of management cadres in the presidia of the workers' councils coupled with the simultaneous concentration of decisions . . . meant that the management could utilise a twin basis of authority – by right of their formal organisational position as well as their position within the workers' councils. . . .[1]

As in the previous study, the workers are well represented in the unions and on the party committee. In the latter we would argue that the workers concerned are the skilled workers.

The third study focuses on the aluminium works in Skawina, an example of modern heavy industry such as the Lenin steel works set up during the period of the six-year plan. This is the most recent of the three studies, having been carried out in the late sixties compared to the early sixties for the other two studies. It was found that the trade union factory council and the factory committee of the PUWP contained a high level of manual worker representation (see Table 26).[2] This does not differ significantly from the other studies except that there is a higher percentage of workers on the union factory council (70 per cent), which is probably due to the fact that there is no separate 'foreman' category. A major difference appears however when we examine the composition of the workers' council and its presidium. In the former there were twenty-two manual workers out of a total number of thirty-three (of the remaining eleven members ten were engineers). In the nine-man presidium of the workers' council however there was not a single manual worker. There were seven engineers (six of them party members), one technician (who was also a foreman), and one chargehand (who was also a party member). All the engineers were under

[1] A. Owieczko, 'Ewolucja samorządu . . .', p. 111.
[2] D. Dąbrowski, 'Organizacja zarządzania', in *Studia nad załogą huty aluminium w Skawinie*, ed. K. Dobrowolski and A. Stojak (Wrocław, 1969) pp. 110–11.

TABLE 25. SOCIO-OCCUPATIONAL COMPOSITION OF SELF-MANAGEMENT ORGANS IN THE TRANSPORT CONSTRUCTION INDUSTRY (PER CENT)[1]

Particulars	Total members	Managers (per cent)	Foremen (per cent)	Engineering-technical (per cent)	Administrative-clerical (per cent)	Workers (per cent)
CWSM	700	16·0	7·4	10·2	14·5	51·9
Workers' council	351	19·1	7·4	11·4	10·8	51·3
Factory council (union)	258	7·8	8·5	9·7	19·8	54·3
Factory committee (PUWP)	161	22·4	5·6	8·1	14·2	49·7
Factory committee (USY)	57	5·3	—	5·3	22·7	66·7
Presidium workers' council	131	42·7	5·3	11·6	12·2	28·2
Presidium factory council	88	11·4	9·1	17·0	27·3	35·2

[1] 'Ocena działalności samorządu robotniczego w świetle badań przeprowadzonych przez Zarząd Główny Związku Zawodowego Transportowców i Drogowców przy współudziale pracowni samorządu robotniczego IGS.' Quoted in Hirszowicz and Morawski, *Z badań nad społecznym . . .*, p. 273, fn. 2

TABLE 26. SOCIO-OCCUPATIONAL COMPOSITION OF THE SELF-MANAGEMENT ORGANS AT ALUMINIUM WORKS AT SKAWINA

Organisation	Total	Industrial socio-occupational groups		
		Engineer	Administrative-clerical	Manual worker
CWSM	67	21	6	40
Workers' council,	33	10	1	22
which includes Presidium of workers' council	9	7	1	1
Factory council (union)	17	3	2	12
Factory committee (PUWP)	11	4	2	5
Supreme technical organisation	3	3	—	—
Union of Socialist Youth	3	1	1	1

forty years of age and held management posts. Only the foreman, who was sixty-four years of age and a member of the United Peasant Party, represented the prewar generation of workers.

The composition of the various workers' councils reflects the differing production and economic functions performed by the councils in their respective industries. The textile industry is a traditional one, located in a prewar factory in an old industrial town (Łódź). The production process is equally traditional, requiring less theoretical expertise and focusing more upon the experience of workers, foremen and managers. Authority is derived from experience rather than qualifications. The foremen who represent the workers tend to be older promoted skilled workers, with elementary education.[1]

The transport construction industry represents an intermediate position with effective authority (located in the presidium of the workers' council) exercised by middle and higher management.

The modern aluminium foundry is a sharp contrast to the textile factory. The presidium members are young and have a higher education appropriate to the tasks which they carry out in this modern industry. They also hold the middle and higher management posts and are predominantly party members.

Throughout the three studies we have observed that the manual workers have been well represented on the trade union factory councils, varying in representation from 50 per cent to 70 per cent of the councils' membership. The power, however, rests not with the council but with its chairman. Here social composition is similar to the workers' council presidium. Table 27 shows the national breakdown of membership of manual workers in trade unions and their organisations. Unions, of course, represent all employees, manual and non-manual. We see that manual workers comprised 61·7 per cent of total union membership, but they constituted only 34·5 per cent of the members of the factory councils, and only 28·8 per cent of the

---

[1] See J. Kolaja, *A Polish Factory* . . ., p. 77, in which the author discusses the relationships between the foremen and the workers. It may be significant that in the industry with the lowest average monthly wage rate there is also a more 'traditional worker' representation. In the highly paid aluminium factory the representation is more 'technicised'.

chairmen of factory councils. In contrast, 27 per cent of chairmen of factory councils are administrative-clerical workers and a further 31 per cent are engineering-technical employees.[1]

TABLE 27. PARTICIPATION OF MANUAL WORKERS IN SELECTED TRADE UNION POSTS AND ORGANS (1965)[2]

	Total (000's)	Manual workers (000's)	Percentage of manual workers
Total employed	7922,2	4947,5	62·5
Total membership in trade unions	7662,7	4730,1	61·7
Members of factory councils	240,0	82,7	34·5
Chairmen of factory councils	32,2	9,3	28·8

It is not surprising that given the above composition of self-management the concern of self-management organs is with production-plan matters.[3] This affects manual workers' attitudes to self-management units and the selection of their officers. In 1966 a sociologist examined the workers' council in a large factory of 10,000 employees. The council was dominated by engineers and department managers. Research showed that the workers insisted upon electing managers, foremen, engineers, economists and technicians even when alternative choices from amongst their fellow manual workers were 'officially sanctioned'. These workers tended to select their immediate superiors for the party, union and self-management functions and in so doing fused the administrative and social functions within the factory.[4] As a result, however, the social functions were being ignored and self-management focused

[1] K. Ostrowski, *Rola związków zawodowych* . . ., p. 76. Unions encompass clerical workers, hence it is difficult to suppose that manual workers will dominate office union organisations.

[2] K. Ostrowski, *Rola związków zawodowych* . . ., p. 75, Table 3.

[3] M. Jarosz, 'Model samorządu robotniczego w świadomości aktywu samorządowego', in *Studia Socjologiczne*, no. 14, 1964.

[4] Reported in K. Krauss, 'Głowy do koronowania', in *Polityka*, 1 Oct. 1966. At the self-management meeting the workers reacted like spectators in a 'gallery', listening to the debate between the professionals and then

exclusively upon economic effectiveness. When the administration did improve the conditions of work and considered the welfare of the manual workers, it usually generated greater productivity, less wastage and a lowering of production costs. We believe that more self-management authorities are coming to realise the benefits of giving priority to the social welfare conditions of the workers. This aspect is being given more prominence than during the first days of WSM.[1] Another study substantiated this belief. It revealed that discussion of such specialised matters as production indices went over the heads of most of the audience, not just the workers. When the discussion turned to problems concerning the everyday working of the factory and the related social and production problems, everyone participated with zest. Questions relating to housing and dismissals, however, which should have been discussed by the unions, were frequently resolved by the top functionaries without any reference to the workers.[2] The more progressive industrial party organisations realised during the mid-sixties that too much time was being spent on problems relating to production plan fulfilment, and they believed that closer links had to be forged with the workers so as to obtain their suggestions and opinions. One party organisation reported its surprise at the size of the response to a questionnaire, circulated by the party committee, in which workers were asked for suggestions about various ways of improving shop-floor conditions and organisation. The workers for their part were equally astonished with the speed with which some of their suggestions were acted upon.[3] In general there appeared to be a rediscovery of the fact that the workers did have something to say, particularly in matters concretely related to their work situation, and that

voting for the point of view which they felt represented them most consistently. They rarely saw themselves as taking part in the proceedings and felt, so the author maintained, that democracy was the freedom to give your mandate to a person in whom you have confidence.

[1] J. Balcerek and L. Gilejko, 'Ekonomiczne efekty . . .', p. 440. According to the authors social-welfare conditions are now third in the list of number of resolutions passed by the CWSM, whereas previously they were hardly ever discussed. The 'December events' have speeded up this process.

[2] A. Gutowski, 'Bez samorządu trudno. W poszukiwaniu drogi', in *Z.G.*, no. 21, 1968.

[3] A. Strońska, 'Nie chcemy wyrobników', in *Polityka*, 5 Nov. 1966.

this form of participation was just as important for the factory as the formulation of a 'good' plan and the juggling with production indices.[1]

We believe that this initiation of shop-floor opinion was closely linked to the development of a particular type of factory activist. The study by Jolanta Kulpińska of a textile factory made some very important observations about the character of these activists. Firstly, the activists did not identify with the organisation which had sponsored them, such as the trade union or the party, but rather identified with the factory department or section in which they worked. This meant that in cases of conflict at the CWSM they 'represented' the finishing shop, or the weaving shop. Furthermore, the activists identified themselves as a group *vis-à-vis* the mass of the employees. They belonged to the 'aktyw' rather than to the party or the unions.[2] It would appear that just as the technical intelligentsia utilised the party and workers' council to increase its managerial control, so also the shop-floor activists used all the organisations at their disposal for the benefit of their section. The existence of this group of activists, owing their first allegiance to themselves as a group and basing their shop-floor power on their authority amongst the manual workers, may explain the rapid mobilisation of the industrial workers in 1970–1.

These activists had already come to the forefront before the eruption of trouble on the northern seaboard. In November 1970 one factory in Warsaw was ordered by the Association (Zjednoczenie) to lay off about 800 workers in the interests of productivity and in the drive to eliminate overemployment. The representatives of the workers refused, maintaining that any overemployment could be dealt with by utilising the production reserves, not by redundancies. Management backed down and the factory remained peaceful during the following months.[3]

[1] A. Gutowski, 'Z badań nad samorządem robotniczym', in *Polityka*, 1 Oct. 1966.

[2] J. Kulpińska, *Społeczna aktywność*..., p. 141. The closest parallel which comes to mind is that of the Shop Stewards Committee which sprung up in British industry in the face of similar 'bureaucratisation' of the means of worker expression.

[3] W. Falkowska, 'W oczekiwaniu lepszego jutra', in *Polityka*, 16 Jan. 1971, p. 4.

The accounts of the disturbances[1] in the shipyards in Gdańsk and Szczecin point to the fact that many of the shop-floor party members retained the confidence of the workers. In Szczecin, where the workers had set up a Workers' Commission to supervise free elections to the various factory organisations, a party activist was made the head of the strike committee.[2] After the workers had 'occupied' the shipyards for well over a month the new First Secretary of the party came to Szczecin to reason with them. It is again significant that when the workers in Gdańsk chose eighty-three delegates to put their demands to Gierek over 40 per cent were party members.[3]

Faced by such open opposition from the party's rank-and-file, Gierek had to admit that there had occurred a crisis of confidence not only between the party and the masses, but '. . . amongst members of the party, amongst its activists, who viewed ever more critically the policy of the leadership'.[4] The increasingly grim social and economic reality of the shop-floor had become less and less plain to the leadership.

On the evidence available it appears that a most important aspect of the December riots and the consequent industrial unrest was not only the deteriorating economic and material conditions of the industrial worker but also the breakdown in formal communication between the workers and the various organisations, and within the different levels of the latter. This had given rise to an informal shop-floor activist group most of the members of which were formally within the party and union organisations. They could not identify with the policies which their leadership espoused. These activists had subsequently moved beyond the control of their formal organisations or, in some cases, out of the organisations altogether.[5] When they were faced with the decision of the leadership to raise the price

[1] The events of Dec. 1970 are discussed in more detail in Ch. 7.

[2] D. Fikus and J. Urban, 'Szczecin', in *Polityka*, 6 Feb. 1971.

[3] S. Kozicki, 'Jak mało jak dużo potrzeba', in *Polityka*, 13 Jan. 1971.

[4] Speech by the First Secretary of the CC PUWP at the VIII Plenum, reported in *Życie Warszawy*, 8 Feb. 1971.

[5] One of the criticisms of the unions had been that they did not include the 'informal group leaders' in the factory council of the trade union. There were therefore informal power centres outside of the formal organisations.

of certain articles of foodstuffs[1] they found themselves answerable to their work-mates but without recourse to their own superiors. The only alternative was to organise full protest and these activists had the ability to do just this.

[1] As one writer reports, when the price increases were read out at the party meetings on 12 Dec. 'the members present swore and hung their heads'. Fikus and Urban . . ., *Polityka*, 6 Feb. 1971. The lower ranks of the party were more aware of the burden these increases put upon them as front line representatives of the policy than were the leadership.

CHAPTER FOUR

The Cultural Intelligentsia: The Writers

By George Gömöri

As has been pointed out in Chapter 1, in the 'official' Marxist-Leninist view of social stratification the 'intelligentsia' is a separate stratum in socialist society performing the leading creative, executive and administrative roles, and it works in full harmony with the manual working class. In this theory the political leadership of society (in practice, the Communist Party) is the expression of the unitary will of the socialist intelligentsia and the manual working class. In practice, however, the intelligentsia is not a unitary social group. There are people in it who are creatively engaged in scholarly or artistic work (such as writers, film directors, poets and sculptors) and others in more technical activities such as executives, organisers of production and other experts with some sort of theoretical training (factory managers, economists, chemists, engineers).[1] Also, the political activists, such as party secretaries and parliamentary leaders, though 'officially' forming part of the intelligentsia, have their basis of authority to some extent in their control of ideology and over political institutions. Such differences in professions stemming from the division of labour influences the views such men have of the world. Also, the traditional culturally determined view of the role of writer, a factory manager or politician also has an effect on the ways in which various members of the 'intelligentsia' behave. One needs, therefore, to investigate how these various groups (cultural, technical and political) act to determine the extent to which their roles are clearly demarcated and congruent and also in what ways they conflict or exchange

[1] This division is similar to the one used by Jan Szczepański, 'Struktura inteligencji w Polsce', *Kultura i Społeczeństwo*, vol. iv, no. 1 (Warsaw, 1960) p. 37.

with each other. It is quite impossible to discuss in any detail every group which might be considered to constitute the general non-manual categories mentioned above. Therefore, here we shall describe the writers and in the next chapter the engineers – as examples of cultural and technical groups – and consider their relationship with the party and political authorities.

THE CULTURAL INTELLIGENTSIA, PAST AND PRESENT

Historically the Polish intelligentsia played a role similar to its Russian counterpart before the 1917 October Revolution, but in Poland the intelligentsia was also indispensable for the actual *survival* of the Polish nation. After the unsuccessful 1830 uprising the remnants of independent Polish statehood were eliminated by the Russian autocracy. Though the 'Polish question' remained a thorn in the side of Imperial Russia, for the Western powers it soon became a dead issue and throughout the nineteenth century, while paying lip-service to the rights of the Poles, no Western statesman felt justified in starting a war for the liberation of Poland. This became apparent in 1848 and even more so in 1863. The Polish-speaking community in partitioned Poland became increasingly exposed to strong political pressures; both Russification and Bismarck's colonisation in the Prussian-held territories were clear signs of the determination of the partitioning powers to stamp out Polish national consciousness. In such a situation, when the importance of the language and national culture became paramount, it was the intelligentsia, especially its writers and philosophers, who fulfilled the 'ideological' and 'didactic' functions of non-existent political leaders. As outspoken critics of social conditions, such intellectuals also became the mainstay of national resistance.

On the whole this intelligentsia had its origins in the land-owning classes. As this stratum became more and more impoverished during the nineteenth century, its members turned towards the free professions and together with a small stratum of educated people of German or Jewish origins formed a new social grouping. As the aims of the nation demanded social cohesion and some measure of national unity, in the second half of the nineteenth century most Polish intellectuals became concerned with social problems, demanding the integration of the peasant into Polish society and furthering the emancipation of all underprivileged groups. Since the nobility was losing its economic base and influence and the bourgeoisie was not strong enough to become a leading force and organise national consciousness, this task was undertaken by the intelligentsia. Through newspapers and literary reviews the intellectuals played an important part in shaping public opinion. They played outstanding roles in democratic and radical movements and formed, for example, the hard core of the leadership of socialist groups and also fought in large numbers in Piłsudski's legions. After 1918 their political role diminished somewhat but as a group they preserved a high social status which was quite unparalleled in France or England.

It is perhaps not surprising then that in present-day socialist Poland the prestige of the cultural intelligentsia is exceedingly high. The three highest rated occupations in 1961 were found to be university professor, doctor and teacher.[1] It is interesting to note that political professions came quite low down the list: a government minister was ranked only eighth.[2] As for the present role of the intelligentsia, in the late fifties most of its members still retained a traditional view of its unusual social importance. A questionnaire answered by journalists revealed that 63 per cent believed in the 'dominant social role' of the intelligentsia.[3] This conviction was justified by references to the special significance of education and to the intellectuals' role in social change. According to at least one journalist: 'The intelligentsia was to a large extent the driving force behind the changes in October.'[4] Although party functionaries in their official declarations speak about the working class as the vanguard of society and the most important class in present-day Poland, they are well aware of the fact that without the consent

[1] W. Wesołowski, 'The Notions of Strata and Class in Socialist Society', in *Social Inequality*, ed. André Béteille (London, 1969) pp. 131–2.

[2] Sarapata, however, found that ministers came fifth in the social hierarchy. See above, p. 27.

[3] S. Dzięcielska, *Sytuacja społeczna dziennikarzy polskich* (Wrocław–Warsaw–Cracow, 1962) p. 172.

[4] Ibid., p. 172. 'October' is a reference to the bloodless revolution in Oct. 1956 which brought Gomułka back into power.

and co-operation and the participation of the intelligentsia no full development of a country's resources is possible. Also, whatever social pressures may exist in East European countries, a serious conflict will erupt only when a significant part of the intelligentsia breaks its alliance with the ruling communist bureaucracy and channels the forces of change into definite political action. The policy of the political leadership therefore, in spite of occasional displays of mistrust and aversion towards intellectuals, is to reward those members of the creative intelligentsia who fully co-operate, while keeping in check the more restless, 'unreliable' elements. The writers are the neuralgic point of the intelligentsia because they have a privileged position in socialist society: they alone are in a position to criticise certain policies or other social groups publicly, if not always directly. Their privileges are partly traditional, and partly tied to the structure of the social system they live in. Polish communists inherited the tradition of writers giving invaluable support to progressive political movements and from the beginnings of the communist movement they attributed great importance to the written word. Most of the founding members of the Party were intellectuals themselves, and already before 1945 the Polish Communists had attracted such writers as Jasieński, Wat, Stawar, Kruczkowski, Broniewski and others. The Communist Party believed in educating the masses and was aware of the significance of writers in the realisation of this task. When a leading communist politician stated in the mid-fifties 'our Party has always set great store by the writers' work remembering that literature was and still is a powerful ideological weapon',[1] he did not exaggerate. Some of the difficulties of the Polish writer prior to 1956 stemmed precisely from the fact that the party set *too great store* by his work and scrutinised every word for political implications. In other words, the political élite of People's Poland needed literature as an 'ideological weapon' and in recognition of this need was ready to ensure the material welfare of any writer willing to obey the party's instructions.

[1] Ochab at the Sixth Congress of the PWA, *Twórczość*, no. 7, 1954, p. 152.

WRITERS' INCOME AND INCENTIVES

It is difficult to state with any certainty just how much the income of a writer is in Poland. No statistical data have been published on this subject and our estimates are based mainly on inference and on personal interviews. Vast differences in income can exist between any two writers, depending on a variety of factors such as age and popularity, town of residence, literary genre in which the writer established himself and last, but not least, the degree to which he is dependent on writing alone. Incomes of free-lance writers tend to be less regular and more dramatically fluctuating than of those having salaried jobs whether as an editor or regular column-writer of a literary paper, or as a reader in a publishing house or literary adviser to a theatre. An established writer will inevitably earn more than a beginner; prose writers and playwrights usually more than poets; and Warsaw writers receive higher fees than their provincial colleagues (though here there might be exceptions). A writer of fiction living in Warsaw, writing one novel of 250 printed pages per year, published in an average 10,000 copies, could get for his book anything between 15,000 and 33,000 złoties depending on 'the artistic, ideological, scholarly or didactic values' of the said work.[1] This payment can be increased by the Ministry of Arts and Culture up to 250 per cent of the original sum and it should be paid out from the 'Authors' Fund'. If we assume that the author had been given such a special premium (*dodatkowe wynagrodzenie*) he could make 82,000 złoties on one edition of his book and would receive further royalties for following editions. Such rights can be used as a powerful incentive and weapon by the Ministry in its efforts to support 'politically constructive' literature.

In all probability an average writer would not make more than 4,000–5,000 zł. per month (48,000–60,000 zł. per year), but a hard-working writer or the author of a bestseller could earn between 8,000 and 12,000 zł. per month. This income, when compared with the average monthly wages in Poland – 2,180 zł. in 1967[2] – is very good. Moreover, writers benefit from State subsidies in other fields such as, since 1952, social

[1] *Zbiór przepisów prawnych. Dla członków ZLP* (Warsaw, 1968) p. 100.
[2] *Poland 1969, Facts and Figures* (Interpress, Warsaw, 1969).

insurance, and 'creative' or rest homes. There is also financial help for writers' families and they may be given loans and scholarships of between 1,000 and 4,000 zł. per month which enables the writer to devote all his energies to creative writing.

Incentives to writers include various awards and prizes. The highest in prestige is the State Prize for Literature, awarded every other year, but the Ministry of Culture and publishers also have their own prizes and awards. Successful writers are often sent abroad as members of professional or State delegations. The books of favoured authors are published in mass-editions, but even in the case of an ordinary edition the degree of approval of the authorities can be measured by the size of the edition and the price of the book. If a writer behaves in a manner which is judged incorrect by the Ministry of Culture or the Central Committee of the Polish United Workers' Party, certain incentives can be withdrawn and others applied selectively. If a serious clash takes place, the recalcitrant author can be 'withdrawn from circulation' – blacklisted for any period of time. Such bans can vary in severity: in some cases they are confined to the mass-media; in other cases the writer is allowed to do translations but no original writing of his can be published; in exceptional cases he is not allowed to do even translations. When a partial ban is imposed upon an individual writer, an unimportant but permanent job or a loan from the Writers' Association can play a vital role in assuring his survival even in unfavourable circumstances.

The writer living in a communist-ruled country is in a paradoxical situation. He is the most exposed producer of culture (it is unlikely that any painter or composer would ever make such an impact on public opinion as a writer) but he may not be fully 'committed' politically to the régime.[1] Like the rest of his social group he is not dependent on the means of production in the same way as the capitalist or the worker – in his eyes the class-struggle may not have paramount importance and his work may not be subordinated to the party's conception of the political struggle. This happens only if the writer resolves to serve a cause with his pen. However, as the writer's main urge is to create new literary values or to defend old and universal

[1] See W. Wesołowski, *Klasy, warstwy i władza* (Warsaw, 1966) p. 175.

ones, he tends to become disappointed when his talent is used by politicians in tactical games dictated by the exigencies of politics. His ambition is to transcend the limitations of society including those imposed on society by the prevailing power structure, giving him a loyalty to the dialectics of change rather than to any political party.

In economic and sociological terms the writer could perhaps be classified as a particular kind of a *small producer*. Like the individual artisan or farmer he too is 'both the owner and the user of his means of production'[1] – he has full control over his work and its marketable product belongs to him. (Resistance against censorship makes economic sense too; the writer resents bureaucratic decisions that reduce the marketability of his product.) In a socialist system, however, there is less and less room for such an anachronistic survivor of the past as the free small producer – sooner or later he will have to be transformed into a worker in the socialised sector. *Mutatis mutandis* this danger hovers above the writer as well. Unless the writer writes books acceptable to his monopolistic super-publisher he may be unable to publish because the market is controlled by the State, which owns most if not all publishing houses. He is under constant pressure to conform to the aesthetic *and* political expectations of the governing élite; the bureaucracy tries to transform him, the free producer of cultural goods, into a salaried State employee, but the writer can defend himself in various ways. As an individual, he can resist making major concessions to official demands which go against his moral commitment, writing, if necessary, for the drawer for shorter or longer periods; in other words he can demonstrate with his silence. Moreover, he can fight back collectively in his capacity as a member of a professional association. By being a member of such an association (in this case the Polish Writers' Association or PWA), he partially submits himself to State control, but precisely because he acts within the existing legal framework and the given social structure, he can maintain some of his creative independence. This supposition is shown to be correct by the postwar history of the Polish Writers' Association, which has been protecting not only the professional rights of writers but time and again has become a crystallisation point of intel-

[1] Ibid., p. 178.

lectual opposition to the unpopular or repressive policies of the political élite.

THE WRITERS' SOCIAL ORIGINS AND STATUS

Before discussing the aims, history and political significance of the Polish Writers' Association, let us first have a look at the social background of writers and their relationship to other classes or groups in Polish society. When speaking of a 'writer' we have in mind a member of the PWA, although the two categories are not always identical, for there are some authors, especially young writers, who may not be members of the PWA, and there are others who, while they are members, can be called writers only in a broad sense, for their main occupation may be that of historian, philosopher, journalist or editor though they may have done some writing at some point of their career.

So far no Polish sociological work has been published on the writers as a separate professional group, though such works have been published on journalists and also on painters and sculptors.[1] Our investigations can give therefore only an incomplete picture.

Recent research on journalists, using a large and certainly representative sample, showed that more than 50 per cent of Polish journalists working in the daily press in 1958 originated from a non-manual background.[2] The corresponding figure for those from working-class origins was 26 per cent and from peasant origins, 13 per cent. These figures could be regarded as broadly indicative of the social origins of living Polish writers as well, with two qualifications. First, the number of writers with peasant backgrounds might be higher than in the journalists' case and those with a working-class background almost certainly lower;[3] moreover, a large number of elderly writers would

[1] Cf. Stefania Dzięcielska's book on the social situation of journalists and Aleksander Wallis's study on painters and sculptors. S. Dzięcielska, *Sytuacja społeczna dziennikarzy polskich* (Wrocław, 1962); A. Wallis, *Artyści plastycy* (Warsaw, 1964). Andrzej Siciński's *Literaci polscy* (Wrocław, 1971) was published after the completion of this study.

[2] Dzięcielska, op. cit., p. 54.

[3] A study of all entries beginning with the letter B of *Słownik Współczesnych Pisarzy Polskich* (Warsaw, 1963) vol. 1, shows that while 54 per cent of the writers listed who were alive in 1963 originated from the intelligentsia, 13 per cent had peasant and only 2 per cent working-class origins.

have come from landowning and upper professional families. These conclusions may be supported by the investigation of the social background of the twenty *most popular* Polish writers of fiction and poetry[1] which reveals that these writers overwhelmingly have intellectual or higher professional family backgrounds.

Such family origin may provide an important link between the values of the traditional Polish cultural intelligentsia and those of contemporary Poland. The new 'socialist' intelligentsia created since 1945 is also characterised by recruitment from the ranks of the manual working class and peasantry. While this process undoubtedly reduced the social distance which had existed between the prewar intelligentsia and the masses, it also had the effect of 'assimilating' the new intellectuals and cutting them off from their social home base in the working class suburb or village.[2] Critics of the writers' political activities in the PWA often refer to the intellectual cohesiveness of the so-called *środowisko*, or literary environment, 'inner society', where professional solidarity is valued more than political expediency or tactical adroitness. In spite of official assurances to the contrary, Szczepański is certainly right in saying that 'the creative intelligentsia . . . has most characteristics of the former prewar intelligentsia'.[3] A distinction may be made between the creative and technical intelligentsia. Among the former not only the tradition of professional independence and solidarity persisted from prewar times, but the organisational structure of each group is different. The career of the technical intelligentsia is closely linked to the hierarchy of office, whether this be in a factory of a research institute, whereas the writer advances through his *individual* efforts.

It has been pointed out earlier in the book that according to the 'official' Marxist interpretation there are no antagonistic classes in present-day Poland. Polish sociologists nevertheless admit the likelihood if not inevitability of social conflicts

[1] The list containing their names was taken from *Nowe Książki*, no. 9, 1969.

[2] Mannheim has pointed out, quite rightly, that 'a proletarian who becomes an intellectual is likely to change his social personality'. K. Mannheim, *Ideology and Utopia* (New York, 1936) p. 158.

[3] J. Szczepański, *Przemiany społeczne w Polsce Ludowej* (Warsaw, 1965) p. 33.

between various groups. These may arise firstly from the unequal consumption of both consumer and cultural goods and secondly from unequal participation in decision-making. The ruling party élite composed also of representatives from various groups, such as managers and technocrats, attempts to regulate and channel the diverse and conflicting interests. Wiatr distinguishes 'sectional' and 'cause-oriented' groups and he lists the 'associations of the creative intelligentsia' as an important interest group in socialist countries.[1] He fails to discuss, however, what makes the writers' association unique amongst the interest groups, namely, its propensity to express more than its own professional interests. In times of political crises or stagnation writers and other creative intellectuals may articulate demands and act as the defender of the non-privileged classes of the population. The non-privileged classes are separated from the creative intelligentsia by a vast gap deriving from differences in income, status and style of life, a fact which makes the intelligentsia in the eyes of the masses look like the ally or the client of the ruling bureaucracy. But there have been occasions when the writer, even at the cost of jeopardising his privileges, became the mouthpiece of social pressures mounting from below.

The peculiar social position of writers in contemporary Polish society was interestingly defined by Jerzy Putrament, himself a writer and also a member of the party élite. According to Putrament, writers are a 'microstratum' of special significance. In both Poland and the USSR before 1956 they enjoyed extraordinary privileges and were also fully engaged politically in justifying the nature of the régime, as it were, 'on the side of the revolution'. After the twentieth Congress of the CPSU many of them were shocked and disillusioned, and though many lost their previous political 'commitment', they preserved their privileges. 'In our conditions,' writes Putrament, 'culture and especially literature belongs to one of the most directly political spheres of life. . . . It is in culture, especially in literature, that the political struggle which has been stifled elsewhere can find for itself a certain possibility for self-expression.'[2] In the absence of any formal political opposition in Communist

---

[1] J. Wiatr, *Społeczeństwo* (Warsaw, 1964) p. 377.
[2] *Literatura na rozdrożu* (Cracow, 1968) p. 39.

countries the writers' professional organisation can easily become an '*ersatz-centre*' of opposition. This is well known to critics in the West and, according to Putrament, is why the Western press pays so much attention to literary affairs in the USSR and in Eastern Europe. Let us now turn then to discuss the official association of Polish writers.

THE HISTORY OF THE POLISH WRITERS' ASSOCIATION BEFORE 1956

The Polish Writers' Professional Association (*Związek Zawodowy Literatów Polskich*) was established first as a writers' trade union in 1920. Its first president was the well-known Polish writer Stefan Żeromski. Until the Second World War, the association was mainly concerned with the protection of the material interests of the writers. This situation changed after the war. The association was re-established and in 1949 it dropped the adjective 'professional'. As the Polish Writers' Association, or PWA, it became concerned 'with the standards and situation of contemporary Polish literature'.[1] The statutes have been changed several times since 1945, and according to the statutes of 1957, 'the aim of the association is the realisation of the ideals of democracy and progress in the field of literary creation, the defence of the freedom of the word and of creation as well as the moral and material interests of writers'.[2] What makes this text rather unusual is the absence in it of any reference to the leading role of the party, or to socialist realism which between 1949 and 1956 was the officially supported creative method in Poland and still is the only approved, though not necessarily enforced, method in the Soviet Union.[3] The main administrative organs of the PWA are the Congress of Delegates, which can take place every year but should take place at least once in three years, and the Executive Board (*Zarząd Główny*). The latter

[1] *Słownik Współczesnych Pisarzy Polskich*, Tom. I.A-I. Ed. Ewa Korzeniowska (Warsaw, 1963) p. 93.

[2] Ibid., p. 94.

[3] Members of the Union of Soviet Writers are supposed 'to participate through their creative work in the class struggle of the proletariat and in socialist construction'. From the statutes of the USW quoted by Harold Swayze in *Political Control of Literature in the USSR (1946–1959)* (Cambridge, Mass., 1962) p. 225.

consists of the President, twenty members elected at the Congress and all heads of local branches.[1] Within the association there are numerous committees of which probably the Admissions Committee (*Komisja Kwalifikacyjna*), the Auditing Committee (*Komisja Rewizyjna*) and the Arbitrations Committee (*Sąd Koleżeński*) are the most important. Until 1969 only the Arbitrations Committee had the right to suspend or expel members, but this was changed at the Bydgoszcz Congress when this right was given to the Executive Board. In 1969 the Polish Writers' Association had fifteen local branches and 1,069 members, of whom over 50 per cent (626) lived in Warsaw.[2]

The PWA has passed through several different phases of political engagement. Between 1945 and 1949 it was not unlike the prewar association and helped facilitate the physical survival of writers in a war-ravaged country lacking the elementary amenities of civilised human life. It fulfilled this task admirably under its first three presidents (Przyboś, Czachowski and Iwaszkiewicz). The turning point came in 1949 at the fourth (Szczecin) Congress of the PWA, where the original professional and humanitarian aims of the association were replaced by new ones more in line with communist cultural policy. In Szczecin, Polish writers were 'mobilised' to further socialist realism which was presented to party spokesmen as the only true method of artistic creation. Leon Kruczkowski became President and the organisation that was originally established to protect authors' rights and professional interests was transformed into a bureaucratic body *controlling* writers. After the Szczecin congress, as Julian Przyboś said a few years later, the association's activities were directed at 'shackling critical thought, turning writers into thoughtless executors of the instructions coming from the central office for propaganda'.[3] In this respect the PWA was on its way to becoming an exact replica of the Union of Soviet Writers, characterised by one critic as 'a powerful political body, ruled by officials who received their instructions from the Party. . . .'[4]

The transformation of the PWA into a fully State-controlled

---

[1] *Rocznik polityczny i gospodarczy 1966* (Warsaw, 1967) pp. 778–9.
[2] *Wielka Encyklopedia Powszechna*, vol. 12 (Warsaw, 1969) p. 764.
[3] *Nowa Kultura*, no. 36, 1956, p. 7.
[4] Marc Slonim, *Soviet Russian Literature* (Oxford, 1964) p. 160.

organisation was carried out by successive administrative steps. In 1950 the 'creative genre sections' (*sekcje twórcze*) were established and at sectional meetings regular discussions would take place about the ideological and other merits of particular books or manuscripts. These sections quickly became unpopular,[1] so that Przyboś in the article quoted above would speak for many of his colleagues, complaining that the Polish writer working in the post-Szczecin period had to pass through four different nets of censorship before publication. The first of these was his 'creative genre section', the second the editorial board of the literary reviews (the weekly *Nowa Kultura* was under the control of the Executive Board of the PWA), the third the publishing house to which he submitted his manuscript and finally the fourth – the formidable Office of Press Control (*Urząd Kontroli Prasy*). Such a state of affairs, while presenting frightful obstacles for each individual writer, led – in Przyboś's view – to the complete 'bureaucratisation of the Writers' Association'.[2]

Another way by which the PUWP hoped to control the Writers' Association was the institution of a liberal admissions policy, the 'democratisation' of membership. In the first post-war decade there was a massive influx of new members into the PWA, and some of these members were recommended and accepted more on grounds of political reliability than on purely artistic excellence. The large influx in membership is illustrated by the fact that at the sixth Congress of the Writers' Association in 1954 amongst the 710 members only 194, that is just over 25 per cent, had been in the association before the war. 'It would be difficult not to notice that the world of Polish creative writing underwent a process of unusually vigorous rejuvenation in the course of the last few years,' said Kruczkowski.[3] The same process was interpreted in rather a different way by the critic Sandauer when, two years later, he claimed that the criterion of quality had been ignored at the selection of new members, most of whom were nothing but graphomaniacs (*grafomani*).[4]

---

[1] Swayze points out that there have been repeated attempts in the Union of Soviet Writers to abolish the creative sections but this was resisted by the (party) authorities. Swayze, op. cit., p. 230.

[2] *Nowa Kultura*, no. 36, 1956, p. 7.

[3] *Twórczość*, no. 7, 1954, p. 167.   [4] *Nowa Kultura*, no. 35, 1956, p. 3.

Though Sandauer perhaps set his literary standards somewhat high, with such a large membership it was inevitable that outstanding writers and critics should be in a minority in a professional association of this kind.[1]

As for the rejuvenation of the PWA, paradoxically it soon turned out to be a mixed blessing for the authorities. After 1954, especially in 1956 and 1957, many young writers, and including party members, became disillusioned with the existing state of affairs in Poland and their disenchantment was reinforced by the shock following the revelations of Stalin's crimes against both Russian and Polish Communists. These revelations upset non-Communists less than Communists, who felt a need to atone for their past gullibility and for their complicity in the lesser but still painfully obvious crimes of the Bierut régime. Consequently, it was mainly the Communist writers who set the tone of the increasingly frank and outspoken debates which took place in the Council of Culture and Arts[2] and in the literary press. In this process both the former members of the group *Kuźnica* (Jan Kott, Andrzejewski, Ważyk, K. Brandys) and the younger Communist writers of the first postwar generation (*pryszczaci* — 'the pimpled ones') played a significant role. It was they who transformed the literary journal *Nowa Kultura* (which apart from *Po Prostu* was the most interesting publication of the Polish Thaw) into a forum of real debate about the 'deformations of socialism' and it was they who formulated the new programme of the Writers' Association in 1956. Adam Ważyk, a former zealot of socialist realism, now became one of the most vocal critics of the system. He described the association's role in the following words: 'In defending the moral rights of the writers the Association should have a task which is diametrically different from the post-Szczecin concept: the protection of the freedom of literary creation.'[3]

[1] The association, by the way, is called ZLP or *Związek Literatów Polskich* in Polish, *literat* meaning a 'literary man', someone professionally engaged in creative writing which in itself, of course, is no guarantee of the truly *creative* character of any person's literary output.

[2] The XIX Session of the council, for instance 'expressed the real views of writers who made critical utterances about the situation that had existed until now in intellectual life'. *Rocznik Literacki 1956* (Warsaw, 1957) p. 622.

[3] *Nowa Kultura*, no. 42, 1956, p. 3.

In the long debate that preceded the Polish October of 1956 and the Writers' Congress in the December of the same year, there were voices demanding the abolition of the association and the establishment of 'literary groups' equal in rights, and in free competition with each other. This model proved to be unacceptable to the new party leadership which now had Władysław Bieńkowski as one of its spokesmen and was also opposed, for practical reasons, by many writers as well. Plans for new periodicals were canvassed and in fact two of them, *Dialog* (an excellent theatrical review edited by Adam Tarn) and *Współczesność* (the literary journal of young writers), even got off the ground during 1956. The third planned periodical, Ważyk's *Europa*, either took too long a time to prepare or ran into administrative difficulties; at any rate, by the time the first number was ready in mid-1957, it was suppressed by the authorities. As a reaction to this new example of official interference in cultural affairs, the founders of *Europa*, who were former members of the *Kuźnica* group and amongst whom were Kott, Ważyk and Andrzejewski, resigned from the party.

Though the PWA, due to the attitude of its conservative leadership, took a cautious stand over political developments, individual writers, and among them many Communists, were in the forefront of the struggle for democratisation. Their activities culminated in the days preceding Gomułka's return to power in October 1956. The role of the writers in the political reform movement that grew out of the de-Stalinisation campaign of the PUWP was not decisive but it was important, for poets like Ważyk, Jastrun, Hertz, Iłłakowiczówna and others, writers like Andrzejewski, K. Brandys and Marek Hłasko expressed not only the disillusionment and frustration of the cultural intelligentsia but also the discontent and even despair of a large segment of the population, including the workers. The writers' contribution to the victory of the liberal forces within the PUWP in October 1956 can be best defined as *mediation* between the political élite and those social forces which had no opportunity to express themselves in any other way than through sporadic direct action such as wildcat strikes and the Poznań disturbances. The changes which took place in October 1956 were the result of an *ad hoc* coalition of liberals, Gomułkists, tactical anti-Stalinists and opportunists. Such groups relied on the writers and journalists for the dissemination of various points of view and for sounding out the mood of the workers and of other social groups. In 1956 some writers therefore performed a valuable task and were later rewarded for this with substantial concessions, the foremost of which was the promise of non-interference by the political authorities in the internal affairs of writers. This meant that literature would enjoy a certain amount of autonomy, and while the party would not cease to suppress views 'harmful to the cause of socialism', it would restrain itself from interfering and, even worse, arbitrating in matters of style and creative method. While asserting the view that 'pure liberalism in cultural policy is . . . a utopia',[1] the party spokesmen on culture nevertheless agreed that such key concepts as 'realism', 'engagement' and 'Party-mindedness' should be broadened and reinterpreted.

The eighth Plenum of the PUWP and Gomułka's election as First Secretary of the party was greeted by the Warsaw writers in a resolution which stated the following: 'After years of lies and injustice a time of hope has arrived. This we owe above all to the bravery and judiciousness of the workers and of the youth. We are united with our thoughts and feelings in the general condemnation of lawlessness and in the popular aspirations to freedom and justice. The Polish road to socialism now lies open.'[2]

One consequence of the October changes was the election of a new Executive Board for the PWA – this time without a list of candidates dictated from above. Kruczkowski lost his position as President and the Writers' Congress voted Antoni Słonimski into his seat. Słonimski was a widely respected figure, a well-known poet, playwright and critic and his prewar liberal and socialist connections and *émigré* past made him an unreliable office-holder in the eyes of orthodox Communists though he was welcomed by the liberals. As for the rest of the Executive Board, the three posts for Vice-President were shared amongst the Catholic Zawieyski, the Avantgardist anti-Stalinist Przyboś and P.E.N. Club Secretary Rusinek, and the board included such writers as Maria Dąbrowska, Jastrun, the Marxist critic Stawar and some non-compromised Catholics like Gołubiew

[1] Stefan Żółkiewski, *Kultura i polityka* (Warsaw, 1958) p. 17.
[2] *Twórczość*, no. 11, 1956, p. 5.

and Kisielewski. Andrzejewski became the President of the Warsaw Branch. The new leadership of the PWA reflected a wide range of political opinion and had a much higher ratio of distinguished writers than any previous board of the association; most of the party-appointed 'administrators' were voted out of office. From the point of view of the party, with its pretensions to ideological supervision, the results were a disaster. Słonimski's new Executive Board carried out certain changes resented by the party bureaucracy. The statutes were changed and to a large extent de-ideologised, the 'creative genre sections' were abolished and the professional character of the organisation was emphasised to the detriment of its presumed political-ideological aims.[1] This liberal 'line of Słonimski' continued up to 1959, enjoying the support of the overwhelming majority of Polish writers, including those who were members of the PUWP. The party organisation of the association, to which about 25 per cent of all Warsaw writers belonged, was in no position to start a campaign against Słonimski or his policies; and apparently many of its members were under 'revisionist' influence.[2]

YEARS OF EQUILIBRIUM: 1957–63

The Thaw and the political changes of 1956 brought about a marked improvement in the atmosphere of Polish cultural life. Scores of interesting books, novels and collections of poetry appeared, a whole generation of talented young writers attracted sudden attention, the Polish cinema and theatre took on a new lease of life and surprised Western Europe with its vitality. Yet the restrictions of the Stalinist period, now usually referred to in the press as the *miniony okres* (the period that has been left behind), did not all disappear, and if some of them seemed to vanish for a short time, they soon reappeared in new forms. The bureaucratic apparatus, including the security service, shaken and frightened by the eruption of popular discontent of 1956, was slowly reorganised and by 1958 strengthened

[1] Janina Dziarnowska, in *Literatura na rozdrożu* (Cracow, 1968) p. 145.

[2] Ibid. 'Revisionist' in this context means party members who oppose 'official' policy on a particular point, i.e. the party's right to interfere on cultural matters.

its control in most fields. The surest sign of the resumption of these controls was the increasing power of the censor.

Freedom of expression had remained restricted even in the heady days of the Polish October when the man in the street might have had the impression that 'everything goes'. In the first weeks after Gomułka's return to power most writers and editors practised some kind of voluntary censorship, fearing for the vulnerability of this new democratic experiment. Soon, however, it became clear that Gomułka had no intention whatsoever to abolish censorship and when, after the *Europa* affair, the outspoken *Po Prostu* was closed down as well in the autumn of 1957, all illusions that may have existed on that score had to disappear.[1] Already in December 1956 the censor suppressed information generally including a book by a Polish journalist eyewitness on the Hungarian uprising.[2] This activity was justified as a preventive step to avoid conflict with the Soviet Union, which was still mistrustful of 'the Polish experiment'. In the course of 1957 several other books and articles were suppressed: the two best-known cases were the non-publication of Wygodzki's *Zatrzymany do wyjaśnienia* (*Remanded in Custody*) and Marek Hłasko's *Cmentarze* (*The Graveyards*), both containing strong critical accents about Bierut's Poland. Though Wygodzki was a verteran party member this made no difference: it was the subject matter, not the author's name, that decided the ban. In later years though, when the interests of the writers and of the PUWP clashed, other sanctions were applied, even against outstanding writers. For instance, a collection of Słonimski's theatrical reviews was withdrawn from circulation a day after publication in 1959. Such retaliation by the authorities for a writer's dissent either within the PWA or through publications was not at all rare. In fact there is probably no Polish writer, with the possible exception of authors of children's books, who would not have had some dealings with the censor, ironically referred to as 'our most faithful reader'. The rights of the censor are extraordinarily wide: the Main Office of Press

---

[1] Nicholas Bethell, *Gomułka, His Poland and His Communism* (London, 1969) p. 240.

[2] The book in question was Hanka Adamiecka's *Prawda o węgierskiej rewolucji* containing her articles printed in *Sztandar Młodych* and some unpublished material.

Control (GUKP) has a veto not only over all newspapers, publications and scripts for the radio and television but it can take specific decisions about the size of the edition to be published and can even stipulate the quality of paper to be used for the book.[1]

The issue of censorship and the censor's arbitrary powers should be viewed against constitutional guarantees concerning the rights of the individual. Article 71 of the Constitution of the Polish People's Republic assures the right of Polish citizens to the freedom of press, thought and expression.[2] This paragraph of the Constitution is constantly over-ruled or violated by the activities of the Main Offices of Press Control, which is under the direct supervision of the Ministry of Internal Affairs. Although in theory deputies of the Sejm could protest against such violations, in practice the role of the Sejm has been very limited in calling the attention of the authorities to particular abuses. Although several writers have been deputies in the Sejm their influence on the cultural policy of the government has on the whole been negligible. Writer-members of the Central Committee of the PUWP would probably exert more influence on cultural issues but even they could be ignored by a hostile majority, as Zółkiewski was at the XII Plenum of the PUWP in July 1968.[3]

By 1959 all the liberal supporters of Gomułka lost their influence and suffered political defeat. Morawski left the Politbureau and Bieńkowski, Minister of Higher Education since 1956, had to resign. In cultural affairs functionaries like Werblan, Starewicz and Kraśko were now advising Gomułka and it was they who decided that Słonimski would have to resign as President of the PWA. According to one source this decision stemmed from the fears of the party leadership about the continuing liberalism of the Writers' Association, which 'was still adhering to the October line when the people in power had already departed from it'.[4] For example, at various writers' meetings demands were voiced about the abolition of censorship; this was impermissible from the point of view of the PUWP just undergoing a political 'freeze'. Werblan and his

---

[1] Paulina Press, *Biurokracja totalna* (Paris, 1969) p. 45.
[2] Quoted by Peter Raina in *Władysław Gomułka* (London, 1969) p. 136.
[3] Ibid., p. 145.   [4] *Kultura* (Paris), nos. 1–2, 1960, p. 169.

colleagues took no chances in getting Iwaszkiewicz elected as the new President and well before the Writers' Congress various forms of pressure were applied against individual writers to toe the line. With the flexible Iwaszkiewicz back in the saddle, both Kruczkowski and Putrament (from 1964 also a member of the Central Committee of the PUWP) were voted back on the Executive Board. In spite of its tactical victory, the party was still not in a very strong position. Żółkiewski's speech advocating Socialist Realism failed to create any response from the writers. Nevertheless, the main aim of the Cultural Department of the Central Committee was *to neutralise* the writers' political influence and to restore some measure of party control over the writers' organisation, and this limited aim was achieved.

The years between 1959 and 1963 were characterised by an uneasy truce between the authorities and the majority of the writers. No progress was made in converting writers to the much resented method of Socialist Realism, moreover the basic party organisation of the Warsaw branch of the PWA was still dominated 'by the Revisionist group' working at the integration of cultural values in the spirit of ideological coexistence.[1] This group, according to its adversaries, was moving towards an alliance with some non-party writers who were 'courting popularity in the West' with oppositionist gestures.[2] In other words, many Polish Communist writers were more interested in a dialogue with non-Marxist colleagues and more concerned with the propagation of cultural values than with furthering party policies with their pen. East–West cultural exchanges were lively in these years, and many Polish writers visited Western Europe. As for *émigré* writers, the years 1957 and 1958 had been a short period of grace and the works of Witold Gombrowicz, a writer of international renown, were reprinted in Poland but this concession was ended in 1959.

After years of discreet tactical manoeuvring in 1963 the party decided to take the initiative and launch an 'offensive'. The two most popular and interesting Warsaw cultural weeklies, *Nowa Kultura* and *Przegląd Kulturalny*, were discontinued[3] and a

---

[1] See Dziarnowska in *Literatura na rozdrożu*, p. 146.

[2] Ibid.

[3] Apparently at the instigation of a group of dogmatists and opportunists in the Executive Board of the PWA. Cf. Raina, op. cit., p. 110.

new paper, *Kultura*, started in their place. For years *Kultura*, which borrowed even its name from the best-known Polish *émigré* review in Paris, was boycotted by most Warsaw writers who saw the establishment of this paper as a kind of provocation, an attempt to break up the solidarity of Communist and non-Communist writers on basic cultural issues.[1] In the early summer of 1963 the party called a plenum to discuss the intelligentsia's disorientation and its lack of support for the policy of the party. Gomułka, speaking at this (the XIII) Plenum stressed the great importance of culture and literature and reprimanded Polish writers for their 'escape from themes connected with the construction of socialism', for their pessimism and lack of engagement 'on the side of socialism'.[2] He put forward the view that in Poland revisionism was a much greater danger than dogmatism.

Gomułka's speech at the XIII Plenum, especially that part dealing with literature, showed the First Secretary's total lack of comprehension of the mood of the literary community. His speech reads in parts like a slightly rehashed version of a speech from 1948; it demands affirmation of the post-1956 course by writers who are either ironical about the achievements of the Gomułka régime or increasingly irritated by and critical of its economic policies and fumbling inefficiency. Thereafter the rift between the PUWP leadership and the intellectuals widened. Until 1959 both Gomułka and Cyrankiewicz repeatedly met delegations of leading Polish writers, and even if they disagreed on certain questions, there was at least an opportunity of person-to-person contacts. These contacts became increasingly rare after 1959; moreover, those people like Putrament or Iwaszkiewicz who as officials of the PWA were still in a position to represent the writers' views *vis-à-vis* the political leadership would neither press the writers' demands nor defend their interests. Consequently, the top party bureaucracy became misinformed about the real situation in literary life and automatically began to impute hostile political motives to any criticism of the régime coming from the writers. In the mid-

[1] The editors of the Warsaw *Kultura* were rumoured to maintain close contacts with the so-called Partisan faction of the PUWP.
[2] Władysław Gomułka, *O aktualnych problemach ideologicznej pracy partii* (Warsaw, 1963) p. 53.

sixties Gomułka and Kliszko, instead of treating the PWA as a democratic socialist interest-group with specific interests, began to regard the more outspoken writers as 'the enemy within', as a bunch of disorientated petty-bourgeois intellectuals ready to sacrifice Polish national interests to 'the imperialists'.

IN OPEN CONFLICT WITH THE PARTY, 1964-8

Yet the fact that some of the more distinguished members of the Writers' Association were unhappy with the party's cultural policy was not entirely lost on the leadership of the PUWP. The writers' dissatisfaction was manifested by the 'Letter of the 34' sent to Cyrankiewicz on 14 March 1964. In this letter thirty-four well-known writers and scholars, amongst them Andrzejewski, Słonimski, Tatarkiewicz, Kotarbiński, Infeld and Krzyżanowski, protested against the growing restrictions on book publication,[1] and the stiffening of censorship and demanded 'a change in Polish cultural policy in the spirit of the rights guaranteed by the constitution of the Polish State'.[2] The text of this letter reached the West soon after Cyrankiewicz received it, and thanks to the publicity given it by the Western press and by radio stations, it could not be hushed up by the authorities. This illustrates the way in which the Western media may be utilised by a group to articulate its own demands. Signatories of the letter were pressed to revoke their signatures but only less than a third did so. The protest of the Thirty-Four was publicly supported by the widely respected author Maria Dąbrowska, who at a meeting of the Warsaw writers urged the re-establishment of the freedom of the press in Poland.[3]

The writers' protest prompted Gomułka to address the next (Fourteenth) Congress of the PWA held in September 1964 in Lublin. There was little new in his speech, but its tone was somewhat less hostile and it contained an appeal to the writers 'to help socialism' rather than threats to those who would go

---

[1] While in 1960 there were 7,305 titles published (in it 1,451 titles of *belles-lettres*), in 1964, for 8,260 book titles, there were only 1,149 titles of fiction, poetry and criticism. There was a corresponding reduction in the size of editions as well. Cf. *Rocznik statystyczny 1966* (GUS, Warsaw) 1966.
[2] Quotes Hans Roos in his *A History of Modern Poland* (London, 1966) p. 288.   [3] Raina, op cit., p. 112.

on ignoring the demands of the party. This was Gomułka's last personal intervention in the tug-of-war lasting from 1964 to March 1968 which witnessed a growing bitterness in the conflict between the political leadership and the Warsaw branch of the PWA. In May 1965 the Warsaw branch passed a resolution, demanding among other things the abolition of preventive censorship and of the Concise Penal Code adopted in 1946. The latter demand was almost certainly the writers' reaction to the Wańkowicz affair. Melchior Wańkowicz, a popular elderly writer who had lived in the West for a long time, was arrested and given a three-year sentence (subsequently commuted) on the strength of some critical remarks made in a *private letter* to his family in the United States. His arrest greatly shocked the literary community, who believed that such trials belonged to the Stalinist past. Wańkowicz did not go to prison, though two less well-known young Marxist intellectuals, Jacek Kuroń and Karol Modzelewski, were sent to jail. They were condemned for their 'Open Letter', which provided a theoretical criticism of the Gomułka régime and contained recommendations for political action to remodel the State on a socialist basis.

The restrictive and unimaginative cultural policy of the Gomułka régime from 1963 onwards reflected, on the one hand, the anxiety of the political élite about Poland's economic difficulties and their determination *not* to embark on a policy of radical economic reform, while it was, on the other hand, the expression of the increased strength of the 'Partisans' headed by Mieczysław Moczar. The 'Partisans' surfaced as a group in the early sixties; their platform consisted of a mixture of nationalism and anti-liberalism. Moczar, who became Minister of Internal Affairs at the end of 1964, was well aware of the significance of the intellectuals in shaping public opinion and he tried to win some writers and distinguished scholars over to his side. Most writers however, and Marxist Revisionists in particular, were suspicious of Moczar's hard-line methods and basic anti-intellectualism. This is not surprising bearing in mind the 'Partisans' aims, which, besides the elimination of centrists and 'internationalists' within the party leadership, included the eradication of all centres of independent opinion or potential opposition in Poland. The Warsaw branch of the PWA was certainly one of these centres.

The conflict between the Writers' Association and the Cultural Department of the Central Committee was however to some extent independent of Moczar's intrigues, for it concerned the rights of writers who belonged to the PUWP. Since many members of the basic party organisation of the Warsaw branch (amongst them such writers as Newerly, Stryjkowski and Konwicki) supported the letter of the thirty-four intellectuals, the Warsaw Party Committee and the Cultural Department of the CC started investigations into this matter and was even considering the explusion of all the 'oppositionists' from the PUWP.[1] There were however still some advocates of 'unity' and the expulsions never took place. The last time when party discipline was successfully imposed upon the party-member writers was in December 1965 at the Writers' Congress in Cracow. Here the Warsaw delegates wanted to propose a list of candidates for the new Executive Board which included the names of some leading 'oppositionists'. Shocked by such an open defiance of the 'official list', Starewicz called a special meeting of the writers' party organisations; some sympathetic non-Communists were also invited to the meeting and denounced the Warsaw writers as enemies of socialism. A compromise list was agreed upon: Iwaszkiewicz was duly re-elected, while Putrament, Centkiewicz and Międzyrzecki were elected Vice-Presidents. Of these three only Międzyrzecki enjoyed the complete confidence of the Warsaw group; after March 1968 even he was ousted from his post.

Less than a year after the Cracow Congress Leszek Kołakowski, Professor of Philosophy at Warsaw University and a member of the PWA, made a speech at a student meeting in which he drew up the balance sheet of the first decade of Gomułka's rule. Kołakowski's speech, deploring 'repressions, the lack of democracy, the régime's intolerance of opposition and the bureaucratic political system',[2] was immediately reported to Moczar and Kliszko. As a result of this speech, Kołakowski was expelled from the party without any consultation with his local party organisation. For many intellectuals Kołakowski was a symbol of 'non-institutional Marxism' and his expulsion was seen by them as a violation of party

---

[1] Dziarnowska in *Literatura na rozdrożu*, p. 151.
[2] Raina, op. cit., p. 129.

democracy and an act of serious implications. Twenty-two party member writers signed a protest against Kołakowski's expulsion[1] – the signatories included such internationally known writers as Newerly, Stryjkowski, Bocheński and Konwicki; Kazimierz Brandys joined the protesters later. The reaction of the party bureaucracy was predictable: Kliszko and Strzelecki formed special 'verification' committees and each writer was individually interviewed and interrogated by these committees. By mid-1967 sixteen of these non-conformist writers had been expelled from the party, though some of them, like the veteran Communist Igor Newerly, handed in their party cards as a sign of protest.

These developments caused considerable anxiety amongst the top party leadership; not only the dissolution of the basic party organisation of the Warsaw branch but the total dissolution of the PWA was contemplated both before and after March 1968.[2] This has happened in other Communist countries: in 1957 the Hungarian, in 1969 the Czech Writers' Association were suppressed. If in the end the PUWP did not dissolve the Writers' Association, this was due to several factors; in the anti-intellectual atmosphere of post-March Poland a combination of purges, blacklistings and denunciations by insignificant 'loyal' writers produced the desired effect and terminated the political role of the organisation.

The long conflict between the writers and the ruling political bureaucracy culminated in late February 1968. The clash was provoked by the official ban on the Warsaw production of Mickiewicz's famous play, *The Forefathers Eve* (*Dziady*). Mickiewicz's drama, which is a Polish classic, contains a few strongly anti-Tsarist and anti-authoritarian passages which were demonstratively applauded by a mainly youthful audience. This incensed Gomułka, who, according to at least one report, was personally responsible for the ban on Dejmek's production of *Dziady*. His arbitrary and politically clumsy decision provoked sporadic demonstrations amongst the students of Warsaw University and soon afterwards it provoked the indignation of the Warsaw writers. An Extraordinary Plenary Meeting was called for the Warsaw branch of the PWA and it took place on

[1] Ibid., p. 130.
[2] Roman Karst in *Na Antenie*, nos. 73–4, vii, Kwiecień-maj 1969, p. 35.

29 February. The atmosphere was tense, the discussion emotional and excited. The case of *Dziady* served to some extent as a pretext to discuss and condemn the entire cultural policy of the régime of which the ban was a particularly crude manifestation. All the pent-up grievances and professional frustrations were aired at the meeting, sometimes in a strikingly outspoken manner – censorship, rigid party control of culture, the falsification of history and the application of police methods against writers were attacked and deplored. The speakers, who included Słonimski, Jasienica, Kisielewski, Andrzejewski and Leszek Kołakowski, pointed out the discrepancies in the party's cultural policy, and condemned the irrational, primitive and anti-cultural aspects of this policy. Kisielewski thundered against the 'dictatorship of the numbskulls'. Putrament tried to calm down his excited colleagues and appealed for caution, but the meeting ignored his warnings and adopted with a large majority a resolution proposed by the critic Andrzej Kijowski – a strong protest against the government's ban on *Dziady*.[1] The Extraordinary Plenary Meeting was followed a few days later by a large-scale police action against the Warsaw students leading to the so-called 'March events' (protest meetings, sit-ins and peaceful student demonstrations) and this proximity in time has led many commentators to point to its role as a catalyst.[2] Some weeks later Gomułka made a rather unusual political speech in which he denounced by name some writers as dangerous political opponents, representing 'Revisionists and Zionist' forces behind the March demonstrations. In other words he accused the Warsaw writers of trying to set up an 'oppositionist centre' – a move which no hegemonistic party could tolerate.[3]

After March 1968 the Warsaw branch of the PWA found itself in a crossfire of ideological attacks and administrative restrictions. Local party secretaries denounced Kisielewski and Słonimski as 'imperialist agents' (Gierek) and told their audience that it was the party, not the writers, who were now

[1] The figures were 221 out of 356 votes for the so-called 'Kijowski resolution'. Quoted by Kossak in *Literatura na rozdrożu*, p. 84.

[2] Cf. 'Pisarze-polityka-kultura', in *Trybuna Ludu*, 27 March 1968.

[3] This is how Putrament characterised the Feb. meeting at another writers' meeting held in Warsaw in Dec. 1969. Quoted in *Litery*, no. 2, 1969.

'the conscience of the nation.'[1] The Cultural Department of the CC blacklisted eighteen authors who spoke at the February meeting of the Warsaw branch; in some cases the ban on their publications lasted for well over two years. Międzyrzecki was forced to resign as editor of the review *Poezja*; the same fate befell Adam Tarn, editor of *Dialog*, who left Poland soon afterwards. Some writers, deprived of their livelihood, unable to get grants or a loan from the Writers' Association, emigrated to Israel (Słucki, Wygodzki, Roman Karst). Others were placed under constant police 'surveillance' and were unable to move about town unescorted.[2] Putrament was given full powers to deal with the Warsaw branch of the PWA without any restraint and he managed to organise the Bydgoszcz Congress, probably the most depressing event of Polish literary life since Szczecin.[3] The conflict between the party and the writers came full circle – but from fruitful engagement to passive submission.

It is interesting to compare the writers' situation in 1956 and in 1968. In 1956 they enjoyed the support of the great majority of Poles and in a sense they were sailing on the waves of popular support. In 1968 they were isolated, supported only by the students and by the more enlightened part of the intelligentsia. While the bulk of the political bureaucracy reacted to the student–writer movement with undisguised hostility, the attitude of the workers could be best described as apathetic. This apathy, according to Zygmunt Bauman,[4] was due to the immaturity and lack of clear political aims of the working class, the majority of which had only recently left rural areas and culturally still belonged to the peasantry. This new working class would not support any kind of piecemeal reform which would not bring about sizeable improvements in the workers' living standards. Also it must be added that the ban on *Dziady* did not create any special indignation in the ranks of the work-

[1] C. Domagała, quoted in *Gazeta Krakowska*, 25 March 1968.

[2] Cf. Roman Karst in *Na Antenie*, nos. 73–4, Rok vii, p. 39.

[3] The delegates to the Bydgoszcz Congress were unrepresentative of the literary community and the pre-congress meetings were, on the whole, boycotted by the more militant writers. At the congress the statutes were amended and the rights of the Executive Board were increased. All the important committees of the PWA were filled by men whose political reliability was beyond question.

[4] *The Second Generation's Socialism* (Mimeograph paper, 1969).

ers; it was a cultural problem beyond the daily interests and practical preoccupations of manual workers, most of whom were simply bewildered and uninterested in the whole affair.

By early 1970 the cultural 'freeze' began to lose its ferocity and most 'oppositionist' writers were, within certain limits, allowed to publish again. This slow normalisation was not upset even by the workers' riots in December 1970 which erupted in several Baltic cities as a consequence of the steep price increases announced by the authorities as a preliminary to economic reform.

The end of the Gomułka régime did not bring any immediate change in cultural affairs. For many months after Gomułka's fall, Edward Gierek, his successor, was too preoccupied with placating the dissatisfied workers and purging the administration of people blamed for the riots to pay much attention to the creative intelligentsia. Gierek's programme included the promise of a continuous 'dialogue with society' which was widely interpreted as invitation to some prudent, but more outspoken, criticism. The scope of this criticism was however circumscribed from the beginning: while the technical intelligentsia was wooed and encouraged to express its opinion more freely, 'the only people for whom the official nod of encouragement has been a little cool were the writers and intellectuals'.[1] In other words, while the ruling bureaucracy, which in early 1971 included as many potential hard-liners as pragmatic reformists, realised the unavoidability of an economic reform, there was no question of making political concessions to those intellectuals who challenged the wisdom of the party's cultural policy in such a forceful fashion in 1968. The Polish Writers' Association was left in Putrament's hands, and no personal changes took place as a result of the change at the top. Nevertheless, if Gierek's present policy of limited reform continues without any serious setbacks for some time, a cautious redressing of the balance can be expected within the Polish Writers' Association between apologists for and critics of the social–political system. In other words, it is not impossible that as in the past, so in the future, the Polish Writers' Association will again be able to play a more active role as a pressure-group and a mouthpiece of the Polish creative intelligentsia.

[1] Richard Davy in *The Times*, 25 May 1971, p. 12.

CHAPTER FIVE

The Technical Intelligentsia

By George Kolankiewicz

In the last chapter we considered the writers and their association as an example of the role and significance of the cultural intelligentsia in People's Poland. The technical intelligentsia, though clearly of more recent origin, is a no less important representative of the intelligentsia in Polish society. As a general guideline, we shall limit the term 'technical' to the twenty-three technical occupations with the title of 'engineer', employed in the state economy.[1] We have omitted economists, medical and health workers, pure scientists and other such groups, not because we believe that they belong in the ranks of the cultural intelligentsia, but simply because they either function outside of the industrial management sector (for example, doctors and pure scientists) or because they warrant attention of a more particular and specialist kind (e.g. economists).

Although we have considered the meaning of the word 'intelligentsia' in chapter 4, it is worth emphasising that the term *inteligencja*, in Polish, is very heavily loaded with both political and social values. The prewar intelligentsia included not only the intellectual children of an 'aristocratic' culture[2] but also a strong middle class, or bourgeoisie. It was the former group which gave the intelligentsia its basically humanistic orientations, its occupational aspirations and its general life-style, and the latter which utilised these features to create class barriers.[3]

With the economic, political and social changes brought

[1] Spis Kadrowy, *Pracownicy z wykształceniem wyższym, No. 2, Zatrudnienie, 1968* (Warsaw, 1969) pp. 2–8.

[2] J. J. Wiatr, 'Inteligencja w Polsce Ludowej', in *Przemiany społeczne w Polsce Ludowej* (Warsaw, 1965) p. 447.

[3] The formation of the 'Intelligentsia Ghetto' is described by J. Chałasiński in *Społeczna genealogia inteligencji polskiej* (Poznań, 1946).

about by the advent of the People's Democracy in Poland, the term intelligentsia was put to different uses and so acquired a more neutral meaning. For Szczepański, 'mental work' became the distinguishing feature of the intelligentsia's socio-occupational activity. This definition was further sub-divided into three major sociological categories: (*a*) cultural creativity in the widest sense; (*b*) the organisation and direction of work; (*c*) the resolution of practical problems requiring theoretical knowledge.[1]

For reasons which will become more obvious as we progress, it is necessary to include into the category of technical intelligentsia persons who lack formal higher education, but compensate for this by holding high political or managerial power in industry. In postwar Poland the parallel goals of the political consolidation of the Communist Party and intensive industrialisation of a relatively underdeveloped country meant that persons involved in each of these tasks overlapped, and only recently has the distinction become more evident. Polish sociologists are well aware of the fact that formal higher education is now the most important criterion for the admission of persons into the socialist intelligentsia. This was by no means always the case, and many persons who held high positions in the organisation and direction of work were not formally qualified to do so, particularly prior to 1956. We shall, therefore, consider in our study the engineers not only in their technological role but also in their organisational and managerial role, and see how the balance between the two reflected political, social and economic development in Polish society.

A foretaste of what we wish to discuss is provided in Szczepański's observation concerning the modern technical intelligentsia in Poland.

[1] J. Szczepański, 'Struktura inteligencji w Polsce', in *Kultura i Społeczeństwo* (Warsaw, 1960) nos. 1–2, pp. 38–42. More recent formulations have grown out of empirical research into social differentiation, and produced the following breakdown of the intelligentsia. (i) Technical intelligentsia-engineers in various fields. (ii) Managers and directors of enterprises, regional administrators and those in management functions within social and political organisations. (iii) Legal and economic intelligentsia. (iv) Teachers and school inspectors. (v) Medical intelligentsia. (vi) Humanistic intelligentsia. (vii) Other intelligentsia with higher education. See K. Słomczyński and W. Wesołowski, 'Próby reprezentacyjne i kategorie społeczno-zawodowe', in *Zróżnicowanie społeczne* (Warsaw, 1970) p. 68.

They [the technical intelligentsia] have become an influential pressure group, with their own ideas of the industrial society, the organisation of enterprises, and the organisation of work, derived from the principles of technological efficiency. They feel restricted by bureaucratic and 'unrealistic' rules imposed on them by the administrative apparatus of the economy, and they voice their discontent in both the professional press and during their organisational conferences and congresses. Their significance in the economy is steadily increasing. They have an ideology of scientific and technological progress. . . .[1]

The principle of technological efficiency was expressed under many guises and in terms of many slogans. We for our part shall focus upon two common expressions of this principle which are conveyed in the ideas (and sometimes demands) of 'the right man for the right job' (*właściwy człowiek na właściwym miejscu*) and its variation, that all holders of positions should possess 'sufficient, as well as the appropriate qualifications' for the post.[2] Plainly the crux of the problem is that there is no independent scale for judging such terms as 'right', 'sufficient' and 'appropriate', particularly in socialist societies where the political imperative is so closely interwoven with the economic. The definition which is eventually accepted provides an expression of the order of priority between political and other demands as well as indicating the relative power of the groups involved in making these demands.

Because of its comparative unimportance in prewar Poland, a discussion of the technical intelligentsia during the interwar period may be limited to some brief remarks about the social origins, social status and economic situation of the engineer.

PREWAR ENGINEER TO POSTWAR PEOPLE'S INTELLIGENTSIA

According to the 1921 census there were in Poland at that time 5,178 registered engineers, who were included in that group

[1] J. Szczepański, *Polish Society* (New York, 1969) pp. 117–18.
[2] Z. Kruszyński, 'Właściwi ludzie na właściwym miejscu', in *Życie Gospodarcze*, no. 47, 1958.

called the 'higher intelligentsia proper', along with representatives of the free professions.[1] Technical studies were lengthy and extremely expensive and entry was consequently restricted primarily to those from well-to-do families. Only 7·7 per cent of students of engineering in 1934–5 were of working-class origins. The main targets of those aiming for upward social mobility from the lower manual and non-manual strata were the lower reaches of the teaching and legal professions. Medicine and engineering were the preserve of those with both high social status and high income.

Between the years 1918 and 1939 the centres for higher education produced a total of over 10,000 engineering graduates, and by the outbreak of war there were between 13,000 and 14,000 engineers in Poland.[2] Despite the fact that the first Polish technical university had been opened as far back as 1818, there were in 1938 still only three higher technical institutions in Poland which turned out, for example, 667 graduates in 1937–8.[3]

War losses and emigration took their toll and it has been estimated that only about 7,000 of the prewar engineers were left to face the task of reconstruction after 1944. The government realised that the losses had to be made good at any cost and by 1950 the nine technical schools which existed before 1945 had been increased to twenty. Until 1950, of the 34,000 or so graduates with higher education, over 20 per cent were technologists, and provided the first additions to the stock of engineering cadres.[4]

The quality of these cadres, however, left much to be desired, not simply because of the lack of teaching personnel and poor material conditions, but also because of the criteria of selection. A significant effort was made by the youth and party organisations to send young as well as experienced workers to the technical colleges for periods of two years' intensive education and then return them to the factories as management personnel.

[1] J. Żarnowski, *Struktura społeczna inteligencji w Polsce w Latach 1918–1939* (Warsaw, 1964) p. 281–6.

[2] Ibid., p. 281.

[3] J. Hoser, *Zawód i praca inżyniera* (Warsaw, 1970) p. 8.

[4] A. Buttler, *Wybrane dane statystyczne o szkolnictwie wyższym w Polsce Ludowej*, Warsaw, April 1969. Unpublished MS., Table 10.

But many of the young workers who were advanced by the party found great difficulty in adapting to the essentially traditional style of learning.[1]

Of all the various educational institutions set up in postwar Poland in the effort to create a people's intelligentsia, the technical colleges for workers best reflected the priorities of the party and government in the years of reconstruction and political stabilisation. These technical colleges, set up in 1945–6 initially to satisfy the requirements of heavy industry, were aimed at those skilled middle-aged workers who were also politically active and eager to learn. In the late forties they fulfilled the need for a body of politically reliable managers at all levels. Later when the situation in the country had become economically and politically more stable these colleges turned to produce more foremen and technical specialists.

The graduates of these colleges, because they lacked formal higher education, were not members of the intelligentsia proper. They were expected to join the ranks of the intelligentsia whilst remaining ideologically aligned, as it were, on the side of the working class. The ways in which the superior authorities used these and other graduates made their position still more difficult. They were variously received by the factories they were sent to, according to whether the latter's needs were political or technical. It was intended that they should break up informal 'power structures' within these factories. Cadres which had graduated from the technical colleges were the 'new brooms which swept clean' and it was not unusual that these very idealistic activists not only upset the local management but the local party organisation as well.[2]

In due course the emphasis upon party membership before entering and on leaving the technical colleges diminished and this indicated that the role of such training was now becoming more technical rather than political. Political control of the work situation and the work forces was being superseded by the necessity for a tighter organisation of the technological process. Table 28, showing the fall of party membership in a selected

[1] J. Chałasiński, *Przeszłość i przyszłość inteligencji polskiej* (Wrocław, 1958) p. 18.

[2] S. Kowalewska, *Przysposobienie do pracy w przemyśle* (Warsaw, 1966) pp. 121–6.

technical school, illustrates this change in need.[1] Many of the graduates of such technical colleges and other special schools reached the highest levels in enterprise management, even becoming directors.[2]

TABLE 28. GROWTH IN THE NUMBER OF PARTY MEMBERS IN A SELECTED TECHNICAL SCHOOL

Year	Total	Joined party		
		Before Technikum (per cent)	*During Technikum (per cent)*	*Members on graduating (per cent)*
1946–7	239	61·1	37·0	98·1
1948	228	77·6	10·0	87·6
1949	275	62·2	4·4	66·6
1950	266	51·5	13·5	65·0
1951	390	46·2	7·4	53·6
1952	335	43·8	20·2	64·0
1953	253	43·4	26·1	69·5
Total	1,986	53·8	15·2	69·0

During the immediate postwar period of reconstruction (1945–8), the top management posts were held by former directors and factory owners of the inter-war years. Resourcefulness and self-reliance were the main qualities required by managers in this period of industrial confusion and political uncertainty when the central planning office had only a co-ordinating function. During 1947–8 the government nationalised over 5,870 enterprises and there could be little doubt as to what the eventual outcome would be of the government's

[1] S. Kowalewska, 'Technikum i jego słuchacze', in *Wykształcenie a pozycja społeczna inteligencji*, ed. J. Szczepański, vol. 1 (Łódź, 1959) p. 227, Table 29.

[2] We discovered relatively little information dealing with the enterprise directors in the immediate postwar period. It is only after 1956 that information dealing with this section of the industrial élite became more readily available. Kowalewski's study did show however that whereas amongst the 1949 graduates of the *technikum* 76 per cent became managers and only 2 per cent foremen, in 1955 the corresponding figures were 19·8 per cent and 63·9 per cent respectively. See Z. Kowalewski, 'Problemy nowej inteligencji (absolwenci technikum dla robotników), in *Wykształcenie . . .*, p. 268, Table 40.

policy in the management and control of industry. Furthermore, whereas the promotion of the manual workers had been restricted until 1948 to the lower management positions of industrial administration, by 1949 the situation was quite radically changed. Figures available for this period show that a very considerable drop in educational level accompanied this industrial mobility of personnel.

The educational level of directors dropped, so that whereas in one sample in 1945 84 per cent of directors had higher education of some sort, by 1949 the figure was 36 per cent. As Table 1 in Appendix 3 shows, party membership became increasingly a prerequisite of top management as also did the 'correct' social origin (only 21 per cent of the directors were of non-manual origin by 1949).[1] The old cadres of directors were replaced by the 'promoted workers' trained at special directors' schools and the technical colleges. The former directors in turn were transferred away from active management to the newly created branch and ministerial apparatus, where '. . . removed from the working class they can serve the national economy with their qualifications and experience'.[2] This transfer of highly qualified specialists and experienced managers may have been politically expedient but it was to have both objective economic consequences for the production efforts of factories and have effects on the status of 'production management' in general, particularly for those young specialists then being trained at the polytechnics and schools of engineering.

POLITICAL STABILISATION AND THE
WORKER-DIRECTOR

The intensification of the class-struggle during the years 1949–1952 was nowhere more evident than in the policy of the party

[1] H. Najduchowska, 'Dyrektorzy przedsiębiorstw przemysłowych', in *Przemysł i społeczeństwo w Polsce Ludowej*, ed. J. Szczepański (Warsaw, 1969) pp. 82–7, and below, Appendix 3, Tables 1, 2, 3.

[2] H. Najduchowska, 'Dyrektorzy . . .', p. 84. It is possible that it was not simply a question of political expediency that the persons who might best provide a focus of opposition to the State's industrial and political policy were transferred to where they could have least influence. A system of centralised planning and management requires experts to be at the centre where the decisions are taken.

towards management personnel in industry. For a time party membership and social origin almost completely replaced other criteria for selection and appointments such as formal education and management experience. It was during this period that the State went part of the way towards creating a new political class and thus sowed the seeds of conflict in the years to come. For it gave power to a group of people whose claims to élite membership were based upon values such as 'political correctness' and 'proper social origins'. Industrial management became synonymous with obedience to the party.

Between 1949 and 1952 the percentage of directors with higher education fell and Najduchowska's sample showed that only 20 per cent of enterprise directors had higher education of any sort. Party membership had become more or less compulsory for directors of industrial enterprises, and by 1952 91 per cent of the above sample were party members and over 70 per cent of these directors claimed working-class or peasant social origins.[1] That many of the promoted directors survived the upheavals of 1956 and had run 'profitable' enterprises does suggest that what they may have lacked in education they made up for by their efforts and the intensity of their commitment.

The resolution of the Council of Ministers (12 May 1950) foresaw, in principle at least, the gradual concentration of decisions concerning technical, industrial and financial planning being put in the hands of the director. With some exceptions and depending upon the complexity of their industrial tasks, the promoted managers were more capable of fulfilling their political functions than their economic ones, and indeed this was not contrary to the role defined for them by the State. Directors were not to be concerned with the cost of production but were to subordinate themselves to the party organisation and leave the task of 'operational management' to the central administration.

It is to this period that we can trace a particular stereotype of management activity, which consisted of such diverse features as cautiousness in decision-making, a keen nose for detecting

---

[1] H. Najduchowska, 'Dyrektorzy . . .', pp. 82–7. Appendix 3 (below), Tables 1, 2, 4. There were some extremely amusing examples of the haphazardness of appointment to responsible management positions. Cf. A. Gutowski, 'Konkurs dyrektorów', in *Polityka*, 14 Oct. 1967.

changes in the political atmosphere and economic irrationality. This may well have been due to the lack of qualifications on the part of the enterprise directors and to the fact that their appointments were primarily political rather than professional, but it was not the whole picture. The proclamation of the principle of 'one-man responsibility of the enterprise director' had been accompanied by the increased use of criminal proceedings against erring directors. In this period of 'Stalinist errors and distortions', the task of protecting the social wealth and executing orders left the director subject to constant suspicion. Complaints to the militia levelled at the director frequently led to his prosecution and since the director was responsible for everything which happened in his factory it was usually possible to find some charge that could be substantiated. The charges might be brought by someone who wished to have the director's job,[1] or the director might be held responsible for some accident which it was completely beyond his power to prevent.[2]

Insecurity and political intrigue, which had little to do with industrial management and engineering, were major causes of the flight of sections of the technical intelligentsia from the provinces and direct production to the cities and to the comparative safety of design offices and ministries.

> This [process of flight] stripped the factories of those people who could have been a basis of support for the young technical cadres and created further disincentives for working in the provinces as well as instilling a tendency amongst the youth to avoid responsibility.[3]

Increasingly, though, the young technical intelligentsia trained in People's Poland were finding themselves on the labour

[1] I. Krzenek, 'Z życia inżyniera', in *Pamiętniki Inżynierów* (Warsaw, 1966) p. 173.

[2] J. Olszewski, 'Pamiętniki inżyniera', in *Pamiętniki . . .*, p. 591.

[3] J. Tymowski, 'O właściwą pozycję polskiej inteligencji technicznej', in *Polityka*, 2 March 1957. Borucki's study showed that prewar engineers did not rise in the management hierarchy during a period which witnessed the heaviest capital investment and industrialisation in Poland's history (i.e. 1949–53). Party membership also did not make a significant difference as to whether such an engineer was promoted though it did guard against demotion. A. Borucki, *Kariery zawodowe i postawy społeczne inteligencji w PRL 1945–1959* (Warsaw, 1967) pp. 91–6.

market, and whereas we could understand the party's lack of confidence in the prewar technical intelligentsia, there could be no such justification in the case of the young engineers. In 1951 the Polytechnics produced 4,759 graduates and well over 50 per cent of these were of working-class or peasant origin.[1] The young engineers were compulsorily posted to factories all over the country and paid wages which were often lower than those of manual workers. This gave rise to conflict and complaint and encouraged the young graduates to leave industry and management of production as soon as they could. This in turn meant that there were factories in the provinces which did not have a single engineer or technician.[2] As J. Tymowski, chairman of the Association of Engineers and Technicians noted in 1957, 'There occurred a paradoxical situation wherein as the number of engineering graduates grew so the percentage of management posts held by engineers decreased.'[3] These newly qualified cadres presented a threat to their immediate superiors, who had neither the qualifications nor the ability to fulfil many of their tasks. By 1954, at the Second Party Congress, one of the causes of the failure of the six-year plan was attributed to the lack of skills on the part of those entrusted with the plan's execution. Pressure had already been exerted as early as the VI and VII Plena in 1952 for the *apparat* to raise the level of their qualifications.

This young technical intelligentsia, free from the stigma of being prewar intelligentsia and frequently belonging to the party,[4] voiced much of the criticism against the distortions of

[1] Figures supplied by the *Międzyuczelniany zakład badań nad szkolnictwem wyższym* (Warsaw, 1969).

[2] In one study, out of a total of 1,488 employees in an enterprise concerned with the repair of railway rolling stock, there were only two engineers in 1950. Quoted in C. Parachatko, 'Awans zawodowy personelu inżynieryjno-technicznego ZNTK "Oleśnica" w Oleśnicy', in *Socjologiczne problemy przemysłu i klasy robotniczej No. 9* (Warsaw, 1969) p. 59.

[3] J. Tymowski, 'O właściwą . . .'.

[4] There is relatively little data available about party membership amongst technical and engineering personnel prior to 1960, though a study of the Academy of Mining and Smelting showed that whereas pre-1958 graduates had higher party membership (attributed to their higher average age) they were more passive in their membership than the post-1958 graduates. In J. Bugiel, *Adaptacja i pozycja społeczno-zawodowa wychowanków AGH w przemyśle* (Kraków, 1970) p. 57.

the preceding three or four years. One engineer, who received his degree in electrical engineering in 1951, wrote in his memoirs that he had had the distinct impression that the management did not quite know what to do with its newly acquired cadres, and that by 1953, as a party member, he and some of his young colleagues had been the subject of quite undisguised malice from the older members.

> During the meeting [of the party] one of the speakers attacked the young engineers in an insulting manner . . . referring sarcastically to their titles as engineers . . . I criticised this attempt to make a clan of the engineers by trying to isolate them. I also took the opportunity to point out the shortcomings of the factory and ways to remedy them. I remember quite clearly that I finished my speech with the following words: 'we need firstly, organisation, secondly, organisation, and thirdly, organisation'.[1]

Whereas the older members of the technical intelligentsia could retreat from the irrationality and conflict characterising the workings of many of the industrial sectors, avenues of escape were not immediately available to the younger members of the technical intelligentsia. They had to serve their time in the factories and posts to which they had been sent, and though they might eventually gravitate away from production to non-production jobs this was not before they had provided some alternative 'professional' approach to management and the solution of industrial problems. In other words there was now arising within the ranks of the lower management and supervisory personnel a new breed of young graduates who were not slow to criticise the organisational, economic and technical shortcomings of their superiors. Before overt changes were noticeable amongst the cultural intelligentsia, the 'specialist *v.* practitioners'[2] conflict within the management of industry was well under way.

[1] Extract from J. Sowiński, 'Z notatnika inżyniera', in *Pamiętniki* . . ., p. 658.

[2] The term 'practitioners', from the Polish 'praktyków', denotes those who hold technical or management positions on the strength of their experience rather than their qualifications, the latter being the specialists.

REFORM 1954–6

June 1954

Tension amongst the management. There are rumours circulating that one of the inspectors is to become departmental manager. Two camps have sprung up. In one of these are to be found only Kazik and myself. Conflict . . . engineers contra practitioners, obviously they have separated themselves off from us. At last the bomb explodes! The chief engineer is Kazik . . . we are all amazed, not least the one promoted.[1]

The above extract from the memoirs of an engineer typifies the uncertainty which surrounded cadres policy after 1953. No one could be sure whether the criteria of the past few years were still dominant or whether change was on the way. Najduchowska shows that although between 1953 and 1955 the percentage of directors with higher education did not increase significantly, there was a slight drop in those who had completed only elementary education.[2]

It seems logical to suppose that pressure should come from below, where more and more qualified engineers were performing lower management and supervisory functions. The engineers and technical intelligentsia in general were becoming increasingly aware of their insignificant role on such representative bodies as local councils, trade unions and the Sejm. Bureaucratisation affected the engineers as much as other groups in society and many were promoted out of production into the middle administrative levels: 'In that structure, elements with initiative, capable of conceptual work did not find scope in the factories. Bureaucratic centralism took them upwards, leaving only executors below.'[3]

The atmosphere of criticism evoked a response from the party, and at the Second Congress of the PUWP in 1954 a statute was introduced which widened the role of the party

---

[1] S. Paczyński, 'Od startu do mety', in *Pamiętniki* . . ., p. 835.

[2] H. Najduchowska, 'Dyrektorzy . . .', Table 2, pp. 86–7. See below, Appendix 3, Table 5.

[3] One study showed that 20 per cent of all engineers at this time were in administration. The same sample in 1955 showed that whereas 36 per cent of the engineers had been born in large towns, 56 per cent finished secondary education in such towns, and 79 per cent finally found work there. 'W sprawie kadr o wysokich kwalifikacjach', in *Polityka*, 29 Sept. 1957.

organisation within the industrial enterprise and gave it control over the administration. A year later the character of the production meetings, which were the only forum of discussion of economic matters within the factory, was widened to examine problems concerning efficiency, productivity and profitability. As one observer noted, the prime feature of these meetings was the desire to demonstrate belief in the possibility of initiative being taken from below.[1] The initiative sought was that of the lower management and technological cadres, not that of the workers. Another reason for extending party control within industry was that of the increasingly apparent incompetence of many sections of the factory administration. The party effectively took over the day-to-day running of the factories, placing itself between the increasingly discontented workers and the equally frustrated lower management and technical intelligentsia. Despite the general liberalisation of party life, it still did not have the respect and authority amongst the young engineers that it might have desired. Amongst other faults they resented the 'double standards' and apparent lack of integrity of some party members.[2]

The party proved itself to be similarly inept and heavy-handed in using the powers which it had given itself and resorted to threats of sanctions against engineers, directors and other employees, if matters did not improve. Though such men readily accepted the hegemony of the party in political life they could not as easily accept party 'meddling' in industry and were particularly resentful of bad management practice on the part of those workers who had been promoted to positions of authority in the industrial administration. To put such matters right, the party early in 1955 was again calling not just for the better education of party activists but was also stressing that professionals, such as engineers and economists, should be absorbed into the party.[3]

[1] W. Morawski, 'Funkcje samorządu robotniczego w systemie zarządzania przemysłem', in *Przemysł* . . ., p. 244.

[2] Expressed in the memoirs of S. Grabowski, 'Wśród ludzi . . .', in *Pamiętniki*, p. 554. The political opportunism and 'double-think' demanded of those who wished to survive in the political arena of the past years, was contrary to the 'positivistic' *weltanschauung* of the engineer.

[3] H. Kozłowska, 'Uwagi o stylu pracy naszego aparatu partyjnego', in *Nowe Drogi*, no. 1, 1955, p. 72.

The party was not blind to the fact that the specialists were to be found in offices and not in production, sometimes fulfilling functions which had nothing in common with their formal training. Consequently they called upon the enterprises to employ more trained cadres.[1] We can here repeat that it was not in the immediate interests of the management in many of these factories to seek to employ more young engineers, as they would pose a threat to the position of the less qualified managers who were increasingly feeling the attack upon their positions. There was a conflict of interests between this group of the 'promoted' technical intelligentsia and those who stressed the wider, objective requirements for an efficient, industrialised economy. Implicit in this conflict was an attack upon the party, which had put many of the directors and managers in the positions which were being attacked. Under the pressure of this situation, the party relieved many worker-directors when politically reliable and better qualified replacements could be found and it ordered others 'back to school'.[2] Some of those directors who were sent back to study could not adapt. Others were formally very successful and confirmed their political success by obtaining higher education. There were also those who were 'relieved' and often returned to the manual jobs which they had not wanted to leave in the first place or were promoted 'out of sight'.[3]

In March 1956 the party journal *Nowe Drogi* printed an article which openly demanded more power for enterprise directors. It argued that the responsibility of the director should be accompanied by appropriate powers[4] and furthermore, since the socialist enterprise is a complex one, it must be made clear who is responsible for what in the factory. In April 1956, therefore, the Central Committee and Council of Ministers accepted a resolution concerning the '. . . widened rights of the directors of state industrial enterprises'.[5]

---

[1] 'Aktualne problemy zatrudnienia', in *Nowe Drogi*, no. 6, 1955, p. 7.

[2] J. Janicki, *Urzędnicy przemysłowi w strukturze społecznej Polski Ludowej* (Warsaw, 1963) p. 166.

[3] H. Krall, 'Optymista z urodzenia', in *Polityka*, 18 April 1964.

[4] 'Directors of industrial enterprises do not have in their hands sufficient rights to undertake operational decisions on matters concerning the factory.' J. Niedźwiecki, 'Dojrzała konieczność zwiększenia uprawnień dyrektorów przedsiębiorstw przemysłowych,' in *Nowe Drogi*, March 1956.

[5] This appeared to be pre-emptive action taken by the party on the path

The directors for their part were warned that they must encourage an atmosphere of discussion and criticism and that independence of the director and the enterprise went hand-in-hand with greater worker participation. We have seen in the chapter on the workers how the new directors and managers used the slogans and spirit of 'democratisation' to carry through organisational changes and to introduce greater efficiency into the enterprises. Opposition to the changes, however, came from those managers who identified themselves with the old system of centralised direction.[1]

The decision to give more powers to directors meant that the party organisation in the enterprise was to restrict its activities to political rather than to industrial matters.[2] The party was to concern itself with choosing better directors, and most urgently it had to give further education to those directors who were keen party men.

A second demand, in addition to that for greater power for the director in the enterprise, was for greater independence of the enterprise as a whole from the higher administrative and planning authorities. In this struggle, the enterprise management eventually found an ally in the workers' councils. As was pointed out in Chapter 3, when the workers' councils were first set up and formally acknowledged in November 1956, they were treated with suspicion by the management and were seen as a threat to the latter's new-found independence. With the passage of time and as the councils became increasingly dominated by the young technical intelligentsia, the management began to press the case for greater rights for the councils and utilised them as an additional weapon in their struggle against the central bureaucracy.[3]

towards democratisation as well as 'decentralisation'. *Dziennik Ustaw*, 9 April 1956. Details of the rights of the enterprise director.

[1] See Maurice Dobb, *Socialist Planning: Some Problems* (London, 1970): '. . . the centralized system will itself have bred attitudes and habits of work of its own together with a structure of relationships between administrative levels that may exercise a strongly conservative resistance to change and to the adoption and cultivation of new attitudes, relationships and methods.' P. 62.

[2] J. Niedźwiecki, 'Dojrzała konieczność . . .', p. 118.

[3] A. Małachowski, 'Jutro rad robotniczych', in *Przegląd Kulturalny*, no. 32, 1957.

Thus at this time the party was subject to pressure not just from the technical intelligentsia and professional associations, but also from within the ranks of the manual working class. Certain groups of manual workers (such as skilled men) and management within the factories were agreed that to achieve greater productivity they must free their enterprises from bureaucratic interference and unprofessional 'political' management. To this end they united to put forward professional engineers and managers of their own choosing. Engineers with higher qualifications and sometimes with prewar education were frequently approached at the desk jobs where they had been employed over the past ten years by delegations from workers' councils, authorised to offer them directors' posts in large production factories.[1] Others were promoted from within the factories' own staff and others still were obtained by means of interviews and advertisements.

'OCTOBER' AND THE FORMULATION OF THE DEMANDS OF THE TECHNICAL INTELLIGENTSIA

It is difficult to generalise, but it would appear that the technical intelligentsia, either managerial or non-managerial, did not take part in the disturbances in Poznań in June 1956.[2] However, October 1956 and the changes resulting from the advent of Gomułka had a profound and stimulating influence upon the technical intelligentsia within the factories. Various members of higher management and socio-political functionaries were removed from their posts and new persons spontaneously elected in their place. Many new people who had previously not been allowed access to, or had removed themselves voluntarily from, the management centres were now considered. The demand for 'verification' (i.e. the close scrutiny of all qualifications possessed by various management and administration personnel) became fashionable and was not confined to 'verification' of party membership. Discussion was particularly enlivened amongst the engineers and technical

---

[1] L. Krznek, 'Z życia inżyniera', in *Pamiętniki . . .*, pp. 186–7.

[2] See for example the memoirs of A. Zimowski, 'Pracowałem w "Stomilu"', in *Pamiętniki . . .*, pp. 924–1025, in which are described events in one of the Poznań factories during the day of 28 June 1956.

supervisory staff, who demanded the defence of their 'professional titles'. The branches of *Naczelna Organizacja Techniczna* (STO, The Supreme Technical Organisation), representing the technical intelligentsia, initiated a series of discussions which were to culminate in the third Congress of Engineers and Technicians in February 1957 in Warsaw.[1]

The STO was a body which drew together most of the technical professional associations and its declared goals were active participation in the building of socialism, the development of technology and the defence of the common interests of the engineering and technical professions.[2] The various demands of the technical intelligentsia were forcefully articulated at the 1957 STO Congress, and this signalled the beginning of a new period in the balance of power in Polish industrial life. The technical and engineering cadres demanded that

> ... the proper position of technicians in society should be returned to us, that there should be confidence shown in our expressed desire to *lead* the building of our fatherland in the direction of socialism. If our just demands are not recognised, then this shall be our last act of faith.[3]

These demands contained two principal themes. The first concerned the position of the technical intelligentsia in such matters as the proper tenure of positions and offices and the education of technical employees. The second related to the wider, more general organisation of the economy. According to Tymowski, then Chairman of the STO, the first set of questions was predominant. He maintained that the fundamental precondition for an improvement in the Polish economy was that its management should be entrusted to professionals, although he clearly realised that such demands would threaten the positions of many persons in high places, whose entrenched

[1] Z. Urych, 'Stary i starcia', in *Pamiętniki . . .*, p. 49. These memoirs describe what took place amongst the engineers in Nowa Huta.

[2] J. Hoser, *Zawód i praca*, p. 193. The STO prided itself on being the only organisation in all the socialist countries which did not have to dissociate itself from its prewar activities and be dissolved prior to reformation. Just as scientific and technical personnel had found it easiest to adapt to the new political system, so also was their organisation more 'neutral'.

[3] J. Tymowski, 'Inteligencja techniczna po III Kongresie', in *Polityka*, 23 April 1957. Most of the following discussion is drawn from this article.

interests would stand in the way of any changes. The question which concerns us here is not just the objective importance of educational qualifications in industrial management, but the methods and accomplishments of the technical intelligentsia in their role as a pressure group demanding such qualifications.

The government and party were prepared to acquiesce to many of the demands of the technical intelligentsia and they obviously treated these demands with some seriousness (as shown by the presence of Gomułka and Jaroszewicz at the Congress). However they were not prepared, or indeed able, to replace all the directors and managers who did not have the 'desired' formal qualifications. It was unthinkable that the party could remove its political control over industry, exercised formally by the party organisation within the factory and frequently informally through the person of the enterprise director. At about this time the STO had formulated and submitted to the Council of Ministers a project concerning the 'proper criteria of appointment to offices and positions'. The government passed a resolution which, though only referring to the machine tool industry, implicitly set the pattern for other industries. The resolution rejected the demands of the technicians' organisation. It exempted directors of factories and enterprises from the necessity of obtaining formal qualifications, arguing that they needed professional *and* political qualifications. It also gave the director the right to exempt from holding the necessary technical qualifications those who were currently in subordinate posts.

Tymowski, commenting upon this obvious rejection of the STO's demands, said that this would only have been justifiable if it was not possible to find among engineers the relatively small number of sufficiently politically reliable men to fill these positions adequately. Tymowski maintained, however, that there were 25,000 positions requiring engineers' qualifications and 80,000 requiring technicians' qualifications currently occupied by people without these qualifications. Amongst top management the situation had certainly improved and was in part due to the pressure from the younger technical intelligentsia. As Najduchowska has shown, between 1956 and 1958 the percentage of directors with higher education had increased from 38·0 per cent to 52·5 per cent, whereas the percentage of those with elementary education dropped from 14·3 per cent to 7·5 per cent.[1]

Throughout 1957 the controversy about qualifications continued. The chairman of the Association of Polish Mechanical Engineers and Technicians (SITMP) published an article in which he advocated first: stringent control over the professional-technical qualifications of directors and subordinate personnel in factories in heavy industry; second: the 'verification' of members in terms of their moral duties; and third: that 'in filling certain posts, the State authorities should primarily be guided by the criterion of professional qualifications [at the expense of political qualifications]'. There also appeared an article in the party daily newspaper, wherein the author of the above demands was accused of '*technocratyzm*'. He, it was said, did not have the right to stipulate what qualifications directors should have and furthermore it was argued that it was essential to apply criteria of selection more elastically and according to the particular attributes of the individual.[2]

[1] H. Najduchowska, 'Dyrektorzy . . .', Table 2, p. 94. See below, Appendix 3, Table 6. The limitations of Najduchowska's study were shown up by Tymowski when he produced figures for 1956–7, showing that in one 'important branch' of industry of 440 enterprises, only 40 directors had higher education, 120 secondary, 220 elementary and 60 incomplete elementary. J. Tymowski, 'O właściwą pozycję . . .', p. 1. In 1956 the Central Statistical Office (GUS) had carried out its own study into over 84,000 management posts at ten levels. Of the posts examined only 16 per cent of their incumbents had higher education, 49 per cent secondary and 35 per cent less than secondary. Of the directors, 15 per cent had higher education, whereas 32 per cent of chief engineers had only secondary education and 10 per cent only elementary. Thirty-five per cent of chief mechanics had less than secondary education, etc. All these facts showed that the demands of the technical intelligentsia were grounded in the reality, as they saw it, of a desperately underqualified industrial management. Quoted in 'W sprawie kadr o wysokich kwalifikacjach', in *Polityka*, 24 Sept. 1957.

[2] M. Kowalewski, *Trybuna Ludu*, 6 Nov. 1957. This party 'view' in turn evoked a most vehement response, despite the fact that it was a very 'authoritative' pronouncement and was meant to set the seal upon public debate. 'Please listen to the complaints of employees against directors who do not understand the functioning of machines ordered by them, who are totally lacking in technological imagination and in the knowledge of technological processes. . . . We are still adding up the losses to our economy of the last period. These [losses] would have been much, much smaller if the management of the factories had been in the hands of professionals with full

It was all very well, however, to demand that positions in industrial management be held by people with formal qualifications; but what if these people had no real experience of industrial production when they came to the factories from the polytechnics and design offices? Over a period of time, the gap between what was taught in polytechnics and what the students faced in industry had been increasing, with the result that many of the new recruits could not cope. This strengthened the hand of those 'practitioners', who, whilst competent, were so steeped in routine as to be unable to promote technological innovation.[1] As a consequence of this and of the hostility and bureaucratic interference already discussed, together with the attractions of non-production work in the capital, recruitment into industry and industrial management suffered severely. Management became the preserve of a privileged group.

Ideological criticisms concerning the levels of income had been levelled at management as a whole as early as 1955. W. Brus, writing in *Nowe Drogi*, was concerned that socialised property seemed to have become more and more under the control of a group of 'industrial managers', primarily through their control of the premiums and payment system. Brus gave examples of three categories of management, according to the level of plan fulfilment, and the premiums advanced in terms of their basic pay (see Table 29).[2]

Table 29 shows that top managers and chief engineers received

qualifications. . . . For the love of God! We are not threatened by technocracy . . . we are ill from the very opposite disease . . . of industrial bureaucratisation. By arguing against the selection of persons with proper qualifications, in case this should lead to technocratisation, the party was like a doctor who forbade his patient to eat essential sugar in case he developed sugar diabetes! . . . The political argument of the need for "political consolidation of party and society" . . . cannot serve but to prolong the weak state of our economy, which constantly has too few professionals and too many persons there by "accident or coincidence" rather than by educational merit.' K. Koźniewski, 'Czy nam grozi technokracja?', in *Polityka*, 24 Nov. 1957.

[1] J. Bukowski (then professor in Warsaw Polytechnic), 'O wstępnym stażu pracy absolwentów szkoł wyższych', in *Polityka*, 30 Aug. 1958.

[2] W. Brus, 'W sprawie bódźców zainteresowania materialnego', in *Nowe Drogi*, No. 12, 1955, p. 68. See also *Przedsiębiorstwo* (Warsaw, 1967), pp. 527–535, where he expands his thesis of the appropriation of socialised property by the management in the context of the decentralisation debate.

bonus payments which could amount to 60 per cent of their basic pay, and for every 1 per cent of over-fulfilment of the plan they received another 6 per cent. Brus also pointed out that in 1954, in some Warsaw factories, premiums paid out came to 110 per cent, 101 per cent and 82·9 per cent of the basic pay of the three groups respectively. Furthermore, for some industries such as iron and steel, for every 1 per cent of over-fulfilment of the plan, 12 per cent of the basic pay was distributed as premium for the management. At the same time, there were severe anomalies in the pay structure at lower levels and incentives for professional advancement below the top ranks were conspicuously absent. Between 1955 and 1960, however, there was an improvement in the earnings of the technical intelligentsia as a whole compared with manual workers. Priority industries (as in the case of the manual workers) were again the greater beneficiaries in wage increases, e.g. the average gross monthly income for engineering-technical staff in mining rose from 3,033 zł. in 1955 to 4,970 zł. in 1960, compared with the average rise of from 1,869 zł. to 2,840 zł.[1]

TABLE 29. MANAGEMENT LEVEL AND PREMIUM PAID AS PERCENTAGE OF BASIC SALARY

	Premia	
Categories of management	100 per cent plan fulfilment	For each 1 per cent of over-fulfilment of plan
(i) Director/Chief engineer	60 per cent of basic salary	6·0 per cent
(ii) Dept. managers and Assistant Directors	55 per cent of basic salary	5·5 per cent
(iii) Lower management	45 per cent of basic salary	4·5 per cent

[1] *Rocznik Statystyczny Pracy 1945–1968* (Warsaw, 1970) p. 419. There were also significant income differences between engineers employed in the cities and those employed outside them which were in favour of the former. The average gross monthly income of engineering technical staff in Katowice województwo in 1960 was 3,464 zł. per month compared to 2,131 zł. in the Olsztyn województwo. *Rocznik Statystyczny Pracy . . .*, pp. 422–3.

After 1956 high earnings were still conspicuously apparent amongst the top managers in Polish industry. This was due to the large bonus payments mentioned above or to illegal diversion of funds, or to profitable side-investments which gave rise to generous profits.[1] It is difficult to calculate the real income of the enterprise directors or top management, since, as we have already stated, much of their income is in the form of premiums and bonuses of various sorts which are not on official salary tariffs. The higher up the management hierarchy, the smaller is the proportion of basic pay in the total take-home pay. This is particularly true in the case of the technological hierarchy, where in some cases basic pay is well below 50 per cent of total income. There is consequently great pressure put upon management for plan fulfilment, particularly in the heavy industries such as iron and steel, electronics and machine tools where the premiums for directors play the greater part. The differences in pay for management cadres vary between various branches of industry, and particularly between heavy and consumption industries. Table 30 gives some indication of the income differentials between directors of various industries (engineers and department managers are added to provide further comparison).[2]

TABLE 30. INTER-BRANCH PROPORTIONS IN INCOME OF CERTAIN TECHNICAL POSTS IN 1964

Branch	Director	Department manager	Senior engineer
	INCOME IN THE CLOTHING INDUSTRY = 100		
Iron and steel	191·5	182·5	105·5
Electrical	174·0	141·0	88·6
Machine-tool	130·0	124·2	87·0
Chemical	119·0	115·0	88·0
Foodstuffs	112·0	117·5	100·0
Textiles	85·7	88·3	71·2

[1] M. Misiorny, 'Dyrektorzy i socjalizm', in *Polityka*, 20 Aug. 1957. Those who criticised the factory clique which was composed of the Director and heads of the Union, Party and Workers' Council organisations were swiftly dealt with. The greater rights of factory management had its negative as well as positive effects. See J. Śmietański, 'Wina duża, mała i najmniejsza, in *Polityka*, 15 May 1959.

[2] B. Fick, *Polityka zatrudnienia a płace i bodźce* (Warsaw, 1970) p. 298.

Table 30 indicates that there are considerable differences in the earnings of individuals in comparable positions from industry to industry. For example, a director in the iron and steel industry is likely to earn twice as much as a director in the textile industry. Fick also indicated, however, that there were large differences in the earnings of individuals in various positions in the same industry. These differences were greatest in the heavy industries. For example, if a steel industry foreman earned 100 units his director's income would be 281 units.[1]

To summarise, the demands of the technical intelligentsia in the period around 1956 concentrated on the recognition of technical expertise, rather than ideological correctness in management, and on the regularisation of the pay structure along more meritocratic lines. Although the demand that industrial management should be better qualified was a slogan very much to the fore and extremely popular amongst the technical intelligentsia, there were various objective as well as subjective obstacles in the path of its implementation. It is these obstacles, amongst other things, which we wish to examine below.

POST-1958 AND THE RESULTS OF THE DEMANDS OF THE TECHNICAL INTELLIGENTSIA

During 1957 and 1958 the recruitment of engineers into the party increased insignificantly, by about 0·2 per cent, and many in the party were understandably worried about how it could continue to exercise control within the industrial enterprises. In the face of the 'alliance' of sections of manual workers and the technical intelligentsia in the cause of productivity and efficiency, the party had no equivalent counter claim to authority. Party members were exhorted to criticise management and not to accept decisions meekly and thus endeavour to re-establish the party's authority in industry.[2] The party justified

---

[1] B. Fick, *Polityka zatrudnienia* . . ., p. 301. We must also point out that the engineer not in a management position was likely to earn significantly less than the foreman, though again, only in heavy industry. In manufacturing and light industry the reverse was the case.

[2] W. Titkow, 'Niektóre problemy rozwoju partii', in *Nowe Drogi*, no. 12, 1958, p. 87. By the time of the third Congress of the party in March 1959 it became necessary to introduce the following statute into the Party Rules:

its administrative intervention by asserting that 'not only are some sections of the technical intelligentsia relegating workers' councils to an advisory capacity, but they are also hostile to the party in that they hold that economic matters should be the preserve of specialists'. The point was made quite plainly in one of the resolutions of the third Congress dealing with the tasks of the party:

> From employees and activists in the State apparatus are demanded not only professional but also political qualifications – the ability to link professional tasks with political ones together with a commitment towards the working class and the party.[1]

The demand for the 'professionalisation' of management and administration was not just a question of status for the young intelligentsia or a simple expression of commitment to the principle of economic rationality. It contained a political challenge, formally unorganised within industry to the hegemony of the PUWP. By January 1960, at the IV Plenum, the party accepted that it would not obtain real co-operation without some form of concession, and so at last it formally called on all those in managerial positions without the necessary qualifications to obtain them within a certain period of time.[2] This in itself was an indication of how important this issue had become and we might infer that the party was moving in the direction of accepting the criteria of professionalism alongside political soundness. Some representatives of the technical intelligentsia clearly interpreted this as a sign that the place of the qualified man in Polish industrial management was secure.[3]

'... party factory organisations have responsibility to the party for the economic condition and the effective working of the enterprise.

'A fundamental obligation of these party organisations is political control and influence of the work of the factory administration in matters concerning key production and economic problems of the enterprise cadres, as well as the living and work conditions of the workers.

'Factory organisations fulfil their role, primarily by active participation in the work of workers' self-management, ensuring the linking of workers' interests with national ones.' R. Zambrowski in *Nowe Drogi*, no. 4, 1959. The Conference of Workers' Self-Management, formed in Dec. 1958, also formally introduced the party into the technical decision-making sphere of the enterprise. See Ch. 3.

[1] Extract from *Nowe Drogi*, no. 4, 1959, p. 657.
[2] *Rocznik Polityczny i Gospodarczy 1960*, pp. 161–2.
[3] J. Tymowski, 'Tradycje NOT', in *Polityka*, 18 Feb. 1961.

Initially, however, the practical effects of the party's resolutions were disappointing. Despite the undertaking by the party at the IV Plenum, a year later there were still complaints about managers holding posts without even secondary technical education. Instances were reported for example of production managers being lawyers by training. The engineers were also conscious of the machinations by which professional criteria were ignored.

> Reference to 'organisational ability' was used in the past, and still is used as a justification for giving a non-qualified person a management position which quite obviously required engineer's training. This non-qualified person of course invariably had 'political' qualifications.[1]

It also became apparent that the greater powers assumed by the director *vis-à-vis* the central authorities did not always lead to greater professionalism or increased innovation. In fact, the widening of the rights of the director in 1956 had become a means by which many of the 'old-style' directors were able to defend themselves against the forces of change and the demands of the young intelligentsia.[2] Nonetheless, from the mid-1950s some young graduates found their way into managerial posts and the 'practicals' with lower formal qualifications became somewhat less dominant. By 1964, the situation had improved considerably, though a degree was still not obligatory for holding a director's post. Out of 420 new directors appointed in 1964, 245 had higher education and only 10 had elementary or lower. While there were still some political appointees, by the mid-sixties the professionalisation of the leading cadres had been accepted in principle.[3] From 1956 onwards, and par-

[1] 'Kompleksy inżynierów' (Nine engineers in a discussion with the editor), in *Polityka*, 2 Feb. 1961. One source of conflict was found to lie in the fact that there were still those who called themselves 'engineers' without being formally entitled to do so. Cf. J. Sikorski, 'Społeczne podłoże autorytetu kierowników przedsiębiorstw przemysłowych', in *Z zagadnień stosunków społecznych w zakładzie pracy* (Katowice, 1968) p. 84.

[2] J. Ambroziewicz and A. Rowiński, 'Nie ma zwycięzców ani zwyciężonych', in *Polityka*, 21 Jan. 1961.

[3] A. K. Wróblewski, 'Tajemnica dyrektorskich dyplomów', in *Polityka*, 11 Sept. 1965. N.B. These were not always directors of *industrial* enterprises. The press during this period was also very vocal in pointing out some of the more scandalous situations. For example, in Łódź, an economist was em-

ticularly after the IV Plenum in 1960 the party became more committed to economic rationality and productivity in industry. J. Rawin describes the ensuing relationship between the industrial party organs and the management sector in the following words:

> The party bureaucracy see their tasks and the tasks of the organisations under their control in terms of economic achievements, chiefly through furthering industrial development. Inevitably this leads them to the adoption of the managerial perspective of industrial problems. The convergence of the party line of activities and that of industrial management is unmistakable.[1]

This idea of unity between party and technical intelligentsia has been emphasised by such commentators as F. Parkin,[2] who consider the alliance of the white-collar experts and *apparatchiki* as an expression of a 'single social entity'. This sort of conceptualisation obscures not only some of the important structural limitations to such a unity but also ignores important social differences between these groups. One of the obstacles to the formation of a unitary social group was that party *apparatchiks* found it difficult to communicate with the young intelligentsia, particularly those in the modern developing industries, such as electronics. Many of the party *apparatchiki* had risen from the ranks of the workers and it was therefore possible for them to communicate with and control those managers and directors of enterprises who had come up by a similar route. The 'bright young experts' however had, as we shall see, different attitudes and expectations towards their own role in industry and towards the 'role' of the party.[3]

ployed as a waiter in the factory canteen and he was the only person in the whole factory with a degree.

[1] S. J. Rawin, 'The manager in the Polish enterprise-accommodation under conditions of role conflict', in *British Journal of Industrial Relations*, iii (1965) p. 11. See also Bauman: 'The party and the technical intelligentsia found a common language in their struggle against irrationality in economic life and in their drive towards sober and purposeful management. . . The party became the spokesman for goals which have their institutionalisation in the social role of technological man.' Z. Bauman, 'Członkowie Partii a aktyw partyjny w zakładzie produkcyjnym', in *Kultura i Społeczeństwo*, vi, no. 4 (1962), cited in Rawin.

[2] F. Parkin, *Class Inequality and Political Order* (London, 1971) p. 152.

[3] S. Kozicki, 'Przemysłem i pomysłem', in *Polityka*, 3 Sept. 1967, p. 3.

It is a fact that after 1958 many engineers did join the party. Between 1958 and 1962 the membership of engineers rose from 14,830 to 28,869 and by 1963 31·7 per cent of all employed engineers were party members. By 1967 over 40 per cent of all employed engineers were party members and in the previous year nearly 19 per cent of the newly recruited party membership were either engineers or technicians. By 1969 this trend had resulted in raising the proportion of party members who were engineers, technicians or technical supervisory staff to 12·8 per cent, from a figure of 8·4 per cent in 1960.[1]

But why did the average engineer who was not concerned with a career in the party *apparat* join the party?

> Engineers through participation in the work of party committees or branches of the PUWP, by working in workers' self-management, realise their desire for influence over the management of the enterprise, in matters which are the subject of their professional activity.[2]

The engineers joined the party, we believe, not so much from political choice but so as to widen their sphere of influence for the good of the enterprise. They felt a responsibility towards Polish industry and the economy as a whole and not necessarily a commitment to the political ideology.[3] Many engineers did not regard formal membership on their part to imply a specific commitment or loyalty to the party. One might generalise that the technical intelligentsia was critical of the party's political role in, and control over, industry, but it also realised that participation in decision-making would be enhanced by party membership. Therefore, it is possible to hypothesise that a high level of occupational commitment might be correlated with a greater degree of active party membership.

[1] Figures taken from M. Marzec, 'Z problemów pracy partyjnej', in *Nowe Drogi*, no. 4, 1964. M. Sadowski, 'Przemiany społeczne a partie polityczne PRL', in *Studia Socjologiczne*, nos. 30–1, 1968, and *Rocznik Statystyczny 1970*, p. 16, Table 9.

[2] J. Burzyński, 'Mentalność inżynierów', in *Polityka*, 4 Dec. 1965.

[3] Another study showed that certain groups of engineers did not view movement into a managerial position as promotion. Instead tenure of management function was another means (as was party membership) to greater independence in their 'professional' activity. Cf. A. Grzelak, 'Kadra urzędnicza FM na tle innych grup zawodowych', in *Człowiek w organizacji przemysłowej*, ed. M. Hirszowicz (Warsaw, 1965) pp. 215–16.

One study found, in support of this hypothesis, that those engineers who had graduated through evening courses and had a less developed 'occupational ideology' and commitment to their profession were also likely to be less active in their party and other organisations. Membership of the party as well as other factory-based organisations (e.g. the STO) was declared by the engineers to be for practical goals. Consequently this activity was confined to the place of work and to matters relating to their occupation.[1] If party membership has an instrumental value then we might hypothesise that we are more likely to find a higher level of membership in those sectors of industry where one may clearly and visibly influence the course of decision-making (i.e. in production enterprises) and a lower level where it does not really count for much (for instance, engineers employed in design and research, in a non-management capacity). The data in Table 31 support just such a hypothesis.[2]

TABLE 31. MEMBERSHIP OF THE SUPREME TECHNICAL ORGANISATION AND PARTY AMONGST A SELECTED GROUP OF ENGINEERS (PER CENT)

Organis-ation	Formal membership (per cent)		Active membership (per cent)	
	Production	Office and Institutes	Production	Office and Institutes
STO	50·5	39·4	15·5	8·4
PUWP	21·4	12·7	11·6	7·5
	100% = 1,325	100% = 1,325	100% = 1,325	100% = 734

Table 31 shows the difference in party membership (PUWP) and membership of the professional organisation (STO) as between production and design departments. Here we see a definite tendency for greater membership of both associations in

[1] L. Aleksa, *Pochodzenie społeczne i rekrutacja środowiskowa wybranej grupy inżynierów* (Katowice, 1969) pp. 62–4. We shall deal below with the question of occupational ideology and its influence upon managerial as well as party group membership.
[2] J. Hoser, *Zawód i praca . . .*, p. 199, Table 1.

production enterprises. In another study Pasieczny discovered a similar tendency.[1] Party membership among engineers holding management positions in enterprises (particularly department and section managers) was as high as 80 per cent, whereas membership amongst independent technical personnel (i.e. non-managerial staff) in design offices was as low as 15 per cent. Party membership also assists the managers of production enterprises to communicate with the workers. As Pasieczny points out, '. . . managers seek other extra-official ways of coming into contact with workers' and co-operation at the party level eases their task to a considerable extent.[2] Hoser likewise maintains that membership of the party is of great importance to engineers because it is '. . . a [source] of access to information and provides possibilities for influencing decisions taken within these organisations. . . .'[3] Though for many engineers party membership is simply a passive affair, as we go up in the management scale party membership and political activity

TABLE 32. PARTICIPATION IN THE PARTY AND STO BY VARIOUS GRADES OF A SELECTED GROUP OF TECHNICAL STAFF

		PUWP		STO	
		Formal	Active	Formal	Active
Position	No.	(per cent)	(per cent)	(per cent)	(per cent)
Director, Ass. Director	28	60·7	35·7	71·4	17·9
Manager of tech. department	32	34·8	16·7	61·4	18·9
Department and Section Manager	139	41·0	20·9	61·9	22·3
Office Manager (Design)	327	21·1	10·7	56·6	20·2
Independent (non-managerial) engineers	550	11·6	5·8	44·0	10·5

Source: J. Hoser, *Zawód i praca* . . ., p. 201.

[1] Out of 3,364 engineers, 36·2 per cent were party members. However, about 20 per cent of those engineers in offices and institutes were members, compared to 44 per cent of those in production enterprises. L. Pasieczny, *Inżynier w przemyśle* (Warsaw, 1968) p. 146.

[2] L. Pasieczny, *Inżynier w przemyśle*, pp. 146–7.

[3] J. Hoser, *Zawód i praca*, p. 200. . . .

increase. The particularly high membership amongst department and section managers in production, as shown by Table
32, indicates that party membership may be a means for smooth-
ing out the particular problems of control, information transmission and reception which such engineer-managers face.

We may suggest, therefore, that as party membership becomes
more necessary for both occupational as well as political reasons
at higher levels of production management, at lower levels it
becomes less necessary. Thus if one does not want to enter
management, then one does not have to become a party member
and a process of self-selection occurs by which those wanting
promotion to management in factories know that it entails
joining the party at some time.

We have examined some of the factors which help us to
understand the reasons for engineers joining the party. We have
suggested that party membership is related to whether the
engineer is involved in production or not and to whether he is
a manager or an independent member of the technical staff.
What then are the social factors which decide whether an
engineer becomes a manager in an industrial enterprise or a
designer at a drawing board?

SOCIAL ORIGIN AND EDUCATIONAL CAREER PATH OF THE TECHNICAL INTELLIGENTSIA

It is popularly imagined that during the period of the 'intensification of the class struggle' (1949–53) the higher educational
institutions would, for political purposes, succeed in excluding
those who were not of working-class and peasant origin. The
figures show on the contrary that those from the 'intelligentsia
and petty-bourgeoisie' were far from being under-represented.
This may be seen by examining Table 33. In 1951, 40 per cent
of first-year students in full-time higher education were of non-
manual origins. With the passage of time the proportion of
students from non-manual backgrounds increased, until in
1967 the 1951 figures had been reversed and only 40 per cent of
those students attending full-time higher education were of
peasant or manual worker social origins. The sudden upsurge
in the proportion of those first-year students of manual-worker

backgrounds in 1968 was a direct consequence of government educational intake policy which quite unequivocally favoured such students. At the same time the graduates of higher technical schools (polytechnics) were also dominated by this group of students of non-manual background which constituted over 50 per cent of the total graduates in 1966. The consequences of such a distribution amongst those who were to be the technical intelligentsia of the future we shall spell out below. Here we would draw the reader's attention to the distribution of students and graduates according to social origin and education in evening as opposed to full-time studies. Whereas the students of non-manual social background comprised the largest group of those in full-time higher education, they in turn constituted only about 25 per cent of those first-year students attending evening classes at degree level in 1969. Conversely, in 1967 over 80 per cent of graduates of higher technical educational evening courses were of manual worker or peasant social origin. This has important consequences. Education is a much more significant determinant of 'social position' (understood in the sense that includes both objective and subjective features) in a

TABLE 33. FIRST-YEAR STUDENTS OF WORKER AND PEASANT SOCIAL ORIGINS* RECEIVING HIGHER EDUCATION (PER CENT)

Year	Day (full-time) (per cent)		Evening (per cent)		Correspondence courses (per cent)	
	Worker	Peasant	Worker	Peasant	Worker	Peasant
1949	23·6	22·0	30·4	18·3	—	—
1951	35·8	24·1	58·4	24·1	—	—
1955	31·5	22·4	58·5	21·1	—	—
1960	26·2	18·3	60·3	20·3	45·2	29·9
1965	27·7	14·8	58·7	18·6	45·2	31·4
1967	25·8	14·9	57·0	18·1	48·0	30·4
1968	31·9	16·7	60·4	17·4	47·3	30·0
1969	31·8	15·6	58·9	16·7	47·3	30·2

* The remaining distribution is amongst students of 'intelligentsia', i.e. non-manual origins, and petit-bourgeois (Drobnomieszczaństwo).

From figures supplied by A. Buttler, *Wybrane dane statystyczne o szkolnictwie wyższym w Polsce Ludowej* (unpublished MS.). Also *Rocznik Statystyczny 1970*, p. 431. See also below, Appendix 3, Table 8.

State socialist society than in Western capitalist society. The *manner* of its attainment is, however, just as crucial as the fact of its attainment. For the former very much 'conditions' the meaning of the latter.

For our present purposes we wish only to focus upon one sector of higher education, namely the technical or, more strictly, the applied sciences. Since we have already introduced the distinction between those engineers employed in direct production and management, and those employed in non-production activity, such as design, we would like to continue and examine the way that various types of higher educational career-paths prepare students for these different kinds of jobs.

In the early sixties a series of research projects examined the adaptation of young engineers to their place of work and looked at the reasons for their discontent. One such study, which questioned 215 young engineers below the age of twenty-five, found that only 2·8 per cent of the engineers consciously foresaw work in a management position and only a few others considered it as part of their 'professional' development. All the engineers questioned stressed the creative character of their work and did not seem to give much thought to the fact that there must also be others who *execute* the expressions of the engineers' imagination. This stereotype of the creative engineer is reflected in the fact that the most attractive jobs defined by over 71 per cent of the sample were seen as research and development, design, etc., and only 27·5 per cent were in favour of factory production work. Since the young engineers stressed that their career aspirations focused around occupational recognition, it is not surprising, therefore, that their main criticism of their superiors concerned the latter's 'undervaluing' of the engineer in the factory owing to, in their opinion, the management's lack of appropriate qualifications. The engineers felt that their initiative was stifled and that they were looked upon as a 'necessary evil'. More often than not this was because their superiors had fears about maintaining their own position. Furthermore, they complained that innovation, which was seen as the life-blood of the professional engineer, was purposely discouraged and hindered.[1] Another author found a marked lack of enthusiasm

[1] A. Grzelak, 'Problemy adaptacji młodych inżynierów', in *Problemy kadry przemysłowej* (Warsaw, 1965) pp. 149–50, 166–8.

amongst young engineers to have anything to do with production management, or in any way to be involved in a situation
where conflict was likely to occur. Others found the existence
of what they termed 'technological patriotism' amongst the
greater section of engineers examined. In one sense this was
seen as a positive feature, as complete occupational indentifi-
cation led to a better exploitation of the engineers' talents. In
the long term, J. Hoser found this high degree of identification
slightly disturbing, he felt that it would lead to a type of
engineer who was isolated from 'the wider social structure' and
lacking in social responsibility.[1] An anti-management perspective in this context demonstrates both the effect of the occupational ideology transmitted during higher education as well
as the strength of the occupational stereotype of what management work entails. This stereotype portrayed management
activity as being desk work, bureaucratic in the worst sense of
the word, non-technical and leading to 'a degeneration of one's
professional capacities'.[2]

Those engineers who graduated through full-time higher
education were shown to possess more clearly defined career
goals (as understood above) than those of their counterparts
who graduated in evening classes.[3] If we remember that the
engineers with full-time educational experience behind them
were largely of non-manual social origin then we would expect
this group to be under-represented in those engineering occupations related to management of production and which clashed
with the occupational stereotype of engineering activity. Conversely those engineers of manual-worker and peasant origins
should predominate in the management of production enter-

[1] Z. Kowalewski, 'Chemicy w Polskiej Rzeczypospolitej Ludowej',
quoted in J. Hoser, *Zawód i praca . . .*, pp. 74–8.

[2] J. Hoser, 'Orientacjc zawodowc inżynierów', in *Studia Socjologiczne*, No.
16, 1965, p. 127. This was one of the consequences of the Stalinist period
of over-centralisation, when untrained personnel held management
position. Also the polytechnics trained their engineers for work in design
and construction offices, whereas 60 per cent of engineers were required for
work in production. See A. Wroblewska, 'Apetyt na inżyniera', in *Polityka*,
1 May 1966.

[3] L. Aleksa, *Pochodzenie społeczne . . .*, p. 45. The author believes that the
lack of clear occupational goals is due to the frequent changes of place of
work by the engineers with part-time educational experience as well as to
the fact that many of their earlier aspirations were unrealised.

prises. Support for this was found in a study carried out in the early sixties in one of the largest precision tool factories in Poland. The bulk of the management staff consisted of engineers under the age of forty-five years (86 per cent) being of peasant and manual-worker social origin (81 per cent).[1] For managers who had only secondary technical education and for those engineers who obtained their education by way of evening studies, a managerial position was considered an 'intrinsic' goal. The engineer who had passed through the polytechnic and had adopted some of the values of an academic environment considered a management position as 'instrumental': it gave him great independence, access to the top management through which he could influence decision-making and also provided him with a much larger income.[2]

So far we have suggested that social origin had a direct influence upon the educational path of some of the engineers and consequently upon their career aspirations. A study of the machine tool industry showed that over the years of centralisation there had occurred a breakdown in communication between the research institutes and the design office (non-production) and the production factories.[3] Consequently, the production enterprises tended to be starved of the better-trained engineers, which amongst other things made it more difficult to apply new techniques and to innovate. The status of those working in design offices and in research was much higher than those working in industry as engineers and managers since the latter frequently had very low educational levels.[4]

Table 34 is based on a sample taken in 1965 of over 3,000 engineers and exemplifies the predominance of engineers of working class and peasant origin in production and of

[1] A. Grzelak, 'Kadra urzędnicza FM . . .', pp. 215–16.
[2] A. Grzelak, 'Kadra urzędnicza FM . . .'. The lower the educational qualification of the managers, the more they saw their management position as social advance. Those engineers in managerial positions considered it as a natural progression in their careers (pp. 218–19). Hoser found that engineers who did move from staff to line functions did so because career mobility in the former was rapidly exhausted. For this reason many engineers also declared that they did not envisage promotion of any sort. J. Hoser, 'Orientacje zawodowe . . .,' pp. 126–7.
[3] 'Jeremiada technokratów', in *Polityka*, 24 Feb. 1962.
[4] L. Pasieczny, *Inżynier w przemyśle*, p. 145, Table 17.

TABLE 34. SOCIAL ORIGIN OF ENGINEERS IN VARIOUS SECTIONS OF
THE ELECTRICAL ENGINEERING INDUSTRY (PER CENT)

Units	Total (per cent)	Intelligentsia	Worker	Peasant	Petit-bourgeois
Industrial enterprises	100	27·0	40·1	27·0	5·9
Construction offices	100	43·5	35·0	14·3	7·2
Design offices	100	40·8	36·2	17·9	5·1
Association	100	37·9	33·8	15·8	12·5

intelligentsia in planning, higher administration and other design
works.[1] It is also interesting that the sectors where the engineers
of intelligentsia origin predominated were also those with the
highest average earnings, i.e. design and research offices, as well
as construction offices.[2] There was a further disadvantage here
for the working-class engineer in his professional career.
Whereas the young engineer of intelligentsia origin could often
afford to work for several years in a design office or research
centre, at low salary, improving his qualifications, and then seek
promotion to much more lucrative jobs, this was not possible
for his working-class counterpart who could not rely upon the
financial support of his family to see him through the lean
years. Consequently, he would generally go directly into the
production sector, in which there were higher *immediate* returns
than in research and design.[3]

[1] Amongst the graduates of the Mining Academy which had an above
average percentage of party members the same sort of pattern could be
identified. Here 50 per cent of graduates of working-class origin worked in
coal-mining, whereas over 40 per cent of graduates of intelligentsia origins
worked as geological engineers, in research institutes, etc., and in generally
more creative, exploratory and more 'suitable' engineering tasks. C. Herod,
Adaptacja wychowanków AGH w przemyśle górniczym (Kraków, 1970), p. 29.
J. Hoser also found that over 70 per cent of engineers under thirty years of
age in design offices and research institutes were of 'intelligentsia' origins.
Cf. J. Hoser, *Zawód i praca . . .*, p. 211.

[2] L. Pasieczny, p. 182, Table 28.

[3] L. Pasieczny, pp. 204–5, Tables 32–5.

We must remember that the engineer was on average the most highly paid individual when compared to other non-manual employees with higher education. Table 35 shows that whereas 70 per cent of engineers earned over 3,500 zł. per month only about 50 per cent of the next highest income group (the economists) were at a similar level. Therefore, regardless of the internal differentiation in earnings the engineers had by 1968 found a recognition of their 'value' in terms of relative income.[1]

There is a great deal of evidence to show that the non-production (staff) functions were more attractive to all groups of the industrial technical intelligentsia than the production (line) functions. Young technicians as well as engineers preferred to move into design and construction offices even if this move entailed a drop in salary. There existed and still exists an added impetus to this kind of mobility in that many of the line positions at lower management levels were held by promoted manual workers. This aroused the status concerns of the young intelligentsia as well as the 'job-security' fears of the old workers and in turn led to conflict and a lack of co-operation at the shop-floor level.[2] This was a consequence of the educational policy of the State, which had created a situation where, with the increasing numbers of engineering cadres, young engineers were compelled to commence their careers low down in the enterprise hierarchy. At the same time the distance between the engineer and the worker was being decreased because, as we have pointed out, many engineers completed evening and correspondence courses enabling them to retain habits and social life-styles not very different to those of the workers.[3]

---

[1] *Rocznik Statystyczny Pracy 1945–1968*, pp. 464–6.

[2] C. Parchatko, 'Awans zawodowy . . .', p. 59.

[3] J. Burzyński, 'Mentalność inżynierów . . .', p. 3. Another author, however, after an examination of the life-styles, acquaintance patterns and occupational aspirations of a group of engineers concluded that 'there [still] exists the traditional stereotype of the intelligentsia, of which some elements in one form or another have survived in the social consciousness'. This was shown by the fact that '. . . in practice social strata which have advanced upwards through higher education (engineers of peasant and manual worker social origins) attempt to make this promotion more evident by accepting the *traditional* signs of their new social positions, e.g. life-style'. Cf. L. Aleksa, *Pochodzenie społeczne . . .*, pp. 68–74.

TABLE 35. THE STRUCTURE OF EARNINGS AMONGST VARIOUS OCCUPATIONAL CATEGORIES WITH HIGHER EDUCATION EMPLOYED WITHIN THE NATIONALISED ECONOMY IN JANUARY 1968

Category	Total	Earnings (złoties)						
		Up to 2,000	2,001– 2,500	2,501– 3,000	3,001– 3,500	3,501– 4,000	4,001– 6,000	Over 6,001
Engineers	136,772	4,804	5,539	11,356	17,582	20,344	48,799	28,348
Agricultural engineers	29,944	2,663	3,084	6,202	5,750	4,434	5,857	1,154
Pure sciences	31,678	4,135	6,155	6,794	4,989	4,196	4,535	874
Health service	61,678	5,032	7,851	13,460	11,664	8,672	13,116	1,881
Humanities	53,570	7,252	9,289	9,931	8,051	5,972	10,470	2,555
Economists	52,399	2,313	3,883	7,818	9,624	9,093	15,705	3,963

Another feature of the internal differentiation of the industrial technical intelligentsia is concerned with party membership. We have pointed out that membership is likely to be higher amongst those engineers employed in production enterprises in a managerial capacity. We have also noticed that it is those engineers of manual working-class and peasant origins who are most likely to rise to management positions. Can we therefore conclude that engineers of manual social origins are more likely to join the party? L. Pasieczny found that over 50 per cent of the group of engineers in the thirty to forty years age group were party members and that it was this group which was most prevalent in industrial enterprises. At the same time about 70 per cent of this age group of engineers were of peasant and manual worker origins. Finally, 45 per cent of those engineers employed in industrial enterprises who were party members were of working-class background compared to 20 per cent of those of intelligentsia origin.[1]

There appears to be a fairly strong correlation between party membership and the social origin of engineers. In the study of graduates of the Academy of Mining it was found for example that in those departments where there was a majority of engineers of non-manual social origins (e.g. in geological work and oil prospecting) there was a party membership of about one in four (22 per cent and 24·9 per cent). On the other hand, in those departments where there was a large percentage of graduates of manual-worker origin (e.g. in coal-mining 50·3 per cent and iron-ore mining 42·6 per cent) there was also found to be a 50 per cent party membership.[2] From the information which we have gathered it appears that there is a distinct tendency for engineers of non-manual social origins to gravitate towards those positions in industry where party membership serves no 'occupational' purpose, i.e. non-management, non-production functions. Conversely, engineers with a manual-worker social background (and to a lesser extent of peasant backgrounds) are to be found frequently in production enterprises in lower and middle management posts and having a higher than average party membership.

We have tried to show that the relationship between the

[1] L. Pasieczny, *Inżynier w przemyśle*, p. 147.
[2] C. Herod, *Adaptacja wychowanków AGH . . .*, pp. 29–32.

'political' element (as expressed by party membership) and the socio-occupational element (social origin, qualifications) in industry is a fairly complex one. Whereas in the fifties the most significant dichotomy was between the technical expert and political activist, in the sixties the chief line of division amongst the engineers was between production and non-production activity. The reason for this we believe was linked to the changing character and meaning of party membership in the latter period. Whereas in the fifties there had occurred a 'politicisation' of technical/specialist functions in the sixties the reverse was the case, there being a 'technicisation' of the party's political function in industry.[1]

Given the importance of the principle of 'one-man authority and responsibility' (which to a great extent defines the role of the enterprise director in Polish industry) it is at the level of the enterprise director that the political, occupational, social and other pressures are focused. It is not possible to speak fully of the technical intelligentsia without examining the career paths, social origins, socio-political and industrial roles of those engineers and technical personnel who achieve this most powerful position in industry.

THE ENTERPRISE DIRECTOR: POLITICAL ACTIVIST OR TECHNOLOGICAL EXPERT?

The enterprise directors were divided on what they considered to be the most appropriate qualifications required to fulfil their tasks. When asked as to what they considered to be the most suitable educational background for directors, their replies fell into two categories. One group considered that a director should

---

[1] Comparing the two generations of socialist intelligentsia, one commentator wrote: '... The most characteristic difference to be observed when comparing the present generation [of intelligentsia] with the previous one appears to me to be the quiet eradication ... of the postulate of equality.' K. Wolicki, 'Twór nieskończony', in *Polityka*, 22 Sept. 1962. The young technical intelligentsia were also found to be the least 'egalitarian', least 'liberal' (in their attitudes to the State's right to limit their personal freedom) and the least committed to Marxism. Cf. S. Nowak, 'Środowiskowe determinanty ideologii społecznej studentów Warszawy', in *Studia Socjologiczne*, no. 5, 1962 (comparison of students' attitudes at the Warsaw Medical School, University and Polytechnic).

be broadly educated, with a technological training being the most essential requirement. In a technocratic society, they argued, ruled by technical people, the only area of initiative open to the director is in the field of technological decision-making. The other grouping of directors considered that a director should be an 'economic politician' and a political activist. He should not require even higher education, some argued, since he has a deputy to make decisions on technical matters. The director also requires some kind of economic orientation, though not necessarily a higher education in economics.

The first type of director was more likely to see himself as representing the good of the enterprise and not as a representative of the workers or of the superior ministry. Here the 'managerial' orientation is predominant, as opposed to the administrative, which is a characteristic of the second type of response. In this second type the director sees himself as the representative of the party and the State. Such directors consider themselves mediators in conflicts between the interests of the workers and those of the ministries. Both types of directors complained of a high level of job insecurity, though the first group with professional managerial orientations, complained of the 'lack of criteria for the objective evaluation of their work'. For their part the second group saw themselves as victims of the whims of their superiors, as the weaker side in a quarrel regardless of the subject matter, so they again conformed to the stereotype of the 'political activist' rather than of the 'committed professional'.[1]

From what we have said earlier it is likely that the older directors would be less well educated than their more youthful counterparts and Najduchowska's study of 1,541 directors of enterprises in key industries shows this quite clearly.[2] Of directors aged under thirty-five, 87 per cent had higher education, whereas of those over fifty-five only 40 per cent had higher education. Despite the widespread conviction that directors

---

[1] H. Najduchowska, 'Dyrektor przedsiębiorstwa', in *Życie Gospodarcze*, 1966, July, nos. 29 and 31. One sees insecurity as caused by lack of 'professional evaluation', the other simply by his lack of power.

[2] H. Najduchowska, 'Dyrektorzy przedsiębiorstw przemysłowych . . .', p. 102, Table 10.

should have some sort of common higher qualifications and that there should exist some recognised criteria for appointment, Najduchowska found that no two directors in her sample of over 1,500 directors had identical career paths. What then were the main routes of access to the position of director? Najduchowska distinguished between four main career patterns and four subvariations:[1]

(a) *Administrative* – those who had obtained their experience by working in government administration; for example local People's Councils (29·0 per cent).

(b) *Professional* – those who had risen up through the production hierarchy whilst completing some form of education – worker, foreman, production manager, production chief, chief engineer, director (32·1 per cent).

(c) *Managerial* – those who had commenced their career from management positions and who had not been linked to any specific occupation or occupational qualification (18·8 per cent).

(d) *Political* – party, trade unions and youth movement activists who had been, for example, in charge of personnel policy in 1945–8 and then during the 1949–53 period were promoted to directors (3·4 per cent).

The four hybrid categories which contained those who had moved between two of the above groups were as follows:

(i)   Professional-political   (4·2 per cent)
(ii) Administrative-political   (3·1 per cent)
(iii) Professional-administrative   (7·3 per cent)
(iv) Managerial-political   (2·1 per cent).

At first glance the professional category seems the most popular route, and the political category the least represented. But in order to present a more realistic view of the politically promoted manager and the weight of the political element, we must bear in mind firstly that some 78 per cent of directors of industrial enterprises in Poland are party members[2] and secondly that if

---

[1] H. Najduchowska, 'Drogi zawodowe kadry kierowniczej', in *Studia Socjologiczne*, no. 3, 1969. This is based upon a random sub-sample of 25 per cent of the 1,541 enterprise directors in key industries, i.e. centrally planned, N = 383.   [2] J. Hoser, *Zawód i praca* . . ., p. 202.

we add up the percentages of all career types containing some political element, the proportion of directors originating from a party background rises to nearly 13 per cent. If we examine the distribution of the various career-paths on the basis of the size of factory and the character of its production, then another pattern becomes clear. The 'administrative' career is most common amongst directors in the smaller factories, whilst the 'professional' career is most typical of those in the larger enterprise. Furthermore it is also the case that the smaller factories are in the consumer and light industry sector, which has a lower level of complexity and less specialised technology, hence the technical abilities required of the 'administrative' manager are of secondary importance. There are fewer engineers with higher education employed in light industry and hence less likelihood of the *authority* of the director being questioned.[1] In heavy industry, on the other hand, the managerial career-path was predominant and this career-path was especially common amongst the younger directors.[2]

Although it was still possible to meet directors who had been promoted directly from worker to director with no intervening stages, Najduchowska found only two such examples of the much publicised though grossly misleading stereotype. As for the other categories of technical intelligentsia, social origin has an important bearing on the type of career path followed by directors as shown by Table 36.[3]

The political and mixed career-paths, as one might expect, are almost the sole preserve of those of working-class and peasant origin, whereas amongst the administrative and managerial career-paths, intelligentsia origin accounts for about one fifth of the group. This of course reflects the large numbers of the intelligentsia receiving higher education. (Industrial enterprise

---

[1] 'O postępie technicznym decydują ludzie', in *Polityka*, 30 Jan. 1960. A discussion of the IV Plenum CC PUWP, which showed amongst other things that the management cadres in heavy industry were much more highly qualified than their counterparts in light industry, which was in turn reflected in the income advantages of the former.

[2] H. Najduchowska, 'Drogi zawodowe . . .', p. 259.

[3] H. Najduchowska, 'Drogi zawodowe . . .', p. 260, Table 4. Of the total 1,541 directors only 20 per cent had ten years or less experience as directors. They were generally men of long and varied work experience. See Appendix 2, Table 7.

directors frequently claim working-class or peasant origins, as this 'looks better' on their personal records.)[1]

TABLE 36. CAREER-TYPE AND SOCIAL ORIGIN OF INDUSTRIAL ENTERPRISE DIRECTORS

Career type	Worker (per cent)	Peasant (per cent)	Intelli-gentsia (per cent)	Petit-bourgeois (per cent)	
Administrative	58·6	12·6	22·5	6·3	100·0
Professional	56·6	23·0	18·0	2·5	100·1
Managerial	44·5	26·4	22·6	6·9	100·4
Political	[53·8	46·2]	—	—	100·0
Mixed	75·0	15·6	7·8	1·6	100·0

While the directors as a group were themselves conscious of the need to raise their status by recruiting highly qualified people, we may also conclude that as a group they were divided into those in the 'managerial and professional' group and those in the 'political and administrative' group. The former had to accept that theirs was a political appointment as well as an economic one.[2] The latter group on the other hand had to come to terms with the fact that their political qualifications had to be supplemented by some other assets such as, for example, a degree in one of the social sciences.

Having said something about the experience which the enterprise director brings with him to his post, let us now turn to examine some of the problems faced by the modern enterprise director.

SOME ASPECTS OF THE ROLE OF THE INDUSTRIAL ENTERPRISE DIRECTOR

One of the consequences of the rapid development of Polish industry over the last twenty-five years (coupled with the primacy of the political imperative during the early fifties) has been

[1] H. Najduchowska, 'Dyrektorzy przedsiębiorstw przemysłowych...', p. 99.
[2] Though many complained about the excess of socio-political matters which took up over 50 per cent of their time. See 'Czy tylko organizator?', in *Polityka*, 17 April 1965. Many among the latter group would spend most of their time at meetings and exercising 'formal' authority in an attempt to safeguard their position. B. Olszewska, 'Dymisja', in *Polityka*, 9 April 1966.

that the enterprise director's training and experience was not of the type to enable him always to fulfil adequately his directorial role. The increasing complexity of management of a socialist enterprise had put more constraints upon the director in the mid-sixties than upon his counterpart ten years earlier. We have seen that the technical intelligentsia itself, which was internally differentiated, did not identify with management as a whole. At the same time, various other groups both within and outside the enterprise were becoming increasingly more articulate in expressing their demands, so that the director's role became more and more one of regulating conflict. The main institutions surrounding him are shown in Diagram 2.

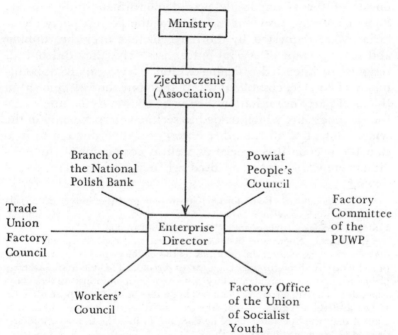

Diagram 2. The Enterprise Director as a Focus of Demands*

Just how well prepared the enterprise director was to handle the intense pressure of these demands which frequently conflicted quite violently is difficult to say. The training of the

* Other organisations making demands upon the director may include the League of Women, Union of Rural Youth and the Supreme Technical Organisation.

director often meant that whereas he could be a good engineer or production manager, it was for that same reason difficult for him to stop being a specialist and become instead a co-ordinator of specialists with the ability to delegate.[1] Most studies of the role of the director emphasise the problem of the director having to maintain his authority within the enterprise on the bais of his qualifications and at the same time being enough of a generalist not to neglect other sectors of enterprise activity.[2]

There were other restrictions upon the activity of the director; for example, the pressure of the superior administration or the zjednoczenie (association)[3] as well as the bank. In one study concerned with the mobility of enterprise directors, the power of the zjednoczenie was demonstrated quite clearly. Some engineers, previous members of the powiat party secretariat, were requested by the party to take over the running and management of several enterprises. This they did but all resigned or intended resigning within a few years of appointment. Their chief complaint was that despite the assistance from the local party organisation they were constantly hampered by the zjednoczenie, which tended to see the enterprise only in the wider context of all the other enterprises subordinated to it so that the peculiarities (social as well as economic) of the individual enterprises were ignored when directives were passed down.[4]

[1] S. Wolff and S. Kalembka, 'Kierowanie przedsiębiorstwem a rola dyrektora', in *Ekonomika i Organizacja Pracy, 1966,* no. 11, p. 518, and A. Matejko, *Socjologia zakładu pracy* (Warsaw, 1969) p. 398.

[2] J. Sikorski, 'Społeczne podłoże autorytetu . . .', pp. 68–9. This study demonstrates the change in priorities as the engineer moves up the enterprise hierarchy through chief engineer to director. The one-man authority principle and its complementary one-man responsibility makes both generalist as well as specialist demands upon the socialist enterprise director. It has also been suggested that 'the generalist' is much more difficult to control than the 'specialist' since he does not fit into the framework loosely defined as 'democratic centralist'.

[3] S. J. Rawin, 'The manager in the Polish enterprise . . .', is possibly the best brief account of the problems associated with the function of the enterprise director in the Polish economy. For a detailed account of the restrictive power of one of these agencies (the State bank) see A. K. Koźmiński, 'Rola zawodowa dyrektora przedsiębiorstwa w aktualnym systemie zarządzania gospodarką socjalistyczną', in *Studia Socjologiczne,* no. 24, 1967.

[4] R. Dudak, 'Płynność dyrektorów', in *Płynność i stabilność kadr,* ed. A. Sarapata (Warsaw, 1967) p. 330.

Another factor militating against the director moving from a technologically oriented style of management to one which was more 'humanised' was the limitations imposed by the enterprise's own technical intelligentsia. The numerous socio-political organisations within the enterprise, such as the workers' councils and the union organisations (which should have been the instrument for the expression of the demands associated with the work-situation), functioned to express the specific demands of production management which were directly linked to enterprise profitability and its own earnings.[1] Studies of workers' self-management (WSM) have shown the widely divergent expectations of the manual workers and the enterprise technical intelligentsia. The latter saw the role of WSM as an aid to improve the production profile to encourage technical innovation and to increase the effectiveness of management decision-making. The manual workers, for their part, looked to the WSM as a representative of their interests, as an organ which would be sensitive to the 'justice' of the division of labour and its remuneration. They were particularly concerned about work-organisation and the social functions of WSM which had been allocated to the trade union, but which the latter tended to ignore.[2]

The position and role of the enterprise director reflect the various tensions inherent within the socialist economy and the Polish political system. The necessities of plan fulfilment conflicting with the social, material, and status demands of various groups lead to a situation which one director describes as follows:

> When there is a build-up of conflict, the director is frequently unable adequately to resolve it . . . at which point the authorities step in. Reaching into the always replete bag of mistakes made by the director in past, they have a change of guard, in the public interest.[3]

One of the unifying features of the enterprise directors as a group is precisely this common experience of the tension involved

[1] See R. Dyoniziak, 'Konflikty międzygrupowe w przedsiębiorstwie przemysłowym', in *Studia Socjologiczne*, no. 16, 1965.

[2] A. Owieczko, 'Działalność i struktura samorządu robotniczego w opinii załóg fabrycznych', in *Studia Socjologiczne*, no. 22, 1966. More is written on this subject in the chapter on the workers.

[3] A. Sarapata, 'Motywacje i satysfakcje dyrektorów-studium porównawcze', in *Studia Socjologiczne*, no. 3, 1970, p. 69.

in their directorial role, though because of their various backgrounds they will deal with these problems in different ways. The other feature which we now wish to examine is the mobility and security (or the lack of it) of the enterprise director, which we suggest is one of the most adequate expressions of the directors' group membership.

Studies of enterprise directors in Poland have indicated a growth in their prestige during the 1960s. This growth is attributed partly to the rising qualifications of directors and partly to a wider recognition of the skills required in industrial management.[1] A further factor, we believe, may be the relative stability of the 'pool' or stratum from which enterprise directors are mainly drawn. Mobility between enterprises is generally seen by the directors themselves to be beneficial, for they believe that most development and innovation takes place during the first few years of the director's tenure of office. This mobility is generally horizontal, for the director is rarely demoted, he appears to move upwards if he is sufficiently ambitious, or sideways if he is not: 'Many mistakes and offences will be forgiven him, provided he does not drastically disturb the elementary principles obligatory in [the circle of persons around him].'[2] In many cases, the enterprise director has direct access to the minister; he is frequently to be found at the plena of the central committee of the PUWP and, depending upon the strategic importance of his enterprise, he may have more or less access to other centres of power.

The directors' security of position was attacked by the current first secretary of the CC PUWP (E. Gierek) in 1968, when he said,

> We must consolidate the conviction that once a person has become a director he has not obtained a life-long patent to this position or, put more simply – he does not always have to be a director. It is not written anywhere that a director must only and exclusively advance, that he must always move upwards.[3]

[1] A. Sarapata, 'Motywacje i satysfakcje . . .', p. 74.
[2] A. Matejko, *Socjologia zakładu pracy*, p. 396. The author stresses that one of the overriding features of the socialist enterprise director's position is that he is nominated by his superiors and can be removed by them at any time. Loyalty to his superiors is therefore essential.
[3] Reported in *Trybuna Robotnicza*, 11 Jan. 1968.

The situation wherein an enterprise director may be sacked from his post in one factory only to be given a similar job elsewhere has been termed the directors' 'carousel'.[1]

Differences in income already discussed point to some inequalities which extend from the ministerial level downward and are another indicator of the difficulty involved in trying to see enterprise directors as a unitary group.[2] If there are differences in income and power of directors there are also differences in their freedom of activity. We can suggest two sets of factors which define and delimit the activity of the enterprise manager. First, there are those features related to his own personal and occupational make-up, such as social origin, education, and career-path and more general occupational values and attitudes which influence the expectations and the behaviour of the director in his office. The second set of features are the limiting conditions presented by the economic and political system which interact with the personality features and mutually condition each other. Kiezun summed up the relationship between these features in these words:

> We shall try to characterise the most common style of management by calling it the 'authoritarian-collegial' type. In this we find an expression of a dialectial contradiction which is the consequence of objective causes connected with the power structure and pressure groups as well as the personal attitudes of managers, which are characterised by a certain dose of conformism and a limited and low level of organisational culture.[3]

The failings of this style of management were exposed by the disturbances of December 1970.

THE EVENTS OF DECEMBER 1970 AND THE
IMMEDIATE CONSEQUENCES FOR THE TECHNICAL
INTELLIGENTSIA

The party suggested that one of the immediate causes of the widespread discontent which followed the explosive riots on the

[1] An example is given in J. Rolicki, 'Karuzela', in *Polityka*, 17 April 1965.

[2] The same inter-industry differences extend right down to the level of the manual workers and produce similar problems of categorisation.

[3] W. Kiezun, 'Styl kierowania na tle zadań organizacyjnych', in *Socjologia Kierownictwa*, ed. A. Matejko (Warsaw, 1969), quoted in A. Sarapata, 'Motywacje . . .', p. 89.

northern seaboard was the deterioration of working conditions in large sectors of industry. This deterioration was attributed to the over-emphasis on the production plan and the weakness of trade unions and workers' self-management in defending the interests of the manual workers.[1] Directors of enterprises were hampered by the unresponsive association, which was itself the target of unrealistic demands from the ministries. The planning commission was blamed for not controlling individual ministries when they drew up unrealistic plans which put management in an invidious position *vis-à-vis* the workers.[2]

The reasons for the failure by the central authorities was not just a result of the party's isolation from the masses and from its own lower organs but was also due to the low qualifications of members of the administrative hierarchy itself.[3] The unprofessional character of the bureaucracy is illustrated by the way in which they would distort information, rather than pass on news which might be displeasing to the higher authorities.[4] This is shown, for example, in the following statement by an executive of the planning commission: 'I eventually asked my superior whether he wanted a cheerful report from me, or a realistic one.'[5] It is not surprising, therefore, that Gierek as first secretary affirmed the meritocratic principle by rejecting claims for the levelling of incomes with the statement that each must be paid according to his qualifications and the social value of his work. He maintained that this was the only way of raising the efficiency and quality of work, which was essential for an intensive development of the economy. Gierek, in his speech to the

[1] R. Kazimierska, 'Samorząd robotniczy', in *Życie Warszawy*, 25 Jan. 1971.

[2] Speech by E. Gierek reported in *Życie Warszawy*, 8 Jan. 1971. As a stop-gap measure, directors were given the power, in Feb. 1971, to create a special wage fund. This restored some of their control over wage policy, and therefore productivity, and also provided an indirect way of increasing wages for some workers.

[3] *Życie Warszawy*, 2 Feb. 1971.

[4] One author had complained earlier that the most common form of conflict in Poland was that between the 'professional' and 'lay' mentality. Bureaucracy was still rare because of the low level of qualifications possessed by the administrative cadres and for that reason there existed only a quasi-bureaucracy in Poland. A. Matejko, 'Społeczny mechanizm konfliktu', in *Organizacja Metody i Technika*, no. 12, 1967, pp. 16–18.

[5] *Życie Warszawy*, 5 Jan. 1971.

VIII Plenum, recognised the disproportions concerning premium payments and stressed that management's remuneration must correspond to its real qualifications. This would require a tighter control of premiums but would at the same time also remove a great deal of discontent amongst the manual workers.[1]

One further cause of the disturbances in December was the proposed introduction of the new system of material incentives. Whilst accepting it in principle, Gierek nevertheless admitted that many of its specific features were unacceptable, since it envisaged too low an increase in wages for the manual workers as well as a reduction in employment in some factories which might lead to unemployment. Whilst this associated Gierek with a 'managerial' viewpoint, it also showed that he realised its limitations.

> ... A class point of view is necessary when taking decisions of political significance. ... In the area of inter-class relations, where there are divergences of social interests, then 'technocratic ability' is not sufficient.[2]

It was the lack of this class perspective and its subordination to technological imperatives, which had characterised decision-making in the latter part of the Gomułka era. To have qualified people taking decisions on the basis of realistic information gleaned from as wide a circle as possible was a necessary but not sufficient condition for sound policy. The political implications of each decision had to be determined and the different interests of various social strata considered at both the macro-level and at the level of the enterprise. The necessity for this was clearly demonstrated by the case of the director who had subordinated the interests of the workers to those of the 'plan' and who was dismissed on the basis of complaints from the workers.[3]

---

[1] As early as 1962 the complaints had been quite vocal about the high and unfair premiums paid to the engineers and technical staff. J. Hellman, 'Dlaczego niesprawiedliwy', in *Polityka*, 7 April 1962.

[2] Report of Warsaw Party Committee conference in *Życie Warszawy*, 11 March 1971.

[3] *Życie Warszawy*, 11 March 1971. Workers at the Żerań factories demanded the resignations of directors who had permitted their interests to be overlooked.

Various party groupings within large factories such as the FSO automobile factory were also demanding that persons promoted to management positions in the economy should have not just ideological qualifications, but also solid professional knowledge and experience.[1] This was the same claim as that made by the technical intelligentsia in 1956, but now it came from party branches. What was the difference, therefore, between the claims made in 1971 and those in 1956–7?

The party was obviously under the same pressure as it had been in 1956 from the specialists and industrial intelligentsia, who were demanding that the party limit its activities to the ideological and 'schooling' tasks and leave industrial management and direction to the managers and qualified personnel.[2] There was obviously some confusion about the sphere of competence of the party, which arose out of the party leadership under Gomułka insisting on the right of the party to interfere in the details of economic and industrial policy. At the same time the lower party organs' ideological role had been neutralised and lower party organisations had become part of the managerial apparatus, geared towards mobilising the work force to fulfil the economic plan. But they suffered from the same handicaps as their administrative counterparts, namely the inability to transmit realistic information upwards and the lack of effective influence upon their superiors. On appointment, Gierek had stated quite clearly that the party should not encroach on the activities of the administration, and this was given further affirmation at the first of the wojewodstwo party conferences following the riots, held in his native Katowice.[3] The party could maintain its control through its power over the selection of administrative and economic personnel and through other direct and indirect means, e.g. through Workers' Self-Management and the unions. To play a fuller part in Polish society the party had to rid itself of passive and careerist ele-

[1] *Życie Warszawy*, 11 March 1971.

[2] T. Jaroszewski, 'Kierownicza rola partii w warunkach intensywnego rozwoju', in *Nowe Drogi*, March 1971. The party has to 'synchronise' the particularistic interests of various groups, of which management was one.

[3] 'Recepta na podział zadań', in *Polityka*, 13 March 1971. See also a discussion by R. Davy, 'New checks without balances in Poland', *The Times*, 25 May 1971.

ments.[1] There was, claimed one writer in *Nowe Drogi*, a great need for active work in the party:

> Those, who for various reasons do not have it in them [to take part in active work] and those who were 'signed on' for various totally unnecessary superficial reasons . . . should leave the party. . . . It should be noted in the party, that they are persons for whom *work properly carried out, or a professional career* are quite sufficient to enable them to serve society in a more general way. These are, after all, particularly worthy values.[2]

This is an indirect reference to the processes which we have tried to identify in this chapter. The party had in fact attracted the technical intelligentsia, but many who joined were passive members or regarded the party as an aid in their professional duties. As a consequence the party had become cut off from the authentic socio-economic problems of factories and the social environment.[3] It was preferable, therefore, that the various groups of intelligentsia should make their contribution in their own right rather than carry out their professional tasks under the guise and auspices of the party. The allegiance of the membership to the party had to be intrinsic, not instrumental.

As Gierek pointed out in his speech to the VIII Plenum, the task of the party was to widen the field of initiative and independent decision-making of the professional cadres in various areas of life[4] without making it necessary for them to have to join the party to achieve this. The lesson which had been re-learned over the fifteen years between 1956 and 1971 was that the first commitment of party members had to be to the party and only in a secondary capacity to occupation or career. In the

---

[1] Gierek had made his dissatisfaction with the selection of party as well as industrial management personnel public on several occasions. In 1967 he was quoted thus: 'It cannot be said that cadre problems are marginal in our political life and yet we feel that the present state of affairs is far from satisfactory. The "sieve" through which various incompetent individuals as well as careerists have been able to squeeze through has not been fine enough.' 'Problemy kadrowe', in *Polityka*, 30 March 1968.

[2] A. Dobieszewski, 'Struktura i zasady działania partii', in *Nowe Drogi*, June 1971, p. 63. Author's italics.

[3] By authentic is meant the problems which concern persons and not the production plan.

[4] Speech by E. Gierek at the VIII Plenum. *Życie Warszawy*, 8 Feb. 1971.

case of the young technical intelligentsia, their allegiance had too often been the reverse. Eventually this had discredited the party in the eyes of those upon whom its long-term power was based – the industrial working class.[1]

[1] The first signs of this had become apparent as early as 1963, particularly in the more modern industries. The engineer, as reported in one article, saw the party 'as an organiser of the socialist economy and the protector of technological advance'. The emphasis was on the production plan and the claims of social matters such as changing rooms, canteens, etc., came later. The final indictment, according to the author, of the professionalisation of the party and its movement away from the revolutionary ideal was that now it permitted the use of television in the supervision of the workers on the production line. From S. Kozicki, 'Pamięć ferrytowa', in *Polityka*, 9 Nov. 1963.

CHAPTER SIX

The Local Political Élites

By Ray Taras

In this chapter we shall turn the focus from the study of social groups to the interaction of these groups in the local community. A fuller study of local People's Councils will follow in another volume of this series which is being prepared at Birmingham University,[1] here we intend to indicate in an introductory way the extent to which social groupings participate in local affairs and also to describe the social characteristics of members of the local political élites. Before embarking on this, however, we need to describe briefly the institutional structure of local government in Poland.

THE INSTITUTIONAL STRUCTURE OF LOCAL AUTHORITY IN POLAND: THE PEOPLE'S COUNCILS SYSTEM

The basic unit of regional and local authority in postwar Poland has been the People's Council ('rada narodowa') and the act establishing its present structure and functions was passed in 1958. In theory, People's Councils 'are organs of State authority of the working people and they express its will'.[2] There are three levels of People's Councils throughout the country: (1) the *wojewodstwo*, or province; (2) the *powiat*, or county; and (3)

---

[1] J. Cave, et al., *Politics and the Polish Economy*, forthcoming.

[2] 'Ustawa z dnia 25 stycznia 1958 r. o radach narodowych', in J. Starościak, *Rady narodowe: Przepisy o organizacji i działalności* (Warsaw, 1966) p. 9, Art. 1.2. For other details see: 'Ustawa z dnia 20 marca 1950 r. o terenowych organach jednolitej władzy państwowej', in *Dziennik Ustaw*, no. 14, poz. 130. J. Dąbrowski, J. Garbala and L. Palczyński, *Organizacja rad narodowych*, cześć 1 (Katowice, 1969) p. 16. Z. Rybicki, *System rad narodowych w PRL* (Warsaw, 1971) pp. 7–71.

the *gromada,* or district. The entire country is divided into seventeen wojewodstwos, but five major cities are excluded from them and constitute wojewodstwo authorities in their own right: these are Warsaw, Kraków, Łódź, Poznań and Wrocław. Within each wojewodstwo are a number of smaller regions, or powiats. Generally towns of over 100,000 inhabitants are also powiat authorities. Finally there is the gromada level, which usually includes between 1,000 and 3,000 people, whether in rural areas, small towns, wards of powiat towns or settlements (such as workers' estates or fishing or health centres). At each level there is a People's Council, elected by the population in the region every four years at the time of the Sejm elections.

What types of activities are the People's Councils responsible for? An act of 1950 specified that they were to direct all the economic, social and cultural activities in their regions. This involved what Jaroszyński has termed a 'localisation of authority' in matters of economic planning, finance and education.[1] Although central government greatly restricted the autonomy of the councils in deciding how to perform these functions, there was still more scope for local initiative than had existed before 1950 when the wojewodowie and starostowie were agents of central administration.[2] The 1958 act added an important residual category of activities assigned to the councils. 'Assigned to them are all matters in the scope of State authority and administration not reserved for other organs.'[3] From the official point of view this has been interpreted as providing the masses with the ability to influence all new issues arising out of the building of socialism,[4] since the councils express the will of the masses.

The specific functions for which People's Councils are responsible, as defined in the 1958 statute, are the following: (1) ensuring order and public security; (2) farming; (3) regional industry and craft; (4) local construction, supervision of construction, development of towns and villages; (5) communal economy and housing; (6) internal trade; (7) purchasing

[1] M. Jaroszyński, *Zagadnienia rad narodowych* (Warsaw, 1961) p. 72.
[2] Z. Leoński, *Rady narodowe* (Poznań, 1969) p. 14.
[3] 'Ustawa z dnia 25 stycznia 1958 r. o radach narodowych', in J. Starościak, p. 10, Art. 3.
[4] J. Dąbrowski *et al., Organizacja rad narodowych,* p. 44.

centres; (8) building and maintenance of roads and road transport; (9) water economy; (10) education and culture; (11) health and social care; (12) physical culture and tourism; (13) employment; (14) finance; and (15) other State administrative matters envisaged in binding regulations.[1] The extent to which a council carries out these functions depends on its level in the organisation structure. Each level has a specified scope of activity assigned to it by statute. For example, in the sphere of education, the gromada councils are responsible for the upkeep of school buildings, the powiat councils are responsible for the functioning of all primary and secondary schools, and the wojewodstwo councils are responsible through their school superintendents for the administration of all matters concerned with higher education.[2] What then is the relationship between People's Councils at various levels in the administrative structure?

The concept of 'dual subordination' of the People's Councils is illustrated in Diagram 3. The first kind of subordination we discuss is vertical; that is, the superordinate relationship of higher level councils to lower level ones. As the diagram indicates, the Sejm is the highest legislative and administrative authority in the country since all organs are indirectly subordinated to it. The Council of State is the second supreme organ of State power and is a 'collective head of State' which performs mostly ceremonial functions. However, it does maintain ultimate supervision over the councils. The Council of Ministers is the government and issues directives and takes decisions of a general policy nature. Each Ministry is responsible for a particular sphere of administration. These are the national institutions to which the councils and their organs are subordinated. In practice, however, the wojewodstwo level is supervised directly by the national institutions whilst other levels are subordinated vertically to their counterparts immediately above.

The forms that vertical subordination take differ according to which organ is being subordinated. For example, both councils and presidia can repeal legal acts passed by their lower counterparts if they are contrary to law or to the 'principal political

[1] 'Ustawa z dnia 25 stycznia 1958 r. o radach narodowych', in Starościak, pp. 10–11, art. 3.
[2] Dąbrowski *et al.*, *Organizacja rad narodowych*, p. 52.

lines of State', but departments can only repeal such acts where specifically authorised by statute. Nevertheless, Leoński claims that councils are least subordinated to their higher equivalents and departments most subordinated.[1] Thus control over administrative organs may be more stringent than control over elected organs. This may be due primarily to the volume of regulations affecting administrative work, which we shall discuss below.

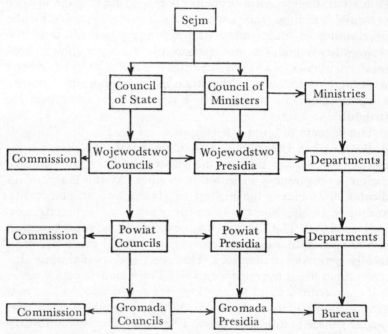

Diagram 3. Structure of Subordination in the People's Council System[2]

The three principal methods of subordinating a council organ to its higher level equivalent are: (1) the issuing of instructions ('wytyczne') by the higher organ to the lower; (2) the exercise of control over lower organs by an examination of their reports; and (3) the repealing of decisions of these lower organs.[3] The

---

[1] Leoński, *Rady narodowe*, p. 90.
[2] Dąbrowski *et al.*, *Organizacja rad narodowych*, p. 26.
[3] Leoński, *Rady narodowe*, p. 91.

purposes served by these methods are, according to Jaroszyński, to share the experience of well-qualified cadres serving in higher councils, and to ensure a necessary standard of uniformity for all councils.[1] This is the basis of the relationship between councils and their organs at various regional levels.

The other half of 'dual subordination' is the horizontal type. All organs of a council are subordinated to the council, the elected body. The internal structure of a powiat People's Council and the various organs functioning alongside it is outlined in Diagram 4. The respective functions and lines of responsibility of the various organs in a particular People's Council are for the most part set down in statute. The relationships between the organs are often complex, and we shall assess only the most important ones. We begin by discussing the role of council meetings. These are held at least once a quarter at the wojewodstwo level, at least once every two months at the powiat level, and at least eight times a year at the gromada level.[2] Council sessions consider '. . . matters having principal significance in the given region', in particular the annual economic plan and budget. They issue instructions to executive organs on the most important local activities undertaken by the council. They also appoint and dissolve their organs and consider their reports.[3] Not only councillors participate in council debate but also representatives from higher level councils, invited persons, directors of economic enterprises or social organisations and department heads. These representatives may be called upon to give information on their enterprises or organisations to the council.[4] However, they cannot vote.

If the council at its meetings considers only general matters affecting the given region and leaves the day-to-day management of the authority's activities to its organs such as the presidium and departments, how does the council achieve subordination of these organs? According to Jaroszyński this is achieved by three methods: (1) Council may issue binding regulations to its organs, especially in matters concerning the economic plan and budget; (2) Council may adopt guidelines

---

[1] Jaroszyński, *Zagadnienia rad narodowych*, p. 299.
[2] 'Ustawa z dnia 25 stycznia 1958 r. o radach narodowych', in Starościak, p. 26, Art. 30.2–4.
[3] Ibid., p. 25, Art. 27.1.   [4] Ibid., p. 28, Art. 35.2.

Diagram 4. Internal Structure of a Powiat Council[1]

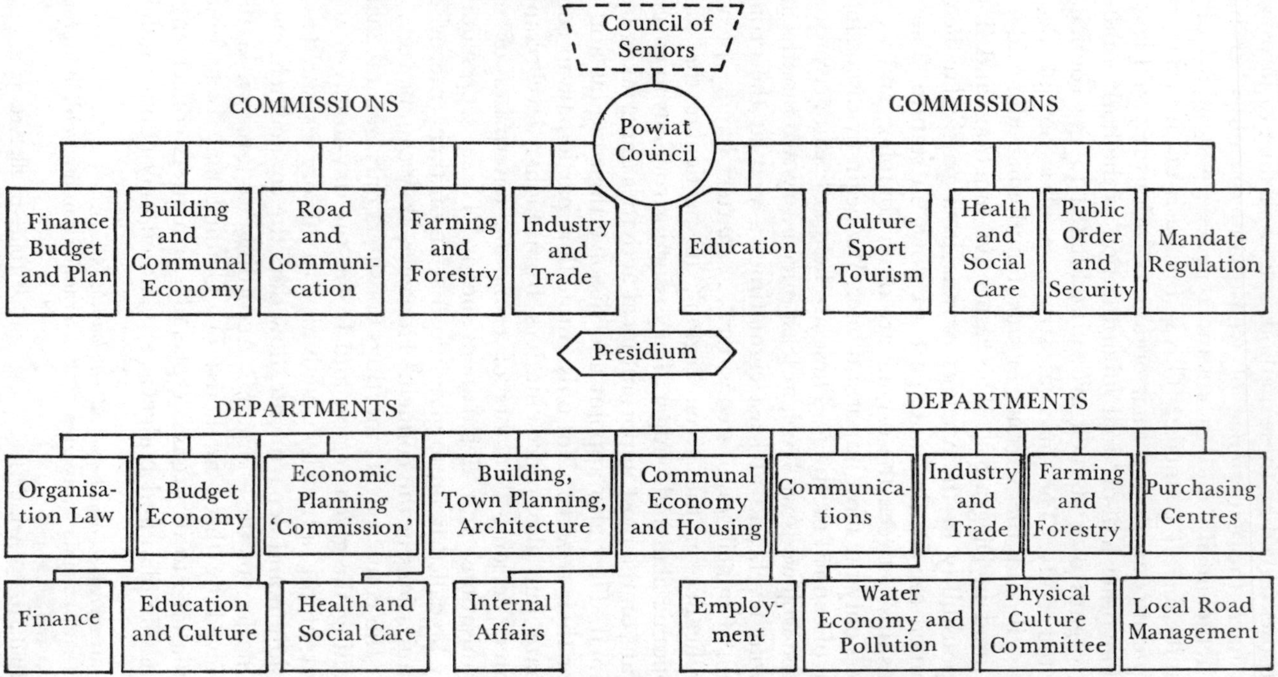

COMMISSIONS

- Finance Budget and Plan
- Building and Communal Economy
- Road and Communication
- Farming and Forestry
- Industry and Trade

Council of Seniors

Powiat Council

- Education
- Culture Sport Tourism
- Health and Social Care
- Public Order and Security
- Mandate Regulation

COMMISSIONS

Presidium

DEPARTMENTS

- Organisation Law
- Budget Economy
- Economic Planning 'Commission'
- Building, Town Planning, Architecture
- Communal Economy and Housing
- Communications
- Industry and Trade
- Farming and Forestry
- Purchasing Centres

- Finance
- Education and Culture
- Health and Social Care
- Internal Affairs
- Employment
- Water Economy and Pollution
- Physical Culture Committee
- Local Road Management

DEPARTMENTS

[1] Dąbrowski et al., Organizacja rad narodowych, p. 38.

on how the most important local functions are to be performed; and (3) Council supervises the activities of its dependent organs by considering their reports.[1] None of these methods has the teeth necessary to ensure council superiority over the other organs.

The executive organ of the council is the presidium. From 1958 onwards the functions of the presidium and departments became distinguished by statute and the presidium became responsible for only the most important administrative matters. At the same time it remained council's executive-managing organ, ensuring that council resolutions were performed (executive function) whilst also organising the performance of those activities which council had not regulated itself (managing function).[2]

The most important function of the presidium is its accountability to council for the work of the departments, which are the regional State administrative organs. It controls and supervises all executive organs, such as departments and locally controlled economic enterprises. Council control is limited to the presidium. As a result the presidium's position is similar to that of the Council of Ministers at the national level: the latter is theoretically subordinate to the elected body (Sejm), supervises the administrative apparatus (Ministries), and is the real power base (government).[3]

An empirical study of councils at various regional levels in Poland's western wojewodstwos based on 1967 data substantiates this analysis.[4] A majority of presidia chairmen questioned thought that most matters were brought before council on the initiative of the presidium or party committees and in many cases only after the presidium had arrived at a decision, which council then ratified. The authors collected other data which indicated that council at its meetings seldom discussed information presented to it by the presidium, and they found that there was never a case of council rejecting a presidium report

---

[1] Jaroszyński, *Zagadnienia rad narodowych*, pp. 149 ff.

[2] W. Sokolewicz, *Rząd a prezydia rad narodowych* (Warsaw, 1964) p. 90.

[3] Jaroszyński makes the same analogy: *Zagadnienia rad narodowych*, p. 206.

[4] A. Patrzałek and A. Seniuta, 'Nadrzędność rady nad prezydium w świetle praktyki', in *PRN 13*, 1969, pp. 93 ff.

or demanding a substantiation of it. In addition, although the presidium is required to inform the council at its meetings of whether its resolutions had been carried out, this information was submitted no more than twice a year in most of the authorities studied. Finally the research showed that there had never been a case of material being presented to council which had not yet been approved by the presidium. The authors concluded that the impression they were left with was of the presidium, not council, acting as the 'landlord in the region'.[1]

The extensive influence that the presidium has over council, rather than vice versa, as the formal relationship between the two would have us believe, is borne out by other studies. These were concerned with the forces which inspired council or the presidium to pass a resolution. The source of initiative which led to a council or presidium resolution is quantified in Tables 37 and 38. The data indicate that the presidium was usually the main instigator of council resolutions, but that council was rarely the instigator of presidium resolutions. There were marked fluctuations in initiative-taking from council to council, ranging from almost equal distribution between council and presidium in Nowy Targ and the five Wrocław wojewodstwos, to the situation in Lublin when in 1955 eighteen of nineteen resolutions were taken on the initiative of the presidium.[2] However, council seldom initiated a presidium resolution: in two of the cases (Nowy Sącz and Wrocław) departments were responsible for initiating more than three quarters of all presidium resolutions, and councils accounted for only 1 per cent. These findings suggest that the popularly elected organ is not in practice the most influential in the People's Council system. Furthermore what data there are indicate that other institutions, such as commissions and public organisations, also have little influence in originating presidium resolutions. There appears to be little scope, therefore, for influential participation by institutions of a public character in presidium decision taking. In contrast, the administrative element *is* influential and we shall return to the representative-administrative relationship below.

[1] Ibid., p. 93.
[2] W. Sokolewicz and S. Zawadzki, 'Wyniki badania uchwał r.n. i ich prezydiów', in *PRN 3*, 1965, p. 165.

Table 37. The Initiators of Resolutions Passed by Councils and Presidia in Kraków Województwo in 1962*

				On initiative of			
	Total res.	Council	Presidium	Commissions	Departments	Public organisations	Statute or higher authority
Kraków City Council	32	5	13	2	0	3	9
Nowy Sącz Powiat Council	21	1	6	13	0	1	0
Nowy Targ Town Council	21	8	9	3	0	0	1
Kraków City Presidium	846	—	—	—	—	—	(40 per cent)
Nowy Sącz Powiat Presidium	257	1	21	0	224	2	9
Nowy Targ Town Presidium	78	—	—	—	—	—	—

(— indicates no data)

* Tabulated from data presented in W. Zakrzewski, 'Z zagadnień działalności uchwałodawczej r. narodowych i ich prezydiów w woj. krakowskim w latach 1955 i 1962', in *PRN 3*, 1965, pp. 11–22.

Table 38. The Initiators of Resolutions Passed by Five Councils and Presidia in Wrocław Województwo in 1955* (in per cent)

				On initiative of			
	Total res.	Council	Presidium	Commissions	Departments	Public organisations	Statute or higher authority
Wroclaw Councils	103	30	33	18	3	0	17
Wroclaw Presidia	1343	1	19	2	76	0	2

* Tabulated from data presented in H. Rot, 'Z problematyki działalności uchwałodawczej rad narodowych i prezydiów woj. wrocławskiego w latach 1955 i 1962', in *PRN 3*, 1965, pp. 108–11.

The extent of council rejection of, or amendment to, proposals submitted to it for ratification can also suggest how autonomous council is. In Białystok wojewodstwo, twenty projects out of 485 were rejected by council. Warsaw City Council rejected only six projects and required that another five be altered substantially of 618 submitted to it in 1962.[1] A survey conducted in 1968 of 139 chairmen and secretaries of gromada councils in Kraków wojewodstwo revealed that 29 per cent thought that council accepted proposals without amendments, 61 per cent thought that amendments did occur, and 9 per cent believed that rejections occurred.[2] From these findings we may conclude that the elected organ is considerably less powerful in practice than in law, but that it still has more influence than many Western writers have suggested.

So far we have discussed aspects of the functioning of councils and presidia. We have suggested that the former are in theory the superior, but that the latter actually exercise the greater authority. Next we consider the regional extensions of the central Ministries – the administrative departments. In 1958 legislation delineated the spheres of responsibility of departments and the presidium. Certain functions were assigned exclusively to departments and as a result they became far more autonomous. However, they still remained subordinated horizontally to their presidium, which set up or dissolved departments and appointed or dismissed their heads. Departments were also, like councils and presidia, subordinated vertically.

An interesting study on the functioning of departments was carried out in 1966 which involved a survey of 269 department heads at the wojewodstwo level. The following data are based on the study of W. Narojek and J. Świątkiewicz.[3] Their impressions on a number of significant topics which interest us are tabulated below.

[1] J. Świątkiewicz, 'Uchwały rad narodowych i prezydiów w 1962 roku', in *PRN 2*, 1964, pp. 105–6.
[2] W. Zakrzewski, 'Gromadzkie rady narodowe oczami swych przewodniczących i sekretarzy', in *PRN 17*, 1970, p. 125.
[3] 'Pozycja wydziału w opinii kierowników wydziałów prezydiów WRN (Wyniki sondażu ankietowego)', in *PRN 11*, 1968, pp. 125–68.

THE POSITION OF DEPARTMENTS ACCORDING
TO OPINIONS OF DEPARTMENT HEADS

Questions Relating to Dual Subordination

	Response %
(1) Which type of subordination influences the functioning of a department to a greater degree?	
(a) Horizontal subordination (council, presidium, commissions)	49·7
(b) Vertical subordination (higher administrative organs)	47·7
(c) Didn't distinguish, no response	2·6
(2) Which type of subordination has greater influence in matters concerning the budget?	
(a) None	12·4
(b) Vertical	14·6
(c) Horizontal	35·9
(d) Equally	8·9
(e) No response	28·2
(3) Is there ever any conflict between viewpoints of regional organs (council, presidium, commissions) and those of higher administrative organs on matters on which the department must decide?	
(a) Yes	47·7
(b) No	49·8
(c) No response	2·5
(4) Which organ has the deciding influence in such cases?	
(a) Regional organs	52·7
(b) Higher administrative	36·5
(c) No response	10·8
(5) What is the assessment of the actual structure of dual subordination?	
(a) Fully correct	21·3
(b) Correct in principle but not without faults	72·3
(c) Incorrect	5·8
(d) No response	0·6
(6) Of those (72·3 per cent) who had critical remarks what were the reasons given for certain 'faults'?	
(a) Meddling of horizontal organs, especially presidium	38·5
(b) Meddling of higher administrative organs	23·0
(c) Entire structure of subordination faulty	38·5

The concept of dual subordination and the departments'
relationship with their presidia and other organs were considered
in the survey. Concerning subordination of departments vertically and horizontally, respondents were divided as to which
was the more influential. Notably heads of economic-budget
departments seemed to indicate that horizontal dependence on
council and presidium was greater, whereas heads of departments concerned with 'administrative jurisdiction' such as
internal affairs and management of shops considered vertical
to be greater. In matters concerning the budget department
heads generally believed horizontal control to be the tighter. In
addition they also thought it to be the more influential subordination where conflict arose between the policies of vertical
and horizontal organs. Further evidence stresses the unnecessary interference that the presidium was thought to exert on
departments. This is tabulated as follows.

THE POSITION OF DEPARTMENTS ACCORDING TO OPINIONS OF
DEPARTMENT HEADS: THE ROLE OF THE PRESIDIUM

Questions	Response (%)
(1) Does the presidium still decide on individual and less significant matters which are not required to be considered at its sessions?	
(a) Yes	36·8
(b) No	41·3
(c) No response	21·9
(2) If yes, what is this a consequence of? (multiple responses permitted)	
(a) Present legislation and executive regulations based on it	33·3
(b) General non-legislative directions of central administrative organs	38·4
(c) Initiative of the presidium	48·9
(d) Initiative of department head in presenting matter to presidium	8·6
(3) Is the presidium member who supervises over a department	
(a) An exponent of the department's viewpoint in relation to the presidium	38·1
(b) A channel of presidium influence on the department	23·9
(c) A mediator between organs	36·1
(d) No response	1·9

(4) What is the form of influence taken by a presidium member supervising over a department? (m.r. permitted)

(a)	Decrees on particular matters	23·2
(b)	Reaching an understanding before a decision is taken	29·7
(c)	Giving general indicators as to how the matter should be resolved	49·7
(d)	Hearing reports of department heads on the matters	50·3
(e)	Other forms	2·3

Nearly as many department heads expressed the opinion that the executive-managing organ still concerned itself with particularistic and insignificant matters as those who denied this. Of those who affirmed the existence of this situation the most common reason offered was that the presidium interfered on its own initiative. This indicates that the 1958 statute dividing functions of presidium and departments was not adhered to in practice.

Two other reasons were cited for producing presidium involvement in less important issues which would have been best left for department jurisdiction. One was central directives demanding presidium consideration of such issues, and the other was legislation and regulations themselves demanding such involvement. A tiny proportion of department heads believed that they were responsible for involving the presidium in departmental affairs. One method of presidium control over departments not yet discussed is the appointment of one of its members to supervise over an individual department. Department heads held the opinion that such members more often represented departmental policy or acted as mediators rather than acting as agents of presidium influence on departments. The methods by which these members influenced departments were generally weak ones, such as through hearing reports or giving general indications as to how certain issues should be resolved. Less often was it required that an understanding be reached between presidium member and department before a decision was taken, and only occasionally did members actually issue decrees as to how matters should be settled. From these data we can suggest, therefore, that department heads were more critical of the control exercised by presidia in scrutinising their individual activities than they were of any rigid general supervision. These results also tell us that the presidium, which we found to be very influential over the elected body, was also viewed as being influential over the administrative apparatus. Its supervisory position over departments (horizontal subordination) was considered to be more influential than the supervisory position of the central Ministries (vertical subordination).[1] It was accused of unnecessary interference in departmental activity. As a result the presidium can be regarded as an influential Cabinet in a local authority in which political power actually resides. An analysis of the elements represented in this organ, which we carry out below, will indicate which groups at the local level are most powerful.

The commissions of the council are organs on which local interests may be represented. They are similar to committees in English local government in that their composition includes both councillors and co-opted members. However, the commissions allow much broader scope for participation by individuals co-opted from the public than do committees: up to 50 per cent of the membership of a commission (excluding, however, its chairman) may be co-opted. Following the 1969 local elections there were still places for some 30,000 such co-opted members on commissions constituted in that year, and there has been an attempt to encourage councils to select more co-opted members than they did in the past. This is not such a straightforward task. Many individuals interested in such public service are functionaries in enterprises and institutions subordinated to council and therefore to commissions also. If these elements were co-opted too extensively – and no legislation exists to prevent this – the danger might arise that the 'independent opinions' which commissions are supposed to express in carrying out supervision over dependent organs could be circumscribed. But as we shall indicate below, the most marked differentiation between co-opted commission members and elected councillors is the over-representation in the former of non-manual workers. This may be due to their tendency to participate more in organisations and it may be due

[1] Since the respondents were department heads at the wojewodstwo level, the organs to which they were subordinated vertically were the Ministries.

to councils' desire to have more specialists on commissions. In co-opting members commissions are faced with the dilemma of selecting to their membership laymen who are representatives of society yet specialists who are knowledgeable in a technical sphere of activity. This dilemma arises out of two fundamental functions assigned to commissions: they are to maintain permanent links with the population and involve it in the functioning of the People's Councils. At the same time commissions are to exercise public control over administrative departments and economic enterprises.[1] The tendency has been to view public elements as being adequately represented by councillors and to choose, therefore, specialists as co-opted members. The commissions, instead, may be an important forum for the articulation and aggregation of professional and specialist interests.

The nature of the relationships of commissions to other organs in the People's Council system must now be discussed for the light it throws on the representative-administrative dichotomy. Firstly, the council acting in session establishes the type, structure, number and membership of commissions within the framework of central directives. In turn commissions exert influence over council by helping to organise its meetings and by formulating some of the resolutions which council will be asked to approve, though we have noted above (Table 37) that in the latter case such influence was minimal. In addition, Sokolewicz describes how commissions may also assist council by critically assessing projects drawn up by departments, thereby helping to formulate an 'autonomous will of the representative organ' and helping to sharpen the confrontation between administrative points of view and the opinions of the public expressed by councillors.[2] Above all, says Sokolewicz, commissions must be regarded as consultative rather than initiative-taking organs in relation to council. This view is given weight by an empirical study which showed that forty-one of ninety-nine speakers (40 per cent) who became involved in discussions at Łódź City Council meetings made statements factually

[1] 'Ustawa z dnia 25 stycznia 1958 r. o radach narodowych', in Starościak, p. 29, Art. 41.

[2] Sokolewicz, *Przedstawicielstwo i administracja w systemie rad narodowych PRL* (Warsaw, 1968) p. 205.

linked with commission work.[1] The primary function of commissions would seem to be, therefore, to allow greater participation by elements of a public character in council work rather than to develop into a power base.

The relationship between commissions and the presidium is not a hierarchical one. It is based more on co-operation between the two organs, and its most common forms are: (1) the expressing of opinions by commissions on presidium matters; (2) recommendations of commissions to the presidium; (3) participation of presidium members in commission meetings; and (4) participation of commission members in presidium meetings. The Łódź study indicated that the first form was the most common and the second the least common, suggesting once again that consultative rather than initiative-taking activity characterised commissions' work. In terms of participation of presidium and commission members in each other's meetings, there was more frequent attendance by presidium members at commission meetings than commission representatives (usually their chairmen) at presidium sessions.[2] The data also showed that commission representatives were not permitted the high degree of involvement in the executive-managing cabinet that they played in the council meetings. The study of Łódź wojewodstwo council found that commission representatives more often refused invitations to participate in presidium meetings than they accepted. No explanation was given for this phenomenon in the Polish study, and we may infer that commission members did not value very highly, perhaps because they were uninfluential, attendance at presidium sessions.

The third relationship of commissions with a principal organ of the People's Council system is with departments. This one is by far the most significant and the most contentious in that it involves continual contact between public and administrative organs. The 1958 statute gave to commissions strong new powers which considerably enhanced the position of represen-

[1] J. Wróblewski, Z. Izdebzki, E. Smoktunowicz and T. Szymczak, 'Problemy działalności komisji rad narodowych m. Łodzi i województwa Łódzkiego', in *PRN 5*, 1965, p. 68.

[2] This tendency was also found in a study of forty Lublin and Rzeszów Councils. See W. Skrzydło, 'Z problematyki organizacji i działalności komisji PRN w Woj. Lubelskim i Rzeszowskim (w latach 1962–1963)' in *PRN 6*, 1966, p. 63.

tative organs in relation to departments. Commissions were now empowered to issue binding advice (*'wiążace zalecenia'*) to department heads in certain matters, agreed to by the Council of Ministers and the local presidium, affecting the execution of assignments by departments or the removal of ascertained deficiencies.[1] This was the first case in which commissions possessed a legal base upon which to enforce their recommendations to departments. In 1964 a Council of Ministers' resolution consolidated these powers and specified cases in which commissions' advice was binding on department heads and stated matters in which department heads were obliged to seek commission opinion before making a decision.[2] Department heads could if they wished appeal against a commission's binding advice to the presidium but in turn commissions could appeal to the full council if the presidium found against them. This authority vested in a representative organ is the clearest illustration of the process of 'democratising' the People's Council system which began in 1955–6 and which we shall have occasion to discuss more fully below (pp. 253–66).

We have stated above that those cases in which department heads are obliged to implement the advice given to them by commissions are determined by the local presidium in agreement with the Council of Ministers. This has led to strong variations from council to council, depending on the extent to which the presidium wishes to assign functions to commissions for binding advice. Chwistek has shown that the number of cases in which commissions give such advice fluctuates from 27 out of 111 cases in Kraków to 10 out of 50 in Rzeszów (in Poznań and Wrocław the comparable figures were 19 out of 76 and 22 out of 115). Similarly the number of issues in which departments must seek commission opinion,[3] varies from 93 in Wrocław to 40 in Rzeszów (57 in Poznań, 84 in Kraków).

The number of matters requiring binding opinion is generally

[1] 'Ustawa z dnia 25 stycznia 1958 r. o radach narodowych', in Starościak, pp. 30–1, Art. 44.

[2] 'Uchwała Nr 158 Rady Ministrów z dnia 6.VI.64 r. w. sprawie zaleceń i opinii komisji rad narodowych udzielanych kierownikom wydziałów', in Starościak, pp. 65–7, Arts. 3–4.

[3] Commission or 'normal opinion' is only binding insofar as its rejection by a department head may lead the commission to appeal to the presidium, and not, as in cases of binding opinion, the head to appeal to the presidium.

low. The explanation for this is that department heads are likely to have influenced the presidia when the latter were determining which matters should be assigned as coming under the 1964 Council of Ministers resolution. Thus legislation to strengthen the power of commissions was not always put into practice. Many presidia, under the influence of departments which had a vested interest in maintaining a low figure, decided that few matters should require commissions' binding opinion.[1] Empirical evidence (Table 39) points out how binding advice and opinion was the least frequent form of commission influence on departments. Far more common were proposals submitted to departments which required only a reply from heads within one month, and the exercise of control ('kontrola') involving the consideration of a department report or fieldwork inspection. However, we can see the variations from one People's Council to the next, particularly between the two powiats concerned. Commissions in each council appear to engage in differing patterns of influencing departmental work. As we may have expected, binding opinions, which result from the initiative of department heads, were lowest of all forms of commission influence.

Our conclusion is that the ethos surrounding the work of commissions remains, despite the attempt to increase their powers in 1958 and 1964, essentially a participatory one. Commissions can make recommendations to department heads and they can examine departmental reports. This consultative and participatory role is extensive. But the actual exercise of power by commissions is circumscribed not only by the presidium and the administrative apparatus but by the subjective assessment by commissions of their perceived role. The assessment appears to be a modest one.

The opinions of department heads on the functioning of commissions substantiates our claim that the latter are consultative organs and not authoritative ones. We might have expected

---

[1] For example, the presidia of Kraków City, Poznań City, Wrocław City, and Lublin, Katowice and Wrocław wojewodstwos considered as issues in which commissions could give binding advice those given only as exemplary by the 1964 resolution. J. Chwistek, 'Wpływ instytucji wiążących zaleceń i opinii na prawną i faktyczną pozycję komisji rad narodowych', in *PRN 12*, 1968, p. 37.

TABLE 39. CONTROLS, BINDING ADVICE AND OPINIONS, NORMAL OPINIONS EXERCISED BY COMMISSIONS BETWEEN 1 JANUARY 1966 AND 31 MARCH 1967*

| | Controls | | Proposals | | Opinions | | Advice |
	Total	In departments	Total	To departments heads	Binding	Normal	Binding
WRN Rzeszów	390	84	813	457	10	85	59
MRN Rzeszów	285	87	253	154	38	123	81
PRN Jasło	67	18	104	76	31	57	38
PRN Przemyśl	197	71	234	142	11	25	66
Total	939	250	1,404	829	90	290	244

* From Chwistek, p. 57. The distinction between binding opinion and binding advice is that the first requires the initiative of the department head, the second the initiative of the commission.

a critical attitude to commissions following the aggrandise-
ment of their powers in relation to departments. It is somewhat surprising, therefore, that research by Narojek and
Świątkiewicz showed that only 2·5 per cent of department
heads believed there to be relatively frequent controversy
between themselves and commissions. In addition 60 per cent
of respondents viewed the mechanism of binding advice and
opinion as having very restricted or no influence in leading to
lively contacts between departments and commissions.[1] Yet
another downgrading assessment of commissions is indicated by
figures showing that over half of department heads responding
considered them to be of very restricted or no assistance at all
for departments. The results of this attitudinal survey, carried
out in 1966, raise doubts as to whether commissions have made
full use of, or have been permitted by their presidia to make
use of, the powers assigned to them by the 1958 and 1964
legislation. It could be postulated that neither the presidium
nor departments wished to share their spheres of authority
with an organ which could potentially develop into a quasi
executive-managing or a quasi-administrative one if it was
permitted to make full use of general powers given to it by law.
There may have been collusion between the two, as is suggested
by Chwistek, in denying to commissions a radical broadening
of their powers. However, if commissions have not evolved into
the powerful organs envisaged by law, they have still served a
useful function in permitting participation by elected representatives of, and co-opted members from, society in the People's
Council system. It is possible, though we have been unable to
show it, that commissions are a means by which professional
and specialist interests are brought to bear on local politics;
and such bodies may in future develop into organs where such
interests are articulated and aggregated.

THE BUREAUCRATIC FRAMEWORK OF THE LOCAL
AUTHORITY

Having described the structure, functions and some of the processes of the People's Councils we can now analyse some of the
key theoretical problems related to them. We are particularly

[1] Narojek and Świątkiewicz, 'Pozycja wydziału . . .', pp. 150–2.

interested in analysing certain patterns in the development of the system such as the supposed trend towards democratisation, viewed as the delegating of authority to representative as opposed to administrative organs. These patterns are concerned with the fundamental aspects of the current doctrine of democratic centralism, the basic organisational principle governing the structure of socialist systems.

The classic Leninist theory of democratic centralism as the principle governing the organisation of the Communist Party was based on the attempt to reconcile the need for firm leadership with the desirability of democratic participation. According to Polish administrative theorists who are concerned with the distribution of authority within the State, such as Leoński, democratic centralism involves on the one hand the need to ensure uniformity in the performance by regional organs of State functions, and on the other hand the need to perform these functions by a method which ensures that authority is exercised in the interests of the working class.[1] Polish administrative theorists have adapted the classic Leninist theory, therefore, to the structure of regional State authority. In the People's Council system, the two conditions cited are fulfilled by dual subordination of all non-representative organs vertically to the higher level organs and horizontally to the council. Vertical subordination has as its main objectives uniformity and efficiency in the administrative apparatus; horizontal subordination is aimed at guaranteeing that the interests and needs within society are considered. Thus the realisation of workers' sovereignty is indirect, as the argument is put, in relation to administrative and executive organs: it is achieved by making these organs structurally dependent upon the representative organs. As Jaroszyński contends, there is no professional élite governing in the interests of a dominant class as occurs in bourgeois States.[2] Nevertheless, a professional element exists, selected indirectly by the people, which must be directed towards managing for the social good, not for its own interests. In addition 'representativeness' in the elected organs includes not just the class criterion (workers, peasants, intelligentsia) but also occupational, and rural-urban, consumer-producer

[1] Leoński, *Rady narodowe*, p. 78.
[2] Jaroszyński, *Zagadnienia rad narodowych*, p. 136.

dichotomies as well.[1] This representative factor is superior to the specialist factor found in the administration, and it constitutes the 'democratic' aspect of the doctrine of democratic centralism.

The problems emanating from the representative-specialist differentiation are numerous and complex. Sokolewicz has classified four kinds, however, which particularly apply to organs in the People's Council system.[2] First, any group tends to place its own interests before wider ones. This may lead to each formulating different objectives so as to satisfy these interests, or it may possibly lead to goal displacement which involves the replacing of original ends with ones designed by and for the executing organ. Second, twofold subordination may make administrative personnel more attentive to higher directives than to those of the representative organ. Sokolewicz has suggested that presidium leaders, though appointed by council, are more conscious of their higher level counterparts which ratified the appointment.[3] The same may apply to administrators who in taking decisions may be influenced more by the requirement to make them acceptable to higher administrators than to local representatives. Third, technical work leads invariably to specialisation and quite frequently as well to exclusion of knowledge concerning the work of other specialists. This may lead to the formulating of means and objectives by one group of specialists possibly in conflict with those of another group, or more likely, superfluous to or repetitive of those of the other group. A fourth major difficulty caused by the existence of representative and administrative elements is that elected members may be so influenced by local interests as to become parochial in attitude. This development may often impede the work of administrators whose experience and training are likely to have involved a more cosmopolitan factor on which many of their projects may be based.

On the other hand, there are a number of factors which are said to lead to a certain degree of integration of work styles of representative and administrative elements within the People's Council system.[4] Specialists may have been socialised through their education and experience to recognise that their

---

[1] Sokolewicz, *Przedstawicielstwo i administracja* . . ., p. 25.
[2] Ibid., p. 39.   [3] Ibid., p. 139.   [4] Ibid., p. 38.

work must be directed to meet the needs and interests of society, not those created by their specialisation. Whether this is so in practice is another issue. Those administrators who have been directly appointed by the presidium are likely to be more sensitive to demands made on them by public organs than are departmental workers appointed by an officer. Since a department is organised into a number of sections the department head has the authority to appoint section heads and they are responsible to him alone. At this level and below may occur a gradient of increasing numbness to public organs. This may closely correspond to the social stratification which is said to exist[1] in the internal structure of administration. Sokolewicz divides non-manual administrative workers into four groups: (1) politico-administrative workers who apply political decisions to the administrative process: they consist of department heads and their equivalents in other administrative organs dependent on council, e.g. directors of locally controlled industry and school and hospital management boards; (2) autonomous administrative workers who take decisions within the limits of the administrative apparatus; (3) non-autonomous administrative workers who simply execute decisions; and (4) experts who take decisions in specialist fields. Only the first group has close links with representative organs and the three lower administrative categories are stratified from both representative organs and the top administrative level. Their careers are considered to be unattractive and their prestige is not great.[2] Consequently their objectives and work patterns may be somewhat differentiated from those of representative organs and top administrators as well. The possible insensitivity of these lower tiers in the administration to representative organs and therefore to any public control at all can lead to the phenomenon of 'bureaucracy' which is frequently attributed to State socialist societies.

Such bureaucratic tendencies may be minimised by the improvement in the qualifications of local councillors, consequently making local councillors a 'better match' for the

---

[1] Ibid., pp. 367–9.

[2] Thus Służewski describes how most people are convinced that anyone so wishing can be an administrator. In university legal departments students directed to administrative practice are hurt by what they believe to be a denigration of their skills. *Nauka administracji* (Warsaw, 1969) pp. 240–1.

full-time administrators. While evidence for this is discussed in more detail below, here we may note that in 1958 28·4 per cent of councillors were non-manual workers; in 1969 this figure increased to 36·5 per cent, which included 10·8 per cent of councillors who were employees in public administration.[1]

The concept of bureaucracy implies, according to Służewski, a functioning of State organs characterised by their becoming divorced from the population and from its needs and interests, their protracted and unconscientious method of settling matters affecting the citizen and their extreme formalism in such activity which harms the settling of the issues involved.[2] Evolution of a bureaucratic State comes about due to certain factors which are inherent in the State itself. A specialist-administrative group is unavoidable in society. When a socialist system was introduced in Poland, the new ruling class, the working class, could only change the composition of the specialist-administrative group, and this it did by saturating it with workers from production. The danger continued, however, that this group might try to isolate itself from other broader social bases. The political-administrative worker, the top level in the hierarchy of administrative workers, might become over-influential. Nevertheless, though the State provides the circumstances for a bureaucracy to exist, it also provides resources to combat it, argues Sokolewicz.[3] One is mass activity, inspired by the party which represents society, in the People's Council system, particularly through institutional channels such as making proposals and submitting complaints about administrative work to the presidium. Another centre for combating bureaucracy is the council itself. This elected organ can exercise social control over administration indirectly through the presidium and thus ensure that a bureaucratic factor does not grow. A third resource is the decentralisation of administrative organs, vesting more authority at lower levels which are closer to the masses. Although the influence of the party on the administrative apparatus is extensive, as we shall see in the next section, and although there has been some administrative decentralisa-

[1] Główny Urząd Statystyczny, *Radni rad narodowych 1958–1969* (Warsaw, 1970) p. 23.
[2] Służewski, *Nauka administracji*, p. 206.
[3] Sokolewicz, *Przedstawicielstwo i administracja* . . ., p. 385.

tion, we believe that perhaps a far more important factor in restricting the development of bureaucratic rule is the extent to which there is rotation of higher-level administrative cadres. Where administrative élites are replaceable it is likely that no permanent bureaucratic ethos will be established. At least, so contends Służewski in describing four justifications of regular rotation of administrative directors.[1] First, he says, such rotation can allow a broader representation of society by including as top administrators individuals who have various social backgrounds. Second, absolute stabilisation of administrative cadres normally leads to an 'authoritative élite' and a technocratic tendency. It prevents the introduction of cadres with newer and higher qualifications of a professional as well as a political kind into the administrative apparatus. Third, where such administrators have held positions for a long period they tend to concentrate around themselves groups of people who hold similar values to their own. This may produce a kind of clique ('kumoterstwo') insensitive to broader-based interests at the top of the structure. Finally, administrative chiefs who have perpetuated their leadership roles may become weary of continually dealing with similar issues in the same ways. They may begin to treat matters superficially and this leads to a routinisation of most of their work. They seldom take novel slants or the more modern and efficient techniques.

Although there are no data as to turnover rates of administrative cadres,[2] it is possible to infer that in the recent period it tended to be high rather than stabilised. For in 1968, the Sejm, on the initiative of the party, passed legislation aimed at limiting extreme fluidity and turnover of administrative workers generally and top administrators in particular. Top administrators and workers could no longer sever contracts with councils as easily as before; they would now receive bonuses and wage increments for long service; and they would be given formal recognition of long-serving work for councils through

---

[1] Służewski, *Nauka administracji*, pp. 238–9.

[2] Some indication as to the level of turnover in administrative cadres is given in a study of Gdańsk wojewodstwo. By 1964 65 per cent of presidium workers employed in 1961 had left. The turnover in executive cadres in each year during this period was 20–25 per cent. See J. Kapliński, 'Instancje partyjne a usprawnienie pracy organów wykonawczych rad narodowych', in *Nowe Drogi*, vol. xx, no. 6 (June 1966) p. 52.

certain rewards.[1] These measures were a response to the growing tide of top administrators who were leaving council work
for better pay and housing benefits offered by industrial enterprises and co-operatives. Służewski has advanced the argument
that rotation of leadership cadres in administration is desirable,
but it should be planned and not an arbitrary rotation. Hitherto
it appears that there was large but unplanned turnover, whereas
ideally it should be moderate and co-ordinated.

The high turnover rate in administrative cadres which existed
recently could not in itself be taken to mean that an im-
planted bureaucratic style of governing was not extant. Although cadres changed, certain modes of operation may have
remained. The onus was left on the individual to collect material
necessary for determining how an issue should be resolved. An
air of superiority persisted in administrators when settling
matters affecting a citizen. They considered it to be doing a
citizen a favour to investigate some issue he had submitted to
them. In addition there was a large volume of regulations,
directives and legislation being received from higher level
administrative authorities which led to an over-complex procedure for resolving issues. This also dissuaded an officer from
taking any decision autonomously; he felt compelled to refer
the matter to other sources as he was so bound by rules. The
situation improved somewhat after 1956.[2] Better forms of
training were available to administrators. In 1960 a Code of
Administrative Procedure was drawn up with which all administrators in People's Councils were expected to be familiar.
It described the procedure to be employed when determining a
matter affecting a citizen. Towards the end of 1966 instructions
issued by the President of the Council of Ministers had the
effect of reducing the number of normative acts by which
departments were bound. The 1968 statute on council workers
gave to them many new responsibilities which were intended to
increase their level of autonomy. These measures removed

[1] Służewski, *Nauka administracji*, p. 237.

[2] For a critical account of bureaucratic conditions existing in the councils
in 1956, see S. Zawadzki, 'O wzrost znaczenia rad narodowych', in *PiP
1956*, nos. 8–9, pp. 263–79, where he claims that bureaucratisation had
led to administrative organs dominating representative ones, central organs
dominating local ones, and the party taking over certain functions of State
administration.

many of the obstructions on administrators which had induced them to be bureaucratic.[1]

However, certain bureaucratic tendencies persisted. In the survey of department heads carried out in 1966, 47 per cent of respondents believed there to be conflict resulting from solutions based on legal regulations and solutions based on fulfilling general goals (Table 40). When legal regulations were

TABLE 40. ASSESSMENT OF LEGAL REGULATIONS BY DEPARTMENT HEADS* (IN PER CENT)

(1)	Is there ever any conflict between solutions to problems which are based on legal regulations and those based on goals?	
	(a) Yes	47·1
	(b) No	32·9
	(c) No response	20·0
(2)	What are the reasons for the violation of laws in departmental functioning? (multiple responses permitted)	
	(a) An excess of regulations	67·1
	(b) Lack of familiarity with regulations	28·4
	(c) Lack of clarity of regulations	50·3
	(d) Giving priority to goals before legality	29·8
	(e) Other reasons	7·1

* Narojek and Swiątkiewicz, 'Pozycja wydziału . . .', pp. 150–2.

violated[2] the most common reasons given were an excess and lack of clarity of regulations. It is significant to point out that the respondents were administrators at the wojewodstwo level, having only central regulations to abide by. We can suggest that at powiat and gromada levels, where central as well as

[1] This improvement was reflected in three surveys carried out at that time. One was conducted amongst citizens leaving the Warsaw City Council building. It found that 33 per cent of respondents said that they had noticed a significant improvement in the work of the executive organs, 48 per cent said there had been a small improvement and only 19 per cent said there had been no improvement. In Warsaw's Wola ward 51 per cent of respondents said administrative work had recently improved significantly. In Łódź a similar finding was recorded. See Kapliński, 'Instancje partyjne . . .', p. 50.

[2] A national study found that in 1962 10 per cent of all council resolutions and 9 per cent of all presidium resolutions infringed some legal regulation. See J. Swiątkiewicz, 1964, p. 17.

wojewodstwo level regulations apply, this perceived excess of regulations would be even greater. Three years later, in 1969, Służewski still argued for better safeguards against an over-abundance of legal regulations directed to administrators and a widening of their decision-taking powers and responsibility for decisions.[1]

The extent to which there is a bureaucratic style of administering in the People's Councils can perhaps be illustrated by the results of a national survey taken of a representative sample of rural and urban populations in 1965. The study encompassed all levels of councils with the exception of wojewodstwo and powiat regions. Altogether 1,850 citizens were interviewed.[2] Table 41 gives respondents' opinions about contact they had had with councils. On the whole, respondents divided evenly between those who perceived that council administrators were kind and friendly and those who considered them to be unfriendly and indifferent. There was a sharp difference in these assessments by rural and urban respondents

TABLE 41. RESPONDENTS' OPINION ABOUT CONTACT WITH THEIR COUNCILS*

	Towns (N = 700) per cent	Country (N = 817) per cent
Assessment of workers' relations to respondents		
Decidedly friendly	10·0	9·4
Rather friendly	31·3	46·3
Indifferent	35·7	26·7
Decidedly unfriendly	13·7	7·0
It differed	9·5	10·6
Assessment of method of settling a matter		
Rather efficiently	30·6	44·6
Rather sluggishly	50·1	32·2
It differed	19·3	23·2

* Dzięcołowska, p. 43.

[1] Sżłuewski, *Nauka administacji*, p. 215.

[2] S. Dzięciołowska, 'Rada narodowa w oczach mieszkańców (Wyniki ogólno-polskiego badania ankietowego)', in *PRN 13*, 1969, pp. 29–88.

however. The latter tended to be more critical because, the author alleges, they did not have the personal, neighbourly form of contact that was more likely to exist in the country. There was also far more anonymity in contact with urban councils in that administrators did not know and were not well known by the electorate. This explanation could equally apply to the low regard held by townspeople for the actual methods used by council administrators in settling issues. A majority found the procedure to be sluggish, whereas in rural areas only a third held this view. As shown in Table 42 a small percentage of respondents, therefore, detected several bureaucratic traits, such as unsympathetic administrators and inefficient methods, in council work.

A final table which may indicate a degree of bureaucratisation of administration perceived by the electorate is its opinion on the reason for shortcomings of, and neglect in, council's administrative work (Table 43). The reason most often attributed is superciliousness and lack of interest and activeness of council workers. This could be interpreted as personal deficiencies in administrators but it also could be regarded as the personalisation of the bureaucratic ethos in council workers. A category which also ranked highly was faulty organisational work of council and bureaucracy as such. Due to the generality of these terms respondents may have been disinclined to specify them as causes of faulty council work. Nonetheless, these data also indicate that many of the shortcomings in administration that existed in the pre-1956 period, before measures were taken to combat bureaucratisation, still existed in 1965. The individual still found it difficult and at times unpleasant to have contact with the administrative apparatus.[1]

---

[1] However, the Gdynia Council recently made concrete attempts at reducing the amount of red tape through which a citizen must pass in order to have a matter considered by the administration. For example, eleven annexes to an administrative code were eliminated, the onus for collecting material, data, testimony and opinions was transferred from the citizen to the department, the period in which an issue took to be resolved was cut from two months (regulated by the official Code of Administrative Procedure) to a few weeks, and a central information point was established in the Organisation-Law department. See T. Kołodziejczyk, 'Oblicza administracji: w stronę obywatela', in *Rada Narodowa*, no. 47 (1118), 21 Nov. 1970, p. 14.

TABLE 42. RESULTS OBTAINED IN COUNCIL SETTLING AN ISSUE AND OPINION ON CONTACT WITH COUNCIL (PER CENT)*

	Method of treating respondents			Process used to settle matter		
	Friendly	Indifferent, unfriendly	Differed	Efficient	Sluggish	Differed
Results on issue						
Favourable	74·4	18·2	6·4	68·4	19·8	16·8
Unfavourable	11·5	79·9	8·6	3·4	85·9	10·7
It differed	30·1	53·7	16·2	11·7	55·8	32·5
No opinion	28·1	53·1	18·8	18·8	34·4	46·8

* Dzięciołowska, p. 59.

TABLE 43. OPINION ON REASONS FOR SHORTCOMINGS AND NEGLECT IN COUNCIL WORK (PER CENT)*

	Town	Country
Independent of council		
Lack of financial resources	20·0	12·0
Difficulty in working with higher-level councils	5·3	6·0
Fault of council		
Superciliousness, lack of interest and activeness	27·4	32·9
Faulty organisational work, bureaucracy	11·0	6·2
Inefficiency, incompetence	6·6	6·5
Moral faults (dishonesty, cliqueness, drunkenness)	7·5	9·8
Other	5·2	6·1
Lack of orientation, no data	16·4	13·9

* Dzięciołowska, p. 41.

It is often claimed that there was a democratisation process in the People's Council system following the 1956 upheavals. We have shown that the influence of representative elements over administrative ones increased in the post-1956 period, but that a bureaucratic style of governing was not completely eradicated.

RELATIONS BETWEEN LOCAL INTERESTS AND THE FORMAL POWER STRUCTURE OF THE LOCAL COMMUNITY

While the style of local councils appears to be bureaucratic and popular participation in decision-making is of a consultative nature, we must also consider the impact of other institutions and groups, such as centrally controlled industrial enterprises and the Communist Party. The result of such an analysis will indicate whether the institutionalised authority structure is as powerful as formal legislation would have it or whether there are 'invisible governments' which really control local affairs. Also a role of such bodies may be to act for the social groups we have considered in this monograph.

In the resolutions of the VIII Plenum of June 1961 concerning decentralisation, a strong emphasis was placed on the supervision of local council work by party committees.[1]

In 1967 the Central Committee's commission on People's Councils described how local party committees might help to strengthen the powers of gromada councils.[2] Criticism was expressed of gromada committees for not helping to 'activise' councillors to meet their electors or to maintain contact with rural organisations. The commission also considered that gromada party committees had minimum contact with councils usually limited to discussions with the presidium leader. Finally committees were criticised for not influencing councils to include in their plans party resolutions passed at higher levels. Nevertheless, the commission found that gromada party committees existed in 91·5 per cent of all gromadas.

The influence of the party is not limited to that exercised by local committees. There are also sections and groups existing in most organisations. Thus the party group existing in a presidium has according to the party statute two basic tasks: to check on the work of the administrative organs and to mould properly workers' political and moral standards.[3] In Rzeszów

---

[1] The most important of these are: (*a*) party committees should work together with councils in giving key socio-political direction to the main activities of councils, particularly in the realm of social mobilisation and major social problems, e.g. food supply, services, housing policy; (*b*) party committees should ensure that councils are properly exercising their co-ordinating function in relation to regional economic policy; (*c*) party committees should ensure that council resolutions, commission opinions and advice and proposals and interpellations of councillors are given appropriate consideration by the presidium, departments and enterprises not subordinated to the council; (*d*) party committees should establish policy which should bind councillors, and the meetings of PUWP councillors should try to include non-party council members; (*e*) party committees should give assistance to the NUF in organising surgeries between councillors and the electorate; and (*f*) party committees should ensure that administrative cadres have a proper political outlook and professional and educational qualifications suited for their jobs. W. Głowacki, *Partyjne kierownictwo i praca partii w radach narodowych* (Warsaw, 1969) pp. 70–5. For an account of the part played by local party committees in the later years of and after the war in the giving of general political direction within a community see A. Kociszewski, 'Powstanie władzy ludowej i walka o jej utrwalenie', in *Ciechanów w okresie władzy ludowej* (Ciechanów, 1970) pp. 9–42.

[2] Głowacki, p. 145.   [3] Ibid., pp. 160 ff.

wojewodstwo, for instance, sections and groups operating in the presidia at all levels had 1,108 meetings in an eighteen-month period in 1965–6, and considered nearly 1,400 items of which about 40 per cent were concerned with the functioning of the administrative apparatus. On the other hand, groups in powiat presidia in Zielona Góra wojewodstwo met on average only four to nine times a year, below the amount required by statute, and of 325 such meetings only 49 had on the agenda an assessment of the administrative apparatus. From this we can see that party activity is not uniform throughout the country and therefore the intensity of its influence is likely to vary from council to council.

Party groups also exist to give political direction to department heads. It was envisaged that there would be close co-operation between such groups which had been set up in the presidium and heads of administrative departments. In this way the presidium would simultaneously be directing departments as executive and *political* superior. However, the Central Committee commission found this relationship lacking amongst wojewodstwo departments in 1965–6. Of seventy-seven department heads questioned as to whether they had *ever* referred to the party branch concerning a particular issue twenty-four (31 per cent) replied they had not, implying that on most issues the party was not consulted. This is not to suggest, however, that administrators preferred to have as little contact as possible with the party; for approximately 75 per cent of all wojewodstwo presidia employees, including 3,500 non-party workers, took part in political training sessions organised by the party.[1] Between 20 per cent and 60 per cent of all presidia employees at all levels were party members, and in wojewodstwos this figure was above 80 per cent. On the whole, the party saturated all other organisations whether internally through affiliation of their members to the party or externally through the influence exerted by party groups, sections or committees running parallel to these organisations.

[1] Not surprisingly, therefore, those citizens trained by or actually belonging to the party tend to know more about local councils. For example, in a national survey which asked what the distinction was between commissions and departments, PUWP members most frequently cited the correct answer, followed by UPP and DP members, those belonging to socialist youth organisations, and finally non-party individuals. From Dzięciołowska, 'Rada narodowa w oczach mieszkańców', p. 69.

Having described certain roles played by the party we now turn to a more dynamic aspect: the actual influence of the party in community politics. This may be examined from various positions: by administrators, by councillors, by the electorate or by the observational approach of an outsider. There are few data on what administrators perceive the influence of the party to be, but the survey of department heads carried out at the wojewodstwo level is fairly instructive.[1] When asked which other agents influenced the manner in which a department was likely to decide an issue 52·2 per cent of heads said there were none outside the formal council structure. The 47·8 per cent who believed that there were outside influential agents most often named the party: of the 54 per cent in this group who actually named such agents 40 per cent referred to the PUWP and the other 14 per cent listed the trade unions, public organisations and the two other parties as being influential. This evidence can be interpreted in two ways: that a majority of department heads consider there to be no interference from any institution outside the council structure, which can signify that the party is not really perceived to be influential in administrative work; or, since nearly half of those who did believe the departments to be influenced by outside agents named the party, this can be interpreted as signifying that it is the most influential institution on administrative work outside of the very council structure. The assessment of the party by administrators is therefore inconclusive.

The influence of the Communist Party in the selection of candidates to elective posts is often said to be dominant, but empirical studies show this to be less important in Poland than perhaps it is in the USSR. In a study of a ward council in Warsaw it was found that 79 per cent of manual workers on council (who numbered nineteen) believed they were selected as candidates by the factory, chiefly because of their occupational activity.[2] Nearly 50 per cent of the technical intelligentsia

---

[1] Narojek and Świątkiewicz, 'Pozycja wydziału . . .', p. 153.

[2] W. Harz and A. Jasińska, 'Problemy reprezentacji grup interesów w radzie narodowej', in *PiP*, vol. xix, no. 3 (217), March 1964, p. 246. This seems particularly paradoxical since another author has claimed that manual workers are not encouraged by their factories to become councillors as the hours for which they would have to be excused to carry out council

(who also numbered nineteen) said that the factory was responsible for selecting them as candidates, about 25 per cent said it was the party and about 20 per cent said it was the citizenry. Finally a majority of office workers (total: twenty-six) named the party as being responsible for their candidatures and 20 per cent said it was the citizenry. There is great occupational differentiation in perceiving how influential the party was in the selection of candidates. The perceived importance of the factory as a source of candidatures supersedes that of the party amongst the majority of people employed in it, such as workers, engineers and technicians. Since only 31 per cent of councillors were non-party it therefore appears that a number of party members still placed factory before party as motivating their candidatures. The role of the party in the nomination process seems far from being an absolute one.

Electors' perceptions of the influence of the party were not homogeneous either. Table 44 gives data of two separate surveys conducted four years apart, the first on a local level (non-powiat town) and the second on a national scale (all councils other than powiat and wojewodstwo). The first asked citizens the question to whom would they turn in cases where they suffered mismanagement at the hands of an official institution or at work; the second asked which channels were used by a citizen unhappy with a decision taken by council. Clearly the two surveys are not measuring precisely the same phenomenon, and respondents' answers were categorised differently in each survey, the second one being more detailed. Nevertheless, some degree of similarity exists, since both concern what channel an aggrieved citizen would use to appeal against some inconvenience caused him. In the 1965 survey the channel most used was appeal to a council of a higher level, a method particularly favoured by rural respondents. This pattern stems from the fact that the issue was made contentious through the decision of council and not some other 'official organ'. In the latter case the tactic most favoured was to contact the party committee concerning the grievance. This channel was the second most frequently cited (if appeals to the Central Committee are included) in the national survey. Invoking central authorities

duties would likely hamper the factories' production plans. Skrzydło, 'Z problematyki organizacji . . .', p. 36.

was a method most frequently suggested by urban respondents in the national survey. Contacting the mass media for assistance was frequently mentioned by respondents in each survey, but appealing to trade unions was only cited by Nakło citizens. This again is due to the different character of the question asked, since in that survey explicit mention was made of mismanagement in place of work. Finally, contacting the local council in Nakło or a local councillor in the national survey concerning a grievance ranked second in the case study, third amongst rural respondents and fourth amongst town respondents. Generally, therefore, the party was considered to be an influential channel to which to appeal by respondents in all three groups.

TABLE 44. CHANNELS OF APPEAL WHICH WOULD BE/WERE USED AGAINST MISMANAGEMENT/UNSATISFACTORY DECISION OF OFFICIAL INSTITUTION/COUNCIL BY CITIZENS IN LOCAL/NATIONAL SURVEY (PER CENT)*

	Nakło (*1961*)	National survey (*1965*)	
		Town respondents	Country respondents
Party committee	35·1	18·5	18·4
Central Committee, PUWP	—	7·7	5·7
Local council/councillor	30·7	14·4	23·0
Higher council	—	49·7	58·6
Press and radio	29·8	23·7	17·8
Central authorities	5·5	10·8	2·3
Sejm deputy	—	3·6	1·1
Trade unions	23·1	—	—
Others	0·0	8·2	2·3

* For the Nakło survey see Z. Suzin, 'Autorytet władzy', in *Polityka*, no. 7, 18 Feb. 1961; for the national survey see Dzięciołowska, 'Rada narodowa w oczach mieszkańców', p. 46. Figures include multiple responses; (—) indicates not applicable.

In a fourth study conducted of political activists in a powiat the same result emerged.[1] Asked to whom they would turn for

[1] J. Wiatr, 'Gospodarze terenu', in *Nowe Drogi*, vol. xxi. no. 1 (Jan. 1967) p. 62.

advice and support activists cited the local PUWP committee (81 per cent), the powiat council presidium (74 per cent), colleagues (52 per cent), wojewodstwo authorities (42 per cent) and higher party authorities (36 per cent). In all the empirical studies described, therefore, local party committees were invariably regarded as a most influential institution to which to appeal.

We have now covered perceptions of the party's role according to administrators, councillors and the electorate, and we now turn to its analysis from the point of view of a sociological researcher. Narojek's study of the party committee in 'Z', a powiat town in eastern Poland, attempts to identify the extent of influence that it possesses in relation to other organisations existing in the community.[1] The most common method of exerting influence over such organisations was found to be through membership of key directors in the party. Of a nineteen-person power group identified in 'Z' sixteen were members of the party. Conversely of an eleven-member town party committee nine held director status in factories, public organisations or service institutions and only two were workers in a factory. Thus there was high overlap between party influentials and directors. The party's influence on the town council was also strong: although only 50 per cent of councillors were party members four of five presidium members were. The author also discovered a positive relationship between issues considered at meetings of the party's councillors' group and those discussed at council sessions. The problems with which council dealt had invariably been studied earlier by the party group of councillors. Finally the town party committee was at the top of a structure which encompassed twenty-eight factories and institutions organised into twenty branches, although only 11 per cent of the population over eighteen years old in the town were party members. Therefore, the infiltration of the party into all organisations and higher management positions was extensive in 'Z'.

The importance of the party committee and the councillor groups in shaping the political life of a community is not limited to 'Z'. In a survey conducted in Kraków wojewodstwo in 1968 the question was asked of gromada council chairmen and

[1] W. Jakubowicz, 'Rola partii w mieście powiatowym', in *Studia Socjologiczno-Polityczne*, 1963, no. 15, p. 199.

secretaries how the PUWP influenced policy decisions in the locality.[1] Nearly four of ten respondents (39 per cent) said that this was achieved through councillors who belonged to the party participating in council and presidium meetings. Almost one quarter (23 per cent) suggested that discussing council work at party committee sessions was the most influential form of directing the gromada's political life. Another quarter (25 per cent) cited miscellaneous types of interaction between party and council, such as having joint meetings of council and the party committee, co-ordinating work in the most important issues, having the presidium chairman attend party committee meetings, or the influencing of council work by the local first secretary. The remainder (13 per cent) gave no response. These results tend to confirm Narojek's finding that the party committee and party councillors are most influential ways of shaping a town's politics.

Narojek also reported a study of a non-powiat town which he named Zawodzie.[2] His conclusions on the role of the party committee were very similar to his first study. Table 45 gives a breakdown of director status of members of the council, co-opted commission members, the primary party committees and other social committees. Three out of every four members in these organisations held director status. If we confine our analysis to the various party committees in the town this proportion extended to nearly nine of every ten members. Of course many directors held membership in more than one organisation. If the party affiliation of first directors is considered we see that of a group of forty-six there were twenty-eight PUWP members, eight UPP, five DP and only five non-party. In this case as well, therefore, a 90 per cent overlap occurred between membership in the first director group and in the party. Finally using a reputational technique to identify an élite which most shaped decisions in the town the author found that of the eleven most frequently cited individuals ten were first directors and the other was a second director. Seven belonged to the PUWP, two to DP, one to UPP, and only one was non-party. The town committee of the PUWP was thus not only found to have a greater sphere of activity than the town council, its influence

[1] Zakrzewski, 'Gromadzkie Rady Narodowe . . .', p. 131.
[2] W. Narojek, *System władzy w mieście* (Wrocław, 1967).

was also strengthened by its members holding top offices in the other organisations in the town.[1]

TABLE 45. MANAGERIAL STATUS OF MEMBERS OF SOCIO-POLITICAL ORGANISATIONS IN ZAWODZIE*

	Total composition	First directors	Other directors	Non directors
Town council	40	15	8	17
Co-opted members, council commissions	14	5	3	6
PUWP town committee	15	9	4	2
UPP town committee	5	2	2	1
DP town committee	3	2	0	1
NUF town committee	24	19	4	1
'Zawodzie Activisation Committee'	37	18	10	9
Other social committees	35	19	11	5
Total	173	89	42	42
Per cent	100	52	24	24

* Narojek, 'Organizacje w układzie miasta', p. 81.

This striking level of coincidence between directors and party committee membership induced the author to conclude that the four primary political organisations (PUWP, UPP, DP, NUF) and particularly the PUWP were the single most important agents bringing about community integration in the local political, economic and cultural life.[2]

Whichever standard was used to identify community influentials the result each time exemplified the prominence of party leaders and directors in the political and economic fabric of Zawodzie. Although this can be interpreted to signify that the manual working class was badly under-represented in the élitist

[1] W. Narojek, 'Organizacje w układzie miasta', in *Studia Socjologiczno-Polityczne*, 1964, no. 17, p. 46.
[2] The influence of the NUF is not always great. Exactly one-half of gromada council chairmen and secretaries found rural NUF committees to be passive or weak in their activity. Zakrzewski, 'Gromadzkie rady narodowe . . .', p. 131. On the other hand the NUF in Łęczna was regarded as the primary agent in activising the town's citizens. J. Kotowicz, 'Decyduje aktyw', in *Rada Narodowa*, no. 50 (1121), 12 Dec. 1970 p. 14.

group there was an associated phenomenon which could have served the interests of the electorate. For the next most noticeably under-represented stratum apart from manual workers was administrators. Having suggested above that there was a danger of bureaucratic rule by politico-administrative workers in local authorities despite recent attempts to give representatives more power, it seems somewhat surprising to find that they were excluded altogether as community influentials in Zawodzie. The eleven-member élite[1] included secretaries of the party committees, the presidium leader and his deputy, and directors of economic and public organisations but no administrative department heads. The three individuals whose opinions were considered most influential consisted of the presidium leader, his deputy and the first secretary of the town party committee. Department heads were again excluded. Even the wider circle of perceived influentials did not include council administrators. Their absence can be taken to signify that administrative and political leadership is not fused, since Narojek's study, which was concerned with the latter, did not reveal administrators playing leading political roles. If political leadership was in fact exercised in Zawodzie by non-administrators then this can serve as strong evidence against the allegation of bureaucratic rule suggested earlier. Instead it suggests that party functionaries and factory managers ensure some measure of social control in a community.

The relationship between council and industry takes on an important character following the findings in Zawodzie. That many first directors who were perceived to be in the local élite were concerned with industrial management requires us to conduct a closer analysis of the formal and informal links between economic notables and the institutional power structure. There are two types of economic State enterprises existing in Poland, those which are controlled centrally and those directed locally.[2] The councils have been given legal

[1] This élite appeared to be not an entrenched one. Five of eleven had served as directors for less than five years. Of the wider forty-member group of influentials only three had served for more than ten years as directors. Narojek, *System władzy w mieście*, p. 199.

[2] For a more detailed analysis see Rybicki, *System rad narodowych w PRL*, pp. 182–95.

powers in certain spheres in relation to both, but as we might expect, centrally controlled industry has a far greater degree of freedom from council interference. The administrative level at which the council is situated is also a significant factor in determining the extent of influence it will have over centrally controlled industry. Wojewodstwo councils have been given most authority. Amongst their powers are giving opinions on the most important tasks performed by centrally managed enterprises which affect regional economic development, making proposals concerning the establishment, organisation and liquidation of such enterprises, offering suggestions on how their productive capacity could best be utilised, co-ordinating their activity with that of locally controlled industry and ensuring that there is integration of assignments included in the local economic plan and assignments included in the enterprises' plans.[1] In appearance these powers seem to lack teeth, though in comparison with the absence of authority vested in English local councils in relation to industry they take on added significance. In fact, however, the institutionalisation of contact in the form of an exchange of opinions, proposals and reports between councils and centrally managed enterprises provides each with a measure of influence over the other. Without this contact the two might be operating in mutually exclusive arenas.

Let us now turn to consider empirical data which quantify the extent of influence that each actor in the relationship has over the other. The major form of influence that council has over non-subordinated units is performing controls, that is, receiving reports from and carrying out fieldwork examination of the activities of these units. In contrast the main form of influence of these units on the council is through participation of their directors in council and presidium meetings.[2] The teeth in these controls are that any inadequacy discovered can be reported to the unit's superior authority, for example, the 'zjednoczenie' (or 'association') in the case of an economic enterprise, which then has the discretion of taking any remedial

---

[1] 'Ustawa z dnia 25 stycznia 1958 r. o radach narodowych', in Starościak, p. 18, Art. 12, 16.

[2] Z. Leoński, *Pojęcie kontroli społecznej i formy jej realizacji przez rady narodowe* (Poznań, 1962) p. 17.

action it may feel is necessary. Controls can be performed on any institution dependent on or independent of council, and they are normally performed by commissions specialising in a particular sphere of activity. Table 46 contains the volume and object of controls performed by commissions at various levels of the council structure in Łódź in 1962–3. The unit which underwent most controls was the one dependent on departments, such as school boards, health centres, libraries, cultural centres and locally controlled factories. The exception to this pattern was the wojewodstwo, which by virtue of the large region over which it has to supervise performed most checks on organs of lower-level councils. In all cases checks were least frequently instituted on departments; this was due to other resources available to commissions to control these units, e.g. giving opinions. Checks on non-subordinated units, which concern us in this section, were not particularly frequent. In the wojewodstwo each commission performed on average only three such controls a year. In the city, where so much key industry is based, each commission performed less than one control a year. In a ward in Łódź this average was slightly over four, whilst in Wielunice powiat it was under three. Generally, therefore, we perceive little use being made of checks over undertakings not subordinated to council. Since the Łódź area has a large concentration of industrial enterprises it appears to be particularly significant that council commissions conducted very few checks on them. It can be taken to signify that such undertakings are large and influential enough to be free from even the most superficial of checks on their activities by local councils. Data on the controls executed by commissions at the powiat level in two more rural wojewodstwo, Lublin and Rzeszów, tend to confirm this view.[1] Here each of about one hundred commissions performed slightly over two checks a year on non-subordinated units. This was even lower than the frequency of controls carried out on departments and indicates that the Łódź analysis is not atypical.

The indicator we chose to illustrate the influence of such undertakings on the work of council is the level of participation of their representatives in presidium sessions. This is not an altogether satisfactory criterion, as there is no way of knowing

[1] Skrzydło, 'Z problematyki organizacji . . .', p. 68.

TABLE 46. TYPES OF UNITS WHICH HAD CONTROLS PERFORMED ON THEM BY COMMISSIONS IN ŁÓDŹ IN 1962–3*

Level (no. commissions)	Year	Total controls	Units controlled			
			Departments	Dependent on Departments	Dependent on lower council	Non-subordinated units
Łódź wojewodstwo (8)	1962	184	13	25	119	27
	1963	150	7	29	94	20
	Total	334	20	54	213	47
Łódź City (9)	1962	171	8	123	35	5
	1963	75	6	41	18	10
	Total	246	14	164	53	15
Łódź ward (8)	Total	458	20	370	0	68
Wielunice powiat (3)	1962	71	9	23	22	17
	1963	97	8	48	13	28
	Total	168	17	71	35	45

* Wróblewski et al. 'Problemy działalności komisji . . .', pp. 123–6.

whether the representatives influenced the presidium or the presidium the representatives. However, as presidium meetings are primarily concerned with executing and managing the activities of all organs in the council structure and only secondarily those outside it this tends to give to representatives from non-subordinated units a channel of influence on council work which would be unavailable to them were they not to attend presidium sessions. That is to say that the more frequent the participation in presidium sessions the more influential the representatives tend to be. Table 47 summarises the participation of representatives from various organisations in presidium sessions in eleven towns from non-powiat to wojewodstwo level in Łódź. Of some twenty organisations which took part in presidium sessions the police organisation (MO) was most frequently represented followed by key industrial enterprises, the Supreme

TABLE 47. REPRESENTATIVES FROM UNDERTAKINGS NOT SUBORDINATED TO COUNCIL WHO PARTICIPATED IN PRESIDIUM SESSIONS IN ELEVEN TOWNS IN ŁÓDŹ WOJEWODSTWO (1962–3)*

State non-subordinated units most represented of twenty	*No. times represented at presidium session*
Police organisation (MO)	29
Key industrial enterprises	20
Supreme Control Bureau (NIK)	14
National Bank of Poland	14
Procurate	13
Zjednoczenie of key industrial enterprises	13

All non-subordinated units most represented of twenty-seven	*No. times represented at presidium co-ordinating meetings*
Association of volunteer firemen	89
Water enterprises	60
PUWP lower level party committee	52
NUF lower level party committee	44
Key industrial enterprises	25
PUWP local party committee	24

Public organisations most represented of thirty	No. times represented at presidium session
PUWP local party committees	64
NUF local party committees	11
Socialist Youth Union (ZMS)	10
Polish Scouts Union (ZHP)	7
SFOS and SFBS	7

Co-operatives and agricultural circles most represented of eight	No. times represented at presidium session
Agricultural circles	34
Peasants' self-help co-operative	23
Workers' co-operative	12
Food co-operative	11
Housing co-operative	10

* J. Borkowski and E. Smoktunowicz, 'Funkcje koordynacyjne prezydium w stosunku do organów i jednostek organizacyjnych nie podporządkowanych radzie narodowej', in *PRN 8*, 1966, pp. 106, 116–18.

Control Bureau (NIK) and the National Bank. This serves to substantiate our premise that representatives of influential organisations are most likely to attend presidium sessions. Participation in co-ordinating sessions organised by the presidium showed a voluntary fireman's association to be most frequently represented[1] followed by water undertakings and party representatives. A similar finding was made amongst public organisations participating in presidium sessions. The party was again seen to be playing a leading role in the authoritative institutions of the towns studied. Finally the agricultural circles were best represented of all co-operative movements. We can interpret the results of this table as implying that the most influential organisations attended presidium sessions most frequently. This may have been motivated by either of two factors: the presidium perceived the organisation to be influential and encouraged its participation, or the organisation participated because it wished to bring its influence

[1] This is freak result, since eighty-eight of the eighty-nine representatives participated in one of the eleven towns studied. Likewise all sixty representatives of water enterprise attended in one town.

to bear on the presidium. In either case we notice the close collaboration of the presidium with such influential organisations, and without doubt the presidium at these meetings received certain demands from these organisations based on their particular interests. That some organisations participated far more intensively than others, for example, party committees, key industrial enterprises and their zjednoczenie, may suggest that these have most demands to articulate.

There is little empirical material concerning the relationship between local councils and the zjednoczenie. The zjednoczenie is a grouping of industries under regional or central management, and the powers of the council over them depend on this division. A council can create a zjednoczenie composed of locally controlled industries and the authority it possesses over it is similar to that it has in relation to individual enterprises subordinated to it and to administrative departments.[1] They are included in the local budget like any administrative section. In fact the director of a zjednoczenie enjoys the same status as a department head, that is, all powers are vested in him. In relation to centrally managed zjednoczenies, council is empowered to co-ordinate and perform controls on their activity but cannot issue any binding directives.[2] The relationship between councils and local zjednoczenie is not considered to be good. One author who studied this relationship wrote that the zjednoczenies tend to complain that wojewodstwo council presidia are too little interested in their problems.[3] Where they are interested, presidia treat production problems in an inexpert manner. In turn the presidia believe that the zjednoczenies offer little assistance to councils as well as to the constituent enterprises. In many ways this malaise is similar to that between representative and administrative organs discussed earlier, that the latter seem to resent the intrusion of a non-specialist element in their work. The zjednoczenies, like departments, would prefer to have less control exercised over them by elected representatives. Nevertheless, the interest of centrally managed

---

[1] 'Ustawa z dnia 25 stycznia 58 r. o radach narodowych', in Starościak, p. 39, Art. 62.3.

[2] Ibid., p. 15, Art. 13.1; p. 18, Art. 16.1.

[3] K. Szwarc, 'Pozycja zjednoczenia terenowego', in *Życie Gospodarcze*, no. 50, 10 Dec. 1961.

zjednoczenies, at least in council work, is quite extensive if the participation of their representatives in presidia sessions is a fair criterion (Table 47).

We conclude this section by describing which interests, if any, are represented in the formal decision-making process, and how such representation occurs, whether through spokesmen for such interests in the institutionalised arena, namely councillors, or through participation of organisations directly. In the study of a Warsaw ward council[1] the authors identified three phases of group representation in the development of the People's Council system in Poland: (1) between 1944 and 1949 the basic conflict of interests was on a political plain, that is, between parties holding different policies; (2) between 1950 and 1956 the struggle turned towards ensuring that the social composition of councils matched those of the electorate, an objective which was prompted by the idea that such a congruence would automatically prove that the masses were participating in government; and (3) from 1956 onwards the battle was to ensure that local interests were not suppressed by central ones (hence decentralisation of authority) and that representative ones were not subordinated to bureaucratic ones; to achieve these ends attempts were made to raise the professional and educational qualifications of councillors. The study found that there was no conflict of interests based on class or strata, nor was there disagreement amongst councillors because of their socio-occupational backgrounds. We should emphasise the fact that councillors did not identify with and thereby did not represent the interests and desires of their socio-occupational group, the only exception being those engaged in private enterprise who defended these interests in council. Factories did not consider any employees who were councillors to be spokesmen for their interests. Instead the process by which such interests were articulated was through direct informal contacts between factory heads and council leaders. However, councillors were found to defend particularistic interests in two cases: when a local inhabitant complained about bureaucratisation in the administration, councillors were likely to take up the case for the complainant; and when there was conflict between ward council interests and Warsaw City Council interests (40 per

[1] Harz and Jasińska, 'Problemy reprezentacji . . .', pp. 424–32.

cent of councillors said such conflict occurred) nearly all councillors (97 per cent) defended the ward. Finally councillors were asked which interest they would support in a hypothetical situation where there was conflict of interests of an individual character with those of a general nature. The majority of councillors who were workers (60 per cent) said they would support individual interests, the majority who were office workers said they would support general interests. From this we can deduce that workers tend to be against centralisation and for local autonomy more than do office workers, due perhaps to a more particularistic kind of consciousness.

The study of powiat activists, most of whom we may suspect to be in the non-manual class if they are at all similar to Zawodzie influentials, reveals that general interests were also placed above individual ones.[1] In reply to the question of what kind of institution or group they considered especially important in their everyday activities, a majority (57 per cent) cited the country as a whole, a third gave the party (33 per cent) and the small remaining group of respondents said the local population (11 per cent) and friends and supporters (0·3 per cent). Although national institutions accounted for nine-tenths of answers there is no implication that this result contradicts the Warsaw ward survey which found almost unanimous support for local before city interests. We can surmise that decision takers are more likely to defend local interests whenever there is specific mention of these conflicting with wider ones, but in a more open-ended question they are likely to cite national wellbeing as most important. In the first case there may be a discrepancy between what activists say and what they actually do.

Some justification for protecting local interests may arise from evidence of decision-taking patterns in various organisations, and not just council, in the Zawodzie study.[2] In 102 matters which affected local organisations Narojek found that in only thirty-five of them was the decision taken locally. Eleven were referred to the powiat level of the organisation for resolution, thirty-two to the wojewodstwo level and twenty to

[1] Wiatr, 'Gospodarze terenu', p. 62.
[2] W. Narojek, 'Mechanizm podejmowania decyzji w mieście', in *Studia Socjologiczne*, no. 13, 1964.

the central level. A large number of cases decided at the central level involved council departments, the zjednoczenie or central co-operatives. Industry was the subject which was most often decided centrally (Table 48). The subject most often decided locally was communal economy. From this we can conclude that decisions affecting industry were most often taken outside of the local arena whilst decisions on less important matters were decided locally. Nevertheless there were few cases (8·5 per cent) where decisions were not in accordance with the recommendations originally made by the organisations which had initiated the issues. Where these organisations were not local ones there were no cases where a contrary decision was taken. As for extent of participation in decisions, we see that decisions taken locally had by far most organisations involved in them. Those taken centrally tended to involve in the vast majority of cases (80 per cent) no more than one organisation. This latter pattern may be a primary cause for some councillors stating that they would defend local before more central interests.

Finally we turn to the representation of interests in rural communities. There have been two major empirical studies conducted in recent years which assessed the role of interest groups in Polish villages. The first was based on the village of Gopło in the middle west of Poland and was completed in 1965.[1] The author found that interest groups emerged as a result of competition amongst families for contracts for agricultural produce, for loans from the Fund for the Development of Agriculture, for non-agricultural jobs, for leases of State land, for long-term credit and for distribution of building materials, fertiliser, seeds and coal. In Gopło the author identified three interest groups.[2] The first was composed of State and local authority officials who had greatest access to the lease of public land and to supplies of building materials. They were recruited

---

[1] W. Adamski, *Grupy interesów w społeczności wiejskiej* (Warsaw, 1967).

[2] The author defined an interest group as the relationship between at least two families which leads to their functioning on a more or less permanent basis with one person in the local authority or influencing a State official outside of the gromada. Adamski, p. 174. As a result the first interest group was composed of only four State or local authority officials (headmaster, teacher, administrator, gromada presidium secretary); the second of four families of farmers; and the third of four farmers. See Adamski, pp. 177–87.

TABLE 48. ASPECTS OF DECISION-TAKING IN ZAWODZIE IN 1962*

Subject matter affecting local organisation	Where decision taken					
	Local	Powiat	Woje-wodstwo	Central	Others	Total
Communal economy	9	3	5	1	2	20
Health	2	3	1	0	0	6
Education	7	1	5	3	0	16
Culture, sport	3	0	5	0	0	8
Housing	4	1	3	1	0	9
Trade and commerce	3	2	4	2	0	11
Industry	6	1	4	12	0	23
Others	1	0	5	1	2	9
Total	35	11	32	20	4	102

TABLE 48 (*continued*)

Manner of resolution of issue	Recommendation on decision made by			
	Same organisation as that affected by decision	Other local organisation	Extra-local	Total
In accordance with recommendation	30	39	18	87
Not in accordance with recommendation	7	5	0	12
Decision in conflicting issues	1	2	0	3
Total	38	46	18	102

Where decision taken	No. organisations participating in decision			
	1	2–5	6+	total
Locally	5	27	3	35
At powiat level	7	4	0	11
At wojewodstwo level	17	10	5	32
Centrally	16	4	0	20
Other	3	1	0	4
Total	48	46	8	102

* Narojek, 'Mechanizm podejmowania decyzji w mieście', pp. 173, 176, 178.

from smallhold farmers and they exercised influence through their leading informal relations with other community leaders. Their objectives, contends the author, were not only material benefits but also upward mobility in the prestige structure in the village. The second group consisted of richer farmers using advanced methods of production who advocated private owner-ship of land. They were the most efficient, or 'rational', of local farmers and they monopolised contracts for the most profitable crops largely because of their outside contacts. The third group was composed of farmers who allocated the ma-chines belonging to the Agricultural Circle. They were centred on the leader of both the circle and the UPP committee and they obtained long-term State loans. Apart from this interest, how-ever, they had little else in common. Considerable conflict occurred between the first two groups, particularly in matters concerning technical-organisational innovation and agri-cultural production, and the entire village was occasionally divided into two. Change of leadership of the Agricultural Circle, however, eliminated much of the influence exerted by the group of rich farmers and transferred it to the less pro-tagonistic group of farmers holding long-term State loans.

A second empirical study of interest groups functioning in a rural setting was completed in 1966 and concerned a village in Kraków wojewodstwo.[1] The author identified the most influential individuals in the village and found that they were closely linked to, although not coincident with, the formal power structure.[2] Several village institutions independent of the gromada council were extremely influential. These included the milk co-operative, commune co-operative, and Agricultural Circle, and because they possessed greater financial resources than the gromada council they frequently took the most im-portant decisions affecting the entire community. The circle

[1] D. Markowski, 'Przemiany władzy lokalnej w społeczności wiejskiej', in *Kultura i Społeczeństwo*, xii, no. 3, 1968, pp. 165–80.

[2] Thus in 1955 the most influential individuals were the local Sejm Deputy, the PUWP secretary and the UPP leader. As a result of the political upheavals in 1956, the new influentials were the chairman and secretary of the gromada council, the head of the Agricultural Circle and the director of the milk co-operative. By 1965 the only changes had been the return of the party secretary into the group, and the departure of the head of the circle and the secretary of the council. Markowski, pp. 171–2.

was, as in Gopło, particularly influential since it made greatest use of the Fund for the Development of Agriculture. An additional interest group was, again as in Gopło, the richer farmers who advocated a return to the prewar system of private property. This group, termed the 'white democracy', was at one time concentrated in the Volunteer Firemen's organisation but was more recently centred on the parish. A further interest group consisted of the teachers. Their influence emanated from their close links with the powiat authority and they managed to successfully oppose the gromada council's housing policy for teachers. Certain hamlets and the local fruit factory played successful roles in articulating their interests. Finally a number of families with relatives in leading positions in authorities outside of the village managed favourably to represent their interests in certain village issues. The author concludes that the pluralist nature of the formal power structure, which included the council, the PUWP, the UPP, the Agricultural Circle and the co-operatives, reflected the real distribution of power in the village.

To summarise our findings in this section, we have seen how important a role local party committees play in community politics. We have also observed how the political élite tends to be saturated with party members and director cadres. We have described the formal and practical relationships between councils and undertakings functioning in the locality which are not subordinated to councils. We have attempted to show that council has less influence on such undertakings than they have on council. Finally we discussed group representation and organisational participation, and we found that those interests most strongly articulated in urban communities involved opposition to a bureaucratic or centralist tendency. The interests most frequently observed in rural communities were those articulated by local authority officials, by the bodies of the Agricultural Circles, and by rich farmers who advocated a system of private property. There was most organisational involvement in locally decided matters but obviously there were other processes which brought about articulation of interests of various groups in society. The most important of these is extent of representation of social groups in the formal power structure, particularly in the presidium, which is council's executive and managing organ. If we can identify the background of members of the various council organs, such as council, presidium, commissions and departments, and find differentiation amongst them we can relate these to our assessment of the authority each possesses. From that we should be able to conclude what the social characteristics are of local influentials and identify thereby the social stratification of authority.

THE CHANGING SOCIAL BACKGROUND OF LOCAL POLITICAL ACTORS

There are four principal groups involved in the People's Council system: councillors, presidium members, commission members and non-manual workers employed in departments (administrators). We propose to describe the social characteristics of these groups over time and at various levels of the council structure, particularly the social background of the key personnel. With these added variables we may be able to identify general patterns of change in social background, which may help us explain what type of person becomes involved in council activity in various capacities.

The first problem is the general distribution of the four groups we have cited in the council system. In Table 49 we see that the lowest level in the structure (gromadas) accounts for over three-quarters of total councils and members of the presidium, and for about two-thirds of total councillors and commission members. Thus overall figures are very strongly influenced by the situation which exists in gromadas. Conversely, that level which has most powers vested in it, the wojewodstwo, is least numerous in terms of units and personnel. Total figures therefore may be misleading and it is necessary to consider, wherever possible, detailed breakdowns.

Since 1958 the number of councils has been reduced and with it the number of councillors. This phenomenon is explained by the amalgamation of many gromada councils between 1955, when they numbered 8,790, and 1969, when they were 4,672. The number of commission members also fell whilst that of the presidia at first decreased but then enlarged in 1969 when councils frequently increased the membership of their presidia. The number of administrators was also reduced.

TABLE 49. NUMBERS OF COUNCILLORS, PRESIDIUM MEMBERS, COMMISSION MEMBERS AND DEPARTMENTAL NON-MANUAL WORKERS IN COUNCILS OVER TIME AND ACCORDING TO ADMINISTRATIVE LEVEL*

	Councils	Inhabitants per councillor	Councillors	Presidium	Commissions	Departments	
Total							
1958	9,595	135ᵃ	205,044	37,780	269,094	135,362	1956
1961	7,602	141	184,023	27,289ᵇ	254,237	115,136	1959
1965	6,502	164	171,724	27,741	245,044	108,175	1962
1969	5,934	180	165,725	31,239	245,907	107,913	1965
		—					
Per cent of those in 1959 engaged in							
Wojewodstwo	0·4		1·5	0·6	1·8ᶜ	15·2ᵈ	
Powiats	5·3		10·6	6·3	11·8	40·0	
Powiat towns	1·2		3·0	1·5	3·5	10·5	
Non-powiat towns	12·7		14·8	13·3	15·2	6·9	
Districts	0·7		1·6	0·8	1·9	5·2	
Settlements	0·9		0·8	0·9	0·8	0·5	
Gromadas	78·7		67·7	76·6	65·0	21·6	

ᵃ Figure is for 1955.   ᵇ Figure is for 1962.   ᶜ For all commissions figures are for 1970.   ᵈ For all departments figures are for 1965.

* From GUS, Rady rad narodowych 1958–1969, pp. 2–4; GUS, Członkowie prezydiów rad narodowych 1958–1969, p. 7; Kancelaria Rady Państwa Biuro Rad Narodowych, Struktura osobowa komisji stałych rad narodowych według stanu w dniu 31.V.70 r., p. 2; Urząd Rady Ministrów, Biuro do Spraw Prezydiów Rad Narodowych, Rady narodowe: Struktura osobowa prezydiów rad narodowych; Struktura zatrudnienia w organach administracji prezydiów rad narodowych (Warsaw, 1966) p. 115; Cześć, ii, pp. 71–96. All figures for years before 1956 are taken from B. Zawadzki and S. Zawadzki, 'Ewolucja składu rad narodowych', in PRN 10, 1967, pp. 5–54.

Between 1958 and 1969 there was an increasing number of women serving in various council capacities. However, very few women at all managed to serve on the presidium, the Cabinet of Council, and this is more the case in relation to the presidium's permanent members, its chairman, deputies and secretary, who are generally the most influential people in the council structure. Women are therefore progressively less represented as the authority of the organ increases. In contrast in 1965 more women worked on administration in council (55 per cent) than men.

In terms of age there is a marked consistency in distribution over time as well as between councillors and commission members. In 1969 about 28 per cent were over fifty, nearly 60 per cent were between thirty and forty-nine years old and only 12 per cent were under thirty. Youth is therefore under-represented on council, though of course this is the case in most countries, including capitalist ones. One significant differentiation in the groups is the smaller proportion of the under-thirty bracket in the presidia, and this is even more telling in the permanent presidium member group. Again we see that the executive-managing organ is composed of the traditionally dominant element in most institutions – elder statesmen. But this claim can be exaggerated in this case, for over two-thirds of presidium members were under fifty. Our most striking discovery is the contrast between administrators and representatives in terms of age. There were more than three times the number of administrators employed by departments who in 1965 were under thirty than there were councillors of that age group. Also there were just over half as many administrators over fifty as there were councillors. The Zawadskis optimistically have interpreted this as having positive effects, indicating greater originality and energy amongst administrators and more life experience and social awareness amongst representatives.

The analysis of the levels of education of groups in council work can indicate which social elements are best represented on council. If the well-educated are over-represented, for example, this may signify that an intellectual élite constitutes a ruling stratum. A psychological chasm may also split the educational élite from the masses and restrict the interaction process of articulating and responding to demands. From a study of the diagram we see that education is a variable which has changed most markedly over time and still sharply distinguishes higher-level councils from their lower counterparts. With the passage of time more and more councillors have better education (see Appendix 4, Table 1). This is particularly true for wojewodstwo councillors, over a third of whom had completed further education in 1969 and only 1 per cent of whom had uncompleted elementary education. This is as sharp a contrast to the situation in 1958 as it is to the present pattern in gromadas, where only 2 per cent had completed higher education in 1969 whilst 79 per cent had no better than completed elementary education. This marks an improvement in the levels of education of gromada councillors from 1958, but it is not a very marked one and still lends much support to the idea that further decentralisation of authority, from the powiat to the gromada, would be premature. If we analyse the pattern from 1949 we see that overall educational standards amongst councillors did not show any improvement until 1958. The Zawadzkis attribute this pattern to the fact that certain objectives have been pursued in each of three distinct periods of the councils' existence.[1] Between 1944 and 1949 the emphasis was on providing means for establishing the victory of socialism in Poland. They point out that although there was a National Front of workers' movements there were two separate workers' parties and other anti-socialist parties opposed to them. Consequently the most important criterion for candidates to council at this time was their political affiliation. Between 1950 and 1956, when the communist party was more firmly entrenched, an attempt was made to change the class character of councils. There was an aspiration to include as many manual workers as possible to exemplify the popular nature of governors and the class basis of the government. Hence education was but a secondary criterion, illustrated by the increase in the number of councillors with uncompleted elementary education from 38 per cent in 1949 to 44 per cent in 1955. Even at the wojewodstwo level, the share of manual workers increased in number, and councillors with unfinished basic education rose from 47 per cent in 1949 to 56 per cent in 1955. Finally, from 1957 onwards the struggle in councils was directed against growing centralisation and

[1] Zawadzka, 'Ewolucja składu . . .', pp. 8–26.

bureaucracy.[1] If more authority was to be vested in local representative organs rather than central or administrative ones it was essential that councillors should be equipped to deal with complex and technical issues. To do this a higher level of education was necessary. Since within the population at large the number who had completed further education and were working in socialised industry increased one and a half times between 1956 and 1964 and those with secondary technical education increased one and a third times in this period, it would have been surprising if council composition did not reflect this tendency as well. Our figures bear this out: those with further education increased from 2·2 per cent in 1955 to 6·7 per cent in 1969, whilst those with unfinished elementary decreased from 43·9 per cent to 10·3 per cent in these same years. However, we have seen that educational standards at gromada level are still relatively poor. In powiats, where decentralisation has taken place most recently, the number of councillors with further education has increased most in recent years.

The pattern of education amongst presidium members since 1947 (Appendix 4, Table 2) is very similar to that amongst councillors, though the sharpest increase in levels of education was recorded in 1962 rather than in 1958. This lag is probably due to the conservative nature of the executive-managing organ within which was included an entrenched local élite. There is only a slightly better education level amongst presidium members than councillors, but it is most noticeable at wojewodstwo level, where from 1958 onwards there were no persons with incomplete elementary education. In terms of education of administrators (Appendix 4, Table 3) our data do not extend beyond 1959. Nonetheless there are indications here also that education of cadres has been improving; it is at a slightly higher level than that of presidium members or councillors, for example, only 0·2 per cent had uncompleted elementary in 1965. However, there is a sharp variation at levels of the council system. For instance under 0·05 per cent of administrators had completed higher education in gromada councils, thus bringing

[1] However by 1971 the main problem facing local councils was not over-centralisation or bureaucracy, but, according to Gierek, innovating and adapting to new methods of work. See S. Zawadzki, 'Kierunki rozwoju systemu rad narodowych', in *Nowe Drogi*, 1971, no. 8 (August), p. 13

about the phenomenon that for every one administrator with higher education there were 224 councillors. In contrast at the wojewodstwo level, though the percentage of councillors with higher education was 36 per cent, as opposed to 31 per cent of administrators, in actual numbers there were six administrators with such a qualification for each councillor.

Let us now consider the type of further education which local government activists and officials have received. We may observe in Diagram 5 that there is striking similarity in the type of higher education of presidium members and administrators. The two most common forms of education amongst both groups were legal training and agronomy. Most councillors, presidium members and administrators who had completed courses in agriculture were based at the gromada or powiat levels, whereas there were most economists at the wojewodstwo level. The similarity between types of higher education of representatives and administrators illustrates once again that elected organs are not without people with suitable qualifications to supervise and direct the work of the administration.

The next factor we would like to discuss is socio-occupational groups of various actors in the council system. In this case, as with education, the pressures applied in the three periods of People's Poland on social composition make themselves very clear. During the political struggle waged before 1950 we observe (see Appendix 4, Table 4) how the working class was widely under-represented on councils and presidia: in 1946–7 only 9·6 per cent of councillors and 5·4 per cent of presidium members were manual workers. However, the number of working-class councillors doubled between 1946 and 1949, and there was a greater than sevenfold increase in the number of workers on the presidium between 1947 and 1951. This was a reflection of the consolidation of power by the Communists and of the primary criterion for selection of candidates to council, i.e. that their political views were in line with those of the envisaged socialist State. Thus in the early 1950s social background was the most important quality which led to upward mobility in political life. This phase was a short-lived one, for already by 1953 we see that the percentage of workers had decreased by half. Only in 1951 and 1958 were manual workers

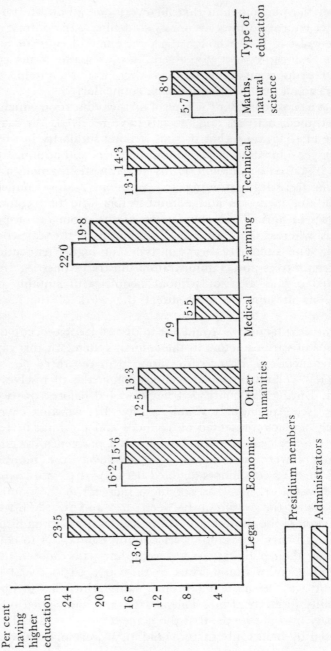

Diagram 5. Types of Further Education of Presidium Members in 1969 and Administrators in 1965*

☐ Presidium members

▨ Administrators

* Członkowie prezydiów . . . , p. 17; Struktura zatrudnienia . . . , p. 145.

better represented on the presidium than on council. And it was in 1951 for the presidium and in 1953 for council that workers were best represented. Since then their share of members has declined, though in 1969 there was a slight increase in their number on council.

The emphasis on political and later social criteria for candidates to council in the pre-1956 period had contributed to the tendency towards bureaucratisation and centralisation at that time. For without emphasis on educational qualifications and personal talents councils could not properly perform many of the functions which were theoretically their responsibility. As a result these powers were gradually taken over by administrative and more centralised institutions. However, with political stability achieved and with due representation of the new ruling class implemented there was after 1956 the freedom to choose cadres on another basis. This was educational standing and consequently class representation was no longer a primary criterion. With higher formal qualifications demanded, manual workers found themselves unable to supply enough suitable candidates for council as in the past. In addition there was less constraint on selecting non-manual workers to council, for this new intelligentsia was not the same as the 1944 one. The values it held were not so violently opposed to the new socialist order and therefore were in harmony with the manual working class. The increase in non-manual workers on council was sharpest during the democratisation and decentralisation phase which took place between 1956 and 1961. Thus in 1961 there were 25 per cent more councillors of non-manual occupation than in 1958, and in 1962 there were 50 per cent more presidium members in that class than in 1958. A very striking differentiation occurred between council levels, however. At wojewodstwo and powiat level there were far more non-manual workers in council and presidium than at gromada level. This pattern was most marked in presidium composition, where in 1969 nearly 97 per cent of wojewodstwo and 92 per cent of powiat members were non-manual workers whilst in gromadas the figure was only 44 per cent. The reason for this was that nearly half of gromada membership tended to be drawn from the peasant and farming strata whilst in wojewodstwos and powiats such groups were negligibly represented. Gromadas, concerned

as they were with agricultural matters and consisting of populations mostly of peasant stock, had little reason or opportunity
to draft non-manual workers. But at all council levels we notice
that non-manual workers were invariably over-represented in
the presidium. Membership in that executive organ tended to
be held, as we have seen, by elder predominantly male non-
manuals with higher education.

We have alluded to the possibility that the monopolisation
of certain political positions by a certain social stratum might
have undemocratic features. We have seen that there is a
tendency for non-manual workers to take a larger share of
representative and directing posts. It should be pointed out that
the very fact of occupational specialisation in administration
leads to the phenomenon of administrators becoming white-
collar workers. To establish whether a stratum monopolises
positions of privilege and influence, we need to consider the
social recruitment of such groups. Table 50 shows the social
origins of the permanent directing members of the presidia of
various types of People's Councils. It shows that only a small
proportion of the total (5 per cent) originate from non-manual
strata. At the more important levels of the wojewodstwos 15 per
cent and powiat towns 17 per cent have non-manual backgrounds; but even here this is not sufficient to conclude that a
social stratum has any monopoly. In fact, Table 50 shows that
in 1969 the overwhelming part of permanent local authority
higher executive personnel were recruited from the ranks of
manual workers and peasants.

Data for employment of councillors and presidium members
in the various sectors of the national economy are not available
until 1969 (Table 51). In that year we see that nearly one half
of all councillors and over 40 per cent of presidium members
were engaged in agriculture, but these figures are skewed by the
gromada councils, in which peasants are strongly represented.
At the wojewodstwo level, the economic sector in which most
councillors worked was industry, and the economic sector in
which most presidium members worked was the political and
social organisations. This indicates again that the party exerts
most influence in the presidium. One other economic sector
which employed a significant proportion (about 10 per cent) of
councillors and presidium members was education and science.

TABLE 50. THE PERMANENT, DIRECTING MEMBERS OF PRESIDIA OF PEOPLE'S COUNCILS ACCORDING TO THEIR SOCIAL ORIGIN IN 1969*

Peoples' Councils	Number	Social origin			
		Manual workers	Peasants	Non-manual workers	Others and no data
		Percentage			
Total	7,576	100·0	33·1	60·8	5·0	1·1
Wojewodstwos	113	100·0	47·8	36·3	15·0	0·9
Powiats	1,036	100·0	34·6	54·8	9·2	1·4
Powiat towns	257	100·0	57·6	23·3	17·1	2·0
Other towns	1,320	100·0	53·4	36·1	9·2	1·3
Gromadas	129	100·0	56·6	21·7	20·9	0·8
Settlements	59	100·0	59·0	36·1	4·9	—
Villages	4,662	100·0	24·4	73·1	1·6	0·9

* Source: K. Zagorski, Social Mobility and Changes in the Structure of Planning Society (Warsaw, 1970) p. 14.

TABLE 51. COUNCILLORS AND PRESIDIUM MEMBERS IN 1969 EMPLOYED IN SELECTED SECTORS OF THE NATIONAL ECONOMY (IN PER CENT)*

	Councillors				Presidium members			
	Total	Wojewodstwo	Powiat	Gromada	Total	Wojewodstwo	Powiat	Gromada
Industry	13·1	27·8	15·6	7·2	8·2	6·5	10·1	5·8
Building	1·3	3·0	1·5	0·7	0·6	1·0	0·7	0·4
Agriculture	48·3	20·7	38·4	62·2	41·1	4·0	12·0	51·2
Forestry	1·5	0·7	1·5	1·8	1·8	0·5	1·1	2·1
Transport and communication	2·7	2·6	2·1	2·1	2·0	1·5	0·9	1·8
Commerce	4·9	2·6	5·2	4·0	4·5	2·0	5·1	3·9
Communal economy and housing	0·8	1·1	0·6	0·2	0·5	0·5	0·4	0·2
Education and science	9·5	9·0	8·4	9·8	10·7	6·5	5·5	11·3
Culture and art	0·6	2·0	0·5	0·5	0·3	0·5	0·2	0·3
Health and social care	2·1	2·6	2·9	0·9	1·5	—	1·1	0·9
Public administration	6·2	8·8	8·5	5·4	—	—	—	—
Finance and security institutions	0·9	1·7	1·9	0·5	—	—	—	—
Political and social organisations	1·4	9·8	5·5	0·2	0·9	14·5	4·2	0·3
Private craftsmen	1·4	2·2	1·7	0·7	—	—	—	—

(— signifies these categories do not appear in the classification)

* *Radni . . .*, pp. 24–7; *Członkowie prezydiów . . .*, pp. 26–7. Totals do not add up to 100 per cent because full information is not given.

There is no occupational breakdown for councillors and presidium members, however, and we are unable to relate manual and non-manual workers to the economic sector in which they are engaged.

Let us now turn to consider the party composition of the various groups in the People's Council system. Again the fluctuations that we observe (see Appendix 4, Tables 6 and 7) reflect the political character of the system in various periods. In 1946 the major parties were competing for power, and although the PWP and PSP combined represented nearly 40 per cent of councillors' political membership no single party at that time could match the 25·8 per cent level of non-party councillors. In the presidium, the PWP encompassed 27 per cent of membership, slightly more than the non-party composition. Between September 1948 and June 1949, however, in which time the two principal workers' parties unified, there was a sharp general change in party affiliation of councillors. The number of party members fell by half and the number of PUWP members increased by nearly a third. The new party submitted a great number of candidates who were elected as councillors. Just before the first elections were held the number of non-party members once again increased, for by 1953 power was firmly in the hands of the socialist forces and policy was then to saturate councils with as many manual workers, party members or not, as possible. In 1954 the first elections were held, and in addition commune councils were replaced with larger, more numerous gromadas. The result of the second fact was an increase in non-party members and a decline in PUWP numbers. For example, though only 1 per cent of presidium members at wojewodstwo level were non-party in 1955, at gromada level in that same year the percentage of non-party members was 36 per cent. Conversely whereas 89 per cent of wojewodstwo presidium members belonged to the PUWP, for gromadas this figure was 47 per cent. However, that year marked the watershed for party membership. Since 1955 PUWP numbers have been gradually increasing on councils and presidia, from 1958 UPP and DP membership has remained constant, whilst non-party councillors and presidia members have remained the same since 1961.

We have already indicated the extent that party membership differed between council levels. By 1969, however, the differences had been considerably narrowed. Exactly 50 per cent of wojewodstwo councillors belonged to the PUWP, as did 49 per cent of powiat councillors, and 45 per cent at gromada level. The non-party proportion differed from about 22 per cent at wojewodstwo and powiat level to 31 per cent in gromadas. The UPP's main sources of strength were at powiat (24 per cent) and gromada (24 per cent) level, whilst the DP included 9 per cent of wojewodstwo councillors and only 0·4 per cent in gromadas. Comparing councils to presidia, we observe that there was a higher proportion of PUWP and UPP members in the latter than on the former. Non-party members were consistently under-represented on the executive organ after 1947. For example, in 1955, when 49 per cent of councillors did not belong to a party, their representation in the presidium was only 33 per cent. In 1969, when 30 per cent of councillors were not party-affiliated, their number in the presidium was cut in half to 15·8 per cent. Once again we see that the composition of the presidia was not representative of that of popularly elected councillors. The social and political characteristics of this ruling élite, not to mention their position on the top of the economic pyramid which we discussed in our previous section, are found to be substantially different from those elected directly by the masses.

Council also is responsible for the recruitment to commissions. The number of women on commissions is generally comparable to that on councils, indicating there was no bias either for or against them in co-opting commission members. There tended to be only slightly more co-opted members with further education than there were amongst councillors, and their specialisations were also similar to each other. In terms of socio-occupational groups co-opted members were more often non-manual workers than were councillors. In addition they were more often drawn from the residual category which included private craftsmen, the retired and some non-working women. Peasants and manual workers were not co-opted as often as they were elected to council. Finally, there was a fair distribution of co-opted commission members of non-party status and in fact slightly more were co-opted in relation to their overall aggregate than amongst PUWP members. Co-option to commissions was therefore less on the basis of certain exclusive characteristics, for example, party membership, higher education, age and dominant sex, than selection to presidium membership. This may indicate that the actual authority held by commissions was not great enough to warrant control by a social élite, or it could suggest that a sincere attempt was made to draft representatives from society for the consultative and participatory purpose which commissions serve.

Although we have demonstrated certain differences in background amongst various actors in the council system and inferred what they signify we must emphasise one important fact not yet mentioned. That is that the high turnover rate observed within administrative cadres is also extant within representative and executive cadres.[1] Amongst councillors elected in 1969 49·6 per cent had not served in the previous term of office.[2] Amongst presidium members 43 per cent were beginning their first term of office in 1969. These figures are proof that there exists no entrenched and irreplaceable élite in the council system. Only one in three councillors was beginning a third term of office in 1969, which means that two thirds were elected no earlier than in 1965. The lack of permanency in presidium membership was even more striking. Over 70 per cent had not served in the presidium for more than four years. As we might expect, there was a smaller proportion amongst permanent presidium members, that is, chairmen, deputies and secretaries. Only 54 per cent in this case had not served in that same position for more than four years. Strangely enough at the wojewodstwo level there were 58·4 per cent of permanent presidium members who had served four years or less. Thus in the presidia

[1] Thus one study found that between 5 and 20 per cent of councillors did not complete their four-year term of office between 1961 and 1965. The highest turnover occurred at the gromada level, due mostly to change in constituencies, and the lowest turnover was at wojewodstwo level. Nearly two of every three councillors who did not complete their term of office at powiat and wojewodstwo level did so through resignation. The much-publicised right of the electorate to suspend their representatives if they so wish was not once exercised. A. Patrzałek, 'Zagadnienia zmian w składzie rad narodowych II i III Kadencji', in *PRN 4*, 1965, p. 121. In the western territories the rate of resignation was higher than the national average and there were more young councillors who resigned, indicating a less stable political development. In T. Kołodziejczyk, 'Zmęczeni kadencją', in *Polityka*, no. 39, 1964.　[2] *Radni* . . ., pp. 34–5; *Członkowie prezydiów* . . ., pp. 29–30.

at the highest level there were slightly fewer permanent members who had served for a long period than the national average. However, we must not ignore the tendency towards less turnover in more recent years. Whereas 50 per cent of councillors elected in 1969 were not new to their position this proportion was only 32 per cent in 1958. More councillors, therefore, were experienced in 1969, indicating a certain stabilisation of representative cadres, but accompanying this was a danger that this local élite was now less likely to be displaced.

The final topic to be discussed in our treatment of the composition of local councils is recruitment. No national studies have been taken of this process and our material is confined to research on the presidia of Lublin, Rzeszów and Łódź wojewodstwos. Tables 52 and 53 summarise sources of recruitment

TABLE 52. SOURCES FOR RECRUITMENT OF PRESIDIUM MEMBERS IN NINETEEN POWIATS AND NON-POWIAT TOWNS IN LUBLIN AND RZESZÓW WOJEWODSTWOS IN 1963*

	Permanent members	Non-permanent members	Total
Party apparatus	8	4	12
Administrative apparatus	40	11	51
Economic apparatus	9	28	37
Teachers	0	5	5
Craftsmen	0	1	1
Workers	0	1	1
Peasants	0	1	1
Total	57	51	108

* W. Skrzydło, 'Prezydium rady narodowej (Skład i system powoływania)', in *PRN 8*, 1966, p. 140.

for permanent and non-permanent presidium members. There were notable differences in the methods of recuitment for each. The party and administrative apparatuses constituted the major source for permanent members. We observe in the Łódź study that the single largest centre for recruiting permanent members was amongst department heads. Our earlier suppositions that department heads have strong influence over the presidium, to the detriment of social organs such as commis-

TABLE 53. SOURCES FOR RECRUITMENT OF PRESIDIUM MEMBERS
IN TWELVE WOJEWODSTWOS, POWIATS, NON-POWIAT TOWNS AND
WARDS IN ŁÓDŹ WOJEWODSTWO IN 1964*

		Permanent members	Non-permanent members	Total
Party apparatus	Party secretaries	5	2	7
	Party instructors, section heads, others	3	0	3
Admini- strative apparatus	Department heads	8	2	10
	Other workers	0	0	0
	Workers in higher level administration	2	0	2
Presidia of other councils	Higher level presidia	0	0	0
	Same level presidia	7	0	7
	Lower level presidia	0	0	0
Others	Directors of social organisations, enterprises	16	34	50
Total		41	38	79

* J. Wróblewski, J. Borkowski, E. Smoktunowicz and T. Szymczak, 'Zagadnienia funkcjonowania, prezydiów rad naradowych', *PRN 9*, 1967, p. 12.

sions or council, appear to be substantiated by this evidence. Of course the close interaction between the presidium and the local party committee discussed earlier is also confirmed by these data on patterns of recruitment. Finally the influence of centrally and locally controlled economic enterprises and the zjednoczenie on presidium work tends to be illustrated by the extent of their representation on the executive-managing organ. In the latter case, however, we note that such representation is largely of a non-permanent kind, that is, representatives of enterprises and zjednoczenie do not occupy as frequently as do administrators and party functionaries the influential functions of chairman, deputy or secretary. This study on recruitment in many ways symbolises what our analysis has found throughout this discussion on the People's Council system: that party control is powerful, the administrative apparatus is extremely influential, the economic directorship cadres are well represented and the doctrine of unity of power vested fully in representative organs is equivocal.

CHAPTER SEVEN

The Role of Social Groups

By David Lane

One of the most powerful theories in political science in recent years has been that of totalitarianism and this model of society has been taken to represent the reality of the USSR and States patterned on her. 'Totalitarianism' may be defined as a social system which 'seeks to politicise all human behaviour and plan all human relationships', its chief features include the obliteration of the distinction between State and society and the destruction of associations and groups which are interposed between the individual and the State.[1] From the mid-1960s, however, thinking among specialists in the West has moved away from this model, which has been recognised as providing 'a set of blinders to the perception of change',[2] to emphasise more the autonomous nature of various groups and their role in influencing the political authorities. As Ionescu has pointed out:

> No society, and especially no contemporary society, is so politically under-developed as not to continue, and reproduce within itself, the perennial conflict of power. No contemporary society can run all the complex activities of the state, political, cultural, social and economic, exclusively, by its own ubiquitous and omniscient servants, without collaboration, and bargains with, or checks by, other interest groups.[3]

Many western scholars, therefore, have turned to consider the

[1] Alfred G. Meyer, *The Soviet Political System* (New York, 1965) p. 471. W. Kornhauser, *The Politics of Mass Society* (London, 1960) p. 123. See also C. J. Friedrich and Z. K. Brzezinski, *Totalitarian Dictatorship and Autocracy* (Cambridge, Mass., 1965).

[2] Dankwart A. Rustow, 'Communism and Change', in *Change in Communist Systems*, ed. Chalmers Johnson (Stanford, Calif., 1970) p. 348.

[3] Ghiţa Ionescu, *The Politics of the European Communist States* (London, 1967) pp. 3–4.

influence of these groups on the political élite. Such studies[1] have been concerned with the articulation of a group interest in the political arena. We have taken a wider frame of reference and have considered the formation and structure of social groups, the demands they make and the ways they have articulated their own 'group' interests.

The research findings of this book bear out the view expressed above by Ionescu. Political conflict is endemic in Polish society and the political élites in addition to the employment of authoritarian methods have to bargain to a greater or lesser degree with various groups. We have been more successful in describing the changing structure of groups than we have been in depicting their involvement in politics. One of the main reasons for this is the closed nature of the political process to the outsider. The 'official' ideology assumes that there is a basic homogeneity of the social and political structure and conflict is not highlighted in the official press. A second reason is the absence of frank reports about the influences which are exerted on the top national and local decision-makers. Theorists supporting the 'totalitarian' theory of society, of course, deny that such 'bargains' or 'checks' by groups actually take place at all. We have been able to show that groups are internally differentiated. They differ in their expectations of activity from the government, in the demands they make, in the kinds of sanctions they may take against the political élite and in the ways they may inhibit it. Following Karl Deutsch, we would suggest that political leadership is a form of steering and that social groups are structures which both limit and influence the direction that steering may take.

The various chapters in this book are a contribution to the description of the political culture of Polish society. By 'political culture' we mean 'the system of empirical beliefs, expressions, symbols and values which defines the situation in which political action takes place'.[2] We have discussed the nature of the various

[1] See *Interest Groups in Soviet Politics*, edited by H. Gordon Skilling and Franklyn Griffiths (Princeton, 1971), and A. H. Brown, 'Policy-making in the Soviet Union', *Soviet Studies*, vol. xxiii, no. 1 (July 1971). These studies are concerned with political interest groups; in this book we have considered wider social groups.

[2] *Political Culture and Political Development*, ed. Lucien Pye and Sidney Verba (Princeton, 1963) p. 513.

groups and the kinds of demands they make and we have, sometimes indirectly, indicated the response of the government. Let us briefly first describe the kinds of demands which flow from the various groups; second, consider the ways these demands were articulated and aggregated in the crisis of December 1970/January 1971 and then third, turn to make some general statement about the relationship of groups to the government in State socialist society.

GROUP DEMANDS

The group considered in this study with least direct involvement in the political process is the peasantry. The representation of this group in the composition of the PUWP is low (in 1968 it came to 11 per cent of total membership and the same proportion of the central committee).[1] Perhaps more important than the small numbers of peasant members is the absence of any social and political *identification* by the political élite with the peasantry. The values of the peasant run counter to those of the political élite. But this does not mean that the peasantry has little influence on the government. It forms an important *veto group*: peasants can effectively sabotage the government's economic plans by refusing to produce for the market and they can turn into themselves, producing for themselves without great costs – at least in the short run. The Communist government is extremely sensitive to this group. A reduction in marketed agricultural produce has serious repercussions through the whole economy and influences the equilibrium of the political system. The Polish government attempted the Soviet solution of collectivisation but due to the resistance by the peasants and difficulties of enforcement this policy failed and was replaced by a modified form of market. The greater reliance placed on a market form of exchange between the government and the peasantry has strengthened certain groups among the peasants. It has given the peasants a belief that private agriculture will continue and those peasants producing for the market are at

[1] Membership of the PUWP in 1967 accounts for about 4 per cent of the peasants, 13 per cent of the manual workers and 27 per cent of non-manual personnel. For further statistics see J. Cave *et al.*, *Politics and the Polish Economy* (forthcoming).

a relative advantage compared to those with self-producing dwarf farms. While the peasantry has played a relatively passive role in the upheavals of 1956 and 1970–1, it has gained considerably in the period following the public demonstrations. After 1956 the peasants felt reassured that collectivisation would not be continued in the short-run. In 1957 some restrictions on private agricultural activity were lifted, compulsory quotas of grain were reduced and deliveries of milk to the government were abolished. But the peasants remained suspicious of the government and its long-term intentions. In 1971 a number of reforms were introduced to improve the position of private farmers and to stimulate their production for the market. From January 1972 compulsory deliveries of produce are to be abandoned and long-term contracts are to replace them, social security and health benefits for private farmers are to be introduced, land tax is to be made less progressive. With the development from a more or less self-sufficient peasant economy into one producing for the market one might predict that the mere 'veto power' of the peasants will increasingly be accompanied by greater participation and more explicit demands. These, however, will be narrow in scope, concerned with the farmers' own well-being and the conditions of agriculture such as minimum price levels and stability of land tenure. The existence of political cliques of rich farmers (see above, pp. 74–6, 281) who seem to be strongly represented in the UPP and are able to bid successfully for loans, State contracts and for the use of machinery, is an indication of the evolution of a more active participant-oriented group among the peasantry. Such farmers are likely to be best placed to take advantage of the agricultural reforms planned in 1971.

At the opposite end of the spectrum of prestige to the peasantry as a social group are the writers forming a part of the cultural intelligentsia. Creative writers are concerned with a very wide range of problems including the political and philosophical; in having a general view of the world, they constitute more than an 'interest group'. Writers in Poland have historically played a leading part in maintaining the unity of the Polish nation and culture; they create and defend literary and human values. Therefore the claims they make on the political leaders are much wider in scope than those of the peasantry. As George

Gömöri has put it, in the events of 1956, they mediated 'between
the political élite and those forces which had no opportunity
to express themselves in any other way than through sporadic
direct action. . . .' They are as concerned with human destiny
as they are with their own status and position. Marxism is a
doctrine which claims for the Communist Party the authority
to make pronouncements and decisions which shape human
destiny, and writers in Poland are expected to identify with
the general party line. If, however, creative writers happen to
disagree with the party line, conflict may take place. While
Western writers adhering to the 'totalitarian' model of State
socialist systems would argue that such claims by writers would
be rigorously and even violently suppressed by the political
élites, we have seen in this study that groups of writers are able
to articulate interests contrary to those of the political élite and
also utilise the Polish Writers' Association to this end. We are
not arguing that the PWA as such is a pressure group for what
are popularly called 'dissident' intellectuals; but rather that the
PWA provides an institutional forum for the articulation of
various interests. While the political élites may manipulate and
change the leadership to meet particular political requirements,
the political élites must make concessions to ensure the compliance and continued participation of writers. In this study we
saw that since 1956 many concessions have been made to writers
and writers as a whole have not been incorporated into the régime; there has been continual conflict between individual
writers and groups of writers on the one side and the political
authorities on the other. We have seen that such conflict occasionally erupts, as in February 1968. We may characterise the
creative writers, then, as a *potentially policy orientated group*: writers
are articulate and may have a wide and general conception of
the social good. In Poland the historical and cultural role of the
creative writer makes him a difficult person for the political
élite to control.

The technical intelligentsia is a social category composed of
people with some sort of theoretical training concerned with
organising the material production of commodities. From a
Marxist viewpoint the 'organising' role of the technical intelligentsia puts it in a crucial position. For the organisational role
may lead to control of the means of production which in turn

may give rise to a managerial or technological class. Indeed, 'managerialist' theorists such as James Burnham[1] have argued that managers, by virtue of their *control* over the means of production, constitute a ruling class under conditions of an advanced technological society. Referring to State socialist societies, such as the USSR, Burnham and his followers have argued that the technical-managerial stratum is more strongly entrenched than in capitalist-type societies. In the latter they say that an opposition of the owners of the means of production continues, though in an attenuated form; in State socialist society, on the other hand, the abolition of private ownership has left the way clear for the rise of the managerial class to a dominant position in the power structure. This view needs to be considerably qualified in the light of the history of People's Poland. From 1948 until the mid-1950s there can be no doubt that managerial personnel were well under the control of the central party and State apparatus. Men lower down the line of command at the level of the enterprise had little initiative, they were workers selected for management because of their political loyalty rather than on the basis of professional managerial-technical qualifications and hence did not constitute a 'technical intelligentsia' proper. It was not until the mid-1950s that the effects of the educational policies and technical training began to be felt in the system of industrial management. The young engineering cadres desired more authority over the running of the enterprise and there was considerable conflict between these men who had a technological orientation and the 'practical workers' who staffed higher management. But though they were discontented with their status, conditions and pay, these grievances were not articulated by the technical intelligentsia in the public demands of 1956. It was a section of the more amorphous working class which caused the disturbances at Poznań. In 1957, however, the technical intelligentsia at the Conference of Engineers and Technicians' Association came out with specific demands for greater independence and for more professional management. These demands were mainly technocratic in perspective – for greater reliance on experts, for tangible rewards to be given to qualified men. We would tentatively suggest that the technical intelligentsia might be

[1] *The Managerial Revolution* (London, 1945).

differentiated into two categories. We might distinguish first those engineers in higher management in the enterprise with a 'professional ethos'[1] whose values are expertise, autonomy, commitment and responsibility. Such men do not question the ultimate goals of production or the State socialist system as such, they come into conflict with superior administrators when they wish to assert their responsibility and the greater autonomy of the enterprise to achieve these goals. Such men in modern Poland hail from working-class or peasant backgrounds, they gain industrial experience on the job and their qualifications by part-time study, their membership of the party is ideational or what we have called intrinsic. The second category is the engineer with the 'ethos of science' who emphasises the 'extension of certified knowledge',[2] impersonal criteria, social collaboration, disinterestedness and 'organised scepticism'. Such engineers tend to be of non-manual origin, they have had a full-time education at a higher technical institution, they gravitate to research or design jobs away from management and if they join the party it is not out of political conviction but for instrumental reasons. The technical intelligentsia as a whole benefited greatly after 1956; their demands for higher pay differentials were met, their authority and status within the enterprise increased. The 'practicals' whose authority was based on political reliability were gradually ousted by professionally qualified engineers. These changes, which also included establishing greater differentials between manual and technical non-manual workers, had (perhaps paradoxically) the support of the manual workers, many of whom believed that a more 'technocratic' approach would improve their own pay and conditions. Have these improvements in the status of the technical and managerial strata at the enterprise level led to the rise of a managerial class? We think not. First, the central bureaucracy in the form of the ministry and zjednocenie (industrial association) is still very much in control of the management of the industrial enterprise – despite the growth in self-management. Second, political control through the political party (PUWP) circumscribes the managerial and technical strata. We also reject the view that there is an 'alliance' between the white-collar specia-

[1] W. Kornhauser, *Scientists in Industry* (California, 1962) p. 1.
[2] R. K. Merton, *Social Theory and Social Structure* (Glencoe, 1959) p. 552.

list and the party official and ideologist, rather we believe that there is considerable tension between these two groups. The fact that many engineers formally join the party does not mean that their commitment is the same as those who join the party out of ideational conviction. There is some evidence to suggest that many technical staff regard the party as an instrument which will help to improve their own career prospects and the smooth-running of the enterprise. Third, one may not define the technical intelligentsia as a 'technocracy': it is not a socially unitary group but is internally differentiated and it is far from constituting a class with an interest inimical to other groups. We might characterise the technical intelligentsia as a *professional interest group*, being primarily concerned with its right to take decisions of a technical nature stemming from a theoretical body of knowledge.

In our chapter on the structure of local politics we saw that in the local political arena the social groups we have considered do not appear directly to articulate their interests. Decentralisation has given power to the presidia of local authorities rather than to the council and the former bodies generally initiate resolutions. What evidence is available suggests that institutions with wider public participation such as the elected councils and commissions play a minor role in decision-making compared to the presidia. The elected council, however, does influence decision-making and does occasionally reject and amend presidia proposals. Commissions, which include many non-manual specialists, influence council presidia and departments by critically assessing projects and thus encourage participation in local decision-making. As Ray Taras points out:' The consultative and participatory role [of public commissions] is extensive.' We focused in the local study on the participation of people as citizens with individual (rather than group) interests. We should conclude that we were unable, as we had hoped, to study a number of local conflicts to show the roles of the various groups included in this monograph. Polish studies have identified political groups in rural communities, these groups include men who have control of various government agencies which lease land and allocate machinery; other social groupings outside the formal political structure are richer private farmers and school teachers. While we have shown that institutions exist for

the aggregation of interests (the presidia, council and commissions), we were not able to indicate with the sources available
the nature or extent of group interest articulation and aggregation. Despite the attempts to 'democratise' the People's
Councils after 1956, there has remained a suspicion of the
administrative apparatus. Participation seemed to be better in
the country than the town and in the latter the results of surveys
indicate a considerable lack of sympathy with administrators.
At the lower levels of the power structure in local authorities, as
opposed to central bodies, the party is an important but not an
overwhelmingly powerful agent; there is some evidence to
suggest that in the nomination of candidates the economic
enterprise is an even more important agency than the party.
While empirical data show that citizens believed factory directors to be the most powerful men in the local community, we
lack detailed studies of the role of such men in the decision-
making process. There is no doubt, however, that the enterprise
is not subject to much supervision (or 'control') by the local
authorities. In our study of local councils there was found to be
little explicit articulation by councillors of social group interests. But it does not follow that social groups are of no
importance politically. Rather, group interests may be implicit
rather than explicit and their relevance may be wider than that
of the arena of a local council. Our study of local councils
brought out that one of the barriers to decentralisation of
decision-making to the lower levels of the State administration
has been the low educational qualifications of councillors. It is
important to note that the absence of a body of competent and
educated citizens contributed to the setting up of a centralised
bureaucratic system and was a major obstacle to the development of participant democracy within the framework of Polish
socialism. The general rise in educational levels of the population has increased the stock of competent lay representatives
and administrators. At the same time, however, the social
composition of councils has been changed in favour of the non-
manual worker at the expense of the manual worker. Finally,
our study of local government showed that there is a strong
bureaucratic element in Polish politics. This was introduced
in the early years of the régime to maintain the integrity of the
élites and to ensure that the goals of industrialisation and

modernisation were carried out; attempts to eradicate a bureaucratic style have not been wholly successful.

THE WORKING CLASS AND THE CRISIS IN DECEMBER 1970/JANUARY 1971

It is not our task here to describe in detail the events in Poland which led to the ousting of Gomułka; rather it is our purpose to use them to illustrate the role of the working class in politics.

In the light of our chapter on the workers we feel justified in using the term manual working class. While in the years after the seizure of power by the Communists there was much collective mobility by manual workers into the strata of non-manual executive and administrative personnel, with the passing of time and the consolidation of communist power, such features of the system of stratification have faded away to be replaced by more traditional barriers between manual and non-manual workers. The boundaries between manual and non-manual are often diffuse and allow for movement but are demarcated by levels of income, life-styles, access to education and to the employment market. Hence we do not consider that in contemporary Poland there has been a significant merging of manual and non-manual strata and a strengthening of barriers between skilled and unskilled. We shall argue that one of the major causes of the upheavals in Poland in December 1970 was the relative deprivation of groups of manual industrial workers. But we do not wish to convey the impression that the manual working class in Poland is a unitary class-conscious social entity. It is internally differentiated. The workers in iron and steel and coal-mining form an aristocracy in terms of real income. The peasant-worker from the country whence he might commute and where he might cultivate a plot is often regarded with contempt by the permanent and mature working class. The workers are also divided on the basis of skill and such divisions have been manifested in representation on bodies set up to serve the workers. The skilled workers have tended to dominate the factory party committee; supervisory and lower management have played a leading role in the workers' councils; even in the trade unions, the skilled workers and supervisory staffs have highly saturated the directing organs. Before 1971 this differentiation left the manual workers too weak to utilise the potential channels of influence. The workers' councils which were set up after 1956 were not institutions through which the workers could express their own needs *vis-à-vis* management but were institutions which management utilised in their struggle for more power against the higher administrative authorities. While in the period prior to 1956 the manual workers had gained in status and income at the expense of non-manual strata, after 1956 they increasingly bore the brunt of Poland's economic difficulties. The growing professionalisation of management made the workers increasingly a victim of the management's near fetishism of plan fulfillment.

The riots in Gdańsk were fundamentally[1] the activity of a stratum of the working class which was conscious of the fact that its place in society was determined by its relationship to the means of production and that its well-being could be enhanced by collective action. Its aims were explicitly political and economic. The workers demanded 'immediate, legal elections' to all trade unions and workers' councils and the recognition of the demands of the members in party and youth organisations at the departmental and factory level.[2] These were demands for greater participation of workers in the political order but the workers were not concerned with the overthrow of the system and thus could not be described as a 'revolutionary class'. They wanted more efficient management: they called for the 'leading cadres' in factories to be 'highly educated and knowledgeable',[3] to be 'efficient and where possible young'.[4] Their wish was for the trade unions and the workers' councils to defend their legitimate interests and they sought changes in personnel which could be achieved by free

---

[1] We say 'fundamentally' because hooligan elements utilised the unrest for arson, looting and assault. The workers organised their own detachments to preserve order and to exclude these elements. *Nowe Drogi* (undated issue, early 1971).

[2] D. Fikus and J. Urban, 'Szczecin', *Polityka*, 6 Feb. 1971.

[3] *Gazeta Białostocka*, 22 Jan. 1971. Cited by Celt, 'The Demands and Grievances of the Polish Population', *Radio Free Europe Background Report*, Poland no. 10, 14 April 1971.

[4] *Głos Szczeciński*, 15 Jan. 1971. Cited by Celt.

elections. But the chief thrust of the manual workers' grievances was economic not political and was for an immediate improvement in conditions. The discontent was a result of 'the worsening economic situation, serious neglect in social policy, stagnation of real wages, shortage of supplies and the rising cost of living'.[1] The 'predominantly workers' demonstrations' had as a 'basis of protest . . . dissatisfaction with the material situation and bad social conditions'.[2] In addition, however, it should be said that the position of the working class was a result of political decisions and the workers' strikes represented a crisis of confidence in the régime. The demands for open elections to union, workers' council and party organisations were of 'great significance to the shipyard workers' in Szczecin.[3]

The immediate precondition was a worsening in living standards. While the official *average* annual rate of growth of national income in Poland between 1961 and 1970 was 1·7 per cent, in 1970 there was a stagnation in money income and a fall in the standards of the poorer strata. There was growing unemployment in Poland and it has been estimated that the projected economic plans put forward by Gomułka would have led to unemployment of about half a million by 1975.[4] In November 1970 the supplies of meat, animal fats and meat products, fish, wool textile goods, leather shoes and building materials were 'significantly lower'[5] than in November 1969. These shortages in supply led to suppressed inflation – to people having money and the shops having empty shelves of certain goods. But in November the supply of other consumer durables, such as radios, tape-recorders, washing machines and other electrical goods rose. The government's action was to raise the prices of goods in short supply (such as food) and to reduce the prices of industrial consumer durables. This action had the effect of redistributing income from the lower paid groups (for whom expenditure on food accounted for a large share of their personal income) to the higher paid strata. Bearing in mind the lower average family income of the manual working class,[6] the price changes of December were an attack on the manual

---

[1] *Nowe Drogi* (undated issue, early 1971).   [2] Ibid.
[3] D. Fikus and J. Urban, *Polityka*, 6 Feb. 1971.
[4] *Trybuna Ludu*, 15 Feb. 1971.
[5] *Gazeta Handlowa*, 1 Jan. 1971.   [6] See above, pp. 135–6.

workers' standards. The local press articulated the manual workers' contention that there was an 'unjust distribution of premiums and bonuses',[1] that there should be a 'more just division of the national income'[2] and that there should be no discrimination between manual and non-manual workers.[3] These demands were the conscious expression of an awareness of structural differences between manual and non-manual workers which we emphasised in chapter 3. The manual workers were not joined in a general public protest by the technical and cultural intelligentsia in December 1970. In Gdańsk a group of demonstrators went to the polytechnic but the students 'refused to join the demonstrators',[4] though on the other hand students showed considerable sympathy for and appreciation of the grievances of the manual workers. The point we are bringing out here is that the support of other social groups was passive in 1970–1, whereas in 1956 it was manifested in active wide-scale public demonstrations. But can our understanding of the position of the working class throw any light on why discontent was to erupt in the coastal towns? We have noted above that the shipyard workers were not any worse off when compared to many other groups of workers. The *average* earnings of manual workers in the shipyards was 3,041 zł. per month compared to the national average of 2,384 zł. and in the Gdańsk shipyards there were 700 workers who earned over 6,000 zł. a month. Like other industrial centres, Gdańsk had a long housing waiting list, the intended economic reforms entailed a raising of work norms and prices of food rose by similar amounts in other places, as they did iṅ Gdańsk. We believe, however, that on the Baltic coast there were structural conditions which created solidarity. The population was made up of youngish rural immigrants;[5] of the 16,000 men employed in the shipyards,

[1] *Głos Wybrzeża*, 19 Jan. 1971. Cited by Celt.

[2] *Trybuna Mazowiecka*, 25 Jan. 1971. Cited by Celt.

[3] *Głos Wybrzeża*, 27 Jan. 1971. Cited by Celt. Manual workers received usually a bonus of 100 złoties for each ship launched compared to 2,000 złoties pocketed by technical and administrative personnel.

[4] Barbara Seidler, *Życie Literackie*, 21 Feb. 1971.

[5] Young workers were reported to have been particularly militant in Szczecin, where they were disappointed with pay and conditions. D. Fikus and J. Urban in *Polityka*, 6 Feb. 1971. Workers on shipbuilding, of course, work outside in the winter and welfare conditions (protective clothing,

3,000 lived in workers' hostels. Thus the working class tended to be socially compact, employed overwhelmingly in one industry which facilitated easy communication. Particular factors on the Baltic coast highlighted the inferior position of the working class. The three-town region (Gdańsk, Gdynia and Sopot) had a considerable tourist industry, providing a reference group with which the workers could compare their own living standards. Despite a waiting period of twelve years for a flat, private villas abounded in the coastal areas. At Sopot dinners at the Grand Hotel sometimes came to several thousand zł., there were 1,400 known black marketeers, and prostitutes could command $20 a night (at the market rate of exchange, the average monthly wage of a manual worker).[1] These facts, even if apparently superficial in character, provided popular talking points for social comparison. The workers high in esteem in the 'official' ideology were underprivileged when contrasted with rich holiday guests – both Polish and foreign. Thus relative deprivation of the manual working class was more strikingly apparent in the coastal areas of the Baltic than it was in industrial towns of Poznań and Nowa Huta. In December 1970, on the Baltic coast, we have a picture of popular discontent, the underlying features of which were the breakdown of regular food supplies, rising prices which led to a fall in living standards, growing unemployment and the expectation that the intended new system of material incentives would mean more work for the same income.

The strikes and riots in the Baltic coast in which the official toll[2] was forty-five dead and 1,165 injured were followed by strikes in other parts of Poland in December 1970 and January 1971. We think that this activity may best be described as class activity. It was distinguished by a part of the working class being conscious of shared social and political underprivilege. But, unlike in October 1956, other social groups did not actively join the manual workers in a national protest. Not only had the technical intelligentsia received many tangible benefits under Gomułka, but perhaps more important was the low expectation

warm food at work, canteens) are relatively more important than in metal working industries, where work is indoors.

[1] Barbara Seidler, *Życie Literackie*, 21 Feb. 1971.

[2] *Nowe Drogi* (undated issue).

of possibilities for change in 1970 and 1971. In 1956 Poland was carried on a wave of optimism which followed after the death of Stalin. In 1970 the Soviet invasion of Czechoslovakia was still fresh in mind and created a more pessimistic climate.

The events of December 1970 again illustrate a theme which has recurred in various parts of this book, namely the tension between social interests and bureaucratic control. In theory, the party machinery should play a role of harmonising group demands with decisions taken centrally. The negative response of the population to the price changes had in fact been communicated by local party groups to the central committee in Warsaw,[1] but the secretariat had disregarded the anxiety which was shown by party members in *aktyws* and in the field generally.[2] This is of some importance because it is evidence that discontent had been articulated and communicated to the central decision-makers, but that in the aggregation process certain demands were ignored. On the Baltic coast many party activists played a leading role in the upheavals, showing that they were responsive to the local workers' demands but were unable to influence central party policy.[3] This may be euphemistically described as resulting in a 'disruption of ties' between the party and the masses.[4] Hence the formal machinery in State socialist society which should articulate and aggregate demands may not function properly because bureaucratic practices and personal preferences may prevail. Violent activity such as the events on the Baltic coast (and strikes later in other parts of the country) had the effect of bringing about a fundamental reappraisal of policy. Under Gierek the monthly minimum wage has been raised from 850 zł. to 1,000 zł.; pensions and family allowances have been increased and factory directors have been ordered to guarantee 'a just distribution of bonuses and monetary

---

[1] Barbara Seidler, *Życie Literackie*, 21 Feb. 1971.

[2] *Nowe Drogi* (undated issue).

[3] Through the disturbances local party activists had considerable authority in the locality. Of eighty-three workers' delegates elected to meet Gierek in Gdańsk, 40 per cent were party members. S. Kozicki, *Polityka*, 13 Jan. 1971.

[4] *Nowe Drogi*, ibid. It should also be noted that no government can satisfy all demands. In this case Gomułka and his supporters felt that the present conditions of the manual workers could be sacrificed to the demands of rationalisation and efficient utilisation of resources in the economy.

rewards'; a higher price is now paid for milk and meat delivered by peasants to the State; retail prices of foodstuffs have been restored to the pre-December levels and a two-year price freeze has been put on non-seasonal foodstuffs; measures have been undertaken to enhance supplies of consumer goods; housing construction is to be increased; full employment is an objective of the new economic plan; factory working conditions are to be improved. On the political side, greater powers are to be given to trade unions[1] and more decentralisation of economic decision-making has been promised; special commissions composed of experts have been set up to consider the ramifications of the new economic plan.[2] Perhaps we might generalise to say that Gierek may try to establish greater political participation of the manual workers in the party. He will try to reduce the influence of the technical groups who try to utilise the party for their own ends[3] and instead reassert its links with the working class.

GROUPS IN THE POLITICAL PROCESS

At the outset of this study we posed the question of whether industrialisation and the economic development of People's Poland led to group differentiation and to the articulation of group demands on the political system. We may summarise our findings by saying first that there is considerable group differentiation in modern Poland and that individuals have a consciousness of group identity. Second, groups may be shown to have 'interests', that is to say, that individuals sharing a given status have common attitudes and views about the ways their status or position should be maintained or enhanced. Third, that social groups become political groups by making claims on the political system. There are social groups active in a way that leads us to reject the categorisation of a citizen in Poland as an

---

[1] The new labour code is to abolish differences in the rights of manual and non-manual workers by equalising upwards. Manual and non-manual workers are planned, for instance, to have equal rights to sickness benefits. The workers' council is to be given a chance to appeal over dismissals of workers.　　　　　　　　[2] For a summary see: *Kultura*, 6 June 1971.

[3] It is noteworthy that the proportion of workers in wojewodstwo party committees has risen from the pre-December figure of 26 per cent to 43 per cent in the spring of 1971. *Trybuna Ludu*, 18 April 1971.

'active robot'.[1] Such viewpoints tend to ignore the ways that political mobilisation of the population is influenced by industrial mobilisation which requires a competent and participant technical intelligentsia. Fourth, that while we may show that groups articulate demands, we have been much less able to show how demands are aggregated in the political system. The aggregation process will remain an obscure part of the Polish political system until studies are carried out in Poland on the regulation of conflict.

We have so far used the term 'group' to refer to a variety of possible social bonds between individuals. There are two aspects of social groups which must be clarified. First, there is the nature of the *relationship* between the members of a group. This is to do with the nature and the frequency of the interactions between persons forming a group. Second, there are the common features and shared characteristics which distinguish one group of persons from another. This aspect is concerned with the goals, sentiments and social characteristics of a group. These two aspects of group membership usually overlap but they *may not* do so. 'Stalinists' (or 'liberals') in State socialist society, for example, may lack any associational links but cognisance is taken of them by the political élite, whose activity they may inhibit or influence; hence we feel justified in defining them as groups.

The group with the weakest bond we may define as a *category group* where mutual dependence and interaction between members may be infrequent and where considerable differentiation exists. Such is the case with the peasantry in Poland. We have suggested that peasants resist authority as a veto group but as an aggregate of individuals rather than as a group making a conscious common claim. The technical intelligentsia might be called from a social point of view an *analytic* group: managers

<hr/>

[1] Frederick C. Barghoorn, 'Soviet Russia: Orthodoxy and Adaptiveness'. in *Political Culture and Political Development*, ed. Lucien W. Pye and Sidney Verba (Princeton, 1968) pp. 494–5. Barghoorn was here writing about the effects of 'the Soviet type of social revolution', which we assume would be the writer's description of Poland after 1945. He takes up an earlier view expressed by Gabriel Almond, who regarded the 'orientation to authority' in the 'totalitarian political culture' as 'some combination of conformity and apathy'. 'Comparative Political Systems', *The Journal of Politics*, vol. 18, no. 3 (1956) p. 403.

and engineers share certain attitudes, they have a similar way of interpreting situations, they make claims on the political system. They are, however, internally differentiated by social origin and career paths and they have only a minimum frequency of interaction as a group. As a political entity we suggest that they be defined as professional interest groups. Perhaps the most cohesive interest group studied in this book are the sub-groups of creative writers. (We say sub-groups because not all creative writers share their views or interact with them.) Such sub-groups are able by virtue of their small size and strategic position to utilise as a forum the Polish Writers' Association in order to make claims on the political system. Manual workers we have categorised as a class rather than as a group. Marxist analysis defines fundamental power relations, and in Poland political authority, as resting on the working class and this is given some saliency by the 'official' ideology. Manual workers as such do not constitute a political interest group: they are internally differentiated by form of work (heavy and light industry, modern and traditional industries, highly and lowly paid occupations), there is no regular interaction because of the large numbers involved and there is considerable 'drainage' to other social groups, such as the non-manual strata. Manual workers in Poland do make up several groups which are constituted of men with common occupational and industrial allegiances. Such groups interact at the place of work and have varied internal cohesion. Politically, however, they perform as *amorphous* interest groups because they have no ideational or professional interests to protect, and they articulate policies in defence of their own welfare and conditions. Thus, paradoxically, their weak capacity for articulation as a political interest group through institutional channels may lead to wider class action. This is because, having common objective life chances and faced by a threat to their own security, groups of workers may spontaneously rebel against the authorities to assert their own rights. Thus in October 1956 and in December 1970 the workers briefly turned from being a fragmented set of groups to become a class 'for itself' – though this was limited in scope and did not include all workers. Social and political groups, it should be emphasised, are dynamic categories, especially in rapidly changing societies such as postwar Poland. Let us now turn, therefore, to consider whether we may be able to relate our study to a more general framework of social and political analysis.

Despite their ideological commitment to the political and social systems of the 'Western democracies' and their condescending tone when describing 'totalitarian' States, Gabriel Almond and Sidney Verba provide us with a number of useful classifications of the political culture of nations and the attitudes of groups of the population towards politics. As these authors point out, the political revolution going on in the world is the 'participation explosion': we hold that similar demands are being made in the socialist States of Eastern Europe. The political order during the period of rapid industrialisation and social change in Poland (1946–51) would seem to fit what these writers have defined as a 'subject' political régime.[1] This of course was not only a result of the political theory of the communist rulers but was also the inheritance from prewar Piłsudski's Poland. The Communists in mobilising the population encouraged the development of a 'subject-participant' culture,[2] both ideologically and as a result of the changes induced by industrialisation. We have seen, for instance, that many became involved in local government and that the new cadres of engineers began to assert their professional interests against the 'political' managers. Almond and Verba have aptly pointed out that a subject-participant culture changes the character of the subject sub-culture, and the authoritarian-oriented groups, in competing with the democratic ones, must develop a 'defensive political infra-structure of their own'.[3] The examples given in *The Civic Culture* relate to States in which authoritarian governments have alternated with democratic ones (i.e. France, Germany, Italy). But there is theoretically no reason why the balance between authoritarian and democratic

[1] A 'subject' political culture is one where the individual is aware of government authority but has an essentially passive relationship to it. *The Civic Culture*, ed. Gabriel Almond and Verba (1963) p. 19.

[2] Such a culture is one where a substantial part of the population has acquired specialist input orientations and an activist set of self-orientations while most of the remainder of the population continue to be oriented towards an authoritarian government structure and have a relatively passive set of self-orientations. Almond and Verba, p. 25.

[3] Ibid., p. 26.

groups should not change within a polity, without a change of legal government.

Our study of Poland would seem to bear out what Almond and Verba say. During the 'Stalin' period the groups with specialist input orientations and activist self-orientations were mainly party functionaries. With the greater industrialisation of Poland and its ensuing social change, to use Almond and Verba's words, the 'participant orientations have spread among only a part of the population and because their legitimacy is challenged by the persisting subject sub-culture and suspended during authoritarian interludes, the participant-orientated stratum of the population cannot become a competent, self-confident, experienced body of citizens. They tend to remain democratic aspirants'.[1] In other words, the authoritarian structure remains tied to the party élites in which legitimacy is enshrined, whereas 'participant orientation' to politics has spread to social groups. In Poland these might be groups of writers, factory directors and workers who without a well-based democratic societal infrastructure lack confidence in pushing their group interests. Changes in State socialist societies since 1956 may be explained by the fluctuating influence of these groups. The political changes instituted by Khrushchev in the USSR and followed by Gomułka in Poland, Dubček in Czechoslovakia, Kadar in Hungary, Ceausescu in Romania and latterly by Gierek are all attempts to reconcile this new 'demand structure' to the hegemony of the party élites. To stay in power the political leaders in these States have to steer a delicate course. To maintain a political equilibrium they must attempt to balance the claims of various groups and also the needs of the present against the future. Leadership must be flexible. The fall of Gomułka in late 1970 perfectly illustrates the fact that bad leadership (in this case resulting in the alienation of sections of the working class) led to unrest which in turn resulted in a change of leadership and reforms to bring together élite and non-élite. When the public continually loses faith in their political leaders, the existing political structure cannot flourish. This applies to States of the socialist bloc as well as to liberal democratic States. Exchange involves commitment, reciprocity and trust.[2] Many Western accounts and those of 'critical

[1] Ibid., p. 25. [2] See P. M. Blau, *Exchange and Power in Social Life* (1964) ch. 4.

Marxists', such as Kuroń and Modzelewski, consider political exchange under State socialism to be characterised by exploitation and fear but they have provided as one-sided an account as have 'official' Polish and Soviet Marxist interpretations almost exclusively stressing harmony. In contemporary Poland, as a result of the changes induced in the Stalin period, the social structure has become more differentiated. Despite the existence of a large peasant population and of private agricultural producers, the groups highly antagonistic to the political order originating from the traditional setting have declined in number and in significance. Allegiance to the régime has grown and the objective need for rigid political control has declined. Indeed, it is also more difficult to enforce policy in an authoritarian fashion as witnessed by the disturbances in December 1970–January 1971. The society is more diverse and more specialised and new groups – e.g. the scientific intelligentsia and the 'new' working class – created by the régime, have come on to the scene. The PUWP is the crucial body through which the demands of these groups must be handled and channelled. The party has the function of maintaining the values and basic institutions of the system and in this respect it is authoritarian but at the same time it has to consult various social interests.

> In the struggle for the goals of socialism the party in power finds itself entangled with various interests: class . . . strata, group, professional, regional, immediate and long-term, generational etc. They create social situations which frequently do not correspond to the situations envisaged and planned for by the party. These various interests have a definite influence upon the party, particularly upon its strategy and tactics, its composition and its authority, as well as upon other elements of its structure.[1]

The party then plays an important role in aggregating group interests and in so doing is similar in character to parties in liberal societies. Rather than providing an exploitative political élite in a mass 'totalitarian' society, we would characterise the Communist Party in State socialist society as being the fulcrum in a consultative but authoritarian political system. We must emphasise that the process of consultation is not smooth and

[1] A. Dobieszewski, 'Struktura i zasady działania partii', in *Nowe Drogi*, no. 6, 1971, p. 66.

frictionless and that 'bottlenecks' occur in the political system as they do in the economy. A Polish writer commenting on the role of social organisations in Poland makes the point clearly.

> ... Their activities have been largely formalised, subjected to a single model, and hence somehow bureaucratised. As a result, many organisations have lost their character as initiative groups, as characteristically socialist 'pressure groups' seeking the realisation of their demands. . . . It often seems that many of the conduits . . . above all, social and civic organisations, are blocked, buried under a mountain of paper, devoid of independence or effectiveness.[1]

Hence we might say that the *political culture* contains groups with participant orientations but the *political system* is often not responsive to their demands and acts in an authoritarian fashion. We would suggest that a system of consultative authoritarianism is being evolved in present-day Poland.

There are four general conclusions to this work which we would like to suggest. First, the character of society before socialist industrialisation had a considerable effect on the kind of régime the Communist political élites could introduce. Cultural factors and the historical heritage may provide limitations on political élites who seek radical change. The mode of State socialism imported from the USSR was difficult to graft on to Polish society. The Polish intelligentsia, weakened though it was by the effects of the Second World War, still carried a tradition of independent intellectual life identified with the Polish nation which the Communist government did not destroy. There were norms at variance with the official view of Marxism–Leninism which exerted considerable influence; for example, on the behaviour of writers, which, in the interests of social harmony, the political élites had to allow to continue.

Secondly, we have seen that industrialisation has involved centralisation and coercion. To no small extent this was due to the need to break down resistance to the Communist model of social and economic change. The changes carried out, however, led to greater structural differentiation. Groups of professional

---

[1] K. T. Toeplitz, *Życie Warszawy*, 22 July 1970. Cited by A. Ross Johnson, 'Polish Perspectives, Past and Present', in *Problems of Communism*, vol. xx, no. 4 (July–Aug. 1971) pp. 62–3.

engineers articulated demands to exercise their professional competence and they wanted financial incentives which would set them off as a social group from unskilled and manual workers. The manual working class, newly recruited from the country-side, also wanted rewards in the form of consumption in return for labour. To enable economic advance to proceed, centralisation had to be weakened. More power was transferred to factory directors: in the first place they were given greater control over the industrial enterprise, later they were allowed more say in the formation of industrial objectives. The style of leadership necessary to accommodate those interests has rested more on persuasion than coercion. This may best be illustrated by the personal intervention of Gierek in the shipyard strike in January. Thus social groups have sanctions which may be utilised against the élites: in extreme circumstances, they may refuse to produce, as peasants; they may work inefficiently, as members of the technical intelligentsia; or they may riot, or absent themselves from work, as the manual working class has done.

Thirdly, the process of adaptation has not been a smooth one and disturbances have illustrated the lack of social integration. The main cleavages in Polish society which have been considered in this monograph have occurred in 1956, 1968 and 1970–1. The first consisted of a major break with the Soviet model. Polish cultural and social values were given a much more important and autonomous role than in the postwar period of reconstruction. The demands of the cultural and technical intelligentsia were met: their role in decision-making was enhanced, their social position was elevated, as was illustrated by the greater differentials between them and manual workers. The events of 1968 again illustrated the tension between groups of the cultural intelligentsia (including students) and the political élites. Here, however, the élites took the initiative by clipping the wings of the more outspoken critics. Obviously, this tension is still a latent factor in Polish politics. Social integration was pursued by a policy appealing to nationalism. In December 1970–January 1971, the explosive outbursts in the Polish Baltic ports brought down Gomułka. The significance of these events was to highlight the role of the manual working class under State socialism. Industrial morale must necessarily be kept high if work is to be efficiently performed. Industrial work is not

intrinsically satisfying and the main motivating factor is re-
munerative. The workers' demands were for the recognition of
their rights to a minimum real wage and to participation and
consultation. The riots also illustrated the fact that mechanisms
for the incorporation of the working class in the Polish political
system were not adequate. The Polish United Workers Party
had 'lost touch' with the masses; demands on the political
system had been ignored. This brings us to our fourth point.

The ideology of State socialism gives pride of place to the
industrial working class which the party leads, but in the actual
social and political structure the working class is fragmented.
Such writers as Kuroń and Modzelewski argue that there is a
fundamental dichotomy between a central political bureaucracy and the exploited masses. We do not agree with the conclusion of Kuroń and Modzelewski for the following reasons. In
the first place, the élites are not unitary but oligarchic: there
is considerable conflict between them which is reflected by
leadership crises and political changes. Second, the surplus
which is extracted from the non-élite is used primarily for re-
investment and further capital formation which eventually
results in greater consumption. It is not utilised to promote
significantly private accumulation by the members of a ruling
class. Third, and most important, the élites, to remain in power,
must to some degree be responsive to demands made on them
which they seek to accommodate within the existing frame-work
of power relations. But they cannot satisfy all interests: every-
body cannot win and have prizes. Under State socialism, political conflict is endemic, and the élites have considerable power,
riches and status which the non-élites do not possess: Poland is
politically and socially stratified. While the ideology of State
socialist society postulates social unity, in practice there are
major political lines of cleavage between the leading party/
State élites and the lower bureaucratic and representative
authorities, and there are limited social boundaries between
manual and non-manual workers and peasants. The major
problem with which the Polish political system must grapple is
how to regulate the social and political conflicts which these
divisions generate. The administration under Gomułka promised greater participation and devolution but its style was in
practice authoritarian and bureaucratic. The party is an

institution whose role it is to regulate these interests. What is overlooked by Western commentators who argue for the relinquishing of power by the party is that the cement which holds together the social system is political: the institution of the party provides for State socialist society what private property supplies for capitalism, namely a value system which is codified into laws and which promotes social and political solidarity. A considerable weakening of the principle of party authority, therefore, might result in the collapse of the régime or in the assertion of other values, either managerial or technocratic, in their stead.

APPENDIX ONE

TABLE 1. POPULATION STATISTICS

Year	Total	Men	Women	Urban No.	Urban %	Rural	Live births Total	Live births Urban	Live births Rural	Deaths Total	Deaths Urban	Deaths Rural	Pop. growth rate Total	Pop. growth rate Urban	Pop. growth rate Rural	Infant mortality Total	Infant mortality Urban	Infant mortality Rural
	(thousands)						(per thousand population)											
1921[a]	27,177	13,133	14,044	6,608	24.6	20,250	—	—	—	—	—	—	—	—	—	—	—	—
1931[a]	32,107	15,619	16,488	8,731	27.4	23,185	—	—	—	—	—	—	—	—	—	—	—	—
1946[b]	23,930	10,954	12,976	7,517	31.8	16,109	—	—	—	—	—	—	—	—	—	—	—	—
1950[b]	25,008	11,928	13,080	9,605	39.0	15,009	—	—	—	—	—	—	—	—	—	—	—	—
1960[b]	29,776	14,404	15,372	14,206	48.3	15,200	—	—	—	—	—	—	—	—	—	—	—	—
1931–32[c]	—	—	—	—	—	—	29.8	21.0	33.0	15.3	12.6	16.3	14.5	8.4	16.7	143.0[d]	121.5[d]	148.2
1936–38[c]	—	—	—	—	—	—	25.3	—	—	14.1	—	—	11.2	—	—	139.2[d]	—	—
1938[a]	34,849	17,000	17,349	10,455	30.0	24,394	—	—	—	—	—	—	—	—	—	—	—	—
1949	24,613	11,718	12,895	8,920	36.2	15,693	30.7	30.0	31.2	11.6	10.9	12.1	19.1	19.1	19.1	111.2	102.6	116.0
1950	25,035	11,942	13,095	9,243	36.9	15,792	31.0	30.7	31.2	11.9	11.5	12.9	19.1	19.2	18.3	117.6	106.3	124.6
1951	25,507	12,183	13,324	10,126	39.7	15,381	30.2	29.7	30.6	11.1	10.4	11.6	19.2	19.3	19.0	96.4	89.2	101.7
1952	25,939	12,437	13,582	10,525	40.5	15,474	29.7	29.2	30.0	10.2	9.4	10.7	19.3	19.8	19.0	88.4	88.4	94.0
1953	26,511	12,700	13,811	10,858	41.0	15,653	29.1	28.7	29.3	9.3	9.5	10.9	19.8	19.2	18.4	88.3	89.1	89.1
1954	27,012	12,955	14,057	11,316	41.9	15,696	29.1	28.6	29.5	9.9	8.9	10.1	19.2	19.7	19.4	82.2	75.5	88.7
1955	27,550	13,232	14,318	12,067	43.8	15,483	28.1	26.8	29.1	8.6	8.3	9.5	19.5	18.5	19.6	77.2	73.3	88.3
1956	28,080	13,506	14,574	12,594	44.9	15,486	27.6	26.0	29.0	8.5	8.6	10.3	19.1	17.4	18.7	72.1	64.6	75.4
1957	28,540	13,745	14,795	12,978	45.5	15,562	26.3	24.5	27.8	8.2	7.7	9.0	18.1	16.8	18.8	71.4	70.0	82.6
1958	29,000	13,980	15,020	13,471	46.4	15,529	24.5	22.4	26.8	7.6	7.9	9.3	17.9	14.5	17.5	70.9	64.2	78.2
1959	29,430	14,226	15,254	13,958	47.3	15,522	24.7	19.9	24.9	7.6	6.9	8.2	16.1	12.9	16.9	64.4	64.4	75.6
1960	29,795	14,414	15,381	14,401	48.5	15,394	22.6	18.1	23.6	7.6	6.9	8.6	15.0	11.2	15.4	54.8	49.7	53.5
1961	30,133	14,504	15,549	14,627	48.8	15,506	20.9	16.9	22.4	7.1	6.9	8.0	13.3	9.8	13.8	53.2	47.0	57.7
1962	30,464	14,768	15,716	14,880	48.8	15,604	19.8	16.3	21.9	8.6	7.1	8.1	11.9	9.4	13.9	54.2	47.8	59.3
1963	30,940	15,008	15,933	15,209	49.2	15,731	19.2	15.5	20.5	8.0	6.9	7.8	11.7	8.5	12.4	48.5	44.2	51.6
1964	31,339	15,208	16,136	15,485	49.4	15,854	18.1	14.9	19.7	8.1	7.0	7.8	10.5	8.0	11.9	47.2	41.6	51.3
1965	31,551	15,319	16,232	15,681	49.7	15,870	17.4	14.4	19.1	7.3	6.9	7.4	10.0	7.4	11.3	41.5	38.8	43.4
1966	31,611	15,453	16,358	15,909	50.5	15,902	16.7	14.0	18.6	7.8	7.3	7.8	9.4	6.7	10.4	38.6	35.1	41.2
1967	32,163	15,620	16,543	16,367	50.9	15,796	16.3	13.8	18.7	7.8	7.2	7.9	8.5	6.6	10.8	37.9	35.7	39.5
1968	32,426	15,754	16,672	16,600	51.2	15,826	16.2	14.1	18.7	8.5	7.7	8.5	8.6	6.4	10.2	33.4	31.4	34.9
1969	32,671	15,877	16,794	16,829	51.5	15,842	16.3	14.1	18.7	8.1	7.5	8.1	8.2	6.4	10.2	33.1	33.1	35.4
1970	32,605	15,843	16,762	17,031	52.2	15,574	16.7	14.7	18.8	8.1	7.7	8.6	8.6	7.0	10.2	33.4	31.6	34.8

[a] 1938 borders. [b] Present borders. [c] Annual average. [d] Incomplete data.

Sources: Glowny Urząd Statystyczny, *Rocznik Statystyczny 1966*, pp. 13, 46; *Mały Rocznik Statystyczny 1967*, pp. 9–10, 22. Ibid., 1970, pp. 21, 42. Ibid., *Rocznik Statystyczny 1971*, pp. 15, 18, 35.

APPENDIX TWO

TABLE 1. RURAL AND AGRICULTURAL POPULATION

	1931	1946	1950	1955	1960	1965	1968
National population (m.)	32·1	23·9	25·0	27·6	29·8	31·6	32·4
Rural population (m.)	23·2	15·6	15·8	15·5	15·4	15·9	15·8
In rural areas (per cent)	72·0	66·0	63·0	56·0	52·0	50·0	49·0
Rural population dependent on agriculture (per cent)	83·0	—	77·0	—	69·0	—	62·0

N.B. 1931 figures for population within prewar boundaries.

Sources: Drugi powszechny spis ludności z dn. 9.XII. 1931 r. (Warsaw, 1938) p. 1. *Rocznik Statystyczny 1969* (Warsaw, 1969) pp. 24 and 46.

TABLE 2. ORGANISATION OF AGRICULTURE

	1950	*1955*	*1960*	*1965*	*1968*
Number of private farms (m.)	3·2	—	3·6	—	3·9
Of agricultural area (per cent)	89·6	77·3	—	85·0	84·5
Of production (per cent)	93·0	82·0	89·0	86·0	85·0
Number of State farms (PGR's)	9,679	10,185	7,876	8,828	8,099
Of agricultural area (per cent)	9·6	13·5	—	13·3	13·8
Of production (per cent)	6·0	11·0	10·0	13·0	14·0
Number of collective farms (prod. co-ops.)	2,199	9,694	1,978	1,251	1,123
Of agricultural area (per cent)	0·8	9·2	—	1·1	1·2
Of production (per cent)	0·5	8·0	1·0	1·0	1·0

Sources: Rocznik Statystyczny, 1956, p. 143; 1966, p. 229; 1969, pp. 218, 222, 239, 249, 252. B. Strużek, 'Problematyka podstawowych procesów rozwojowych wsi i rolnictwa', in *Rocznik Dziejów Ruchu Ludowego*, 11, p. 35.

TABLE 3. STRUCTURE OF PRIVATE AGRICULTURE

Size (ha.)	0·1–0·5	0·5–2	2–5	5–10	10–15	15 and over
Number of farms (ooo's)						
1931	788		1,171	744	195	138
1950	200	622	992	968	246	133
1960	348	830	1,092	938	248	101
1968	1,467		1,091	922	390	
Percentage of total						
1931	26		38·6	24·5	6·4	4·5
1950	6·3	19·6	31·3	30·8	7·8	4·2
1960	9·7	23·1	30·4	26·1	7·9	2·8
1968	37·9		28·2	23·9	10·0	
Percentage of area						
1950	0·3	4·5	21·1	44·0	17·1	16·0
1960	0·5	5·8	21·7	39·5	20·1	12·4
1968	—	—	—	—	—	—
Population resident on farms supplying *main* source of income (ooo's)						
1950	1,181		3,209	4,113	1,139	621
1960	1,355		3,164	3,698	1,298	478

Sources: Drugi powszechny spis ludności z dn. 9 Dec. 1931 r., p. 2. Rocznik Statystyczny, 1969, p. 239; 1968, p. 46. B. Strużek, 'Problematyka . . .', p. 35.

TABLE 4. POLITICAL MOBILISATION OF THE PEASANTRY

	1950	1955	1959	1964	1968
Rural membership (ooo's):					
PUWP				290	587 ('66)
UPP					315
Peasant membership (ooo's):					
PUWP	269 ('48)	175	117	168 ('63)	222 ('67)
UPP	130	156	174	237	260
Peasants in national membership (per cent):					
PUWP	15·8 ('48)	13	12·2 ('58)	11·2 ('63)	11·5 ('67)
UPP	67	74·2	74·2	69·3	70·3
Villages with branches of (per cent):					
PUWP		35	56	55	75
UPP			44		63 ('70)
Gromadas with committees of (per cent):					
PUWP				90	94
UPP					96

N.B. Figures for 1948–50 concern combined peasant membership of PWP and PSP before the unification to form PUWP.

Sources: M. Sadowski, *Przemiany społeczne a system polityczny PRL* (Warsaw, 1969) p. 202. A. Mariańska, 'Wiejskie organizacje PZPR', in *Roczniki Socjologii Wsi*, vii, pp. 181, 177. *V Zjazd* (Warsaw, 1969) p. 214. W. Dąbski, 'ZSL w latach 1949–65', *Wieś Współczesna*, April 1966. B. Dyląk and W. Dąbski, 'ZSL w latach 1965–70', in *Wieś Współczesna*, Nov. 1970. *VIII Plenum NK ZSL – Materials*, Warsaw, LSW, 1969, pp. 22–3. A. Korbonski, *The Politics of Socialist Agriculture in Poland* (New York, 1965) pp. 194–5.

TABLE 5. COMPOSITION OF SMALL-HOLDING PEASANT MEMBERS (1965)

	Up to 2	*2–5*	*5–10*	*10 and over*
Small-holding peasant members (000's):				
PUWP	54,032	76,433	71,265	15,773
UPP	43,764	79,529	80,108	26,552
Proportion of small-holders in:				
PUWP (per cent)	4·4	7·0	7·6	4·1
UPP (per cent)	3·1	7·3	8·5	7·0

Sources: Z. Mikołajczyk and E. Patryn, *Struktura i funkcje partii Chłopskiej*, p. 125. A. Mariańska, 'Wiejskie organizacje PZPR', p. 179.

Table 6. Rural Party Membership (1965)

	Members in rural areas (per cent)	Peasants in rural membership (per cent)	Incidence of group membership (per cent)	In collectives (per cent)	Of which PGRs (per cent)	Are peasant-workers (per cent)
PUWP	31·4 (1966)	37·5	3·8 (1966)	n.a.	n.a.	n.a.
UPP	85·2	80·2	4·5 (1966)	1	—	10·1
Of all UPP membership of rural PUWP membership:	Education			Age		
	Basic (7–14)	Middle (–18)	Higher	Under 40	Over 40	Women
PUWP (per cent)	83·6	15·0	1·4	56·8	43·4	n.a.
UPP (per cent)	83·5	14·1	2·4	40·6	59·4	15·1

Sources: A. Mariańska, 'Wiejskie organizacje PZPR', pp. 177, 181–4. W. Dąbski, 'ZSL w latach 1949–65', pp. 156–9. M. Sadowski, 'Przemiany społeczne a partie polityczne', pp. 91–7. S. Dziabała, 'Metodologiczne problemy badań organizacji politycznych na wsi', in *Studia Socjologiczne*, 1968, pp. 3–4.

APPENDIX THREE

DATA OF DIRECTORS OF ENTERPRISES

TABLE I. ENTERPRISE DIRECTORS AND PARTY MEMBERSHIP (1945–55)

Year	No.	PWP	PSP	Non-party	Lack of data
1945	25	24·0	4·0	52·0	20·0
1946	35	28·6	17·1	37·1	37·1
1947	40	40·0	10·0	35·0	35·0
1948	39	53·8	7·7	20·5	20·5
		PUWP*	UPP*		
1949	47	76·6	—	17·0	6·4
1950	44	84·5	—	9·1	6·4
1951	47	85·0	4·4	4·2	6·4
1952	45	91·1	2·2	2·2	4·4
1953	46	89·1	2·2	2·2	6·5
1954	44	90·9	2·3	—	6·8
1955	41	95·2	2·4	—	2·4

* Post-1948 PWP and PSP combined to form the PUWP.
Sources: H. Najduchowska, 'Dyrektorzy przedsiebiorstw przemysłowych . . .',
Tables 1, 2, pp. 82 and 86. Ibid., p. 95. 'By 1964, out of the 1,541 directors
examined "nearly all" were party members.'

TABLE 2. ENTERPRISE DIRECTORS AND SOCIAL ORIGIN (1945–64)

Year	No. in sample	Worker	Intelligentsia	Peasant	Petit-bourgeois
		per cent	per cent	per cent	per cent
1945	25	12·0	24·0	—	—
1946	35	22·9	39·4	—	—
1947	40	22·5	27·5	—	2·5
1948	39	33·3	20·5	5·1	2·6
1949	47	53·7	17·0	4·2	2·1
1950	44	50·0	13·6	4·5	4·5
1951	47	55·4	12·8	10·6	4·2
1952	45	62·2	8·9	8·9	6·7
1953	46	65·2	8·7	8·7	6·5
1954	44	68·2	11·3	11·3	—
1955	41	68·3	14·6	14·6	—
1956	37	75·7	8·1	16·2	—
1957	30	70·0	6·6	23·3	—
1958	34	67·7	8·8	20·6	2·9
1959	31	67·8	6·4	22·6	3·2
1960	31	61·3	6·4	20·0	3·2
1961	31	58·1	9·7	29·0	3·2
1962	32	56·2	15·6	28·1	—
1963	30	66·5	13·5	20·0	—
1964	29	65·5	10·4	24·1	—

Source: H. Najduchowska, 'Dyrektorzy . . .', Table 1, pp. 82–3 and 86–7.

TABLE 3. ENTERPRISE DIRECTORS AND EDUCATIONAL QUALIFICATIONS (1945–8)

Year	No. in sample	Type of education (per cent)						
		Higher technical	Higher other	Secondary technical	General secondary	Other secondary	Vocational	Elementary
1945	25	76·0	8·0	4·0	4·0	—	—	—
1946	35	57·2	8·6	5·7	8·5	2·9	2·9	5·7
1947	40	62·5	2·5	5·0	10·0	2·5	2·5	7·5
1948	39	48·7	5·1	7·7	12·8	—	7·7	12·8

Source: H. Najduchowska, 'Dyrektorzy . . .', pp. 82–3, Table 1.

TABLE 4. ENTERPRISE DIRECTORS AND EDUCATIONAL QUALIFICATIONS (1949–52)

Year	No. in sample	Type of education (per cent)						
		Higher technical	Other higher	Secondary technical	General secondary	Other secondary	Vocational	Elementary
1949	47	29·8	6·4	10·6	23·4	—	12·0	12·8
1950	44	29·2	4·6	11·3	20·5	—	20·5	9·1
1951	47	14·9	6·4	14·9	23·4	2·2	14·9	17·0
1952	45	13·3	6·4	9·0	28·9	4·5	11·1	17·8

Source: H. Najduchowska, 'Dyrektorzy . . .', Table 2, pp. 86–7.

Table 5. Enterprise Directors and Educational Qualifications (1953–5)

Year	No. in sample	Type of education (per cent)						
		Higher technical	Other higher	Secondary technical	General secondary	Other secondary	Vocational	Elementary
1953	46	15·2	8·8	15·2	21·7	4·4	8·8	15·2
1954	44	15·9	9·1	20·5	25·0	4·5	4·5	13·7
1955	41	14·6	12·2	19·5	19·5	4·9	9·8	14·6

Source: H. Najduchowska, 'Dyrektorzy . . .', Table 2, pp. 86–7.

Table 6. Enterprise Directors and Educational Qualifications (1956–8)

Year	No. in sample	Type of education (per cent)							
		Higher technical	Higher economic	Other higher	Secondary technical	General secondary	Other secondary	Vocational	Elementary
1956	42	26·2	2·3	9·5	16·7	19·0	4·8	7·1	14·3
1957	37	29·7	5·4	8·1	13·0	16·2	5·4	8·1	13·5
1958	40	32·5	5·0	15·0	10·0	17·5	5·0	7·5	7·5

Source: H. Najduchowska, 'Dyrektorzy . . .', Table 3, p. 94.

TABLE 7. POSITIONS HELD DIRECTLY PRIOR TO PROMOTION TO POST
OF ENTERPRISE DIRECTOR (1965)

		Persons	
		No.	*Per cent*
(1)	Assistant director for technological problems (chief engineer)	351	22·8
(2)	Managers of technical and production departments	282	18·3
(3)	Management position outside of industry	175	11·4
(4)	Ministry and Zjednoczenie (Association) employees	156	10·0
(5)	Assistant director for administrative, trade, etc., matters	100	6·5
(6)	Managers in the economic-trade depts.	72	4·7
(7)	Factory managers (sub-unit of enterprise)	60	3·9
(8)	Party, social and political organisation apparatus employees	59	3·9
(9)	Employees from State administration and People's Councils	53	3·4
(10)	Managers of *finance* departments	48	3·1
(11)	Clerical personnel	28	1·8
(12)	Foremen, technicians, etc.	26	1·7
(13)	Managers of cadre (personnel) administrative, economic and social departments	21	1·4
(14)	Directly after completing studies, to which they were directed *whilst working*	20	1·3
(15)	Manual workers	2	0·1
(16)	Others	88	5·7

Source: H. Najduchowska, 'Dyrektorzy . . .', Table 6, p. 97.

TABLE 8. GRADUATES OF HIGHER TECHNICAL COLLEGES (WYŻSZE SZKOŁY TECHNICZNE) BY DAY (FULL-TIME) COURSES ACCORDING TO SOCIAL ORIGIN

Year	Total	Worker		Peasant		Non-manual		Craft		Other	
1955	5,690	2,451		1,474		2,552		164		48	
1956	7,771	—		—		—		—		—	
1957	5,232	—		—		—		—		—	
1958	4,550	1,563	(34·3)	908	(20·0)	1,917	(42·1)	130	(2·9)	32	(0·7)
1959	3,520	1,168	(33·2)	701	(19·9)	1,527	(43·4)	97	(2·7)	27	(0·8)
1960	6,219	2,161	(34·7)	1,313	(21·1)	2,532	(40·7)	198	(3·2)	15	(0·3)
1961	5,979	1,929	(32·3)	1,288	(21·5)	2,530	(42·3)	214	(3·6)	18	(0·3)
1962	4,483	1,262	(28·2)	972	(21·7)	2,068	(46·1)	163	(3·6)	18	(0·4)
1963	4,256	1,267	(29·8)	864	(20·3)	1,971	(46·3)	138	(3·2)	16	(0·4)
1964	4,296	1,367	(31·1)	797	(18·1)	2,069	(47·1)	138	(3·1)	25	(0·6)
1965	4,082	1,184	(29·0)	784	(19·2)	1,935	(47·4)	163	(4·0)	16	(0·4)
1966	3,350	977	(29·2)	581	(17·3)	1,679	(50·1)	101	(3·0)	12	(0·4)
1967	4,802	1,438	(29·9)	836	(17·4)	2,324	(48·5)	169	(3·5)	35	(0·7)

Sources: A. Butler, *Wybrane dane . . .* and also L. Aleksa *Pochodzenie społeczne,* Table 4, p. 23.

APPENDIX FOUR

TABLE 1. LEVEL OF EDUCATION OF COUNCILLORS AT WOJEWODSTWO, POWIAT AND GROMADA LEVEL BETWEEN 1949 AND 1969*

	1949	1951	1953	1955	1958	1961	1965	1969
Per cent of councillors who had completed higher education								
Total	3·1	1·5	1·6	2·2	3·5	4·6	6·1	6·7
Wojewodstwo	—	—	—	—	28·8	31·7	36·3	36·1
Powiat	—	—	—	—	9·9	11·6	14·9	16·3
Gromada	—	—	—	—	0·9	1·3	1·9	2·0
Per cent of councillors who had completed secondary education								
Total	13·6	9·2	19·2	13·7	16·9	20·4	22·1	24·2
Wojewodstwo	—	—	—	—	32·7	28·3	27·5	25·0
Powiat	—	—	—	—	32·6	31·2	32·3	31·8
Gromada	—	—	—	—	11·9	16·3	17·2	19·0
Per cent of councillors who had completed elementary education								
Total	45·1	—	56·1	40·2	37·0	41·6	48·5	56·1
Wojewodstwo	—	—	—	—	31·6	36·5	33·8	37·8
Powiat	—	—	—	—	38·8	44·6	44·8	47·3
Gromada	—	—	—	—	35·2	47·5	55·7	65·2
Per cent of councillors who had not completed elementary education								
Total	38·2	—	23·1	43·9	42·6	27·6	19·1	10·3
Wojewodstwo	—	—	—	—	6·9	3·5	2·4	1·1
Powiat	—	—	—	—	18·7	12·6	8·0	4·6
Gromada	—	—	—	—	52·0	34·9	25·2	13·8

(—) No data

* *Radni*, pp. 0—111 Zawodzka, 'Ewolucja składu...' p. 48

BETWEEN 1947 AND 1969*

	1947	1951	1953	1955	1958	1962	1965	1969
Per cent of presidium members who had completed higher education								
Total	4·9	1·4	1·6	1·2	2·7	5·0	7·1	8·7
Wojewodstwo	41·2	22·5	10·5	24·4	44·0	53·2	66·2	73·0
Powiat	15·0	6·9	2·6	6·2	14·6	23·2	32·6	42·2
Gromada	2·2	0·2	0·1	0·4	0·8	1·3	2·0	2·9
Per cent of presidium members who had completed secondary education								
Total	21·8	11·4	19·2	15·9	18·0	22·4	26·3	28·9
Wojewodstwo	38·8	40·0	52·3	59·2	47·0	40·0	30·4	22·5
Powiat	42·5	39·2	39·5	45·3	49·2	49·3	52·8	47·3
Gromada	16·3	7·0	13·0	12·4	13·0	16·6	20·1	23·8
Per cent of presidium members who had completed elementary education								
Total	46·7	—	56·1	45·2	43·4	51·7	54·6	54·6
Wojewodstwo	20·0	—	34·9	15·9	9·0	6·8	3·4	4·5
Powiat	38·6	—	54·8	45·1	35·2	27·2	14·4	10·1
Gromada	48·3	—	62·0	44·2	43·7	54·7	62·1	63·3
Per cent of presidium members who had not completed elementary education								
Total	26·6	—	23·1	37·7	35·9	20·9	12·0	7·8
Wojewodstwo	0·0	—	2·3	0·5	0·0	0·0	0·0	0·0
Powiat	3·9	—	3·1	3·4	1·0	0·2	0·2	0·4
Gromada	33·2	—	24·9	43·0	42·5	27·4	15·8	10·0

(—) No data

* *Członkowie prezydiów . . .*, pp. 11–12; M. Wendlandt, 'Struktura osobowa prezydiów rad narodowych w latach 1944–1965', in *PRN* 10, 1967, p. 55, passim. Since gromada councils were only established in 1954 references in 1954 are to commune ('gminna') councils.

TABLE 3. LEVEL OF EDUCATION OF NON-MANUAL WORKERS
EMPLOYED BY PRESIDIA AT WOJEWODSTWO, POWIAT AND GROMADA
LEVEL*

	1959	*1962*	*1965*
Per cent of non-manual workers who had completed higher education			
Total	9·6	9·5	10·0
Wojewodstwo	26·7	29·6	31·2
Powiat	7·4	7·9	9·0
Gromada	0·1	0·0	0·0
Per cent of non-manual workers who had completed secondary education			
Total	32·9	38·1	44·1
Wojewodstwo	36·9	41·4	45·5
Powiat	39·2	47·7	56·8
Gromada	14·7	14·0	18·2
Per cent of non-manual workers who had completed elementary education			
Total	55·8	51·8	45·7
Wojewodstwo	36·0	28·7	23·2
Powiat	52·2	44·1	34·1
Gromada	80·6	84·1	81·2
Per cent of non-manual workers who had not completed elementary education			
Total	1·7	0·6	0·2
Wojewodstwo	0·4	0·3	0·1
Powiat	1·2	0·3	0·1
Gromada	4·6	1·9	0·6

* *Struktura Zatrudnienia* . . ., p. 145.

TABLE 4. SOCIO-OCCUPATIONAL GROUPS OF COUNCILLORS AT WOJEWODSTWO, POWIAT AND GROMADA LEVEL BETWEEN 1946 AND 1969*

	1946	1949	1953	1955	1958	1961	1965	1969
Per cent of councillors who are manual workers								
Total	9·6	18·7	21·0	18·7	11·7	13·3	12·3	15·4
Wojewodstwo	—	—	—	—	18·7	21·5	19·6	23·0
Powiat	—	—	—	—	9·8	13·7	13·3	16·2
Gromada	—	—	—	—	10·0	10·6	9·6	12·1
Per cent of councillors who are peasants								
Total	44·4	45·3	48·0	49·1	53·2	47·4	44·9	43·0
Wojewodstwo	—	—	—	—	14·5	15·9	15·4	15·5
Powiat	—	—	—	—	30·7	29·8	28·6	29·8
Gromada	—	—	—	—	64·8	59·1	57·7	56·4
Per cent of councillors who are non-manual workers								
Total	29·1	30·8	27·5	28·2	28·4	35·0	37·1	36·5
Wojewodstwo	—	—	—	—	58·6	59·5	60·6	56·6
Powiat	—	—	—	—	49·6	52·5	52·4	49·1
Gromada	—	—	—	—	20·4	26·7	28·0	27·7
Other councillors (private craftsmen, having no occupational work, retired)								
Total	16·9	5·2	3·5	4·0	—	4·3	5·7	5·1
Wojewodstwo	—	—	—	—	—	3·0	4·4	4·9
Powiat	—	—	—	—	—	4·0	5·7	4·9
Gromada	—	—	—	—	—	3·6	4·7	3·8

(—) No data.

* *Radni . . .*, pp. 2c–3; Zawadzka, 'Ewolucja składu . . .', pp. 42–3.

TABLE 5. SOCIO-OCCUPATIONAL GROUPS OF PRESIDIUM MEMBERS AT WOJEWODSTWO, POWIAT AND GROMADA LEVEL BETWEEN 1947 AND 1969*

	1947	1951	1953	1955	1958	1962	1965	1969
Per cent of presidium members who are manual workers								
Total	5·4	41·2	19·7	11·2	13·5	7·8	6·6	6·6
Wojewodstwo	5·0	52·5	17·7	6·5	6·0	1·1	1·5	2·5
Powiat	5·9	49·0	10·7	4·1	6·1	1·4	1·0	2·4
Gromada	4·9	35·3	18·8	11·0	13·3	8·4	7·2	6·7
Per cent of presidium members who are peasants								
Total	54·9	51·5	28·3	45·3	52·6	43·1	39·8	36·6
Wojewodstwo	5·0	25·0	2·1	0·5	3·0	0·0	0·0	1·0
Powiat	22·7	39·1	4·3	3·2	7·5	3·0	2·7	4·2
Gromada	68·6	59·6	37·3	52·6	62·1	56·1	52·0	46·6
Per cent of presidium members who are non-manual workers								
Total	22·1	4·1	48·1	41·3	30·7	45·2	49·8	53·3
Wojewodstwo	66·1	19·2	78·8	92·0	88·6	96·3	98·5	96·5
Powiat	51·4	8·7	82·2	90·0	82·8	93·9	94·5	92·3
Gromada	13·9	2·7	40·2	34·4	21·9	32·1	37·6	43·7
Other presidium members (private craftsmen, having no occupational work, retired)								
Total	17·6	3·2	3·9	2·2	3·2	3·9	3·8	3·5
Wojewodstwo	23·9	3·3	1·4	1·0	2·4	2·6	0·0	0·0
Powiat	20·0	3·2	2·8	2·7	3·6	1·7	1·8	0·5
Gromada	12·6	2·4	3·7	2·0	2·7	3·4	3·2	0·6

* *Członkowie prezydiów* . . ., pp. 22–5; Wentlandt, 'Struktura osobowa . . .', passim.

TABLE 6. PARTY MEMBERSHIP OF COUNCILLORS BETWEEN 1946 AND 1969*

	1946[a]	1948[b]	1949[c]	1953	1955	1958	1961	1965	1969
Non-party	25·8	25·4	12·9	33·5	48·8	36·6	31·2	29·1	30·0
PUWP	39·2	47·0	62·1	44·2	38·1	40·5	45·3	46·8	46·5
UPP	10·5	—	20·9	19·5	12·1	21·2	21·5	21·6	20·9
DP	4·6	—	2·7	2·8	1·0	1·7	2·0	2·5	2·6
Other parties	19·9	—	1·4	0·0	0·0	0·0	0·0	0·0	0·0
	100%	100%	100%	100%	100%	100%	100%	100%	100%

[a] PUWP figure is the aggregate of PWP, PPS; UPP figure refers to PP figure; other parties include Popular Party of Poland and Labour Party.

[b] PUWP figure is the aggregate of FWP and PSP; no data of 27·6 per cent.

[c] Other parties include Popular Party of Poland (PSL) and Labour Party (SP).

* *Radni . . .*, pp. 14–15; Zawadzka, 'Ewolucja składu . . .', pp. 42–3.

TABLE 7. PARTY MEMBERSHIP OF PRESIDIUM MEMBERS BETWEEN 1947 AND 1969*

	1947	1951	1953	1955	1958	1962	1965	1969
Non-party	25·9	11·1	15·6	32·5	26·4	13·8	14·3	15·8
PUWP	47·9	64·9	63·2	51·6	46·7	58·3	57·7	56·4
UUP	20·8	21·8	19·5	15·4	25·1	25·5	25·4	25·3
DP	3·1	2·2	1·7	0·5	1·8	2·4	2·6	2·5
Other parties	2·3	0·0	0·0	0·0	0·0	0·0	0·0	0·0
	100%	100%	100%	100%	100%	100%	100%	100%

* *Członkowie prezydiu . . .*, pp. 17–18; Wentlandt, 'Struktura osobowa . . .', passim.

Terms and Abbreviations

AC   Agricultural Circle (Kółko Rolnicze: KR)

ACCPS   Agricultural Centre of the Co-operative 'Peasants' Self-Help' (Centrala Rolnicza Spółdzielni 'Samopomoc Chłopska': CRSSC)

Aktyw   Activists (either in the unions, party or other socio-political organisations)

Association (Zjednoczenie) Comprised of groups of industrial enterprises within a particular Ministry and superior to the enterprise in planning and management.

Association of Polish Engineers and Mechanics (Stowarzyszenie Inżynierów i Mechaników Polskich: SIMP)

CCTU   Central Council of Trade Unions (Centralna Rada Związków Zawodowych: CRZZ)

Chief Board of Supervision (Naczelna Izba Kontroli: NIK)

Civic Militia: the police force (Milicja Obywatelska: MO)

Combine (Kombinat) A combination of factories and enterprises which endeavours to bring into one industrial unit all the elements involved in the production cycle of a particular product.

CWSM   Conference of Workers Self-Management (Konferencja Samorządu Robotniczego: KSR)

Democratic Party (Stronnictwo Demokratyczne: SD)

Departmental (or section) Workers' Council (Oddziałowa Rada Robotnicza: ORR)

DPO   Departmental Party Organisation (Oddziałowa organizacja partyjna: OOP)

Enterprise (Przedsiębiorstwo) The enterprise is usually formed out of several smaller factories or 'work-shops' (zakłady).

Factory Committee (of the PUWP) (Komitet Zakładowy: KZ PZPR)

Factory Council (of the Trade Union) (Rada Zakładowa (Związków Zawodowych): RZ ZZ)

FDA   Fund for the Development of Agriculture (Fundusz Rozwoju Rolnictwa: FRR)

IAE   Institute of Agricultural Economics (Instytut Ekonomii Rolnej: IER)

MOPC   Main Office of Press Control (Główny Urząd Kontroli Prasy: GUKP)

NPB   National Polish Bank (Narodowy Bank Polski: NBP)

NUF   National Unity Front (Front Jedności Narodu: FJN)

One Hektar (1 ha.) = 10,000 square metres. One acre = 0·4 ha.

OPC   Office of Press Control (Urząd Kontroli Prasy: UKP)

PCNL   Polish Committee of National Liberation (Polski Komitet Wyzwolenia Narodowego: PKWN)

PP   Peasant Party (Stronnictwo Ludowe: SL)

PPP   Polish Peasant Party (Polskie Stronnictwo Ludowe: PSL)

PPO   Primary Party Organisation (of the Polish United Workers' Party) (Podstawowa Organizacja Partyjna: POP)

PSA   Polish Scouts Association (Związek Harcerstwa Polskiego: ZHP)

PSP   Polish Socialist Party (Polska Partia Socjalistyczna: PPS)

PUWP   Polish United Workers' Party (Polska Zjednoczona Partia Robotnicza: PZPR). Formed by an amalgamation of the PPS (PSP) and the PPR (PWP) in 1948.

PWA   Polish Writers' Association (Związek Literatów Polskich: ZLP)

PWP   Polish Workers Party (Polska Partia Robotnicza: PPR)

SC   Supreme Committee (Naczelny Komitet: NK)

Social Fund for the Building of Day and Boarding Schools (Stołeczny Fundusz Budowy Szkół i Internatów: SFBSiL)

State Farms (Państwowe Gospodarstwa Rolne: PGR)

STO   Supreme Technical Organisation (Naczelna Organizacja Techniczna: NOT)

UPP   United Peasants' Party (Zjednoczone Stronnictwo Ludowe: ZSL). Formed by an amalgamation of the PSL (PPP) and SL (PP) in 1949.

UPY   Union of Rural Youth (Związek Młodzieży Wiejskiej: ZMW)

USY   Union of Socialist Youth (Związek Młodzieży Socjalistycnej: ZMS)

VPC   Village People's Council (Gromadzka Rada Narodowa: GRN)

Workers' Council (Rada Robotnicza: RR)

WPC   Wojewodstwo People's Council (Wojewódzka Rada Narodowa: WRN)

zł.   złoty(ies).

Bibliography

DOCUMENTS AND REFERENCE WORKS

Third Congress PZPR (1959), Gomułka's speech at, reprinted in *O naszej partii* (Warsaw, 1969).

Fourth Congress PZPR (1964), report of KC, reprinted in *O naszej partii*, 1969.

Fifth Congress PZPR (1968), materials in *V Zjazd polskiej Zjednoczonej Partii Robotniczej* (Warsaw, 1969).

Third Congress ZMW (1966), materials in *III Krajowy Zjazd Związku Młodzieży Wiejskiej*, Iskry (Warsaw, 1966).

Fourth Congress ZSL (1964), materials in *IV Kongres Zjednoczonego Stronnictwa Ludowego*, Stenogram (Warsaw, 1965).

Third Congress ZSL (1959), materials in *III Kongres Zjednoczonego Stronnictwa Ludowego*, Stenogram (Warsaw, 1960).

Concise Statistical Yearbook of Poland 1939–1941 (London, 1941).

Główny Urząd Statystyczny (G.U.S.), *Budżety rodzin pracowników zatrudnionych w gospodarce uspołecznionej*, no. 53 (Warsaw, 1969).

Członkowie prezydiów rad narodowych 1958–69 (Warsaw, 1970).

Drugi powszechny spis ludności z dn. 9.XII.1931; stosunki zawodowe-ludność w rolnictwie (Warsaw, 1938).

Mały Rocznik Statystyczny 1971 (Warsaw, 1971).

Polska w liczbach 1944–1966 (Warsaw, 1966).

Radni rad narodowych 1958–1969 (Warsaw, 1970).

Rocznik polityczny i gospodarczy 1966 (Warsaw, 1967).

Rocznik Statystyczny 1966 (Warsaw, 1966).

Rocznik Statystyczny 1970 (Warsaw, 1970).

Rocznik Statystyczny Pracy 1948–1968 (Warsaw, 1970).

Rocznik Statystyczny Przemysłu 1968 (Warsaw, 1970).

Sołectwa i sołtysi (Warsaw, 1968).

Spis kadrowy 1968, Pracownicy z wykształceniem wyższym (Warsaw, (1969).

I.E.R. *Zmiany społeczno-ekonomiczne wsi w Polsce Ludowej* (Warsaw, 1961).

'Kancelaria Rady Państwa, Biuro Rad Narodowych', in *Struktura Osobowa Komisji Stałych Rad Narodowych* (Warsaw, 1966).

Petit annuaire statistique de la Pologne 1939 (Warsaw, 1939).

XII Plenum KC (1958), Gomułka's speech 'Zadania organizacji

partyjnych w akcji przed III Zjazdem partii', reprinted in *O naszej partii* (Warsaw, 1969).

XII Plenum KC (1963), *W sprawie zwiększenia inwestycji w rolnictwie i zapewnienia dalszego wzrostu produkcji rolnej* (Warsaw, 1963).

IX Plenum KC (1957), Gomułka's speech, 'Węzłowe problemy polityki partii', reprinted in *O naszej partii*.

IV Plenum NK ZSL (1956), materials in *IV Plenum Naczelnego Komitetu ZSL* (Warsaw, 1956).

VII Plenum NK ZSL (1957), materials in *VII Plenum Naczelnego Komitetu ZSL* (Warsaw, 1957).

II Plenum NK ZSL (1960), materials in *II Plenum Naczelnego Komitetu ZSL* (Warsaw, 1960).

IV Plenum NK ZSL (1961), materials in *IV Plenum Naczelnego Komitetu ZSL* (Warsaw, 1961).

VI Plenum NK ZSL (1962), speeches by Wycech, '*Aktualne zadania polityczne i organizacyjne ZSL*' (Warsaw, 1962).

VIII Plenum NK ZSL (1968), *Zjednoczone Stronnictwo Ludowe przed V Kongresem* (Warsaw, 1969).

'KC PZPR, NK ZSL, Uchwała w sprawie węzłowych zadań rolnictwa w latach 1959–1965', reprinted in *Programy stronnictw ludowych*, ed. S. Lato and W. Stankiewicz (Warsaw, 1969).

Rocznik Literacki 1956 (Warsaw, 1957).

Wielka Encyklopedia Powszechna, vol. 12, Usa-Z (Warsaw, 1969).

Wieś w liczbach 1962.

Zbiór przepisów prawnych. Dla członków ZLP (Warsaw, 1968).

NEWSPAPERS

Gazeta Krakowska, 25 March 1968. C. Domagała.

Polityka, 21 Jan. 1961. J. Ambroziewicz and A. Rowiński, 'Nie ma zwycięzców ani zwyciężonych.'

Polityka, no. 19, 1961. J. Banaszkiewicz and A. Owieczko, 'Kto wstępuje do partii?'

Polityka, 24 April 1957. J. Barski, 'Niemowlę chce rosnąć?'

Polityka, 17 Aug. 1957. B. Borkowski 'Padają i takie pytania-no a robotnicy?'

Polityka, 30 Aug. 1958. J. Bukowski, 'O wstępnym stażu pracy absolwentów szkół wyższych.'

Polityka, 17 April 1965. 'Czy tylko organizator?' (Discussion.)

Polityka, 16 Jan. 1971. W. Falkowska, 'W oczekiwaniu lepszego jutra.'

Polityka, 6 Feb. 1971. D. Fikus and J. Urban, 'Szczecin.'

Polityka, 31 Jan. 1959. J. Gredzielski, 'Kompleksy inteligencji technicznej-Kogo się w Polsce favoryzuje?'

Polityka, 14 Oct. 1967. A. Gutowski, 'Konkurs Dyrektorów.'

Polityka, 1 Oct. 1966. A. Gutowski, 'Z badań nad samorządem robotniczym.'

Polityka, 7 April 1962. J. Hellman, 'Dlaczego niesprawiedliwy?'

Polityka, 14 Dec. 1957. S. Jakubowicz, 'Kierunek i zwiększona samodzielność przedsiębiorstwa.'

Polityka, 30 June 1962. A. Jędrzejczak, 'Wielka czwórka.'

Polityka, 24 Feb. 1962. 'Jeremiada technokratów.'

Polityka, No. 39, 1964. T. Kołodziejczyk 'Zmęczeni kadencją.'

Polityka, 11 Feb. 1961. 'Kompleksy Inżynierów.' (Discussion.)

Polityka, 16 Jan. 1971. S. Kozicki, 'Jak mało, jak dużo potrzeba.'

Polityka, 28 May 1966. S. Kozicki, 'Niech no towarzysz powie.'

Polityka, 9 Nov. 1963. S. Kozicki, 'Pamięć ferrytowa.'

Polityka, 3 Sept. 1967. S. Kozicki, 'Przemysłem i pomysłem.'

Polityka 24 Nov. 1957. K. Kóźniewski, 'Czy nam grozi technokracja?'

Polityka, 18 April 1964. H. Krall, 'Optymista z urodzenia.'

Polityka, 27 Feb. 1957, no. 1. 'O radach robotniczych.'

Polityka/Statystyka, no. 5, Nov. 1970. H. Krall, 'Pobieżny szkic do portretu klasy.'

Polityka, 20 Sept. 1958. J. Machno, 'O partii, samorządzie i dyrektorach.'

Polityka, 2 Aug. 1957. M. Misiorny, 'Dyrektorzy i socjalizm.'

Polityka, 9 April 1966. B. Olszewska, 'Dymisja.'

Polityka, 30 Jan. 1960. 'O postępie technicznym decydują ludzie.'

Polityka, 13 June 1970. S. Podemski, 'Jak po grudzie.'

Polityka, 13 June 1964, no. 24, 'Portret klasy.'

Polityka, 30 March 1968. 'Problemy kadrowe.'

Polityka, 10 April 1957. 'Program działania organizacji partyjnej huty im. Lenina.'

Polityka, 18 April 1970. H. Rafalski, 'Chłopskie zdrowie.'

Polityka, 17 April 1965. J. Rolicki, 'Karuzela.'

Polityka, 21 Aug. 1957. S. J., 'Nakaz chwili.'

Polityka, No. 41, 1968. 'Socjalistyczny kodeks pracy.'

Polityka, 18 April 1970. A. Strońską, 'Życie i okrycie.'

Polityka, 5 Nov. 1966. A. Strońska, 'Nie chcemy wyrobników.'

Polityka, No. 7, 18 Feb. 1961. Z. Suzin, 'Autorytet władzy.'

Polityka, 16 May 1959. J. Śmietański, 'Wina duża, mała i najmniejsza.'

Polityka, 8 June 1957. M. Tempczyk, 'O radach-praktycznie.'

Polityka, 1 March 1958. 'Towarzyszowi w odpowiedzi.'

Polityka, 2 March 1957. J. Tymowski, 'Inteligencja techniczna po III Kongresie.'

Polityka, 2 March 1957. A. Tymowski, 'O właściwą pozycję polskiej inteligencji technicznej.'

Polityka, 18 Feb. 1961. J. Tymowski, 'Tradycje NOT.'

Polityka, 20 May 1967. A. Tymowski, 'Zarobki w przemyśle.'

Polityka, 26 June 1957. A. Werblan, 'Od tragedii poznańskiej upłynął rok.'

Polityka, 28 Aug. 1957. A. Werblan, 'Świadomość klasowa.'

Polityka, 16 Nov. 1963. M. Wierzyński, 'Środek ale nie złoty.'

Polityka, 24 April 1957. K. Wigura, 'Kto daje tę broń do ręki.'

Polityka, 31 Jan. 1959. J. Winnicki, 'Spocić się monża nie tylko przy dźwiganiu ciężarów.'

Polityka, 22 Sept. 1962. K. Wolicki, 'Twór nieskończony.'

Polityka, 1 May 1966. A. Wróblewska, 'Apetyt na inżyniera.'

Polityka, 11 Sept. 1965. A. K. Wróblewski, 'Tajemnica dyrektorskich dyplomów.'

Polityka, 24 Sept. 1957. 'W sprawie kadr o wysokich kwalifikacjach.'

Pravda, 4 Feb. 1957. 'V derevnie polskoi.'

Przegląd Kulturalny, no. 32, 1957. A. Małachowski, 'Jutro rad robotniczych.'

Rada Narodowa, no. 47 (1118), 21 Nov. 1970. T. Kołodziejczyk, 'Oblicza administracji: w stronę obywatela.'

Rada Narodowa, no. 50 (1121), 12 Dec. 1970. J. Korowicz, 'Decyduje aktyw.'

The Times (London), 25 May 1971. R. Davy, 'New checks without balances in Poland.'

Trybuna Ludu, 18 April 1971. E. Babiuch, 'Główne kierunki działania partii.'

Trybuna Ludu, 12 Dec. 1956, 'KC PZPR, NK ZSL, Deklaracja o zasadach współpracy między PZPR i ZSL.'

Trybuna Ludu, 9 Jan. 1957. 'KC PZPR, NK ZSL, Wytyczne w sprawie polityki rolnej.'

Trybuna Ludu, 21 May 1969. J. Kraśniwski, 'Gdy organizacja odmładza się.'

Trybuna Ludu, 6 Nov. 1957. M. Kowalewski.

Trybuna Ludu, 27 March 1968. 'Pisarze-polityka-kultura.'

Zielony Sztandar, 23 May 1956. W. Fołta, 'Z wyborczych analiz.'

Zielony Sztandar, 14 Nov. 1956. S. Ignar, Report of speech to the Sejm.

Zielony Sztandar, 23 Dec. 1956 (102). 'V Plenum NK ZSL (1956).

Zielony Sztandar, 25 Nov. 1956. Reversal of decree (unsigned).

Zielony Sztandar, 19 June 1969. M. Wilczak, 'Dlaczego coraz mniej społeczników?'

Zielony Sztandar, 16 Dec. 1956. P. Ziarnik, 'Dramat aktywisty.'

Życie Gospodarcze, no. 22, 1966. S. Frenkel, 'Czy uchwały załatwiają sprawę.'

Życie Gospodarcze, no. 21, 1968. A. Gutowski, 'Bez samorządu trudno. W poszukiwanie drogi.'

Życie Gospodarcze, 13 Jan. 1957. S. Krajewski, 'Samorząd zrzeszeniowy.'

Życie Gospodarcze, no. 47, 1958. Z. Kruszyński, 'Właściwi ludzie na własciwym miejscu.'

Życie Gospodarcze, no. 51, 1957. E. Lipiński, 'Rady robotnicze, przedsiębiorstwo i inne sprawy.'

Życie Gospodarcze, 2 June 1957. Z. Mikołajczyk, 'Rady robotnicze a alienacja.'

Życie Gospodarcze, 8 Sept. 1957. G. Pisarski, 'Trzeba usunąć źródła zadrażnien.'

Życie Gospodarcze, no. 50, 10 Dec. 1961. K. Szwarc, 'Pozycja zjednoczenia terenowego.'

Życie Warszawy, 25 Jan. 1971. R. Kazimierska, 'Samorząd robotniczy.'

BOOKS IN POLISH

W. Adamski, *Grupy interesów w społeczności wiejskiej* (Wrocław, 1967).

Ludwik Aleksa, *Pochodzenie społeczne i rekrutacja środowiskowa wybranej grupy inżynierów* (Katowice, 1969).

H. Adamiecka, *Prawda o węgierskiej rewolucji.*

L. Beskid and K. Zagórski, *Robotnicy na tle przemian struktury społecznej w Polsce* (Warsaw, 1971).

K. Bidakowski (ed.), *Pamiętniki Inżynierów* (Warsaw, 1966).

C. Bielecki and B. Winiarski, *Gospodarka rad narodowych* (Warsaw, 1960).

W. Bielicki and K. Zagórski, *Robotnicy, wczoraj i dziś* (Katowice, 1966).

W. Bieńkowski, *Motory i hamulce socjalizmu* (Paris, 1969).

M. Biernacka, *Potakówka* (Warsaw, 1962).

J. Borkowski, *Postawa polityczna chłopów polskich w latach 1930–1935* (Warsaw, 1970).

A. Borucki, *Kariery zawodowe i postawy społeczne inteligencji w PRL 1945–59* (Warsaw, 1967).

J. Bugiel, *Adaptacja i pozycja społeczno-zawodowa wychowanków Akademii Górniczo-Hutniczej w przemyśle* (Kraków, 1970).

J. Chałasiński, *Przeszłość i przyszłość inteligencji Polskiej* (Warsaw, 1958).

H. Chołaj (chief ed.), *Lenin a kwestia agrarna* (Warsaw, 1967).

H. Chołaj, *Leninizm a polityka rolna PZPR* (Warsaw, 1969).

M. Ciechocińska, *Położenie klasy robotniczej w Polsce 1929–1939* (Warsaw, 1965).

E. Ciupak, *Kult religijny i jego społeczne podłoże* (Warsaw, 1965).

S. Czarnowski, *Dzieła Vol. I. Kultura: Powstawanie nowej kultury* (Warsaw, 1965).

M. Czerniewska, *Gospodarstwa rolne i ludność o mieszanym źródle dochodu* (Warsaw, 1964).

D. Dąbrowski, 'Organizacja zarządzania', in *Studia nad załogą huty aluminium w Skawinie*, eds. A. Stojak and K. Dobrowolski (Warsaw, 1969).

J. Dąbrowski, J. Garbala and L. Palczyński, *Organizacja rad narodowych*, Part I (Katowice, 1969).

R. Dyoniziak, *Społeczne uwarunkowania wydajności pracy* (Warsaw, 1967).

J. Dziarnowska, *Literatura na rozdrożu* (Cracow, 1968).

M. Dziewicka, *Chłopi-robotnicy* (Warsaw, 1963).

S. Dzięcielska, *Sytuacja społeczna dziennikarzy polskich* (Wrocław, 1962).

S. Dzięcielska-Machnikowska and J. Kulpińska, *Awans kobiety* (Łódź, 1966).

B. Fick, *Polityka zatrudnienia a płace i bodźce* (Warsaw, 1970).

I. Frenkel, *Zatrudnienie w rolnictwie polskim* (Warsaw, 1968).

D. Gałaj, *Aktywność społeczno-gospodarcza chłopów* (Warsaw, 1961).

D. Gałaj, *Chłopski ruch polityczny w Polsce* (Warsaw, 1969).

B. Gałęski, *Chłopi i zawód rolnika* (Warsaw, 1963).

B. Gałęski, *Socjologia wsi* (Warsaw, 1966).

B. Gałęski, *Społeczna struktura wsi* (Warsaw, 1962).

L. Gilejko, 'Formowanie się i rola samorządu robotniczego', in *25 lat Polski Ludowej: struktura i dynamika społeczeństwa polskiego*, ed. W. Wesołowski (Warsaw, 1970).

W. Głowacki, *Partyjne kierownictwo i praca Partii w Radach Narodowych* (Warsaw, 1969).

J. Gołębiowski, 'Problemy nacjonalizacji przemysłu', in *Uprzemysłowienie ziem polskich W XIX i XX wieku* (Warsaw, 1970).

Władysław Gomułka, *O aktualnych problemach ideologicznej pracy partii* (Warsaw, 1963).

W. Gomułka, *Przemówienie dożynkowe* (Warsaw, 1962).

A. Grzelak, 'Kadra urzędnicza na tle innych grup zawodowych', in *Człowiek w organizacji przemysłowej*, ed. M. Hirszowicz (Warsaw, 1965).

Anne Grzelak, 'Problemy adaptacji młodych inżynierów', in *Problemy kadry przemysłowej*, ed. M. Horszowicz (Warsaw, 1965).

Z. Grzelak, *Zależność między studiami a pracą absolwentów szkół wyższych* (Warsaw, 1965).

R. Halaba, *Stronnictwo Ludowe, 1944–46* (Warsaw, 1966).

Bibliography 355

C. Herod, *Adaptacja wychowanków AGH w przemyśle górniczym* (Kraków, 1970).

Z. Hiedrich, *Zasady organizacji i kierownictwa* (Warsaw, 1967).

M. Hirszowicz and W. Morawski, *Z badań nad społecznym uczestnictwem w organizacji przemysłowej* (Warsaw, 1967).

Jan Hoser, *Zawód i praca inżyniera* (Warsaw, 1970).

Z. Izdebski and J. Tudrej, *Kierownicy przedsiębiorstw kapitalistycznych* (Warsaw, 1968).

M. Jagielski, *O nowej polityce partii na wsi* (Warsaw, 1957).

J. Janicki, *Urzędnicy przemysłowi w strukturze społecznej Polski Ludowej* (Warsaw, 1968).

M. Jaroszyński, *Zagadnienia rad narodowych* (Warsaw, 1961).

H. Jędruszczak, 'Odbudowa potencjału przemysłowego w latach 1945–1949', in *Uprzemysłowienie ziem polskich W XIX i XX wieku* (Warsaw, 1970).

A. Jezierski, 'Warunki rozwoju przemysłu w Polsce międzywojennej (1918–1939)', in *Uprzemysłowiebie ziem polskich w XIX i XX wieku* (Warsaw, 1970).

Witold Kieżun, *Dyrektor, Z problematyki zarządzania instytucją* (Warsaw, 1968).

A. Kociszewski, 'Powstanie władzy ludowej i walka o jej utrwalenie', in *Ciechanów w okresie władzy ludowej* (Ciechanów, 1970).

J. Kordaszewski, *Pracownicy umysłowi: Dynamika zatrudnienia i metody badań trudności pracy* (Warsaw, 1969).

E. Korzeniowska (ed.), *Słownik Współczesnych Pisarzy Polskich*, vol. i. A–I (Warsaw, 1963).

S. Kowalewska (ed.), *Nowatorzy w zakładzie przemysłowym* (Warsaw, 1968).

S. Kowalewska, *Przysposobienie do pracy w przemyśle* (Warsaw, 1966).

J. Kulpińska, *Społeczna aktywność pracowników przedsiębiorstwa przemysłowego* (Wrocław, 1969).

J. Malanowski, *Stosunki klasowe i różnice społeczne w mieście* (Warsaw, 1967).

Z. Leoński, *Pojęcie kontroli społecznej i formy jej realizacji przez Rady Narodowe* (Poznań, 1962).

Z. Leoński, *Rady narodowe* (Poznań, 1969).

K. Lutyńska, *Pozycja społeczna urzędników w Polsce Ludowej* (Warsaw, 1965).

A. Łopatka (ed.), *Organizacja społeczeństwa socjalistycznego w Polsce* (Warsaw–Poznań, 1970).

W. Makarczyk, *Czynniki stabilizacji w zawodzie rolnika i motywy migracji* (Wrocław, 1964).

J. Marczak, *Młodzież robotnicza w łódzkim przemyśle włókienniczym* (Łódź, 1969).

W. Matuszewska, *U źródeł strajku chłopskiego w roku 1937* (Warsaw, 1962).

Z. Mikołajczyk, *Struktura i funkcje partii chłopskiej* (Warsaw, 1968).

S. Misztal, 'Zmiany w rozmieszczeniu przemysłu na obecnym obszarze Polski w latach 1860–1960', in *Uprzemysłowienie ziem polskich w XIX i XX wieku* (Warsaw, 1970).

F. W. Mleczko, *Z badań nad aktywnością zawodową i społeczni chłopów* (Wrocław, 1964).

W. Morawski, 'Funkcje samorządu robotniczego w systemie rządzania przemysłem', in *Przemysł i społeczeństwo w Polsce Ludowej*, ed. A. Sarapata (Warsaw, 1965).

H. Najduchowska, 'Dyrektorzy przedsiębiorstw przemysłowych', in *Przemysł i społeczeństwo w Polsce Ludowej*, ed. A. Sarapata (Warsaw, 1965).

H. Najduchowska, *Pozycja społeczna starych robotników przemysłu metalowego* (Warsaw, 1965).

W. Narojek, *System władzy w mieście* (Wrocław, 1967).

S. Nowakowski, *Narodziny miasta* (Warsaw, 1967).

A. Olszewska, *Wieś uprzemysłowiona* (Wrocław, 1969).

K. Ostrowski, *Rola związków zawodowych w polskim systemie politycznym* (Warsaw, 1970).

A. Owieczko, 'Ewolucja samorządu robotniczego', in *Socjologiczne problemy przemysłu i klasy robotniczej*, ed. S. Wilderszpil (Warsaw, 1967).

L. Pasieczny, *Bodźce materialnego zainteresowania w przedsiębiorstwie* (Warsaw, 1970).

Leszek Pasieczny, *Inżynier w przemyśle* (Warsaw, 1968).

C. Parchatko, 'Awans zawodowy personelu inżynieryjno-technicznego ZNTK "Oleśnica" w Oleśnicy', in *Socjologiczny problemy przemysłu*, ed. S. Wilderszpil (Warsaw, 1967).

Paulina Press, *Biurokracja totalna* (Paris, 1969).

I. Pietrzak-Pawłowska (ed.), *Uprzemysłowienie ziem polskich w XIX i XX wieku. Studia i materiały* (Wrocław, 1970).

S. Pigoń, *Z Komborni w świat* (Kraków, 1957).

M. Pohoski, *Migracje ze wsi do miast* (Warsaw, 1963).

A. Preiss, 'Robotnicy a pracownicy inżynieryjno-techniczni', in *Socjologiczne problemy przemysłu i klasy robotniczej*, ed. S. Widerszpil (Warsaw, 1967).

Z. Pucek, 'Konflikt w zakładzie przemysłowym', in *Z zagadnień stosunków społecznych w zakładzie pracy* (Katowice, 1968).

P. Raina, *Władysław Gomułka* (London, 1969).

M. Sadowski, *Przemiany społeczne a system partyjny PRL* (Warsaw, 1969).

A. Sarapata, 'Klasa robotnicza w Polsce Ludowej', in *Przemiany społeczne w Polsce Ludowej*, ed. A. Sarapata (Warsaw, 1965).

R. Siemieńska, *Nowe życie w nowym mieście* (Warsaw, 1969).

J. Sikorski, 'Społeczne podłoże autorytetu kierowników przedsiębiorstw przemysłowych', in *Z zagadnień stosunków społecznych w zakładzie pracy* (Katowice, 1968).

K. Słomczyński and W. Wesołowski, 'Próby reprezentacyjne i kategorie społeczno-zawodowe', in *Zróżnicowanie społeczne*, ed. W. Wesołowski (Wrocław, 1970).

J. Służewski, *Nauka administracji* (Warsaw, 1969).

W. Sokolewicz, *Przedstawicielstwo i administracja w systemie rad narodowych PRL* (Warsaw, 1968).

W. Sokolewicz, *Rząd a prezydia rad narodowych* (Warsaw, 1964).

J. Starosciak, *Rady narodowe: Przepisy o organizacji i działalności* (Warsaw, 1966).

E. Strzelecki, 'Rozwój ludności Polski w dwudziestoleciach 1944–1964', in *Przemiany społeczne w Polsce Ludowej*, ed. A. Sarapata (1965).

J. Szaflik (ed.), *70 lat ruchu ludowego* (Warsaw, 1967).

J. Szczepański, *Odmiany czasu teraźniejszego* (Warsaw, 1971).

J. Szczepański (ed.), *Przemysł i społeczeństwo w Polsce Ludowej* (Warsaw, 1969).

J. Szczepański (ed.), 'Wykształcenie a pozycja społeczna inteligencji' (part i) (Łódź, 1959).

J. Szczepański, 'Zmiany w strukturze klasowej społeczeństwa Polskiego', in *Przemiany społeczne w Polsce Ludowej*, ed. A. Sarapata (Warsaw, 1965).

A. Szemberg, *Przemiany w strukturze agrarnej gospodarstw chłopskich* (Warsaw, 1966).

S. Szostkiewicz, *Przemiany w strukturze załogi fabryki samochodów w latach 1956–61* (Warsaw, 1965).

R. Turski, *Między miastem a wsią* (Warsaw, 1965).

J. Wacławek, *Socjalistyczne stosunki w zakładzie pracy* (Warsaw, 1970).

W. Wesołowski (ed.), *29 lat Polski Ludowej. Struktura i dynamika społeczeństwa polskiego* (Warsaw, 1970).

W. Wesołowski, *Klasy, warstwy i władza* (Warsaw, 1966).

J. Wiatr, *Społeczeństwo* (Warsaw, 1964).

S. Widerszpil, *Skład polskiej klasy robotniczej. Tendencje zmian w okresie industrializacji socjalistycznej* (Warsaw, 1965).

S. Widerszpil (ed.), *Socjologiczne problemy przemysłu i klasy robotniczej*. 2 (Warsaw, 1967).

S. Widerszpil and A. Preiss-Zajdowa, *Uprzemysłowienie i stosunki społeczne w zakładzie pracy* (Warsaw, 1966).

Z. T. Wierzbicki, *Zmiana w pół wieku poźniej* (Wrocław, 1963).

R. Wilczewski, 'Dynamiczny rozwój przemysłu w latach 1950–1965', in *Uprzemysłowienie ziem polskich* . . .

W. Witos, *Moje wspomnienia* (Paris, 1964).

K. Zagórski, 'Warunki materialno-bytowe robotników i inteligencji', in *25 lat Polski Ludowej*, ed. W. Wesołowski (Warsaw, 1970).

J. Żarnowski, *Społeczeństwo Polski międzywojennej* (Warsaw, 1969).

J. Żarnowski, *Struktura społeczna inteligencji w Polsce w latach 1918–1939* (Warsaw, 1964).

S. Żółkiewski, *Kultura i Polityka* (Warsaw, 1958).

BOOKS IN LANGUAGES OTHER THAN POLISH

Gabriel Almond and Sidney Verba (eds.), *The Civic Culture* (1963).

H. Arendt, *On Revolution* (London, 1962).

Federick C. Barghoorn, 'Soviet Russia: Orthodoxy and Adaptiveness', in *Political Culture and Political Development*, ed. Lucien W. Pye and Sidney Verba (Princeton, 1963).

André Beteille (ed.), *Social Inequality* (London, 1969).

N. Bethell, *Gomułka, His Poland and His Communism* (London, 1969).

P. M. Blau, *Exchange and Power in Social Life* (New York, 1964).

James Burnham, *The Managerial Revolution* (London, 1945).

A. V. Chayanov, *Theory of Peasant Economy* (Homewood, Ill., 1966).

M. Dobb, *Socialist Planning: Some Problems* (London, 1970).

M. K. Dziewanowski, *The Communist Party of Poland* (Cambridge, 1959).

S. H. Franklin, *The European Peasantry* (London, 1969).

C. J. Friedrich and Z. K. Brzezinski, *Totalitarian Dictatorship and Autocracy* (Cambridge, Mass., 1965).

A. Gieystor *et al.*, *History of Poland* (Warsaw, 1968).

M. Gluckman, *Order and Rebellion in Tribal Africa* (London, 1963).

R. Hiscocks, *Poland: Bridge for an abyss* (London, 1963).

Ghiţa Ionescu, *The Politics of the European Communist States* (London, 1967).

J. Kolaja, *A Polish factory—A case study of workers' participation in decision-making* (New York, 1960).

A. Korbonski, *The Politics of Socialist Agriculture in Poland 1945–1960* (New York, 1965).

S. Korboński, *Warsaw in Chains* (New York, 1959).

W. Kornhauser, *Scientists in Industry* (California, 1962).

W. Kornhauser, *The Politics of Mass Society* (New York, 1960).

R. D. Laird and B. A. Laird, *Soviet Communism and Agrarian Revolution* (London, 1970).

F. Lewis, *The Polish Volcano* (London, 1959).

K. Mannheim, *Ideology and Utopia* (New York, 1936).

K. Marx and F. Engels, *Selected Works* (London, 1963).

R. K. Merton, *Social Theory and Social Structure* (Glencoe, 1959).

Alfred G. Meyer, *The Soviet Political System* (New York, 1965).

M. Miller *et al.* (eds.), *Communist Economy under Change* (London, 1963).

J. M. Potter, *Peasant Society* (Boston, 1967).

Lucien Pye and Sydney Verba (eds.), *Poltical Culture and Political Development* (Princeton, 1963).

Radio Free Europe: Background Report, Poland No. 10, 14 April 1971. E. Celt, 'The Demands and Grievances of the Polish Population.'

S. J. Rawin, 'Changes in Social Structure in Poland under Conditions of Industrialisation 1945–1963', Ph.D. thesis (University of London, 1965).

R. Redfield, *Peasant Society and Culture* and *The Little Community* (Chicago, 1960).

Hans Roos, *A History of Modern Poland* (London, 1966).

Dankwart A. Rustow, 'Communism and Change', in *Change in Communist Systems*, ed. Chalmers Johnson (Stanford, Cal., 1970).

H. Gordon Skilling and Franklyn Griffiths (eds.), *Interest Groups in Soviet Politics* (Princeton, 1971).

Marc Slonim, *Soviet Russian Literature* (London, 1964).

J. Słomka, *From Serfdom to Self-Government* (London, 1941).

Nicholas A. Spulber, 'National Income and Product', in *Poland*, ed. Oscar Halecki (New York, 1957).

Richard F. Staar, *Poland 1944–1962* (Louisiana State University Press, 1962).

W. J. Stankiewicz and J. M. Montias, *Institutional Changes in the Postwar Economy of Poland* (New York, 1955).

H. Swayze, *Political Control of Literature in the USSR* (1946–59) (Cambridge, Mass., 1962).

J. Szczepański, *Polish Society* (New York, 1969).

E. Szyr *et al.*, *Twenty Years of the Polish People's Republic* (Warsaw, 1964).

J. Taylor, *The Economic Development of Poland 1919–1950* (Ithaca, N.Y., 1952).

W. Thomas and F. Znaniecki, *The Polish Peasant in Europe and America* (New York, 1958).

U.S. Congress, *Trends in Economic Growth: A Comparison of the Western Powers and the Soviet bloc* (Washington, D.C., 1955).

W. Wesołowski, 'Changes in the Class Structure in Poland', in *Empirical Sociology in Poland*, ed. J. Szczepański (Warsaw, 1966).

J. Wiatr (ed.), *Studies in Polish Political System* (Wrocław, 1967).

E. R. Wolf, *Peasants* (Englewood Cliffs, N.J., 1966).

K. Zagórski, *Social Mobility and Changes in the Structure of Planning Society* (Warsaw, 1970).

A. Zauberman, *Industrial Progress in Poland, Czechoslovakia and East Germany* (London, 1964).

P. F. Zinner, *National Communism and Popular Revolt in Eastern Europe* (New York, 1956).

F. Zweig, *Poland between the Wars* (London, 1944).

ARTICLES

Contemporary Studies in Society and History, xi, no. 3, 1969. J. C. Scott, 'The Analysis of Corruption in Developing Nations.'

East Europe, no. 2, 1968. M. Celt, 'Another Round: Peasant and Party in Poland.'

Ekonomika i Organizacja Pracy, no. 11, 1966. S. Wolff and S. Kalembka, 'Kierowanie przedsiębiorstwem a rola dyrektora.'

Gospodarka Planowa, no. 3, 1957. W. Krencik and C. Niewadzi, 'O właściwą rolę rad robotniczych w polskim modelu gospodarczym.'

The Journal of Politics, vol. 18, no. 3 (1956). G. Almond, 'Comparative Political Systems.'

Kultura i Społeczeństwo, vol. iv, no. 1, 1960. J. Szczepański, 'Struktura inteligencji w Polsce.'

Na Antenie, nos. 73–4, VII Kwiecień-maj 1969. Roman Karst (Radio Free Europe).

Nowe Drogi, no. 6, 1955. 'Aktualne problemy zatrudnienia.'

Nowe Drogi, no. 2, 1958. J. Balcerek and M. Borowska, 'Załoga a rada robotnicza.'

Nowe Drogi, no. 4, 1954. B. Bierut, 'II Zjazd, PZPR.'

Nowe Drogi, no. 12, 1955. W. Brus, 'W sprawie bodzców zainteresowania materialnego.'

Nowe Drogi, no. 6, 1971. A. Dobieszewski, 'Struktura i zasady działania partii.'

Nowe Drogi, no. 3, 1971. T. Jaroszewski, 'Kierownicza rola partii w warunkach intensywnego rozwoju.'

Nowe Drogi, no. 6, 1966. J. Kapliński, 'Instancje partyjne a usprawienie pracy organów wykonawczych rad narodowych.'

Nowe Drogi, no. 4, 1971. W. Kawalec, 'Narodowy spis powszechny 1970: pierwsze rezultaty i pierwsze wnioski.'

Nowe Drogi, no. 5, 1958. J. Kofman, 'Związki zawodowe w świetle IV Kongresu.'

Nowe Drogi, no. 1, 1955. H. Kozłowska, 'Uwagi o stylu pracy naszego aparatu partyjnego.'

Nowe Drogi, no. 10, 1965. J. Majchrzak, 'O pracy politycznej na wsi województwa bydgoskiego.'

Nowe Drogi, no. 4, 1964. M. Marzec, 'Z problemów pracy partyjnej.'

Nowe Drogi, no. 3, 1956. J. Niedźwiecki, 'Dojrzała konieczność zwiększenia uprawnień dyrektorów przedsiębiorstw przemysłowych.'

Nowe Drogi, nos. 7–8, 1956. J. Ochab, 'Uchwała o sytuacji politycznej i gospodarczej kraju i zadaniach partii.'

Nowe Drogi, no. 1, 1955. J. Olszewski, 'O niektórych biorokratycznych wypaczeniach w stylu pracy partyjnej.'

Nowe Drogi, no. 11, 1966. T. Rolf, 'Organizacja partyjna w zakładzie przemysłowym.'

Nowe Drogi, no. 1, 1962. F. Siemiankowski and J. Grajewski, 'W POP na wsi województwa poznańskiego.'

Nowe Drogi, no. 12, 1958. W. Titkow, 'Niektóre problemy rozwoju partii.'

Nowe Drogi (Undated issue, early 1971).

Nowe Drogi, no. 2, 1959. J. Wacławek, 'W sprawie koncepcji roli partii w zakładach pracy.'

Nowe Drogi, no. 1, 1967. J. Wiatr, 'Gospodarze terenu.'

Nowe Drogi, no. 4, 1959. R. Zambrowski (Third Party Congress).

Organizacja, Metody i Technika, no. 12, 1967. A. Matejko, 'Społeczny mechanizm konfliktu.'

Państwo i Prawo, no. 4, 1959. J. Topiński, 'Zmiany w systemie planowania i zarządzania gospodarką panstwową PRL w latach 1956–1958.'

Państwo i Prawo, nos. 8–9, 1956. S. Zawadzki, 'O wzrost znaczenia rad narodowych.'

Państwo i Prawo, vol. xix, no. 3 (217), March 1969. W. Harz and A. Jasińska, 'Problemy reprezentacji grup interesów w radzie narodowej.'

Paper presented at the Third Annual SSC, New York, 1967. E. R. Wolf, 'Peasant Problems and Revolutionary Warfare.'

Polish Sociological Bulletin, no. 2, 1964. M. Pohoski, 'Interrelations between Social Mobility of Individuals and Groups in the Process of Economic Growth in Poland.'

Polish Sociological Bulletin, no. 16, 1967. J. Tarkowski, 'A Study of the Decisional Process in Rolnove Powiat.'

Problemy Rad Narodowych (PRN), 8, 1966. J. Borkowski and E.

Smoktunowicz, 'Funkcje koordynacyjne prezydium w stosunku do organów i jednostek organizacyjnych nie podporządkowanych radzie narodowej.'

PRN, 12, 1968, J. Chwistek, 'Wpływ instytucji wiążących zaleceń i opinii na prawną i faktyczną pozycję komisji rad narodowych.'

PRN, 13, 1969. S. Dzięciołowska, 'Rada Narodowa w oczach mieszkańców (Wyniki ogolno-polskiego badania ankietowego).'

PRN, 11, 1968. W. Narojek and J. Światkiewicz, 'Pozycja wydziału w opinii kierowników wydziałów prezydiów WRN.'

PRN, 4, 1965. A Patrzałek, 'Zagadnienia zmian w składzie rad narodowych II i III kadencji.'

PRN, 13, 1969. A. Patrzałek and A. Seniuta, 'Nadrzędność rady nad prezydium w świetle praktyki.'

PRN, 2, 1965. H. Rot, 'Z problematyki działalności uchwałodawczej rad narodowych i prezydiów woj. wrocławskiego w latach 1955 i 1962.'

PRN, 8, 1966. W. Skrzydło, 'Prezydium rady narodowej (Skład i system powoływania).'

PRN, 6, 1966. W. Skrzydło, 'Z problematyki organizacji i działalności komisji PRN w woj. lubelskim i rzeszowskim (w latach 1962–1963).'

PRN, 3, 1965. W. Sokolewicz and S. Zawadzki, 'Wyniki badania uchwał r.n. i ich prezydiów.'

PRN, 2, 1964. J. Swiatkiewicz, 'Uchwały rad narodowych i prezydiów w 1962 roku.'

PRN, 10, 1967. M. Wendlandt, 'Struktura osobowa prezydiów rad narodowych w latach 1944–1965.'

PRN, 9, 1967. J. Wróblewski, J. Borkowski, E. Smoktunowicz and T. Szymczak, 'Zagadnienia funkcjonowania prezydiów rad narodowych.'

PRN, 5, 1965. J. Wróblewski, Z. Izdebski, E. Smotkunowicz and T. Szymczak, 'Problemy działalnosci komisji rad narodowych m. Łodzi i województwa łodzkiego.'

PRN, 17, 1970. W. Zakrzewski, 'Gromadzkie rady narodowe oczami swych przewodniczących i sekretarzy.'

PRN, 3, 1965. W. Zakrzewski, 'Z zagadnień działalności uchwałodawczej rad narodowych i ich prezydiów w woj. krakowskim w latach 1955 i 1962.'

PRN, 10, 1967. B. Zawadzka and S. Zawadzki, 'Ewolucja składu rad narodowych.'

Przegląd Socjologiczny, no. 1, vol. xv, 1961. Aurelia Jankowska-Polańska, 'Rybacy morscy jako grupa zawodowa.'

Przegląd Socjologiczny, no. 1, vol. xv, 1961. E. Lenkowski, 'Badanie nad strukturą i postawami pracowników fizycznych zawodu malarskiego.'

Przegląd Socjologiczny, vol. xii, 1958. S. Nowakowski, 'Hotel robotniczy na tle procesów urbanizacji.'

Roczniki Dziejów Ruchu Ludowego, no. 11, 1969. B. Strużek, 'Problematyka podstawowych procesów rozwojowych wsi i rolnictwa w okresie 25-lecia PRL.'

Roczniki Socjologii Wsi, no. 8, 1970. K. Adamus-Darzewska, 'Z zagadnień aktywności społeczno-gospodarczej wiejskiej parafii w Polsce.'

Roczniki Socjologii Wsi, no. 7, 1969. A. Mariańska, 'Wiejskie organizacje PZPR w działaniu.'

Roczniki Socjologii Wsi, no. 8, 1970. A. Pawełczyńska, 'Postawy ludności wiejskiej wobec religii.'

Roczniki Socjologii Wsi, no. 5, 1967. J. Poniatowski, 'O społeczno-ekonomicznych procesach integracji w PGR.'

Roczniki Socjologii Wsi, no. 2, 1965. A. Wyderko, 'Zmiany w strukturze wieku ludności wiejskiej.'

Ruch Prawniczy, Ekonomiczny i Socjologiczny, no. 1, 1963. S. Nowakowski, 'Przemiany postaw w stosunkach wieś-miasto w Polsce.'

The Second Generation's Socialism, by Z. Bauman (mimeograph paper, 1969).

Slavonic and East European Review, no. 43, 1964. W. Stankiewicz, 'The Agrarian Problem in Poland between the Two World Wars.'

The Socialist Register, 1965 (ed. R. Miliband and J. Saville). H. Alavi, 'Peasants and Revolution' (London, 1965).

The Socialist Register, 1970 (ed. R. Miliband and J. Saville). V. G. Kiernan, 'The Peasant Revolution: Some Questions.'

Studia Socjologiczne, no. 16, 1965. R. Dyoniżiak, 'Konflikty międzygrupowe w przedsiębiorstwie przemysłowym.'

Studia Socjologiczne, nos. 3–4, 1968. S. Dziabała, 'Metodologiczne problemy badań organizacji politycznych na wsi.'

Studia Socjologiczne, no. 4, 1967. B. Gałęski, 'Typy uprzemysłowienia.'

Studia Socjologiczne, no. 16, 1965. J. Hoser, 'Orientacje zawodowe inżynierów.'

Studia Socjologiczne, no. 14, 1964. M. Jarosz, 'Model samorządu robotniczego w swiadomości aktywu samorządowego.'

Studia Socjologiczne, no. 24, 1967. A. K. Kózmiński, 'Rola zawodowa dyrektora przedsiębiorstwa w aktualnym systemie zarządzania gospodarką socjalistyczną.'

Studia Socjologiczne, no. 2, 1961. W. Makarczyk, 'Czynnyki stabilności i aktywności zawodowej rolników w gospodarstwach indywidualnych.'

Studia Socjologiczne, no. 4, 1967. D. Markowski, 'Zagadnienia zróżnicowania społecznego-studium wybranego wsi.'

Studia Socjologiczne, no. 3, 1969. H. Najduchowska, 'Drogi zawodowe kadry kierowniczej.'

Studia Socjologiczne, no. 13, 1964. W. Narojek, 'Mechanizm podejmowania decyzji w mieście.'

Studia Socjologiczne, no. 5, 1962. S. Nowak, 'Środowiskowe determinanty ideologii społecznej studentów Warszawy.'

Studia Socjologiczne, no. 22, 1966. A. Owieczko, 'Działalność i struktura samorządu robotniczego w opinii załog fabrycznych.'

Studia Socjologiczne, nos. 30–1, 1968. M. Sadowski, 'Przemiany społeczne a partie polityczne PRL.'

Studia Socjologiczne, no. 3, 1962. A. Sarapata, 'Iustum Pretium'.

Studia Socjologiczne, no. 3, 1970. A. Sarapata, 'Motywacje i satysfakcje dyrektorów-studium porównawcze.'

Studia Socjologiczne, no. 2, 1961. W. Wesołowski and A. Sarapata, 'Hierarchia zawodów i stanowisk.'

Studia Socjologiczne, no. 18, 1965. J. Ziołkowski, 'Miejsce i rola procesu urbanizacji w przeobrażeniach społecznych w Polsce Ludowej.'

Studia Socjologiczno-Polityczne, no. 19, 1965. W. Adamski, 'Koncepcja "grup interesu" w środowisku wiejskim.'

Studia Socjologiczno-Polityczne, no. 14, 1963. Z. Kitliński, 'Popularność różnych kierunków kształcenia wsród młodziezy i rodziców w środowiskach społecznych Warszawy.'

Studia Socjologiczno-Polityczne, no. 17, 1964. W. Narojek, 'Organizacje w układzie miasta.'

Studia Socjologiczno-Polityczne, no. 15, 1963. W. Narojek, 'Rola partii w mieście powiatowym.'

Studia Socjologiczno-Polityczne, no. 15, 1963. W. Wesołowski, 'Prestiż zawodów-system wartości-uwarstwienie społeczne.'

Studia Socjologiczno-Polityczne, no. 19, 1965. Z. Zebrowski, 'Społeczno-zawodowa aktywność chłopów.'

Twórczość, no. 7, 1954. (Ochab at the Sixth Congress of the PWA.)

Wieś Współczesna, no. 10, 1969. Z. Adamowski, 'Stosunek chłopów do członkostwa KR.'

Wieś Współczesna, no. 6, 1967. I. Adamski and L. Makiela, 'Zjazdy powiatowe Stronnictwa w 1967 r.'

Wieś Współczesna, no. 9, 1968. S. Asanowicz, 'Z problematyki sesji gromadzkich rad narodowych w województwie białostockim.'

Wieś Współczesna, no. 3, 1968. L. Cegielski, 'Nowe ustawy agrarne uchwalone przez Sejm.'

Wieś Współczesna, no. 1, 1966. W. Dąbski, 'O niektórych sprawach

organizacyjno-politycznych Stronnictwa w województwie łódzkim.'

Wieś Współczesna, no. 4, 1966. W. Dąbski, 'ZSL w latach 1949–
1965.'

Wieś Współczesna, no. 11, 1970. W. Dąbski and B. Dylak, 'ZSL
1965–1970.'

Wieś Współczesna, no. 5, 1963. M. Kuzakiewicz, 'O kryzysie
społecznej pozycji nauczyciela wiejskiego.'

Wieś Współczesna, no. 4, 1969. R. Mackowski and R. Wysocki, 'Z
myślą o skuteczniejszym działaniu.'

Wieś Współczesna, no. 12, 1969. A. Potok and G. Madej, 'Pozycja
służby rolnej w gromadzie.'

Wieś Współczesna, no. 1, 1967. 'Dziesięć lat nowej polityki rolnej.'

Wieś Współczesna, no. 12, 1970. 'Gospodarstwa indywidualne a
sytuacja w rolnictwie.'

Wieś Współczesna, no. 10, 1966. J. Szczepański, 'Rola chłopów w
rozwoju społeczeństwa polskiego.'

List of Contributors

GEORGE GÖMÖRI was born in Hungary and was educated at Budapest and Oxford. He is now teaching Polish language and literature at the University of Cambridge and is a Fellow of Darwin College, Cambridge. He is author of *Polish and Hungarian Poetry 1945 to 1956* (1966) and co-editor of *New Writing of East Europe* (Chicago, 1968).

GEORGE KOLANKIEWICZ was educated at the University of Leeds. Between 1969 and 1971 he was SSRC research fellow in the Department of Sociology at Essex University and is currently lecturer in Sociology at the University of Essex.

DAVID LANE studied at Birmingham and Oxford Universities and is currently reader in Sociology at the University of Essex. He is author of *The Roots of Russian Communism*; *Politics and Society in the USSR*; *The End of Inequality? Social Stratification under State Socialism*.

PAUL LEWIS lectures at The Open University. He is a graduate of Birmingham University and has studied at the Rural Sociology Department of the Academy of Sciences in Warsaw. He is currently writing a Ph.D. thesis on the politics of the Polish peasantry between 1956 and 1971 with particular reference to the sociology of rural political organisations in Poland.

RAY TARAS is Canadian and studied at the Universities of Montreal and Sussex. He is currently lecturer at Lanchester Polytechnic and is completing a study at Essex University on internal and external communication in English local government.

Index

Academy of Mining and Metallurgy (AGH), party membership in, 217
activisation of peasants, 72
activists and organised protest, 149, 151
Adamiecka, Hanka, 169
Adamski, J., 76-7
Adamski, W., 72
age structure, 15
aggregation of demands, 316
aggregation of interests, 310, 322
'agraryzm', 60
Agricultural circles
  and People's Council, 277, 284, 285
  and rationalist vs. traditionalist peasant groups, 80
  as thin end of Socialist wedge, 74
  controlled by UPP, 79
  dominated by wealthy peasants, 68
  formation of, 54
  management of, 77
  unease over, 55
agriculture, 16-17, 305
aktyw
  and CWSM, 149
  mobilisation of workers, 149
Alavi, H., 33
Almond, G., 320
amorphous interest groups, 319
analytic group, 318
Andrzejewski, Jerzy, 165, 166, 168, 173, 177
anti-management perspective of engineers, 212
apparat, 189
apparatchiki and white-collar experts, 205
Arendt, H., 104-5
articulation of demands, 318

articulation of interests, 309
Association of Engineers and Technicians, 189
Association of Polish Mechanical Engineers and Technicians (SITMP), 198
Association (Zjednoczenie), 149
authoritarian political system, 322
authority
  of enterprise director, 221
  of the Party, 116, 326
automobile workers, 132
average real wages
  drop in, 130
  growth of, 120

Bauman, Zygmunt, 178
Białystok Council, 242
Bieńkowski, Władysław, 166
Bierut, Bolesław, 169
Bismarck (Chancellor of Prussia), 153
Bocheński, Jacek, 176
boundaries, 5-6
Brandys, Kazimierz, 165, 166, 176
Broniewski, Władysław, 155
Brus, W., 199-200
bureaucracy, 255-63, 272, 279, 285, 290, 293, 316
  trimming of, 98
bureaucratic
  centralism, 191
  opposition to workers' councils, 110-11
  style, 311
Burnham, J., 307

cadres, administration, 255, 256, 257, 258, 261, 272, 286, 287, 288, 290, 291, 292, 294